China and Sustainable Development in Latin America

ANTHEM FRONTIERS OF GLOBAL POLITICAL ECONOMY

The **Anthem Frontiers of Global Political Economy** series seeks to trigger and attract new thinking in global political economy, with particular reference to the prospects of emerging markets and developing countries. Written by renowned scholars from different parts of the world, books in this series provide historical, analytical and empirical perspectives on national economic strategies and processes, the implications of global and regional economic integration, the changing nature of the development project, and the diverse global-to-local forces that drive change. Scholars featured in the series extend earlier economic insights to provide fresh interpretations that allow new understandings of contemporary economic processes.

China and Sustainable Development in Latin America

The Social and Environmental Dimension

Edited by

Rebecca Ray, Kevin Gallagher, Andrés López
and Cynthia Sanborn

ANTHEM PRESS

Anthem Press
An imprint of Wimbledon Publishing Company
www.anthempress.com

This edition first published in UK and USA 2017
by ANTHEM PRESS
75–76 Blackfriars Road, London SE1 8HA, UK
or PO Box 9779, London SW19 7ZG, UK
and
244 Madison Ave #116, New York, NY 10016, USA

British Library Cataloguing-in-Publication Data
A catalogue record for this book is available from the British Library.

Library of Congress Cataloging-in-Publication Data
Names: Ray, Rebecca (M. E. Rebecca), editor.
Title: China and sustainable development in Latin America : the social and environmental dimension / edited by Rebecca Ray, Kevin Gallagher, Andrés López and Cynthia Sanborn.
Description: London ; New York, NY : Anthem Press, 2016. | Series: Anthem frontiers of global political economy | Includes bibliographical references and index.
Identifiers: LCCN 2016039292| ISBN 9781783086139 (hardback) | ISBN 9781783086146 (paperback)
Subjects: LCSH: Sustainable development—Latin America. | Latin America—Foreign economic relations—China. | China—Foreign economic relations—Latin America. | International trade—Environmental aspects—Latin America. | International trade—Social aspects—Latin America. | BISAC: SOCIAL SCIENCE / Developing Countries. | BUSINESS & ECONOMICS / Development / Economic Development. | BUSINESS & ECONOMICS / Development / Sustainable Development.
Classification: LCC HC130.E5 C55 2016 | DDC 337.5108—dc23
LC record available at https://lccn.loc.gov/2016039292

ISBN-13: 978-1-78308-613-9 (Hbk)
ISBN-10: 1-78308-613-0 (Hbk)

ISBN-13: 978-1-78308-614-6 (Pbk)
ISBN-10: 1-78308-614-9 (Pbk)

This title is also available as an e-book.

CONTENTS

ILLUSTRATIONS

Figures

Tables

ACKNOWLEDGMENTS

This book and project could not have been completed without the hard work and support of numerous people. The editors thank all of the chapter authors and their respective institutions, as well as the Global Development and Environment Institute at Tufts University in the United States for collaborating. We also thank Victoria Chonn, Victoria Puyat, Iryna Ureneck and others on the staff at Universidad de Pacifico and Boston University's Global Economic Governance Initiative for supporting this work. Cesar Gamboa, Jeronim Capaldo, Denise Leung and others made useful inputs into our initial thinking and final execution of this work. We thank Jennifer Turner, Janine Feretti, Mauricio Mesquita Moreira, Shouqing Zhu and Lu Guoqiang for hosting workshops based on the results from this project. The editors also sincerely thank the John D. and Catherine T. MacArthur Foundation and the Charles Stewart Mott Foundation for the financial support, especially Sandra Smithey, Steve Cornelius, Traci Romine and Amy Rosenthal.

Part I
INTRODUCTION AND REGIONAL OVERVIEW

Chapter 1

CHINA IN LATIN AMERICA: LESSONS FOR SOUTH–SOUTH COOPERATION AND SUSTAINABLE DEVELOPMENT

Rebecca Ray, Kevin Gallagher, Andrés López
and Cynthia Sanborn

1. Introduction

Latin America's recent commodity boom was associated with a sharp increase in social and environmental risks. The boom was largely driven by trade and investment with China and concentrated in the petroleum, mineral extraction and agricultural sectors – sectors strongly linked to environmental degradation and social conflict. With some notable exceptions, Latin American governments have fallen short of mitigating these risks and costs of the boom. While China should not be blamed for the bulk of Latin America's environmental and social problems, it would be wise to mitigate the impacts of its overseas activities to maintain good relations with host countries and to reduce the risks of international investment. Some Chinese firms have demonstrated an ability to adhere to best practices in these arenas, but overall, thus far, they lack the experience or policies to manage their impacts in the region. As the boom tapers off and Latin American economies slow down, there is increasing pressure on governments to streamline approvals for new export and investment projects, and to ignore civil society organizations working to hold governments and foreign firms accountable. It is in the interests of the Latin American and Chinese governments, as well as Chinese firms, to put in place adequate social and environmental policies to maximize the benefits and mitigate the risks of China's economic activity in Latin America.

In this context, the present study asks two research questions. First, to what extent has China independently driven environmental and social change in Latin America? Second, to what extent do Chinese firms perform differently from their domestic and foreign counterparts when they invest in Latin

America? We and our colleagues have explored these questions through a series of eight country-level case studies – in Argentina, Bolivia, Brazil, Chile, Colombia, Ecuador, Mexico and Peru – laid out in the chapters that follow.

2. China as a Driver of Social and Environmental Change in Latin America

China has recently grown into a major export destination for the Latin America and Caribbean region (LAC), second only to the United States. In 1993, China consumed less than 2 percent of LAC exports, but by 2013 it accounted for 9 percent. However, that importance was quite uneven across different export sectors. As Figure 1.1 shows, over the last decade China has nearly tripled its market share of total LAC exports, more than tripled its share of extractive exports and nearly doubled its share of agricultural exports. But its demand for manufactured LAC exports has barely moved, staying at about 2 percent.

In fact, China has been an important driver in the expansion of LAC export agriculture and extraction. As Figure 1.2 shows, while agricultural and extractive exports to China from LAC have been rising as a share of gross domestic product (GDP), for the last decade those exports to the rest of the world have been stagnant or even falling overall. Not only did Latin America's extractive and agricultural sectors boom due to China's demand, but Chinese demand also played a role in increasing the general price level of major commodities during this period, significantly increasing the terms of trade across the Americas.

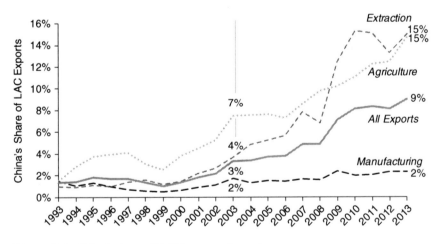

Figure 1.1 China's share of LAC exports, by sector
Source: Authors' calculations based on UN Comtrade data.

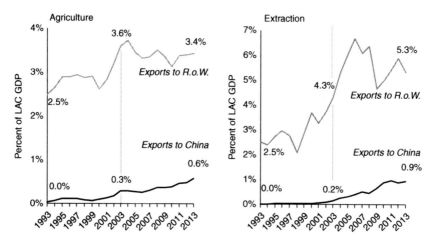

Figure 1.2 Agricultural and extractive exports as a share of LAC GDP, by market
Source: Authors' calculations based on UN Comtrade and IMF data.

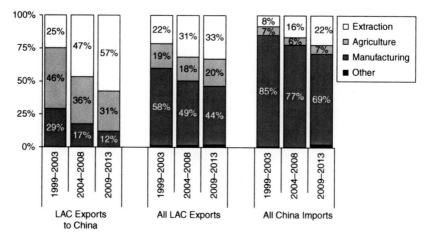

Figure 1.3 LAC export basket composition, by market
Source: Authors' calculations based on UN Comtrade data.

As a result, LAC exports to China have become increasingly concentrated in extraction and agriculture. As Figure 1.3 shows, from 1999 to 2003 LAC exports to China were fairly balanced among the three major sectors, but a decade later they were dramatically different, with extraction accounting for over half of all LAC–China exports. Nor do they reflect the composition of China's imports overall, which are predominantly manufactured goods. But this increasing concentration in extractive goods does reflect China's

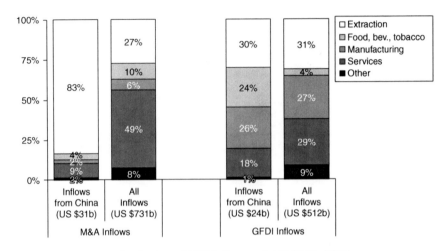

Figure 1.4 Sector distribution of FDI inflows to LAC (2008–2012)
Source: Authors' calculations using DeaLogic (left), fDIMarkets (right) data.
Note: Food, beverages and tobacco include food-product production. Extraction includes oil, natural gas, mining and basic metal processing. Percentages may not add up to 100 due to rounding.

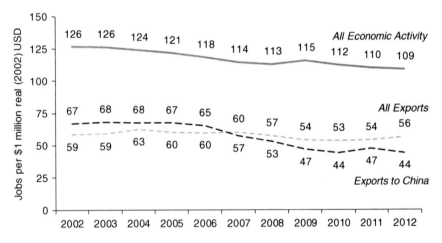

Figure 1.5 Jobs supported by overall LAC economic activity and exports
Source: Ray (2016a, forthcoming).

increasing thirst for minerals, which rose from 8 percent to 22 percent of its imports over the same time period.

Chinese investment in LAC has been similarly concentrated in primary sectors. Figures 1.4 and 1.5 show the sector distribution of FDI inflows from mergers and acquisitions (M&As) and greenfield projects, respectively. Most

Chinese direct investment into LAC has been through M&As, and over two-thirds of this investment has been in the oil and gas sector. In contrast, only 15 percent of overall M&A inflows to the region have been in that sector. Among greenfield FDI (GFDI) projects, China's difference is most visible in agriculture. Food and tobacco comprise a quarter of Chinese GFDI into LAC, but only 2 percent of overall GFDI inflows.

2.1 Employment creation

Because the LAC–China export basket is so different from overall LAC exports, the employment impact of LAC–China exports is also different. Specifically, because of the heavy concentration in extractive industries, LAC exports to China support fewer jobs per US$1 million. Figure 1.5 shows the labor intensity of LAC overall economic activity, exports and, specifically, LAC exports to China. Over the last decade, total economic activity has supported far more jobs than exports. This is largely due to the extremely labor-intensive nature of peasant agriculture, which is pervasive in the region but absent from production for export. Total exports support fewer jobs, but the labor intensity has remained fairly stable – falling from 59 to 56 jobs per US$1 million. Exports to China, however, have fallen by over a third in the number of jobs they support for every US$1 million – from nearly 70 in 2002 to fewer than 45 in 2012.[1]

2.2 Environmental impacts

The disproportionate, and growing, concentration in extractive and agricultural products of LAC exports to China give them a distinctly different environmental footprint than other exports. This section looks more closely at two environmental impacts, one global (greenhouse gas (GHG) emission) and one local (water use). As Figure 1.6 shows, LAC–China exports cause more greenhouse gas emissions and use more water per dollar of output than other exports, and much more than overall economic activity.

---

1   It is worth noting that Figure 1.5 includes only direct rather than indirect employment. Direct labor intensity across the region has an average of 60.1 jobs in agriculture, 11.6 jobs in extraction and 71.8 jobs in manufacturing for every US$1 million output in each sector. Estimates of indirect employment vary dramatically, even within each sector. According to the World Input-Output Database (Timmer, 2012), for every dollar of output, extraction creates about twice as much demand for upstream (indirect) industries as agriculture in Brazil, only about a third as much in Mexico, and about three-fourths as much in non-OECD countries. Based on these estimates, it is highly unlikely for the total (direct and indirect) employment from extraction to rival the other sectors shown here for employment generation.

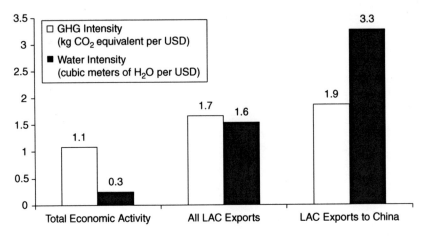

Figure 1.6 Environmental impact of overall LAC economic activity and exports
Source: Ray (2016b, forthcoming).

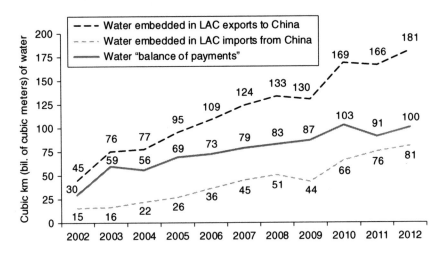

Figure 1.7 LAC "balance of payments" in water with China
Source: Authors' calculations from Water Footprint Network and UN Comtrade data.

The data in Figure 1.6 are from 2004, the last year of directly measured data on each indicator. However, as Figure 1.2 shows, LAC exports to China have continued to become more and more concentrated in a few sectors since that time. Figure 1.7 applies the 2004 intensities to the changing trade-basket composition to create a water "balance of payments" between China and LAC. It shows a positive balance of 100.4 billion cubic meters of water in 2012, meaning that LAC sent China much more water in its exports than

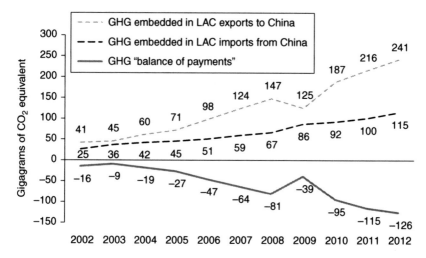

Figure 1.8 LAC "balance of payments" in greenhouse gas emissions with China
Source: Ray (2016b).

what was embedded in imports. For reference, the volume of Lake Nicaragua is approximately 108 billion cubic meters. In other words, if LAC had not traded with China in 2012 (by producing domestically everything it imported from China and consuming locally everything it exported to China), it would have saved roughly 90 percent of the volume of Lake Nicaragua. This has major ramifications, not only environmentally, but also socially, as the case studies in this book show that competition for water is a frequent source of conflict between communities practicing peasant agriculture or small-scale ranching and large-scale plantations and mines.

Figure 1.8 shows a similar environmental "balance of payments," but for GHG emissions. LAC exports to China are responsible for far fewer GHG emissions than Chinese exports to LAC. Of course, the impacts of GHG emissions are global rather than local. It makes little difference to climate change whether those emissions originate from LAC or from China. However, the scale is still very interesting. As much as LAC exports to China (and their embedded GHG emission) have risen in the last decade, the GHG emissions embedded in LAC imports from China have risen at an even faster pace.

Box 1.1 Chile, China and solar panels

Sometimes, the environmental impact of the LAC–China relationship can be felt more acutely on the import rather than the export side. This is the case in Chile (Chapter 8), where imports of Chinese photovoltaic

(PV) panels have had a major impact on greening the Chilean energy matrix. In the mid-2000s, Chile lost its main source of low-emissions energy when Argentina restricted its exports of natural gas and eventually closed its pipeline to Chile altogether. But China was experiencing a major oversupply of PV panels at the same time. The concurrence of these two events gave Chile an opening to rapidly expand its use of solar power. In 2013, Chile imported US$40.9 million in Chinese PV panels, more than half of its total PV imports. While solar power is still a small share of total energy generation in the country, it is poised to expand rapidly: over half of the 10,000 megawats of new power projects with approved environmental permits are solar (Borregaard et al., 2015).

Figures 1.6 and 1.8 measure GHG emissions in CO_2 equivalency, including the effects of land-use change. In LAC, land-use change is one of the most important factors in net GHG emissions changes. According to the FAO, LAC deforestation accounted for 1.7 megatons of CO_2 equivalence in GHG emissions in 2010, or about 41 percent of the region's total for that year. Our case study of China's relationship with Brazil shows that exports to China are a statistically significant driver of deforestation in the Brazilian Amazon, together with the total soybean-planted area. In turn, China has been an important driver in the expansion of the soy area: in 2013 China accounted for three-fourths of Brazil's oilseed exports (see Chapter 7 for more information).

In terms of deforestation, Figures 1.6 and 1.8 actually understate the GHG emissions from LAC's relationship with China, because while they account for deforestation directly linked to exports, they do not account for the most important cause of deforestation: roads, canals and railroads to get those products to ports. Research by Philip Fearnside (one of the authors of Chapter 7, on Brazil) and others (2013) show that access roads are the most important cause of Amazonian deforestation, as they open the forest to human settlements and interrupt animal migration patterns. Thus, in order to adequately account for the GHG impact of the "China boom" in Latin America, it is important to include not just exports to China but also Chinese-financed roads, canals and railroads designed to get those products to ports, as well as dams to provide power to mines and oilfields.

Figure 1.9 shows South America's most biodiverse areas and indigenous territories, with Chinese-financed infrastructure and Chinese FDI projects added. The biodiversity of these areas is reflected in the various shades of grey: the darkest grey patches (present only in eastern Ecuador and the northern extreme of Peru) represent areas with the highest biodiversity in four different groups of species: mammals, birds, amphibians and plants. The second-darkest shade, present near the border of Peru and Brazil, indicates areas with the highest biodiversity in three of the four species groups, and so forth. Indigenous territories are reflected in stripes.

As Figure 1.9 shows, two major Chinese investments may pose serious risks to highly biodiverse areas and indigenous territories: the western half of the transcontinental railway and oilfields in eastern Ecuador. The transcontinental railway is still in the planning stage, so it does not yet have a finalized path. Two possibilities exist for the route of its western end: one through Piura in northern Peru and another through Puno in southern Peru. The northern route crosses into Brazil through an area with extremely high biodiversity in three out of the four species groups shown here in the darkest shade in Figure 1.9. The southern route largely avoids this environmentally sensitive region. The final choice of route for this railway will be crucial in determining its environmental impact.

The other major Chinese investment in a highly biodiverse area is oil development in eastern Ecuador, much of which also occupies traditional indigenous territory. The southernmost two Chinese oil concessions in Ecuador are

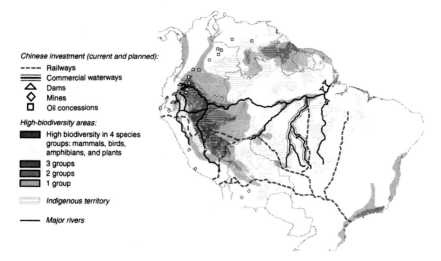

Figure 1.9 High biodiversity areas, indigenous territory and Chinese investment
Source: Compiled from Bass et al. (2010), Cruz Fiestas (2014), Fearnside and Figeiredo (Chapter 7), International Rivers et al., Ministério dos Transportes (2009), Ministerio de Transportes y Comunicaciones and Red Amazónica de Información Socioambiental Georreferencial.
Note: Mines and some oil concessions are already in operation. Railway locations are approximate, as most plans are not yet final. High biodiversity is defined as the top 6.4% of South American land area for species richness.

new, and their contracts have not yet been finalized. If these concessions do in fact go through, the terms of their contracts will be extremely important for both their social and environmental impacts.

2.3 Rising to the challenge: Social and environmental safeguard innovations

In the face of this tremendous growth in sectors intrinsically linked to high environmental impacts and risks for social conflicts, we find that several Latin American countries have developed important policy responses to minimize the risks. Three of the most innovative of these responses are Brazil's new environmental oversight measures, Ecuador's new labor standards and Peru's transparency measures and indigenous protections.

Brazil (Chapter 7) dramatically enhanced the enforcement power of its environmental regulations in 2008 without changing the current environmental laws themselves. Instead, Brazil's Central Bank changed its rules to no longer allow public bank loans to operations with unpaid fines for environmental irregularities reported by government agencies. Public-agency fines for environmental violations can be postponed through appeals, but this more proactive approach has immediate effect.

Ecuador (Chapter 4), in 2008 and 2010, enacted a series of labor protections for its petroleum sector – enactments that form one of the most progressive packages of labor protection in the LAC region. In 2008, Ecuador strictly curtailed the use of subcontracted labor, limiting it to "complementary" work such as security and custodial services. The 2010 Hydrocarbon Law further boosted labor protections in the oil and gas sector by requiring foreign investors to hire Ecuadorian workers for 95 percent of unskilled and 90 percent of skilled jobs. Moreover, this law required profit-sharing with all employees, including contract workers. Taken together, these laws eliminated two of the most important sources of labor conflicts facing Chinese (and other international) investment projects across the LAC region: the use of foreign laborers and differences in the labor conditions between directly hired and subcontracted employees working at the same project.

Peru (Chapter 6) has made important strides in transparency and indigenous rights over the last decade. Peru joined the Extractive Industries Transparency Initiative (EITI) in 2007 and in 2011 became the first country in the Americas to be declared compliant within that framework. Also in 2011, it became the first LAC country to enact legislation to implement International Labour Organization (ILO) Convention 169, which grants indigenous communities the right to prior consultation on any state policies that directly affect them, including concessions and permits for extractive projects within their traditional territories. To comply with its EITI commitments, the Peruvian government and participating companies publish detailed reports of revenue flows related to the extractive industries, available online for concerned citizens and civil society. Furthermore, the Peruvian government assigned staff from the Ministry of Energy and Mining to the EITI process, including working with non-participating companies to encourage participation. Starting in 2014, three Chinese companies confirmed their involvement in the process: Shougang, China MinMetals and China National Petroleum Corporation (CNPC). These two measures put Peru in a leadership position regionally for public participation in the resource boom.

2.4 Progress under fire: Challenges to existing protections

The LAC–China export boom has been supported by high world prices for the commodities involved, which has boosted the value of minerals reserves and increased bargaining power for countries interested in enacting social and environmental standards for their use. However, the same phenomenon has boosted the power of sectors associated with the boom that have incentives to resist these standards.

Within governments, the extractive boom has prioritized mining and hydrocarbons ministries, as executive branches face pressure to speed up the process of beginning new investment projects. To that end, Peru has recently curtailed the authority of the Environment Ministry over the approval and supervision of extractive projects. The objective is to streamline the process of getting new extractive investments under way and accelerate production in the face of flagging world prices, but this change has not incorporated safeguards to prevent conflicts of interest from corrupting the process and diminishing the power of environmental oversight (see Chapter 6 for more on Peru).

In Brazil, the China boom has also had major impact on the agricultural sector. There, Chinese demand has enriched and empowered the "ruralist" voting block, representing large landholders in Congress. This newly strengthened voting block has exerted powerful influence on the current administration's environmental stances (Santilli, 2014; Smeraldi, 2014). For example, it has mounted an effort to roll back the new Central Bank rules cited above, which have proven useful in strengthening enforcement of environmental safeguards.

3. The Performance – and Incentives – of Chinese Investors in Latin America

Our research shows that Chinese firms do not perform significantly worse relative to domestic or other international firms. In fact, despite relatively weaker levels of regulation at home in China, and a fledgling set of guidelines for overseas companies, our case studies found some instances of Chinese firms outperforming their competitors, especially with proper incentives from governments and civil society. This section explores lessons from each of these case studies. Overall, they show that Chinese firms are flexible, able to adapt to new environments and perform up to local standards. However, several of the cases show that as these investments continue to expand, major challenges still lie ahead.

The remaining chapters in this volume explore each of these case studies. Three case studies involve oil production. First, the Argentina chapter involves the China National Offshore Oil Corporation (CNOOC) and the China Petroleum and Chemical Corporation (Sinopec). The Colombia chapter follows the investments of Sinopec as well as the Chinese petrochemical firm Sinochem. The Ecuador chapter also includes Sinopec, together with the CNPC. Two additional chapters explore Chinese mining operations. In Bolivia, China has been present through tin mining, including Jungie Mining, and in the planned development of the nation's large lithium reserves. Three separate mining projects are profiled in the Peru chapter, including the Marcona iron mine (run by the Shougang Corporation), the Toromocho copper mine (run by Chinalco), and the Rio Blanco copper and molybdenum mining project (run by the Zijin Mining Group). The Mexico chapter stands alone as a case study of a Chinese manufacturing company, Golden Dragon Associates. Finally, two additional chapters do not involve Chinese investors, but rather trade: agricultural exports from Brazil to China, and manufactured Chinese imports in Chile.

Among these Chinese firms is one that our case studies examine in three different Latin American countries: Sinopec. The case studies show that Sinopec has had very different experiences under different regulatory regimes and with different incentives. Sinopec's labor relations in Argentina and environmental performance in Ecuador have been more positive than either in Colombia.

- Sinopec's labor challenges in Colombia (Chapter 3) have involved the local community action boards, which are common in rural Colombia and control the hiring of oil workers. Allegations abound of powerful local figures trading employment for favors or even fees, or unfairly favoring workers from other areas over local workers, but the regional Labor Ministry officials state that these complaints have not been formalized for fear of endangering the very employment positions they involve. The Colombian national government is considering removing hiring authority from community action boards, but the proposal faces vigorous opposition by the boards themselves, unsurprisingly. In contrast, Sinopec faces no such issues in Argentina (Chapter 2) or Ecuador (Chapter 4), because of the regulatory framework in each country. In Argentina, Sinopec has signed an agreement with the local government ensuring that all workers will have had residency in the Santa Cruz province for at least two years prior to their hiring. In Ecuador, subcontracted labor is tightly regulated, as discussed above.

• Environmentally, Sinopec has a better record in Ecuador than most of its competitors, with fewer local protests over spills than most of its competitors, either foreign or domestic. This record is partly due to the incentives it faces there: it bought oil concessions that were initially owned by Chevron and therefore receive a great deal of attention. Sinopec's ability to maintain a low profile has been key to its ability to continue operations for nearly a decade. In contrast, the Comptroller General of Colombia cited Sinopec in 2014 for never paying the US$500,000 investment in conservation required by law and pledged in 2008. These two cases show the importance of establishing – and enforcing – an effective regulatory framework for international investment. Fortunately, Colombia appears to be taking this to heart, as its 2014 environmental finding and the recent proposed change in labor regulation show.

Other positive outcomes in the case studies show that Chinese investors are capable of living up to high standards, especially when the proper incentives are in place. These case studies show the importance of cooperation between governments, investors, local communities and Chinese regulators in creating those incentives. Areas where this cooperation can be especially helpful include oversight by lenders, community engagement at the outset of projects and training investors in compliance with local laws.

3.1   Incentives from home: The role of lender oversight

China should be credited for enacting guidelines for its overseas economic activities. When Western countries were at middle-income status such guidelines were not on government radar screens. Other middle-income countries (like Brazil, discussed above) prevent public lending to *domestic* projects with outstanding environmental fines, and *multilateral* lenders have long required borrowers to meet environmental performance standards. But these kinds of standards for *outbound* international investment sets China ahead of its middle-income country peers. Nonetheless, China is a relative newcomer to international investment, and its environmental and social safeguards still lag behind those of the traditional multilateral lenders.

There are three levels of safeguards for Chinese outbound investment. First, the Ministry of Commerce (MOFCOM) has published voluntary "Guidelines for Environmental Protection in Foreign Investment and Cooperation" for all investors, regardless of whether they are public or private, or how they are financed. While these are not binding, they carry moral authority for state-owned enterprises (Tao, 2013). For projects that are bank-financed, the China Banking Regulatory Commission (CBRC) has set "Green Credit Guidelines" for all Chinese banks that finance investment projects abroad, which include requiring investments to meet host country and international environmental laws. Finally, the China Development Bank (CDB) and the Export-Import Bank of China (China Ex-Im Bank), state-owned "policy banks" that fund overseas investments in the name of the Chinese government, have developed safeguard practices for projects within their portfolios.

Table 1.1 compares Chinese guidelines to those of major multilateral lenders: the World Bank, the International Finance Corporation, and the Inter-American Development Bank. While the Chinese lenders and regulators have fewer requirements than the multilateral lenders, there is one notable exception: only the Chinese policy banks require ex-post environmental impact assessments.

The regulations shown in Table 1.1 demonstrate a major step forward for Chinese lenders, but those lenders still face steep challenges in enforcement. For example, without a grievance policy, lenders may not know about violations of other requirements such as compliance with international environmental laws. Furthermore, even requiring compliance with host-country law – arguably the least challenging of the requirements in Table 1.1 to enforce – can be challenging if local governments are not enforcing their own laws. For example, in the Sinopec case in Colombia discussed above, the comptroller general cited not only Sinopec but also the national environmental licensing agency, for not enforcing its own regulations sufficiently. In a situation like that, it is not clear that MOFCOM has the grounds to claim that Sinopec is in violation of their guidelines. Latin American civil society groups have begun educating communities about the Green Credit Directives and other environmental and social safeguards attached to Chinese lending, but without a formal method for receiving and investigating complaints, banks have little immediate incentive to follow up on any communication they receive. Given the difficulty in policing investor behavior abroad, it could be extremely helpful for Chinese lenders to approach Latin American civil society and governments as partners in holding investors accountable to these guidelines, perhaps through introducing a formal grievance mechanism.

Table 1.1 Chinese and multilateral regulations compared

	Multilateral lenders			Chinese banks and regulators			
	World Bank	**IFC**	**IDB**	**MOFCOM***	**CBRC**	**CDB**	**Ex-Im Bank**
Ex-ante environmental impact assessments	X	X	X	X		X	X
Project review of environmental impact assessments	X	X	X			X	X
Industry-specific social and environmental standards	X	X					
Require compliance with host country environmental regulations	X		X	X	X	X	X
Require compliance with int'l environmental regulations	X				X		
Public consultations with affected communities	X	X	X	X			X
Grievance mechanism	X	X					
Independent monitoring and review	X						
Establishing covenants linked to compliance	X	X	X				X
Ex-post environmental impact assessments						X	X

Note: *MOFCOM policies are voluntary in nature.
Source: CBRC, 2012; Gallagher et al., 2012; Leung and Zhao, 2013; State Forestry Administration, 2010.

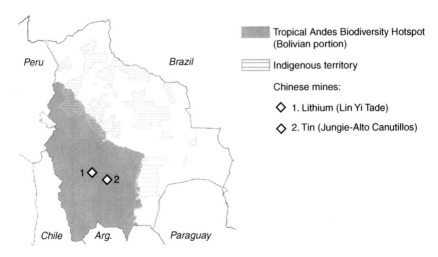

Figure 1.10 Bolivia: Biodiversity hotspot, indigenous territory and Chinese mines
Source: Compiled from Red Amazónica de Información Socioambiental Georreferencial and Zador et al., 2015.

3.2 The importance of community engagement

Our case studies show that an investor's willingness to work with governments and local communities from the outset of their presence, especially when deciding where to build, is one of the most important aspects of establishing positive community relations. Three examples highlight this lesson particularly well: the Toromocho copper mine owned by Chinalco in Peru, the Jungie tin mine in Bolivia and Andes Petroleum in Ecuador. Each case illustrates the importance of government incentives and assistance in the negotiation process.

In Bolivia (Chapter 5), China's Jungie Mining and the local Alto Canutillos mining cooperative formed a joint venture to mine tin in Tacobamba in 2010. While the mine does not appear in the extremely biodiverse areas shown in Figure 1.9, it does lie within threatened land: the Tropical Andes Biodiversity Hotspot.[2] Figure 1.10 shows the Bolivian segment of the Tropical Andes Biodiversity Hotspot in grey, and indigenous territory in stripes.

Before operations could begin, surveys showed that the local community was opposed to the establishment of a processing plant and tailings dam

---

2   Biodiversity hotspots are defined as areas with at least 1,500 endemic plant species that have lost at least 70 percent of their original habitat. For more on biodiversity hotspots, and on the Tropical Andes hotspot specifically, see Zador et al. (2015).

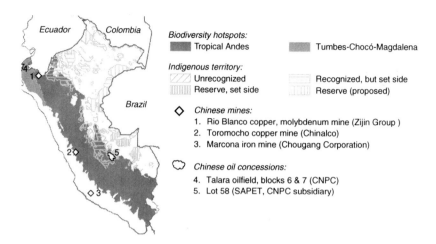

Figure 1.11 Peru: Biodiversity hotspots, indigenous territory and Chinese mines
Source: Compiled from Red Amazónica de Información Socioambiental Georreferencial
and Zador et al., 2015.

in Tacobamba. In response, the state-owned COMIBOL mining company donated land over 25 miles away for the facility, in Agua Dulce, Villa de Yocalla, where a public consultation showed that the community accepted its presence. This move took cooperation among the investors, the government and the local community, and prevented a major potential source of conflict (see Chapter 5 for more on this process).

In Peru, Chinese SOE Chinalco's Toromocho mine also borders the Tropical Andes Biodiversity Hotspot, as Figure 1.11 shows.[3]

In 2007, Chinalco inherited a commitment to relocate the 5,000 residents of the existing city of Morococha to make way for the mine construction. Morococha is a former mining camp, and its water and soil have been badly contaminated from decades of nearby mining operations. Prior to Chinalco's purchase of this project, the Peruvian government was expected to build a new town for the residents, but Chinalco took on the obligation as part of the investment. While the old Morococha had communal latrines and a limited water supply, "Nueva Morococha" promises a modern water and sanitation system. Perhaps most importantly, the move was largely voluntary and the product of dialogue and negotiation among community members, their elected authorities, the central government and the investor – considered the first example

---

3   For more on biodiversity hotspots, and specifically on the Tropical Andes hotspot, see
    Zador et al. (2015).

of voluntary, participatory community relocation in modern Peruvian history. While it has not been without problems (for example, Chinalco offered each moving family a title to their new homes, but the municipality has been delayed in issuing them) and there continue to be a number of holdouts, it represents a step forward in Peruvian mining community relations (Sanborn and Chonn, 2015).

The community consultation process has not gone so smoothly in Ecuador, where Andes Petroleum (a joint venture between Chinese SOEs Sinopec and CNPC) won two new concessions in early 2014. As shown in Figure 1.9, Ecuador is the only South American country where major Chinese investments exist in an area with extremely high biodiversity in four different species groups as well as traditional indigenous territory (Figure 1.12 shows this situation in more detail). So its respect for social and environmental safeguards is especially important, perhaps more so than any other Chinese investments in this project. Until now, Andes has had better community relations than most of its competitors (including Ecuadorian SOEs), with fewer protests due to contamination or unfulfilled social obligations. But its real challenge lies ahead, as its current expansion is beginning under acrimonious circumstances, without the proper community consultation.

Ecuadorian law requires the Secretary of Hydrocarbons (SHE) to seek majority approval within the affected community, and in particular among the Sápara and Kichwa indigenous nations, whose authority over developments in their traditional territory Ecuador enshrined when it signed onto

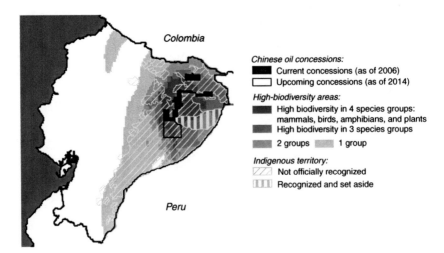

Figure 1.12 Ecuador: Chinese oil concessions, biodiversity and indigenous territory
Source: Ray and Chimienti, 2015.

ILO Convention 169. However, SHE circumvented these obligations by getting the approval of the Sápara president instead of seeking the majority approval of the Sápara and Kichwa communities. SHE also opened temporary outreach offices in the affected area and claims that 16,469 people participated in workshops or submitted comments – a number equal to about one-fourth of the local adult indigenous population, or about one-eighth of the total adult population in the new concession blocks. Sápara and Kichwa community leaders have responded by mounting an international struggle to reclaim authority over their traditional lands and reject all oil development there. The possibilities for Andes Petroleum to establish a positive relationship with the local community are extremely slim at this point, because good-faith negotiations involving the government and the local community are almost impossible (Ray and Chimienti, 2015).

3.3 Government–firm relations and the importance of outreach and learning

Another important venue for cooperation between investors, governments and civil society is in training new arrivals regarding local environmental and social regulations, customs and available local resources. Recent examples in Peru, Argentina and Mexico show that this is a promising area that Latin American governments are just beginning to bring to explore.

In March 2014, Chinalco's Toromocho mine project in Peru (noted above for its community-relocation process) suffered a major setback when the Organism for Environmental Evaluation and Enforcement (OEFA), within the Ministry of the Environment, ordered it to halt operations following a leak of acid wastewater. The problem was generated by unexpectedly heavy rainfall, which Chinalco had apparently not taken into account. After the cleanup, which happened in a period of a few days after rapid action by regulators and Chinalco, the Association of Chinese Companies in Peru, asked the Environment Ministry to organize a series of conferences for all of their members about Peru's environmental regulations. This was an opportunity for the government to address environmental concerns in a proactive way as well as to form working relationships with environmental safety personnel at the investing firms and to lay the groundwork for future cooperation.

Argentina is a unique case: negotiations over oil royalties and environmental and social commitments happen at the provincial level. This arrangement has important drawbacks, in that it creates an incentive for provincial government negotiators to treat short-term royalties and long-term environmental commitments as trade-offs. But it also creates an opportunity for local civil society groups, which have much more access to the negotiators than they would if negotiations happened at the national level. This has allowed for small-business groups to successfully press for foreign oil companies to develop more linkages with local suppliers. For example, Pan American Energy (CNOOC's joint entity with BP) has developed the "SMEs of Golfo San Jorge" program to build capacity for local small businesses and incorporate them into PAE's supply chain. This kind of cooperation requires the presence of the provincial government officials to help recently arrived foreign investors connect with local organizations. Another important opportunity for training and capacity building in Argentina involves facilitating learning between more experienced and more recent investors: in this case, CNOOC and Sinopec, respectively. Our case study shows that CNOOC has a better environmental record than Sinopec, partly because CNOOC partners with BP, which has a long history of pursuing foreign investment and receiving global scrutiny for its environmental record. Even though both CNOOC and Sinopec are Chinese SOEs, one benefits from its cooperation with more-experienced investors while the other does not. Argentina can help bridge these differences by facilitating training for foreign investors, by which new arrivals can learn from their more-experienced peers.

The Mexico case study (Chapter 9) is another situation where training may be very useful. Generally speaking, the Golden Dragon copper tube manufacturing company has abided by environmental and labor law, and has even introduced important new energy efficiency innovations. Nonetheless, it has run into labor difficulty due to cultural barriers. One major obstacle springs from the fact that the firm's Chinese employees do not speak Spanish, the Mexican employees do not speak Chinese and very few members of either group of employees speak a common third language such as English. Another important stumbling block has come from Chinese managers' unfamiliarity with Mexican customs. Chinese minimum wages are quite low, and employees compensate by working extremely long hours. In contrast, Mexican workers tend to be less willing to work on weekends and holidays. Golden Dragon has a history of requiring workers to work on those days, and not compensating them appropriately for their overtime, largely because they are not accustomed to workers expecting that time off. These cultural differences between Golden Dragon's Chinese and Mexican workers are unlikely to be resolved without being specifically addressed, because the two groups of workers do not speak the same languages or socialize together. But they are the types of misunderstandings that can be addressed rather straightforwardly with training to ensure that Mexican labor laws protect workers, and Chinese investors need to respect those labor laws.

4. Lessons for Policy

Our study has shown that the China-led commodity boom in Latin America has accentuated environmental and social conflict in the region. Although Latin American governments, Chinese firms and civil society can be credited for some innovations during the China boom, by and large the benefits of China-led trade and investment have come with significant environmental and social costs. These costs can be reduced by concerted action of Latin American governments, the Chinese government and Chinese firms, and by civil society in Latin America, China and across the world.

4.1 Latin American governments

For Latin America to truly benefit from this commodity-led growth, Latin American governments will need to capture and invest more of the windfall into social and environmental protections. Civil society organizations in the region will need to hold governments more accountable. Our case studies found numerous examples of Latin American governments developing innovative policy responses to the China boom. Ecuador's labor laws, Bolivia's implementation of community consultation and Peru's leadership on transparency stand out as particularly important policy steps. There is tremendous room for Latin American civil society groups to take advantage of these examples to push for higher standards everywhere.

Chinese oil companies have shown in Ecuador that they are capable of operating with almost entirely Ecuadorian staff. Bolivia has shown that it is possible for Chinese mining companies and local SOEs to collaborate to honor communities' decisions about where processing plants should – and should not – be located. Peru has shown that Chinese mining and oil companies are capable of reaching high levels of transparency. Latin American civil society and government can push for these standards to be adopted in countries that do not yet have them, knowing that these standards are not only reasonable, but that Chinese investors are perfectly capable of reaching them.

This progress is being threatened, however, by the very sectors enriched by the China boom, such as mining ministries and large-landowner voting blocs. For example, regulatory reforms in Peru are cutting back the Environment Ministry's oversight of extractive projects, doing so without putting in place safeguards to prevent conflicts of interest in the approval process. In Brazil, the progress in environmental law enforcement faces strong resistance from the "ruralist" landowner voting bloc that has benefited so much from China's demand for soy. Proposed labor-law protections for oil workers in Colombia may not go through because of pressure from the community action boards that have been the target of so many abuse complaints. It is crucial for Latin American governments to hold the line against these deregulation efforts.

Specifically, we recommend that Latin American governments prioritize:

- Enforcement and upgrading of existing environmental and social protections.
- Defending and strengthening the capacity of environmental and social ministries to enforce and upgrade laws, such as with the Ombudsman program in Peru.
- Joining the Extractive Industries Transparency Initiative and encouraging Chinese firms to participate.
- Implementing ILO Convention 169 (which most Latin American governments have signed), by enacting and enforcing requirements for prior consultation with indigenous peoples regarding state policy measures that affect their interests and welfare.
- Requiring foreign investors to hire local workers wherever possible, perhaps through quotas or floors, and limiting the use of subcontracted labor.
- Spearheading collaboration between Latin American governments, local civil society and foreign investors to seek informed consultation before extractive projects begin, and to address local concerns in good faith.
- Investing in capacity building for local businesses and encouraging foreign investors to incorporate them into their supply chains.
- Developing mechanisms by which Latin American governments, the Chinese government and local civil society can collaborate in holding Chinese investors to the standards in China's guidelines and local regulations.
- Creating opportunities for new foreign investors to learn local regulations and customs from governments, civil society and investors that have been present for longer.
- Defending and strengthening the capacity of civil-society organizations for capacity building, networking and taking other opportunities to serve as actors who can monitor the social and environmental behavior of firms and governments alike.

4.2 China and Chinese investors

Safeguarding the social and environmental impacts of Chinese investment overseas helps Chinese firms and the government better identify risk and expand market share. Driving the Latin America–China boom are billions of dollars in Chinese investment in mines, oil and gas fields, dams to power them and railways to get the products to port. These massive projects will take years to come into operation and even more years to pay for themselves. In order to reach that point, Chinese investors will need to mitigate risks to these projects' longevity, especially risks of environmental damage or social conflict that could jeopardize their relationships with host countries.

Our case studies show that Chinese firms are capable of meeting – and beating – the environmental and social standards set by their host countries. In fact, we have found some instances of Chinese investors outperforming their local and international competitors, especially when given the right incentives and regulatory framework. China has taken important steps toward making sure all Chinese investors have incentives to act with corporate social and environmental responsibility, through the CBRC's Green Credit Guidelines and MOFCOM's Guidelines for Environmental Protection in Foreign Investment and Cooperation. Furthermore, making these processes more transparent is also paramount to success, allowing Chinese companies, Latin American governments and civil society to have a better understanding of the true benefits and risks of various investments. However, overseeing investor behavior abroad is extremely difficult without the collaboration of host-country governments and civil society. For that reason, we specifically recommend that China and Chinese investors prioritize:

- Implementing existing social and environmental guidelines and making their use more widespread as Chinese firms and development banks increase their presence in the Americas.
- Working to make the results of social and environmental guidelines more transparent for company representatives, governments and civil society.
- Upgrading current guidelines with independent monitoring, a formal grievance process, enforcement mechanisms for investors who fall short of the standards and other safeguards that have become commonplace among other major foreign investors across the globe.
- Participating in transparency programs in their host countries, such as the environmental reporting requirements in Colombia or the voluntary EITI program in Peru.
- Establishing working relationships with Latin American governments and civil society groups to learn the local regulations and customs.

4.3 Civil society

Policy improvements like these – on both the Latin American and Chinese sides of the Pacific – will only be enhanced by participation from all walks of civil society:

- Direct NGO actions that highlight both the successes and limitations of government and company policies can bring issues to the attention of policymakers and the media. NGOs should expand their networks to monitor new economic actors in their region and link with their counterparts in China and across the world to bring further attention to these issues.
- Academic research and workshops can help derive a more empirically based understanding of these complex issues and serve as a neutral space where governments, companies and civil society can join in dialogue. Academics can also form international networks to compare findings with other analyses and disseminate their work more widely.
- Academic researchers and universities can also play a role by promoting educational and cultural exchange, joint research and training for governments and other members of civil society.
- NGOs, academia and other organizations can collaborate with governments and companies to learn best practices and lessons from past mistakes.
- Business-to-business collaboration such as the association of Chinese enterprises in Peru can meet to learn of best practices and pending regulation and to learn from mistakes.
- Finally, the media can move beyond general discussions of the China–Latin America economic relationship and conduct more empirical reporting efforts that hold governments and firms accountable.

The studies in this project underscore the importance – and the promise – of collaboration between governments, Chinese investors and Latin American civil society. The most successful stories uncovered here are of these groups working together: Bolivia's successful community consultation process, Chinese companies in Peru joining the EITI program and CNOOC's development of a local small-business association in Argentina. China needs Latin American governments and civil society as their eyes and ears for the implementation of their guidelines for overseas investors. Chinese investors need Latin American governments and civil society to train them on local regulations and customs, thereby to prevent environmental and social conflicts from erupting in the first place. Latin American governments need Chinese investors and community groups to come together to find solutions that work for everyone involved. It is imperative for all stakeholder groups to establish working relationships with each other, in order for the China-Latin America relationship to have the greatest benefit and the least risk.

References

Databases

ECLAC (UN Economic Commission for Latin America and the Caribbean). "CEPALStat." Accessed 20 January 2015 from http://estadisticas.cepal.org.

European Commission. "World Input Output Database." Accessed 20 January 2015 from http://www.wiod.org/new_site/home.htm.

Financial Times. "fDiMarkets." Accessed 20 January 2015 from http://www.fdimarkets.com/.

IMF (International Monetary Fund). "World Economic Outlook Database: October 2014 Edition." Accessed 20 January 2015 from http://www.imf.org/external/pubs/ft/weo/2014/02/weodata/index.aspx.

International Rivers, Fundación Proteger and ECOA. "Dams in Amazonia." Accessed 20 January 2015 from http://dams-info.org/.

Red Amazónica de Información Socioambiental Georreferenciada. "Amazon 2012 Protected Areas and Indigenous Territories." Accessed 20 January 2015 from http://raisg.socioambiental.org/mapa-online/index.html.

FAO (Food and Agriculture Organization of the United Nations). "FAO Food Price Index." Accessed 20 January 2015 from http://www.fao.org/worldfoodsituation/foodpricesindex/en/.

FAO (Food and Agricultural Organization of the United Nations). "FAOStat." Accessed 20 January 2015 from http://faostat3.fao.org.

UN Statistics Division. "UN Comtrade." Accessed 20 January 2015 from http://comtrade.un.org/.

Water Footprint Network. "WaterStat: National Water Footprints." Accessed 20 January 2015 from http://www.waterfootprint.org/?page=files/WaterStat.

World Bank. "GEM Commodities." Accessed 20 January 2015 from http://data.worldbank.org/data-catalog/commodity-price-data.

World Bank. "World Development Indicators." Accessed 20 January 2015 from http://databank.worldbank.org/data/home.aspx.

World Resources Institute. "Climate Analysis Indicators Tool 2.0." Accessed 20 January 2015 from http://cait2.wri.org/.

Published works

Bass, Margot S., Matt Finer, Clinton N. Jenkins, Holger Kreft, Diego F. Cisneros-Heredia, Shawn F. McCracken, Nigel C. A. Pitman, Peter H. English, Kelly Swing, Gorky Villa, Anthony Di Fiore, Christian C. Voigt and Thomas H. Kunz (2010). "Global Conservation Significance of Ecuador's Yasuní National Park." *PLoS ONE* 5(1): e8767. doi:10.1371/journal.pone.0008767. http://journals.plos.org/plosone/article?id=10.1371/journal.pone.0008767.

Borregaard, Nicola, Annie Dufey, Maria Teresa Ruiz-Tagle and Santiago Sinclair (2016). "Chinese Incidence on the Chilean Solar Power Sector." Boston University Global

Economic Governance Initiative Working Paper 2015-5. http://www.bu.edu/pardee-school/files/2014/12/Chile1.pdf.

Cruz Fiestas, Darwin (2014). "Empresas Chinas se Interesan en el Tren que Unirá Brasil y Perú," *El Comercio*, 14 August. http://elcomercio.pe/economia/peru/empresas-chinas-se-interesan-tren-que-unira-brasil-y-peru-noticia-1749808.

Fearnside, Philip, Adriano Figueiredo and Sandra Bonjour (2013). "Amazonian Forest Loss and the Long Reach of China's Influence," *Environment, Development and Sustainability*, 15: 325–38.

Hoekstra, A. Y. and Mekonnen, M. M. (2012). "The Water Footprint of Humanity," *Proceedings of the National Academy of Sciences*, 109(9): 3232–37.

Leung, Denise and Yingzhen Zhao (2013). "Environmental and Social Policies in Overseas Investments: Progress and Challenges for China." Washington, DC: World Resources Institute Issue Brief. http://www.wri.org/sites/default/files/pdf/environmental_and_social_policies_in_overseas_investments_china.pdf.

Lódola, Agustín, Rafael Brigo and Fernando Morral (2010). "Mapa de cadenas agroalimentarias de Argentina" in *Cambios estructurales en las actividades agropecuarias: de lo primario a las cadenas globales de valor*, Guillermo Anlló, Roberto Bisang and Guillermo Salvatierra, eds. Santiago: ECLAC. http://repositorio.cepal.org/bitstream/handle/11362/3804/lcw350.pdf.

Ministerio de Energía y Minas (2013). "Ministro Merino Destaca Importancia de Ciudad Nueva Morococha en Actividad Minera." Press Release, 5 September. http://www.minem.gob.pe/_detallenoticia.php?idSector=1&idTitular=5659.

Ministerio de Transportes y Comunicaciones (no date). "Ferrocarril Transcontinental Perú – Brasil (FETAB)." http://www.mtc.gob.pe/portal/home/concesiones/FETAB.html.

Ministério dos Transportes (2013). "Mapa Ferroviário PNV – 2013," http://www2.transportes.gov.br/bit/03-ferro/6-mapas-ferro/ferro-tabela2013.pdf.

Ojos Propios (2013). "Talleres en Morococho." http://www.ojospropios.pe/index.php/talleres/item/156-talleres-en-morococha.

Peters, Glen, Jan Minx, Christopher Weber, and Ottmar Edenhofer (2011). "Growth in Emission Transfers via International Trade from 1990 to 2008," *Proceedings of the National Academy of Sciences*, 108(21): 8903–08.

Ray, Rebecca (2016a, Forthcoming). "Working for the Panda: The Employment Impact of the China Boom in Latin America." Boston University Global Economic Governance Initiative Working Paper.

Ray, Rebecca (2016b, Forthcoming). "The Panda's Pawprint: The Environmental Impact of the China boom in Latin America." Boston University Global Economic Governance Initiative Working Paper.

Santilli, M. 2014. Ruralismo de fronteira. Instituto Socioambiental (ISA), 27 February 2014. Brasília, DF, Brazil: ISA. http://www.socioambiental.org/pt-br/blog/blog-do-ppds/ruralismo-de-fronteira.

Smeraldi, Robert (2014). "Para sair da estaca zero," *Folha da São Paulo*, 26 February. http://www1.folha.uol.com.br/opiniao/2014/02/1417853-roberto-smeraldi-para-sair-da-estaca-zero.shtml.

State Forestry Administration (2010). "A Guide on Sustainable Overseas Forests Management and Utilization by Chinese Enterprises." 26 January. http://www.forestry.gov.cn/portal/main/s/224/content-401396.html.

Tao, Hu (2013). "A Look at China's New Environmental Guidelines on Overseas Investments." Washington, DC: World Resources Institute. http://www.wri.org/blog/2013/07/look-chinas-new-environmental-guidelines-overseas-investments.

Timmer, Marcel P. (2012). "The World Input-Output Database (WIOD): Contents, Sources and Methods," WIOD Working Paper Number 10. http://www.wiod.org/publications/papers/wiod10.pdf.

Zador, Michele, Patrick Comer, Marta Echevarría, Carmen Josse, Jon Hak, Kevin Moull, Jacob Olander, Alexandra Sanchez de Lozado, Regan Smyth, Margaret Stern, Sigrid Vasconez, Bruce Young (2015). "Ecosystem Profile: Tropical Andes Biodiversity Hotspot." Critical Ecosystem Partnership Fund. http://www.cepf.net/SiteCollectionDocuments/tropical_andes/Tropical_Andes_Profile_Draft.pdf.

Part II

CHINA'S AND LATIN AMERICA'S HYDROCARBONS SECTORS

Chapter 2

FDI AND TRADE: IS CHINA RELEVANT FOR THE FUTURE OF OUR ENVIRONMENT? THE CASE OF ARGENTINA

Julian Donaubauer, Andrés López and Daniela Ramos

As with many other Latin American countries, China's economic presence in Argentina has become very significant over the past decade. Most significantly, China has become the main export destination for Argentina's soy products. Increasingly, Argentina is also becoming a strategic location for Chinese firms to invest in oil and gas.

After providing an overview of these trends, this chapter examines in two ways the social and environmental ramifications of Chinese economic engagement in Argentina. First is an aggregate statistical analysis of the greenhouse gas and water intensity of Chinese economic activity in Argentina. Second is a field-based case study of the performance of Chinese firms in Argentina's oil and gas sector.

In terms of greenhouse-gas emissions, we find that China is Argentina's only major export destination for which emissions intensity is growing, and total emissions to China rank second (to Brazil) in terms of trade-based emission from Argentina. In terms of China's water footprint in Argentina, we find that by 2012 China had the second-largest water footprint (to Spain) in 2012, due to the concentration of Chinese imports from Argentina's water-intensive soy sector.

Our case study on Chinese investment is also revealing. Of course it must be acknowledged that oil extraction in Argentina (indeed anywhere) is endemically environmentally degrading. Moreover, due to the fact that Chinese investment in Argentina's oil sector is in the form of mergers and acquisitions (M&As) it is difficult to assign responsibility to environmental damage and liability because environmental damage could be a function of previous ownership. Nevertheless, we find that Chinese firms have been assigned blame for increasing amounts of environmental damage, although they may not be responsible for such damage.

Our fieldwork gives some indication that Chinese firms tend to be more environmentally responsible when in a merger with a Western firm. For example, Sinopec partners with British Petroleum, which has the capabilities to adhere to stricter environmental standards and is under intense scrutiny for its overseas operations by global governments and non-governmental organizations (NGOs). Our interviews also indicate that Chinese firms have tended to respond when civil society and provincial governments apply pressure. However, we also find that there is an institutional mismatch between the federal and provincial governments with respect to the incentives and capacities on the environmental regulation of foreign firms. Provincial governments and civil societies have sought to respond to local water issues around Chinese firms but have lacked institutional and political support from national authorities.

Chinese activity is not necessarily categorically more environmentally degrading within a sector than other domestic or foreign counterparts. That said, as Chinese demand continues to grow in the soy and energy sectors, Argentine authorities will need to strengthen efforts to maximize the benefits and mitigate the environmental risk stemming from economic activity in these sectors. More specific policies might be to:

- Foster "learning" among firms with stronger environmental capabilities with their Chinese counterparts to speed up the environmental learning curve.
- Better align national and provincial efforts at environmental policy in the extractive sector.
- Encourage all foreign firms, including Chinese, to engage with EITI and other mechanisms for transparency and accountability.
- Generally upgrade social and environmental policy, particularly in the extractive sector.

1. Introduction

The emergence of China as a global economic power has had strong impacts on most countries and regions worldwide. Latin America and Argentina have been no exceptions. In a few years China became Argentina's second most important trading partner, behind Brazil. Argentina's trade with China is based on a clear pattern: Argentina exports natural resource-based products (mainly soybeans and soybean oil), while China exports manufactured goods to Argentina. This is the 'standard pattern' of bilateral trade relations with China for all Latin American countries.

In turn, China's investments in Argentina have been growing significantly in recent years, although China is still far from being one of the major investors in the country. The lag of foreign investment relations vis-à-vis trade is not surprising, as undertaking foreign direct investment (FDI) operations requires more experience, internal capabilities and knowledge of potential host countries.

The growing relevance of China as a trade and investment partner of Argentina has generated a number of concerns, including: (a) domestic firms complain that their home and global market share is threatened by China, sometimes going so far as to accuse China of deploying unfair trade practices; (b) employees of those industries are in danger of losing their jobs; (c) environmental and social movements warn about the possible abuses of Chinese firms in light of China's weak domestic legislation in those areas and the antecedents of poor environmental and labor standards applied by Chinese firms when they invest abroad; (d) as many Chinese firms investing abroad are state-owned, fears in the political arena emerge, mainly related to sovereignty issues; (e) as bilateral trade and FDI with China are strongly concentrated in natural resources, concern about the sustainable use of those resources and the environmental impacts of their exploitation have emerged.

This study focuses mainly on the environmental impacts of Argentina's trade and FDI relations with China. The next section briefly describes the main trends associated with those relations. Section 3 analyses the environmental impacts of exports to China. Section 4 deals with the case of Chinese FDI in the oil industry. Section 5 concludes.

Before proceeding, some caveats are needed. First, there are still very few Chinese firms in Argentina, and their presence is very recent. Hence, this is an incipient phenomenon, and great caution must be used in comparing the behavior of Chinese firms with FDI from traditional investor countries whose multinationals have been in the region for a long time – those from Europe, the United States and from other Latin American countries. Second, there is evidence of a wide difference between actual and officially recorded flows of Chinese FDI, so caution should be used in any analysis of this FDI.

Third, Argentina's exports have always been strongly related to its natural resources endowment. Chinese demand is indisputably the leading factor behind the commodity prices boom, but Argentina is a traditional agricultural producer and exporter, and the oil industry in Argentina dates from more than 100 hundred years ago. Soybean and petroleum production in Argentina, as well as concerns about their environmental impacts, started prior to the emergence of China as a global power.

Fourth, although agriculture and oil sectors often have serious environmental impacts, the technology employed by soy, soybean oil and petroleum producers does not differ depending on whether or not the buyers are Chinese. Although in the case of petroleum it could be that different firms differ in their technologies and environmental management systems: as explained below in more detail, this information is not available in the case of Argentina. While Chinese firms are often reluctant to give information on their activities, environmental NGOs criticize all oil firms operating in Argentina with more or less the same determination.

2. Bilateral Trade and Investment Flows

Bilateral trade between Argentina and China has been growing quickly in recent years (Table 2.1). China's share in Argentine exports increased from 1.4 percent to 6.4 percent between 1995 and 2012, having peaked at 9.2 percent in 2007. Currently, China is tied with Chile as the second-largest buyer of Argentina's exports (Brazil is first). The fall in China's share in recent years is related to the reduction in soybean oil exports. In 2009, 45 percent of Argentina's exports of soybean oil went to China (USD 1,440 million), but afterwards exports to China fell dramatically (USD 255 million in 2010), to later recover, but without reaching the 2009 levels (USD 853 million in 2012, less than 20% of total Argentina's exports of soybean oil) –more on this below.[1]

Argentina's exports to China are strongly concentrated in a handful of natural-resource related products. Just five products represented 89 percent of Argentina's exports to China in 2012, and 20 products (at six-digit level of the trade harmonized system classification) amounted to 95 percent. In 2012 Argentina sold 407 different products to China, in contrast with 1,465 products sold to the United States and 1,712 to the European Union (CEPAL, 2013). However, it is important to note that this is a common trend for almost all South American countries, Brazil being the only case with a higher diversification.

Natural-resources value chains are much more relevant in exports to China than in total Argentinian exports (97% compared to 66% in 2012 – see Table 2.2 for details). Soybeans accounted for 56.2 percent of Argentina's exports to China 2012, while soybean oil and crude oil's share reached 13.4 percent and 15 percent, respectively. Other natural resource-related exports include

---

1   This fall reflects two causes. First, China reduced imports of soybean oil as a consequence of increased domestic crushing capacity. Second, Argentina lost market share in the Chinese market: Chinese imports fell from USD 3,300 million in 2008 to USD 1,300 million in 2013, but Argentina's share in those imports fell from 67% to 55% in that period.

Table 2.1 China's relevance as Argentina's trade partner
(1995–2012)

Year	Exports to China		Imports from China	
	Share	**Rank**	**Share**	**Rank**
1995	1.4%	17th	3.0%	8th
1996	2.6%	9th	2.9%	8th
1997	3.3%	5th	3.3%	8th
1998	2.6%	8th	3.7%	8th
1999	2.2%	11th	3.9%	8th
2000	3.0%	6th	4.6%	4th
2001	4.2%	4th	5.2%	3th
2002	4.3%	5th	3.7%	4th
2003	8.3%	4th	5.2%	4th
2004	7.6%	4th	6.2%	3th
2005	7.9%	4th	7.8%	3th
2006	7.5%	4th	9.1%	3th
2007	9.2%	2th	11.4%	3th
2008	9.1%	2th	12.4%	2th
2009	6.6%	3th	12.4%	3th
2010	8.5%	2th	13.5%	2th
2011	7.4%	2th	14.3%	2th
2012	6.4%	2th	14.6%	2th

Source: Authors' calculations using INDEC (National Institute of Statistics and Census) data.

tobacco, leather, poultry, wool, wine, groundnut oil, barley, whey, mollusks and, to a lesser extent, minerals.

As an origin of imports, in 2012 China ranked second (as in the case of exports, Brazil ranked first). China's share in Argentina's imports went from 3.0 percent in 1995 to 14.6 percent in 2012 (see Table 2.1). China's exports to Argentina are almost totally composed of industrial goods. Moreover, the composition of those exports has been gaining diversification and complexity during the last two decades, following the trends in Chinese exports to the world (and the transformation of the Chinese economy). Hence, while in 1995 China's exports to Argentina consisted mainly of consumer goods, China currently is a key provider of capital goods and intermediate inputs (e.g., petrochemicals, chemicals, steel, etc.); in both cases China's share in Argentina's total imports went from less than 2 percent in 1995 to around 22 percent in 2012 (see Table 2.3).

As a result of this divergence between exports and imports, Argentina has developed a growing trade deficit with China (see Table 2.4). In this context, Argentina has adopted various protectionist measures that were met with

Table 2.2 Composition of Argentina's exports (2012)

	Exports to the World	Exports to China
Primary goods	24%	57%
Agriculture-based manufactures	34%	29%
Industry-based manufactures	34%	3%
Petroleum, energy and gas	8%	11%

Source: Authors' calculations using INDEC data.

Table 2.3 China's share in Argentina's imports (2012)

	1995	2000	2007	2012
Capital goods	1.9%	4.3%	15.6%	21.8%
Intermediate inputs	1.7%	2.6%	9.1%	22.5%
Parts and accessories for capital goods	1.0%	2.8%	9.9%	11.6%
Consumer goods	11.6%	11.9%	24.1%	24.7%
Others	0.1%	1.0%	0.6%	0.3%
	3.0%	4.6%	11.4%	14.6%

Source: Authors' calculations based on INDEC data.

similar Chinese initiatives. For example, in 2010 China suspended imports of Argentina's soybean oil during several months and, while later on the ban was lifted, Argentina's presence in the Chinese market never regained the previous levels.

In contrast to the relevance of bilateral trade, FDI flows (when measured by official investment statistics) are very low. According to Argentina's Central Bank (BCRA), Chinese FDI in Argentina reached around USD 500 million between 2005 and 2012, barely 0.7 percent of all FDI inflows to Argentina in that period, although Chinese FDI has been growing tremendously in that period and recorded an acceleration in 2010–2012 (see Table 2.5).

As is well known, to a large extent Chinese FDI goes to Hong Kong, Macau, Taiwan and other tax havens and offshore financial centers. However, if we include Chinese FDI made through these countries (again on the basis of BCRA estimations), China's share remains approximately at the same level (0.7%) of total FDI arrived at Argentina between 2005 and 2012.

Taking into consideration this pattern of Chinese FDI outflows, Chen and Pérez Ludeña (2013) have re-estimated the destinations of those outflows. Their

Table 2.4 Bilateral trade between Argentina and China (1990–2012)

Period	Annual average value (USD million)			Annual growth rate	
	Exports	Imports	Balance	Exports	Imports
1990–1994	201	412	−211	−1.7%	119.1%
1995–1999	591	894	−303	15.5%	13.0%
2000–2004	1,625	935	690	34.8%	4.9%
2005–2009	4,372	4,476	−104	3.5%	21.2%
2010–2012	5,679	9,417	−3,738	−3.6%	7.0%

Source: Authors' calculations using INDEC data.

results suggest that actual Chinese FDI in Argentina is considerably higher than that reported in official statistics. Chen and Pérez Ludeña's estimates confirm that until 2009 Chinese investments in Argentina were very low (just USD 143 million between 1990 and that year). However, the authors, using press reports regarding two large Chinese takeovers in Argentina's petroleum industry (including the purchase of 50 percent of local oil firm Bridas by CNOOC, China National Offshore Oil Corporation, and the purchase of the Argentine assets of Occidental Petroleum by Sinopec, China Petroleum and Chemical Corporation), estimate that in 2010 and 2011 Chinese FDI in Argentina reached USD 3.1 and 2.45 billion, respectively. In fact, due to these large investments, Argentina was second to Brazil as a destination for Chinese FDI in Latin America. In contrast, estimations by Yue (2013) – based on MOFCOM data – suggest that Argentina ranked fifth in Latin America in terms of Chinese FDI stock (2010 data), also behind Peru, Venezuela and Panama.

However, even when Chen and Pérez Ludeña's estimations are taken into account, Chinese FDI in Argentina is well below the bombastic figures announced at different times, both officially as well as through the media. At present, there are only a dozen Chinese firms in Argentina, mostly with commercial offices only. To this, we may add the peculiar phenomenon of the Chinese supermarkets, which have gained a widespread presence in Buenos Aires and other Argentinean cities in recent years.

According to official figures, and in great contrast with the case of trade, Chinese investments in Argentina are less concentrated in natural resources than total FDI in the country (see Table 2.6). In 2012, according to official BCRA figures, mining accounted for 11 percent of Chinese FDI stock in the country – the main Chinese investor in this sector is China Metallurgical Group Corporation – and petroleum for another 13 percent – the already mentioned cases of Sinopec and CNOOC, although a huge difference exists between the official figures of Chinese FDI in this sector and the above-mentioned

Table 2.5 China compared with the five main origins of FDI inflows to Argentina (2004–2012, FDI stock and flows in USD billions)

Country	2004	2005	2006	2007	2008	2009	2010	2011	2012	Growth in FDI stock (2004–2012)
Stocks:										
Spain	17.0	18.9	21.1	23.1	23.1	22.6	23.2	22.6	20.2	19%
United States	10.3	11.7	12.2	13.9	14.1	14.4	15.2	16.8	19.4	89%
Netherlands	4.2	5.2	5.3	5.7	6.7	6.9	7.0	7.3	9.6	129%
Brazil	1.8	2.5	2.8	3.7	5.0	4.3	5.4	6.8	7.0	250%
Chile	2.0	2.7	3.1	3.6	4.2	4.4	5.5	6.7	6.8	282%
China	0.0	0.0	0.0	0.1	0.1	0.1	0.2	0.2	0.6	4,439%
TOTAL	56.9	63.0	69.1	78.3	81.4	80.9	88.7	96.1	102.3	79%
China (Flows, USD million)	-	-2.8	30.7	39.5	26.4	0.0	100.5	38.3	274.4	

Source: Central Bank of Argentina (BCRA). Note: China inflows measured in USD millions.

Table 2.6 China's investment pattern compared with the main origins of FDI inflows in Argentina (2012, FDI stock in USD million)

	Spain	United States	Netherlands	Brazil	Chile	China
	Millions of USD					
Petroleum	2,392	6,345	1,239	248	67	76
Manufacturing	5,599	4,946	2,515	1,499	3,451	53
Banking	1,838	1,050	1,123	0	702	308
Commerce	1,287	714	156	1,287	238	54
Communications	2,765	1,194	304	37	17	1
Mining	193	454	2,294	1,572	482	65
Grains	584	437	427	3	12	0
Other	5,550	4,240	1,493	2,372	1,791	28
Total	20,206	19,380	9,552	7,018	6,760	584
	Percent of whole					
Petroleum	12%	33%	13%	4%	1%	13%
Manufacturing	28%	26%	26%	21%	51%	9%
Banking	9%	5%	12%	0%	10%	53%
Commerce	6%	4%	2%	18%	4%	9%
Communications	14%	6%	3%	1%	0%	0%
Mining	1%	2%	24%	22%	7%	11%
Grains	3%	2%	5%	0%	0%	0%
Other	28%	22%	16%	34%	27%	5%
Total	100%	100%	100%	100%	100%	100%

Source: BCRA.

figures reported in the media related to Sinopec and CNOOC investments in Argentina. Although no official data on Chinese investments in agriculture exist, on the basis of media information we know that various Chinese firms, such as Noble Grain and Chongqing Grain Group, have been buying land and investing in grains trade in Argentina.[2] In 2012, 30 percent of total FDI in Argentina was concentrated in the natural-resource related sectors of oil, mining and grains, while China's corresponding FDI figure was 25 percent. The bulk of Chinese FDI was in banking (more than 50%, reflecting the acquisition in 2012 of the Standard Bank by the ICBC), and the other relevant sectors were industry (9%, concentrated in assembly operations in the electronic industry in Tierra del Fuego island,[3] such as those by Huawei, TCL and Ambassador Fueguina) and commerce (9%, including the above-mentioned Chinese supermarkets).

If we turn now to Chen and Pérez Ludeña's estimations, although they do not disaggregate their figures by sector, we may infer that the concentration of Chinese FDI in natural resources is much higher than that suggested by the official data, considering that the bulk of Chinese investments in Argentina, according to the authors' figures, is associated with the above-mentioned takeovers by CNOOC and Sinopec. These purchases highlight the dominant presence of state-owned firms (SOEs) in Chinese FDI, especially in strategic industries such as oil – more on this below (Dussel Peters, 2013).

2.1 Environmental impacts of bilateral trade

Environmental damages of bilateral trade can be measured along several dimensions: emissions, energy consumption, water use and pollution, land degradation, deforestation and so on. Due to a lack of cross-country data regarding most of these aspects, the vast majority of the existing literature examining the effect of trade on the environment focuses on emissions (e.g., Antweiler et al., 2001; Frankel and Rose, 2005). We follow this approach and use data on carbon emission intensities from Peters et al. (2011).[4] In

---

2   In 2012 a law was passed limiting the acquisitions of lands by foreign owners, which led to the cancellation of some Chinese projects in this sector.

3   A special regime promoting the manufacturing of electronic products in Tierra del Fuego was enacted some years ago, fostering investments, but without generating any significant linkage with the local economy (beyond employment generation) – since all components except those related to packaging are imported – and totally oriented to providing the domestic market.

4   Alternatively, data on emissions of noxious gases are available from the UN Framework Convention on Climate Change (UNFCCC) Secretariat (available at http://unfccc.int)

Table 2.7 Greenhouse gas emissions (GHG)* and emission intensity** of Argentinean exports 2007 and 2012, by export market

	Total GHG emissions from exports			GHG emissions intensity of exports		
	2007	**2012**	**Change, 2007–2012**	**2007**	**2012**	**Change, 2007–2012**
Brazil	7,950	10,614	+33.5%	0.76	0.64	−15.8%
Chile	3,199	3,233	+1.1%	0.77	0.64	−16.9%
China	2,087	2,335	+11.9%	0.40	0.47	+17.5%
USA	5,438	4,767	−12.4%	1.25	1.15	−8.0%
Spain	1,342	1,487	+10.7%	0.65	0.56	−13.8%

* In 1,000 tons of CO_2 equivalents; based on 2007 emission data.

** In kg of CO_2 equivalents per USD.

Source: COMTRADE; GTAP database; Peters et al. (2011).

addition, we use data on the water footprint of production to estimate the water content of Argentinean agricultural exports to its major trading partners. Among Argentina's major export markets, we find that China is the only one associated with a growing carbon intensity and is the second most water-intensive export destination.

To measure the impact of exports to China on Argentina's emissions (compared to other export destinations) we use data from the Global Trade Analysis Project (GTAP) (Peters et al., 2011). This project provides information on emission intensities (MT of CO_2 equivalent per USD of output) for 57 production sectors in Argentina. Table 2.7 relates the latest available data on overall greenhouse gas emissions (for the year 2007) to Argentina's exports to its main trading partners at two points in time (2007 and 2012).

The first thing that stands out is that the overall amount of greenhouse gas emissions embodied in bilateral trade increased in Argentina's trade with all its main trading partners except with the United States, where a sharp decline in emissions (exceeding 12 percent) has taken place.[5] At the same time, the emission intensity dropped in all export markets except China. The emissions intensity of exports to China rose significantly in this five-year period, from

---

and in the World Bank's World Development Indicators (WDI) database (available at http://data.worldbank.org/data-catalog/world-development-indicators). However, sector-disaggregated information is rarely available. The same is true for data on energy consumption across different sectors (e.g., UN Energy Statistics, available at http://unstats.un.org/unsd/energy/edbase.htm).

5   However, this is also due to reduced trade flows over that period (−4.88%).

the equivalent of 0.40 metric tons of CO_2 per USD to the equivalent of 0.47 metric tons: an increase of 17.5 percent. However, this intensity is still the lowest among major export markets. Argentina's exports to China are less polluting than exports to all other major trading partners. Exports to the United States are for example more than twice as polluting as exports to China (1.15 vs. 0.47 kg of emissions per USD of goods exported).

Table 2.8 shows Argentina's exports to its main trading partners with emission intensities on a sectoral basis. Overall, in terms of total emissions (in thousands of metric tons of CO_2 equivalents), agricultural and petroleum products seem to be most harmful to the environment. The share of these products in total Argentinean exports to China is higher than its share in exports to the world as a whole (see Table 2.2 and the discussion in Section 2).

Next, we focus on the water consumption and pollution of Argentinean exports. For that purpose, we calculate the water content of Argentinean agricultural exports to its major trading partners, using data from the water footprint network:[6] "The water footprint of a product is the volume of freshwater used to produce the product, measured over the full supply chain" (Aldaya et al., 2012, 2). It takes into account both water consumption (green and blue water footprint) and pollution (grey water footprint). This indicator is widely accepted and used for example in Aldaya et al. (2010) to calculate the virtual water content of primary crop exports of three major exporting countries: the United States, Argentina and Canada. Here, we use data on the total water footprint (henceforth WFP), which is the sum of the green, blue and grey water footprint.[7]

Table 2.9 matches exports (on a product level) to Argentina's five most important trading partners with data on the WFP associated with the production of the respective good[8] in Argentina. As can be seen in Table 2.9, the most water-intensive sectors are biodiesel (with a total WFP of 11,214 liters/liter of biodiesel), soy (between 1,751 and 4,041 m^3 of water/MT of soy), wheat (about 1,900 m^3/MT), and meat (almost 5,800 m^3/MT). While Argentinean exports to most of its main trading partners are relatively diversified across product categories, agricultural exports to China and Spain are concentrated in a few products. In the case of China more than 70 percent of the goods that are exported from Argentina are soy based. Spain imports

---

6   Mekonnen and Hoekstra (2010a, 2010b).

7   Alternative sources are the WDI on water pollution or FAO's Aquastat (available at http://www.fao.org/nr/water/aquastat/main/index.stm), where information on water withdrawal by sector can be found. In both datasets, however, the sectoral breakdown is on a rather aggregated level. In addition to that, data are not available per kilogram or USD of output in each sector.

8   Irrespective of the trading partner.

Table 2.8 Greenhouse gas emissions of Argentinean exports 2007–2012, most polluting sectors for each trading partner

	Top Exports, 2007			Top Exports, 2012		
	Sector	Emission intensity*	Total emissions**	Sector	Emission intensity*	Total emissions**
Brazil	**Total exports**	**0.76**	**7,950**	**Total exports**	**0.64**	**10,614**
	Vegetables, fruit, nuts	6.57	3,186	Vegetables, fruit, nuts	6.57	5,170
	Petroleum, coal products	1.60	2,646	Petroleum, coal products	1.60	1,997
	Crops, NEC	7.25	921	Crops, NEC	7.25	1,777
	Wheat	0.33	378	Wheat	0.33	460
	Ferrous metals	1.27	113	Ferrous metals	1.27	288
Chile	**Total exports**	**0.77**	**3,199**	**Total exports**	**0.64**	**3,233**
	Petroleum, coal products	1.60	916	Crops, NEC	7.25	813
	Gas	1.58	627	Oil	0.74	733
	Electricity	8.73	343	Petroleum, coal products	1.60	451
	Crops, NEC	7.25	284	Vegetables, fruit, nuts	6.57	385
	Vegetables, fruit, nuts	6.57	235	Mineral products, NEC	2.29	225
China	**Total exports**	**0.40**	**2,087**	**Total exports**	**0.47**	**2,335**
	Oilseeds	0.38	1,002	Oilseeds	0.38	1,025
	Wool, silk-worm cocoons	14.50	550	Wool, silk-worm cocoons	14.50	601
	Oil	0.74	313	Oil	0.74	444
	Vegetable oils and fats	0.05	85	Vegetables, fruit, nuts	6.57	71
	Vegetables, fruit, nuts	6.57	34	Fishing	0.80	60

(continued)

Table 2.8 Continued

	Top Exports, 2007			Top Exports, 2012		
	Sector	Emission intensity*	Total emissions**	Sector	Emission intensity*	Total emissions**
USA	**Total exports**	**1.25**	**5,438**	**Total exports**	**1.15**	**4,767**
	Vegetables, fruit, nuts	6.57	2,324	Vegetables, fruit, nuts	6.57	2,901
	Petroleum, coal products	1.60	1,769	Oil	0.74	591
	Oil	0.74	524	Ferrous metals	1.27	438
	Ferrous metals	1.27	183	Petroleum, coal products	1.60	202
	Crops, NEC	7.25	125	Crops, NEC	7.25	175
Spain	**Total exports**	**0.65**	**1,342**	**Total exports**	**0.56**	**1,487**
	Vegetables, fruit, nuts	6.57	713	Vegetables, fruit, nuts	6.57	986
	Fishing	0.80	281	Fishing	0.80	301
	Cereal grains, NEC	0.35	91	Metals, NEC	0.44	54
	Ferrous metals	1.27	71	Food products, NEC	0.08	54
	Food products nec	0.08	69	Chemical, rubber, plastic prods	0.05	48

* In kg of CO_2 equivalents per USD
** In 1,000 tons of CO_2 equivalents; based on 2007 emission data
Source: COMTRADE; GTAP database; Peters et al. (2011).

Table 2.9 Water footprint* of Argentinean agricultural exports, main products for each trading partner, 2012

	% of total bilateral exports	Total WFP** (in m³/MT)
Brazil		
Wheat and meslin	8.37	1.891
Wheat or meslin flour	1.39	1.913
Malt, not roasted	1.29	2.086
Pears	0.96	0.370
Milk and cream powder	0.73	2.668
Chile		
Animal feed prep.	3.71	1.603
Soya-bean oil-cake	3.52	1.751
Animal/veg fats & oils	3.46	6.640
Bovine cuts boneless	3.36	5.791
Wheat and meslin	2.82	1.891
China		
Soya beans	54.22	2.110
Soybean oil	16.96	4.041
Tobacco, unmanufactured	1.94	1.508
Poultry	1.47	2.661
Ground-nut oil	1.47	9.101
USA		
Grape wines	9.07	0.531
Honey, natural	2.94	2.592
Grape juice	2.60	0.609
Black tea	1.79	0.531
Cranberries	1.61	0.664
Spain		
Biodiesel***	37.03	11.214
Soya-bean oil-cake	22.99	1.751
Frozen shrimps, prawns	9.80	NA
Molluscs	2.40	NA
Resid. of legum. plants	1.82	NA

* Average, 1996–2005.
** Total water footprint (WFP) is the sum of green, blue and grey water footprint.
*** litre/litre of biodiesel.
Source: COMTRADE; Mekonnen and Hoekstra (2010a, 2010b).

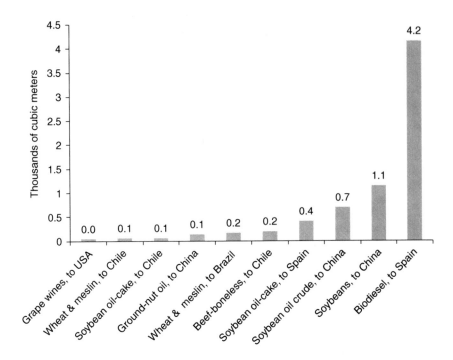

Figure 2.1 Total* water footprint of Argentinean agricultural exports, main products for major trading partners 2012 (in m³/ton, weighted by product shares in total bilateral exports)

Source: COMTRADE; Mekonnen and Hoekstra (2010a, 2010b).

* Sum of green, blue and grey water footprint, using intensity data for 1996–2005.

more than 60 percent biodiesel and soya products. Thus, in terms of water consumption, trade with these two countries seems to be more biased towards water-intensive goods. This becomes even clearer when we weigh Argentinean exports to its major trading partners (on a product level) with the respective product shares in total bilateral exports (see Figure 2.1).

All in all, given the limitations of the available data and the respective analysis, it is difficult to assess whether Argentinean exports to China are more polluting than those to the country's other main trading partners. Although greenhouse gas emission intensities of Chinese imports are rising, they are still low compared to other countries' imports' emission intensities. Thus, the most critical aspect regarding the environmental effects of trade is water consumption and water pollution. Particularly, the disproportionately high share of soya products in total exports in combination with the water-intensive cultivation of soya is a major concern.

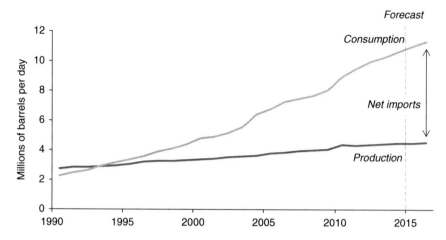

Figure 2.2 Production and consumption of oil and gas, China (1990–2013, thousands of daily barrels)
Source: EIA International Energy Statistics and Short-Term Energy Outlook, February 2015.

3. Chinese Investments in the Oil Industry in Argentina (CNOOC and Sinopec)

China was a net oil exporter until the early 1990s, later becoming the second-largest oil importer after the United States. This change was strongly related to its rapid economic growth, increasing urbanization, the expansion of its transport system and the growing demand of its refineries.[9]

Chinese oil production has seen sustained growth since the mid-1980s, and its current volume is twice that of the earlier period, as shown in Figure 2.2. Hence, its share in global oil production has increased from 3.3 percent in the 1980s to 5.0 percent currently. According to the US Energy Information Administration (EIA), in 2012 China was the world's fourth-largest oil producer and the second-largest consumer (with 11.5% of total consumption). Natural gas production has also expanded rapidly, and China's share in world production rose from 0.6 to more than 2.5 percent between 1990 and 2012, while China is currently the fourth world consumer with a 3.9 percent of the global natural gas demand. Hence, in both cases, China is a net importer of energy.

---

9   According to IHS Global Insight, refining capacity in China (currently 11.6 million barrels per day) has doubled since 2000 and is projected to reach 14 million in 2015. FACTS Global Energy estimates that China will add another 5 million from 2015 to 2020. In contrast, Argentina's refining capacity is 700,000 barrels per day.

Three large oil SOEs are the key players in the energy sector in China. First, CNOOC, (founded in 1982) controls the largest part of offshore oil production and exploration. Second, Sinopec (created in 1983), focuses on refining and marketing. Third, CNPC (China National Petroleum Corporation) was established in 1988 as a spin-off of the Oil Industry Ministry and focuses on *onshore* production (Strecker et al., 2000). In the late 1990s the Chinese government aimed at creating global, vertically integrated firms, forcing CNPC and Sinopec to restructure: CNPC transferred oil fields to Sinopec in exchange for refineries. Notwithstanding, CNPC is still dominant in the upstream segment[10] while Sinopec controls the downstream stage.

Although the three big oil companies are SOEs, they manage themselves to some extent, applying private managerial criteria, and they operate in a dual price system in which they are able to sell any oil and gas exceeding the quotas fixed by the government at market prices. Investments are financed through retained earnings or loans, so public financial support is being gradually reduced (Houser, 2008). In turn, the refining sector has been modernized and consolidated in recent years, as public policies have promoted mergers and closures of smaller refineries for economies of scale and higher efficiency.[11]

The growing need for energy has led Chinese firms to increase offshore exploration and production and to embark upon international expansion (Xu, 2007). The government supports this goal through strengthening bilateral relations with target countries. The Ministry of Trade and the National Development and Reform Commission (NDRC) have defined a list of (mostly developing) countries and resources eligible for investment subsidies (Zweig and Jianhai, 2005).

Another objective of internationalization in this sector is to develop technical expertise in non-conventional resources and gain access to profitable segments of the upstream market (EIA, 2013). According to Wu (2008) other drivers include: (a) the need to survive through continuous expansion both at home as well as abroad; (b) the aim of diversifying business, which is higher abroad (where competition is more open) than in China; (c) the search for higher profits (which, even if they are below those obtained by other oil companies, are still higher than those obtained in the Chinese market) and (d) full employment of their technology and labor force.

---

10 CNPC and its subsidiary PetroChina have 60% and 80% of the oil and gas markets, respectively.

11 The increased diversification of the oil import sources led Chinese refineries to adapt new technologies able to process different types of crude oil, like the Venezuelan and other Latin American crudes, which are usually heavier than those coming from the Middle West.

In general, Chinese oil companies pursue FDI through M&As. Firms finance their projects with their own resources except in highly strategic projects in which access to public funding is available (Wu, 2008). It is often the case that, as these firms have highly diversified business interests, they compete in bids in which they end up offering much more than their competitors can justify, taking advantage of their huge financial capacity, their lower profit expectations, and the access to public financing. According to Wu (2008), this is does not reflect the Chinese government's geopolitical strategy, but domestic political considerations and inter-agency competition. In fact, the Chinese government has been pushing firms to form partnerships for investing abroad instead of competing among themselves.[12] Finally, it must be noted that Chinese firms are willing to invest in countries considered too risky by other international oil companies.

Summing up, Chinese oil FDI is seemingly guided by a mix of market-based decisions by SOEs, by competition among them for the favor of the government, and by political pressures to increase access to energy sources. This combination of factors, jointly with the above-mentioned aggressive attitude in search of new businesses, has generated concerns regarding China's growth in the global energy market in coming years.[13]

Outward Chinese FDI has grown since the beginning of the twenty-first century: since 2009 Chinese firms have bought assets in Africa, Asia, Latin America, the United States and the Middle East. According to EIA data, in 2011 alone those firms invested USD 18 billion in energy assets, mainly related to natural and non-conventional gas. As a result, Chinese oil production abroad went from 140 million barrels per day in 2000 to more than 1.5 billion in 2011 and forecasts suggest that its share will keep growing in coming years. Currently, 20 percent of oil and gas production of Chinese firms comes from abroad and it is estimated that this figure will grow to 30 percent in 2015 (see EIA, 2013 using PFC Energy data). According to press information in 2010 alone Chinese oil firms bought more than USD 38 billion in assets, more than one-third of which pertained to operations in Latin America (diariodefusiones. com, 2010).

Regarding Latin America, the first firm to invest in the region was CNPC, which has operated oil wells in Peru and Venezuela since the 1990s and in Ecuador since 2006. Sinopec started operations in the region in 2006 in Colombia while CNOOC was the last to invest in the region (Argentina,

---

12 While CNOOC and Sinopec competed for bidding in Brazil, Petrochina, Sinopec and Sinochem associated to buy oil assets in Ecuador.
13 Some authors, however, argue that this strategy is not very different from that applied by other state oil firms like those of India, Brazil and Malaysia (see Wu, 2008).

2010). According to CEPAL (2013), FDI in Latin America of these three firms amounts to more than USD 23 billion and they currently have investments in all producing countries except Bolivia and Mexico.

3.1 *The Argentinean oil sector*

Argentina contributes less than 1 percent to worldwide oil production (EIA data, 2012). This figure has been stable during the last three decades. Natural gas production has fluctuated but with a long-term growth trend, allowing a slight increase in the share of world production (1.1% in 2012, according to EIA data).

The hydrocarbons sector has been a key activity for Argentina's economic development since the discovery of the first oil well at the beginning of the twentieth century. On the one hand, the oil and gas industry has generated employment, wealth and, in recent decades, exports. On the other hand, Argentina's energy matrix is highly dependent on hydrocarbons.[14] This dependency has grown in recent decades after the discovery of large natural gas fields in the mid-1970s. This trend has not reversed in spite of the fact that gas reserves have been steadily falling since the mid-2000s.

The fall in oil and gas production during the last decade, as shown in Figures 2.3 and 2.4, emerged *pari passu* a strong increase in energy consumption, resulting from high growth and strong subsidies that dis-incentivize energy savings. Hence, Argentina a net energy importer in recent years.[15] For its part, refining capacity is limited. Argentina has ten oil refineries – with four of them accounting for three-quarters of total refining capacity[16] – but their production is not sufficient to meet domestic demand, leading to the need of importing fuels – though a trade surplus in oil still exists.

Although Argentina produces more natural gas than any other South American country, production levels have been falling since the 2006 peak, and the country became a net importer in 2008, as shown in Figure 2.5. This in turn puts strong pressures on the external accounts: in 2012 the energy trade deficit reached USD 7 billion and remained slightly below

---

14 Argentina's reliance on petroleum is not very different from the world's matrix, but Argentina's gas dependency is much higher than the world average, while the use of coal is much less extensive.

15 Both the oil and gas prices in the domestic market have been systematically below the international ones since 2002.

16 YPF (La Plata and Luján de Cuyo), Shell (Buenos Aires) and Exxon Mobil (Campana).

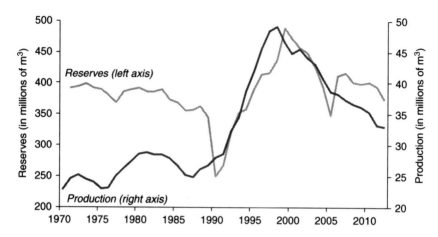

Figure 2.3 Oil production and reserves
Source: Authors' calculation using IAPG data.

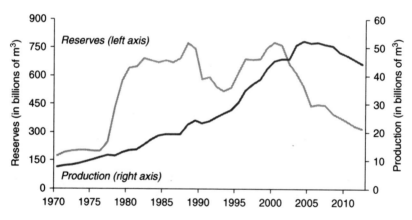

Figure 2.4 Natural gas production and reserves
Source: Authors' calculation using IAPG data.

USD 6 billion in 2013 and 2014.[17] The recent announcement regarding the start of the exploration of supposedly very large shale oil and shale gas fields could signal the possibility of a reversal of this situation in the medium and long term.[18]

---

17 By the mid-2000s the surplus in the energy trade balance reached USD 5,600 million/ USD 6,000 million (INDEC's data for 2005 and 2006, respectively).

18 The first drilling of a non-conventional hydrocarbon field was made in 2010 in Loma de la Lata, Neuquén. Shale gas and oil were discovered in the 1960s in Argentina, but

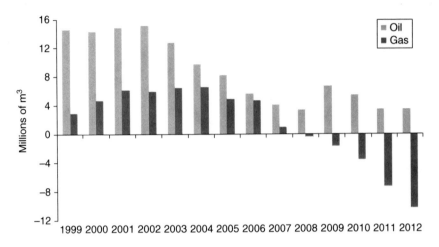

Figure 2.5 Oil and natural gas trade balance (in m³)
Source: IAPG.

Hydrocarbon sector deregulation[19] began in the late 1980s and early 1990s.[20] Many exploration and production areas that were previously owned by the SOE YPF[21] were privatized, and through Law 24,145 hydrocarbon resources were federalized, giving the dominion of the wells to the respective provinces. As a result, oil production grew significantly and self-reliance was attained by mid-1990s (which was later lost in mid-2000s). YPF itself was first sold to private investors through IPOs in different stock exchanges, but later the Spanish firm Repsol took control of the company until its renationalization in 2011.[22]

At present, many domestic and foreign firms operate in the hydrocarbon sector in Argentina, including two Chinese SOEs, CNOOC – through its share in Pan American Energy (PAE) – and Sinopec, as shown in Tables 2.10

---

the technology to exploit them was not available, and hydrocarbon prices were not high enough, to allow their profitable exploitation (Di Sbroiavacca, 2013).

19 In fact, this allowed free entry for private companies to the oil industry, the granting of new concessions for oil areas and freedom to invest in refineries and gas stations.

20 Decree 1,055/89 created a free crude oil market in the exploration and production stages (upstream). Decree 1,212/89 defined new rules of the game for the refining and marketing stages (downstream). Finally, Decree 1,589/89 established free trade and eliminated tariffs and other trade taxes for oil and its derivatives (http://www.ecopuerto.com/petroleo07/informes/infoPetrolero.html).

21 YPF is the largest Argentinean firm by sales and assets.

22 The renationalization was based, according to the official arguments, on the fact that Repsol had not been investing enough in Argentina and diverted funds to make investments abroad. Previously, some provinces had cancelled exploration and production licenses owned by Repsol. Repsol still has 12% of the YPF capital stock.

Table 2.10 Argentina's main oil producers (2012, % of total production)

Producer	% of total production
YPF S.A.	35.0
Pan American	**17.9**
Petrobras Argentina S.A.	6.8
Pluspetrol S.A.	6.7
Sinopec Argentina Exploration Inc.	**6.6**
Chevron Argentina S.R.L.	5.2
Tecpetrol S.A.	4.0
Total Austral S.A.	3.1
Petrolera Entre Lomas S.A.	2.6
Compañías Asociadas Petroleras S.A.	1.9

Source: IAPG.

Table 2.11 Argentina's main natural gas producers (2012, % of total production)

Producer	% of total production
YPF S.A.	23.4
Pan American	**12.0**
S.A.	9.0
S.R.L.	3.9
S.A.	3.3
S.R.L.	3.1
S.A.	2.9
S.A.	2.8
Sinopec Argentina Exploration Inc.	**1.7**

Source: IAPG.

and 2.11. These firms rank second and fifth in terms of oil production in Argentina, respectively.

3.2 Main features of the Chinese oil firms investing in Argentina

According to Houser (2008), Sinopec had 700,000 employees in 2006, and by 2011 its payroll had surpassed one million employees (Fortune data).[23] The

23 CNPC, the largest Chinese oil firm, had 1.7 million employees in that year (Houser, 2008).

firm commands 46 percent of the Chinese refining market, and it is the second-largest firm globally in refining capacity (with five million barrels per day in China alone in 2012). It is also the second-largest firm globally by number of gas stations. Since 2000 Sinopec stock has been listed in the New York and Hong Kong stock exchanges. In recent years the company has focused on quality and efficiency improvements and expanding into other chemical market segments (ICIS Chemical Business, 2013)

Sinopec was the last of the three large Chinese oil firms to invest abroad. The firm operates more than 30 oil and gas projects abroad, including in Iran, Algeria, Saudi Arabia, Kazakhstan, Brazil, Canada, Egypt, Colombia, Oman, Nigeria, Cuba, Venezuela and Argentina (Wu, 2008). In the case of Latin America, Sinopec has expanded its operations through flexible contracts and agreements with oil companies already in the region (Xu, 2007). It is estimated that Sinopec production capacity abroad reached nearly 450,000 barrels per day in 2011.[24]

CNOOC is the third Chinese oil company in terms of sales, and it has specialized in offshore exploration and production (Xu, 2007). Although it is a much smaller company – Houser (2008) estimates that it has 37,000 employees – CNOOC has proven to be a major competitor for CNPC and Sinopec, due not only to its projects offshore in South China but also its growing participation in downstream operations.

Internationalization has been a key objective of the firm since its creation, and its overseas activities have been steadily growing since the first operation abroad started in 1993 in Indonesia. CNOOC has a highly professionalized management that has shown great ability to find profitable businesses abroad and establish strategic M&As, which have been its preferred channel for FDI (Xu, 2007).

CNOOC's production capacity abroad reached 150,000 barrels per day in 2011, and grew further in 2012 through new acquisitions of oil and gas companies.[25] These acquisitions aimed not only at increasing proven reserves and production capacity but also at gaining access to technical expertise in non-conventional gas fields and deep-water oil.[26] At present, it is estimated that around 20 percent of CNOOC's proven reserves are located abroad. (EIA, 2012)

---

24 http://www.eia.gov/countries/cab.cfm?fips=ch
25 In 2012, CNOOC signed an agreement to acquire the Canadian TNC Nexen.
26 In this scenario, one of the main operations of investment abroad was the acquisition of offshore areas in Indonesia by REPSOL-YPF in 2005.

3.3 History of Chinese FDI in the oil sector in Argentina

The first Chinese oil company to invest in Argentina was CNOOC. In March 2010 it acquired 50 percent of the local oil company Bridas for USD 3.1 billion. Some months later, Bridas aimed to acquire the 60 percent of Pan American Energy (PAE) owned by British Petroleum (the remaining 40% was owned by Bridas itself) for USD 7.1 billion, but this acquisition was later abandoned.[27]

According to CNOOC sources, the association with Bridas allowed the firm to combine its experience in offshore operations with Bridas's knowledge in onshore production and exploration (OPSur, 2011). However, according to press sources, CNOOC is considering selling its stake in PAE, to free up money for other projects. Note must be taken that PAE is currently under investigation by the US Securities and Exchange Commission for bribes allegedly paid seven years ago to extend the Cerro Dragón oil field concession in Argentina. If a judge rules against CNOOC, the extension could be considered void and the company's concession would expire in 2017.[28]

PAE is Argentina's second-largest producer of oil and third-largest producer of gas, with 18 percent and 12 percent of the country's production, respectively (IAPG data, 2012), and operating in the main oil area of Argentina – Cerro Dragón – located in Golfo San Jorge. Until recently, the firm had been steadily increasing its share of the domestic oil market, although in recent years it has been affected by several labor and social conflicts.[29] PAE has also recently acquired the Exxon Mobil local affiliate (Esso) as part of a strategy of vertical integration (Esso owned a refinery and several gas stations).

According to Nosis data PAE has around 1,500 employees, as well as the employees of those firms that supply services to PAE. Personnel firings in contractor companies are often attributed by labor and social movements to decisions of the oil companies, creating strong conflicts that affect production (more on this below).

---

27 According to Laufer (2013) the reasons behind the agreement's failure are not very clear, but possibilities include resistance from some members of the Argentine government, changes in BP's financial situation and the decision by the Argentine government to force oil companies to liquidate 100% of their export incomes in Argentina's official currency exchange market (formerly part of those incomes could be held abroad).

28 http://www.bloomberg.com/news/2014-04-07/cnooc-said-to-weigh-sale-of-bridas-stake-bought-for-3-1-billion.html

29 Due to the conflicts in Chubut province and the discussions regarding the new provincial Hydrocarbon Law, only one oil field was explored in 2012.

Table 2.12 PAE's exports (USD million)

	2008	**2009**	**2010**	**2011**	**2012**	**2013**
Crude petroleum oils	3,750	5,110	5,581	4,574	3,389	886
Natural gas	636	420	16	25	6	4
Liquefied gas (propane)	15	28	24	25	0	13
Gas turbines	7	5	7	3	9	2
Butane gas	11	5	0	0	0	12
Gas oil	1	9	8	8	2	0
Aviation kerosene	0	0	1	0	1	1
Petrol	1	0	0	0	0	0
Total	4,421	5,578	5,639	4,635	3,408	918

Source: Nosis.com.

Note must be taken of the fact that Bridas and PAE management are still in hands of the Bulgheroni family (the founders of Bridas). This arrangement avoided a possibly long adaptation process for CNOOC managers who are newer to onshore operations in Argentina.

PAE's exports, like those of its competitors, have been falling, as shown in Table 2.12. In contrast, the firm has imported machinery and equipment and scientific and precision instruments for the oil industry, as well as tubes and pipes (Nosis data).

Sinopec also arrived in Argentina in 2010, through two major acquisitions: the oil fields operated by US TNC Occidental Petroleum Corporation (Oxy) for USD 2.45 billion and 40 percent of Repsol Brazil for USD 7.1 billion. The Oxy acquisition came first, and was among the first Chinese investments in Argentina[30] – and the second one in the oil sector – and it accounted for around one-third of the FDI received in Argentina that year.[31]

When Oxy was acquired, its proven reserves reached 393 million barrels and it had 23 oil and gas production units in Santa Cruz, Chubut and Mendoza, 19 of which were operational. By then Oxy accounted for 6.4 percent of Argentina's oil production (it ranked fifth among oil producers) and 1.5 percent of natural gas production (IAPG data).

---

30 One of the main antecedents was the acquisition of the iron mine of Sierra Grande by China Metallurgical Corporation.

31 Although this figure does not match official FDI data coming from the Argentina's balance of payments, as mentioned above, it is likely that the operation was channeled through a tax haven or an offshore financial center. Unfortunately, we have no means to corroborate this data, although different sources, both from the firms as well as from the media, agree on the above-mentioned figure.

Table 2.13 Sinopec's exports (USD million)

	2008	2009	2010	2011	2012
Crude oil	146.1	1,160.8	1,814.7	452.2	1,131.5
Petroleum oils, other than crude	6.9	13.9	11.3	3.5	13.3
Total	153.0	1,174.7	1,825.9	455.8	1,144.8

Source: Nosis.com.

The sale of Oxy's Argentina's affiliate to Sinopec was a relative surprise since the US firm had announced its aim of renewing its oil concessions and had agreed with the Santa Cruz provincial government an extension of its contract in exchange for USD 100 million in royalties and USD 30 million for provincial infrastructure works.

After three years of investing in the country, Sinopec has kept its market share (6.6 percent in the case of oil and 1.7 percent in natural gas in 2012) – in 2013 it apparently became the fourth-largest oil producer in Argentina – and has around 550 employees (Nosis data) and more than 3,000 contract workers. Agreements signed with the provincial government stipulate that direct and indirect Sinopec employees must have at least two years' residence in Santa Cruz.

Sinopec exports have had wide fluctuations in recent years but are mostly composed by crude oil, as shown in Table 2.13. In fact, Sinopec has no refineries in Argentina. Regarding imports, Sinopec buys capital goods and accessories, including precision equipment, valves, tubes, telecommunication equipment and so forth.

Summing up, the arrival of CNOOC and Sinopec to Argentina did not generate major changes in the operations of the acquired firms in the productive, technological and trade areas. It is likely that the acquired firms would have continued their operations even without the infusion of Chinese capital, as their assets were attractive to many other oil companies. Notwithstanding, in the case of CNOOC (assuming the firm decides not to sell its stake at PAE), the presence of the company could contribute in the future to the expansion of offshore activities, as the Chinese company is an industry leader in offshore exploration.

4. The Case Studies

Before beginning our analysis, we must highlight the fact that the oil industry has strong environmental impacts, and that oil firms usually rank high in terms of environmental incidents, complaints and penalties. In fact, during the last two years the "winners" of the Public Eye Awards,[32] given to companies with the worst environmental and ethical behavior, were oil firms: Gazprom and Royal Dutch Shell. Moreover, oil firms often work in countries where human rights abuses are common: this is because oil is often found in developing countries with weak institutional structures and low democratic standards (in fact, some econometric studies have blamed oil abundance for severe institutional failures, and for even increasing the probability of civil wars – see Ross, 2013). However, the large economic impacts of the oil industry and the power of big oil firms make this industry especially prone to regulatory capture, corruption and other government failures even in countries with strong, well-enforced environmental standards.

In this context, it is very difficult to establish which oil companies are "greener." In fact, the second place in the 2011 ranking of the greenest oil firms elaborated by the environmental organization Greenopia was granted to Royal Dutch Shell.[33]

Media information indicates that CNOOC and Sinopec are no exception, with less than satisfactory environmental and labor management records worldwide. Complaints have been raised of CNOOC's persecution of workers belonging to the Falun Gong movement in China, of human rights abuses and environmental contamination in Myanmar and of serious environmental incidents in China (including oil spills in the Bohai Bay and an oil refinery explosion in Guandong).[34] Complaints regarding Sinopec include its having begun oil exploration in the Loango National Park, Gabon – a nature sanctuary – before the Environmental Impact Assessment (EIA) had been approved by the Ministry of Environment (Kotschwar et al., 2012). Both firms have had to pay fines and reach agreements with affected communities and governments. However, as mentioned above, the same could be said of other oil companies around the world (in fact, in its Bohai Bay operations CNOOC was associated with Conoco Philips).

Complaints about CNOOC and Sinopec ignoring or bypassing national and international corporate and legal standards in areas such as labor, corruption and the environment do not make them unusual among Chinese SOEs. In fact, Sinopec is one of ten firms on the 2008 Fortune China 100

---

32 These prizes are hosted by the Berne Declaration, a Swiss NGO, and Greenpeace.

33 Greenopia defines itself as "the leading directory for eco-friendly businesses and services making sustainable shopping easier. Greenopia provides the market's only independent rating system that ranks businesses and products according to their sustainable practices."

34 http://www.sustainalytics.com/sites/default/files/sustainalytics_corporate_action_alert_cnooc_to_buy_nexen_26july2012.pdf

lists that Greenpeace cites as having violated the Measures on Environmental Information Disclosure (for Trial Implementation) adopted in China.[35] However, as reported in Kotschwar et al. (2012), some signs of improvement in Chinese domestic and international environmental policy (including SOEs' behavior abroad) are slowly emerging, which comes as no surprise given the growing international pressures on the subject. In a similar vein, Urban et al. (2013) point out that growing pressures from civil society and international financial institutions are forcing Chinese companies to demonstrate a commitment to addressing environmental impacts of their overseas projects. Consequently, some Chinese TNCs are getting involved in Corporate Social Responsibility programs (CRS), focused on environmental issues.[36]

In the specific case of Argentina, uncovering the impacts of the recent investments of China's oil firms is difficult due to a number of reasons, including: (a) the investments are very recent; (b) in both cases they have been channeled through total or partial takeovers of existing firms, and in the case of CNOOC the management is still in the hands of the Argentine partner company (so it is not clear whether changes have been introduced after the takeover); (c) Chinese firms have shown reluctance to give information on this or any other aspect of their businesses; (d) as in other countries, the oil industry in Argentina has a record of poor environmental behavior, and all firms in the sector are affected by complaints, lawsuits and governmental sanctions.[37]

We have had no opportunity to meet with CNOOC's or PAE's representatives, since the firms refused our requests. As far as we know, this is the standard behavior of Chinese firms in all sectors (at least in Latin America). We had the opportunity to speak with the president of ASSUPA (Asociación de

---

35 http://www.greenpeace.org/eastasia/press/releases/toxics/2009/silent-giants

36 In the case of Chinese investments in Africa, Tan-Mullins and Mohan (2013) suggest that the outcomes of these CSR strategies are very heterogeneous and rely on specific local political and social structures.

37 See www.opsur.org. For example, ASSUPA (Asociación de Superficiarios de la Patagonia) has sued a dozen firms operating in the main five oil basins in Argentina. ASSUPA is an NGO created by land owners in Patagonia affected by activities of oil firms, which later broadened its objectives to include the protection of the environment from the consequences of oil and mining activities in Argentina (http://www.assupa.org.ar/ASSUPA/Principal.html). The first suit by ASSUPA involved a UNDP report that estimated an environmental liability of USD 545 million from the activities of the oil industry in the Argentinean province of Neuquén between 1991 and 1997. As a result, Repsol finally agreed to a remediation plan in 2011, which is apparently currently suspended after the re-nationalization of the firm (http://www.opsur.org.ar/blog/2014/03/18/la-mega-causa-ambiental-en-la-cuenca-neuquina-y-la-negociacion-con-repsol).

Superficiarios de la Patagonia) (see previous footnote). We also met representatives of firms providing environmental services to the oil firms. In spite of our efforts to speak with government officials of Chubut and Santa Cruz, we did not have access to information from those sources (beyond what is published in official media).

Our research also benefited from information available in the media and opinions from various stakeholders, mainly environmental NGOs. Not surprisingly, this led to a rather gloomy picture regarding the behavior of Chinese oil firms in Argentina. Moreover, we have to consider that, given the importance of oil activities in Patagonia (the main region of oil production in Argentina) politicians often use the subject in their campaigns and personal branding. Hence, caution is needed when analyzing complaints and statements made in the political arena.

4.1 Environmental enforcement and negotiation at the province level

Provincial governments are the most directly involved in terms of environmental regulation of the oil industry and negotiating oil concessions and royalties. This fragmented approach to enforcement, coupled with the provinces' need for royalty revenue, creates a conflict of incentives in which environmental standards can easily fall by the wayside. Nonetheless, oil provinces have pursued strategies to hold oil companies accountable, and with varying degrees of success.

According to the current legal framework regulating the oil industry in Argentina, an EIA must be undertaken before any project can begin; each province has its own standards for this assessment. Water pollution is regulated on the federal level under the Hazardous Waste Law, which sets permitting regulations and acceptable quality levels, although each province has its own water code for basins that do not cross provincial borders (Bareisaite et al., 2013). Although, as seen below, various actions have been taken at the provincial level in order to create standards and regulations and remedy existing environmental damage, some of the people consulted for this study stated that the effective enforcement of these regulations is weak.

As the oil-rich provinces are highly dependent on oil revenues (in Santa Cruz, for example, oil royalties amount to 12% of the provincial budget), addressing environmental liabilities and other impacts of the oil industry (employment, local linkages, social responsibility actions, etc.) are part of complex negotiations in which both the government and the private firms exchange commitments in various areas, a process in which environmental objectives could be sacrificed in exchange for other government objectives such as more royalties, more local employment and so forth. (Note must be taken, however, that some recent statements by public officers in Patagonian provinces show that they have discovered that remediation and environment protection activities also generate employment opportunities).[38]

The province of Chubut has tried to address some of these conflicting incentives through greater transparency, but with limited results. PAE is the major oil operator in Chubut province, so it comes as no surprise that PAE has received a number of complaints regarding not only its environmental behavior but also on the alleged lack of accomplishment of investment commitments (besides the alleged bribes mentioned above). Naturally, criticisms of PAE's environmental action are prior to CNOOC's investment and have continued after the entry of the Chinese firm. Chubut passed a law creating a special Parliament commission in 2012 to monitor investments, environmental liabilities and other aspects of the oil provincial activity, but it has not yet published a report.

The province of Santa Cruz has taken a different, but related, strategy for environmental enforcement. Last year the Santa Cruz government announced that it would require oil firms to draft investment plans to deal with their environmental liabilities at the time of granting or renegotiation of oil concessions. Sinopec has faced sanctions and complaints in recent years[39] and, according to press reports, the amount of those liabilities was preliminarily estimated around USD 150 million at the current peso–dollar exchange rate.[40] In the case of PAE no precise figure has been published (the firm's last renegotiation of concessions was prior to the passing of this new legislation). YPF's liabilities were estimated around USD 3.5 billion in 2012 (considering that year's exchange rate).[41] The environmental liabilities were the result of lack of investment in equipment maintenance, human resources training and remediation activities. A large part of the remaining environmental issues involves inactive wells that have not been appropriately cleaned and whose wastes were disposed of in unsafe ponds, leading to contamination of several aquifers (it is estimated that there are 13,000 inactive wells in Santa Cruz).[42] In the case of Sinopec, the remediation plan has established a five-year period

38 http://magnamedia.com.ar/index.php?option=com_content&view=article&id=18392:pasivos-ambientales-95-de-las-piletas-de-crudo-estarian-mal-saneadas&catid=110:cat-locales-03&Itemid=532

39 The firm has stated that some of the recorded environmental incidents are the result of sabotage actions (http://www.laopinionaustral.com.ar/diario.asp?Modo=Noticia&NId=6096&texto=&A=2012&M=10&D=11).

40 http://www.santacruzdigital.net/nota.asp?n=2013_8_18&id=16556&id_tiponota=4

41 See http://www.santacruzdigital.net/nota.asp?n=2013_8_4&id=16556&id_tiponota=4.

42 See http://www.santacruzdigital.net/nota.asp?n=2013_8_4&id=16556&id_tiponota=4.

to undertake the works needed to remedy the identified liabilities (including nearly eleven hundred contaminated wells). This requirement of estimating environmental liabilities and presenting remediation plans was a consequence of Law No. 3122 in 2010 (Santa Cruz is the only province with such kind of legislation). Notwithstanding legal obligations, press reports state that oil firms are reluctant to make the required investments and, in many cases, argue that those liabilities are the result of the operation of the former owners of the oil fields (as in the case of Sinopec and YPF).[43]

Another key issue in both Santa Cruz and Patagonia regarding the impacts of oil activity has to do with water availability. Given the lack of appropriate infrastructure in the region (in particular, dams and water pipes), there has historically been a strong controversy between civil society and oil companies for the use of water, especially in Patagonia, due to the fact that oil companies use huge amounts of drinking water for oil production while some cities face shortages of clean water for agriculture and consumption. In December 2012 the governor of Santa Cruz and the president of Sinopec Argentina signed an agreement to build water wells and new pipes in Caleta Olivia and Pico Truncado and deliver the equipment needed to operate them, train the required employees and provide their maintenance. However, press reports stated that the works schedule in 2013 had not been met. In Patagonia, oil firms were blamed for not helping when an aqueduct serving many southern Patagonia cities broke and left thousands of citizens without water for almost two weeks.[44]

On a related note, Santa Cruz has also had to deal with alleged negative impacts of the oil industry on fishing. Complaints have been made accusing PAE of damages to fisheries due to offshore operations. The firm elaborated a report for the Santa Cruz government that apparently shows fishing activity has in fact increased in recent years.[45] However, in 2013 PAE stopped a seismic prospecting project in San Jorge Gulf due to a lawsuit by fishing firms, which alleged negative impacts on their activity due to a similar previous project undertaken in 2009 (trade unions and the Santa Cruz government also opposed the project).

4.2 Voluntary measures by CNOOC and Sinopec

Beyond their relationships with provincial governments, it is worthwhile to note the overall environmental behavior of CNOOC and Sinopec. Some sources

43 http://www.empresasnews.com/noticia-2714.html

44 http://www.lavanguardiadelsur.com/index.php/politica/2860-claudio-vidal-cargo-contra-las-operadoras-petroleras-que-se-desentendieron-de-la-crisis-hidrica-de-caleta

45 See http://www.prochubut.com.ar/node/1274.

consulted for this study stated that, after the acquisition of Oxy, Sinopec lowered the budget dedicated to environmental activities. At the same time, during this research we were also told that PAE's environmental commitment is stronger than Sinopec's, due to the participation of British Petroleum in PAE and the fact that, as a consequence of having accumulated a number of important environmental incidents in the past that damaged its reputation, BP has a stronger commitment to the environment than Chinese firms. As always, it bears emphasizing that we have no hard evidence supporting these statements.

Finally, both PAE and Sinopec have embarked on CSR programs. In 2008 Oxy launched a program to protect biodiversity in the area, Reserva Natural Loayza y Duraznillo. After the acquisition of the company, the program was upheld by Sinopec and later recognized as the best environmental conservation program by the Ecumenical Forum in December 2013. Other CSR programs by Oxy PAE focus on helping preserve endangered bird species,[46] preventing drug addiction,[47] reducing the digital gap by facilitating access to computers and computer training[48] and building parks in Patagonian cities.[49]

4.3 Looking to the future: Shale oil and gas

The most relevant issue regarding the future of environmental impacts of the oil industry in Argentina involves the exploration and exploitation of shale oil and gas wells. According to various sources Argentina has one of the world's main reservoirs of shale gas. The biggest concentration of these resources is located in Vaca Muerta, Neuquén province. YPF has been trying to form partnerships with various major private companies to promote the development of this area. PAE as well as CNOCC itself have been among the firms that showed interest in establishing associations with YPF, although so far only Chevron has signed a formal agreement.

The development of shale hydrocarbons is based on the use of hydraulic fracturing (or "fracking"). According to Mares (2012), since these techniques are relatively new, there is no scientific consensus on the degree of associated

---

46 http://www.vocesyapuntes.com/nuevo/index.php/noticias/politica/5509-pae-suma-esfuerzos-para-la-preservacion-del-maca-tobiano-un-emblema-de-la-patagonia-pan-american-energy-colaborara-con-aves-argentinas-y-ambiente-sur-en-su-proyecto-para-evitar-la-extincion-de-esta-especie-endemica-que-es-exclusiva-de-la-argentina-

47 http://patagoniaenergetica.com/2014/05/sinopec-argentina-curso-preventores-comunitarios-en-adicciones/

48 http://www.patagonianexo.com.ar/v2/labor-conjunta-entre-pae-y-la-fundacion-proyecto-puente/#sthash.K5oDW5v6.dpuf

49 http://patagoniaenergetica.com/2012/05/sinopec-inauguro-la-plaza-david-charles-en-las-heras/

risks. Nevertheless, it is well-known that fracking requires large amounts of water, and that the water used in fracking contains potentially hazardous chemicals and must be managed properly. Large amounts of toxic wastewater must be treated and disposed of. Disposal of such wastewater into deep wells can cause earthquakes and other damage. Moreover, competition for water affects other human and economic activities, including drinking water, recreation and agriculture, and could have a negative effect on wildlife habitat. The development of shale gas also carries emissions consequences, including NOx, SO_2, volatile organic compounds, particulate matter, and methane. The only environmental benefit reported by Mares is that, vis-à-vis vertical drilling, horizontal drilling significantly reduces the number of well pads, access roads, pipeline routes and production facilities.

Fortunately, Argentina's shale gas reserves are largely in sparsely populated regions of Patagonia, making some of the environmental issues less pressing (Mares, 2012). Nevertheless, there is a growing NGO movement against the use of fracking in Patagonia as well as in the rest of Argentina.[50] Some provincial affiliates of center-left political parties[51] as well as one of Argentina's trade union confederations (CTA) are also (formally or informally) part of this alliance. However, as noted above, the exploitation of these resources is still on a prospection and exploration phase and, except for the case of Chevron, no other oil firm has signed agreements with YPF to operate in this area, and the list of possible partners includes firms from many different countries.

4.4 Other aspects

National Law 17319 (reformed by Law 26197) establishes that oil and natural gas producers must pay a 12 percent royalty based on the crude oil price in the field (that figure may be reduced to 5% according to the location and productivity levels of the fields). Although provinces may not legally increase royalties above that ceiling, some of them, like Neuquén and Chubut, create "special fees" that are added to the 12 percent established by law. In the case of Chubut this fee amounts to 3 to 4 percent of the crude oil price in the field.[52] Some

---

50 Some of the involved NGOs include Coordinadora de Comunicación Audiovisual Indígena Argentina (CCAIA), Grupo Ambiental Nogoyasero, Ambiente Comarca, Asamblea Ambiental Ciudadana (AAC) of Rio Gallegos, Asamblea Popular of Zapala, Asamblea Popular Colon-Ruta 135, Movimiento por la Recuperación del Petróleo en Neuquén, Asamblea Permanente por el Agua del Comahue, Foro Ambiental y Social de la Patagonia, and Mesa Entre Rios Libre de Fracking.

51 Proyecto Sur, Frente Amplio Progresista and Coalicion Civica ARI.

52 Contracts also include additional royalties that must be paid by oil firms to local governments where the oil activity is undertaken.

provinces also include extra royalties and lump-sum payments when they negotiate concessions with the oil operators. For example, Santa Cruz's 2008 renewal of PAE's oil field concession for 40 more years required the firm to pay another 3 percent in royalties and an initial payment of USD 40 million for infrastructure projects and educational programs. As mentioned above, the extension of PAE's concessions in Patagonia is under investigation in the United States due to alleged bribes.

Regarding labor relations and wages, note must be taken that workers in the oil industry are among the best paid in Argentina's economy, and the same holds in Chubut and Santa Cruz (salaries in the oil extraction sector are double the average salary in both provinces). However, oil firms operating in those provinces have had a long series of conflicts with workers and supplier firms, triggering strikes, picketing and occupation of oil fields and plants. The main origin of these conflicts is the outsourcing process initiated with the restructuring and later privatization of YPF in the 1990s, but they also include complaints regarding the tax burden of oil workers and complaints that small contracting firms in Patagonia usually lack the resources to meet the technical demands of the oil companies. This situation is aggravated insofar as oil communities in Patagonia tend to see oil firms as the main source of employment generation in their territories.[53]

Conflicts have been especially fierce in the case of PAE. In 2012 a group called "Los Dragones" (The Dragons), a breakaway from the construction workers union of Chubut, ransacked the Cerro Dragón oilfield and blocked several roads, demanding wage increases (the workers belonging to this group work for subcontractors and earn lower salaries than those directly employed by the oil industry) and the reinstatement of 40 workers who had been fired after PAE terminated contracts with two suppliers.

In this context, in 2012 a new Hydrocarbons Law was passed in Chubut[54] that, among other objectives, regulates the relations between the oil firms and their goods and services providers, with the aim of promoting more linkages with the local economy. Currently, Chubut's government is trying to adapt the oil licenses in force to the new criteria introduced in the above-mentioned law.

---

53 As an illustration, Sinopec has been recently involved in three labor conflicts that affected their subcontractors. In all cases the origins of the conflicts were personnel firings which were due in one case to complaints of poor labor conditions while in the other two cases the workers claims were about mismatches between salaries and skills required for certain jobs – subcontractors alleged that workers' protests were illegal so firings were justified (http://www.elciudadanodelasheras.com/?p=39580).
54 Law XVII No. 102 and Decree No. 91/13.

To reduce social conflict, PAE, has implemented various CSR programs aimed at improving the relations with suppliers, training the local labor force and promoting technology transfer. All these programs existed before the arrival of CNOOC but have been preserved after the entry of the new Chinese partners. The main program is SMEs of Golfo San Jorge, which started in 2005 and aims to improve the performance of local SMEs (focusing on organizational and technological capacity), increase value added and local content of production, and improve employment in the region. The program contains five main actions: (a) preferred procurement for local SMEs; (b) technical capacity-building of local suppliers and upgrading in the value chain; (c) development of new suppliers for PAE; (d) creation of a network of local institutions and companies aimed at promoting cooperation and collective actions in the region, and (e) technical and financial assistance for SMEs.

The program has been quite successful. Since 2005, the number of participating companies has increased from 34 to 90, the number of locally produced products grew from 12 to 28,[55] and the number of services provided by firms within the region grew from 3 to 15. Moreover, the program offered more than 23,000 training hours and 18,000 hours of in-house training. Several participating SMEs obtained quality-assurance certifications. Finally, according to PAE, the program has allowed a substitution of certain local producers for products previously imported (PAE, 2013).

Regarding NGO involvement, there are many like the above-mentioned ASSUPA, which campaign against the environmental damages generated by the oil industry and are especially active in Patagonia. In turn, oil firms (including PAE and Sinopec) often seek alliances with local NGOs in order to jointly develop CSR programs.

5. Conclusions

As stated in the introduction, this study is an exploration of relatively new subjects. Argentinean exports to China have grown quickly and, currently, China is among its major trade partners, but exports are extremely concentrated on soybean and its derivatives. This export basket produces less carbon emissions per dollar than exports to other markets, but that difference has been narrowing, as China is the only major trading partner associated with rising carbon emissions intensity. China's impact on water consumption is more direct, as soy is a high water-consumption crop, and its water footprint is relatively large.

---

55 Note that not all the products are specific to the oil industry.

In our view, Santa Cruz's recent adoption of a law demanding that oil firms remedy their environmental liabilities is an example of the type of action that should be taken to reduce the environmental impacts of the oil industry. Although Chinese firms may be less conscious of the need to adopt greener practices than other established oil firms, it is the responsibility of the local authorities to foster the use of better environmental management systems. Although the evidence suggests that provincial (and national) governments in Argentina have often been more interested in maximizing royalties or tax collection, growing pressure from local communities and other stakeholders could bring more attention to the environmental impacts of this industry.

In addition, more transparency is needed for a better evaluation of our research issues. Neither governments nor private firms are prone to disseminating relevant information on these matters, and no legal framework pushing for more transparency in the relations between both parts exists in Argentina, making it difficult to have a good assessment of the current situation and its prospects.[56]

Both more transparency and more active policies are needed in face of the opportunity (and challenges) associated to the apparently huge gas and oil reserves existing in Vaca Muerta, which need to be exploited through the use of fracking techniques. If forecasts are correct, Argentina could be one of the major reservoirs of those resources at the world level, which would give the country leverage to establish favorable negotiation conditions – not only in terms of royalties, technology transfer and other economic variables – but also in terms of the preservation of the environment and the protection of local communities and producers. The main antecedent in this regard, however, is not very auspicious, since the terms of YPF's exploration contract with Chevron have not been made public. Moreover, the government of Argentina has been the target of complaints and a new investigation, due to allegations that a decree was signed to give specific benefits to Chevron.[57]

As China consolidates its role as a major economic and political superpower, there is a need for strategic consideration of the role of Argentina in this new international context, and how to handle the opportunities and risks presented by China's growing role in trade and investment. Long-term vision is needed, since the temptation of short-term profit opportunities in spite of long-term risks is very strong in countries with fragile institutional settings. More research on these issues could help to inform the public debate and

---

56 In this regard, one option for Argentina is to join the Extractive Industries Transparency Initiative (EITI), following the steps of Peru.

57 http://www.lanacion.com.ar/1690219-la-camara-federal-impulsa-una-investigacion-sobre-cristina-kirchner-por-el-acuerdo-con-chevron

help politicians and decision makers adopt more informed and better policy choices aiming at taking advantage of the trade and investment opportunities under an inclusive and sustainable development framework.

References

Aldaya, M. M., Chapagain, A. K., Hoekstra, A. Y. and Mekonnen, M. M. (2012). *The Water Footprint Assessment Manual: Setting the Global Standard.* London: Routledge.

Aldaya, M., Allan, J., and Hoekstra, A. (2010). "Strategic Importance of Green Water in International Crop Trade." *Ecological Economics* 69(4), 887–94.

Antweiler, W., Copeland, B. R., and Taylor, M. S. (2001). "Is Free Trade Good for the Environment?" *American Economic Review* 877–908.

Bareisaite, A., Cook, E, Fathieh, R., Landstrom, E., Lilinshtein, J., Pagkalou, E. and Wallace, T. (2013), "The Business Landscape for Unconventional Natural Gas in Argentina, Australia, Canada, France, Poland and the United Kingdom," a Report to Credit Agricole.

Cárdenas, G. (2011). "Matriz energética argentina. Situación actual y posibilidades de diversificación." *Revista Bolsa de Comercio de Rosario.* Año C (1514): 32–36.

CEPAL (2013). "Promoción del comercio y la inversión con China: Desafíos y oportunidades en la experiencia de las cámaras empresariales latinoamericanas." Santiago, Chile: United Nations.

Chen, T. and Pérez Ludeña, M. (2013). "Chinese Foreign Direct Investment in Latin American and the Caribbean." *World Economic Forum*, 18–20 November. Abu Dhabi. CEPAL.

Chidiak, M., R. Rozemberg, C. Filipello, V. Gutman, G. Rozenwurcel, y M. Affranchino (2012). "Sostenibilidad de biocombustibles e indicadores GBEP: un análisis de su relevancia y aplicabilidad para la Argentina," *Documento de iDeAS*, No. 11, UNSAM, Buenos Aires.

Diario de Fusiones y Adquisiciones (2020). "Sinopec de China compra la unidad de Occidental Petroleum en Argentina." Accessible in http://www.diariodefusiones.com/?page=ampliada&id=239

Di Sbroiavacca, N. (2013). "Shale oil y shale gas en Argentina. Estado de situación y prospectiva." Department of Energy Economics. Fundación Bariloche – CONICET. August.

Dussel Peters, E. (2013). "Características de la inversión extranjera directa china en América Latina (2000–2011)." In E. Dussel Peters (coordinator). *América Latina y El Caribe – China Economía, Comercio e Inversiones.* Mexico, D. F.: Red ALC-China. Unión de Universidades de América Latina y el Caribe.

Ederington, J., Levinson, A., and Minier, J. (2004). "Trade liberalization and pollution havens." *Advances in Economic Analysis and Policy* 3(2).

EIA (2012). "China Analysis Brief." Energy Information Administration. United States. www.eia.gov.

EIA (2013). "China Analysis Brief." Energy Information Administration, United States: www.eia.gov.

Frankel, J. A., and Rose, A. K. (2005). "Is Trade Good or Bad for the Environment? Sorting Out the Causality." *Review of Economics and Statistics* 87(1), 85–91.

Gallagher, K. (2000). *Trade Liberalization and Industrial Pollution in Mexico: Lessons of the FTAA.* Boston: Tufts University.

Grether, J.-M., Mathys, N. A., and de Melo, J. (2012). "Unravelling the Worldwide Pollution Haven Effect." *The Journal of International Trade and Economic Development* 21(1), 131–62.

Hettige, H., Martin, P., Singh, M., Wheeler, D., and Mundial, B. (1995). "The Industrial Pollution Projection System." World Bank.

Houser, T. (2008). "The roots of Chinese oil investment abroad." *Asia Policy* 5(1), 141–66.

ICIS Chemical Business (2013). www.icis.com.

Jenkins, R. and Dussel Peters, E. (2009). "China and Latin America. Economic Relations in the Twenty-First century." Bonn/Mexico City: German Development Institute/ Deutsches Institut für Entwicklungspolitik (DIE).

Kotschwar, B., T. Moran and J. Muir (2012), "Chinese Investment in Latin American Resources: The Good, the Bad, and the Ugly," Working Paper Series WP12-3, Peterson Institute for International Economics.

Laufer, R. (2013). "Argentina–China: New Courses for an Old Dependency." *Latin American Policy* 4(1), 123–43.

Mani, M., and Wheeler, D. (1998). "In Search of Pollution Havens? Dirty Industry in the World Economy," 1960 to 1995. *The Journal of Environment and Development* 7(3), 215–47.

Mares, D. (2012), "The New Energy Landscape: Shale Gas in Latin America," IDB, Discussion Paper No. IDB-DP-253, Washington, DC.

Mekonnen, M., and Hoekstra, A. (2010a). *The Green, Blue and Grey Water Footprint of Farm Animals and Animal Products*, UNESCO-IHE, Institute for Water Education, Research Report Series No. 48.

Mekonnen, M., and Hoekstra, A. (2010b). *The Green, Blue and Grey Water Footprint of Crops and Derived Crop Products*, UNESCO-IHE, Institute for Water Education, Research Report Series No. 47.

Muradian, R., O'Connor, M., and Martinez-Alier, J. (2002). "Embodied Pollution in Trade: Estimating the 'Environmental Load Displacement' of Industrialised Countries." *Ecological Economics* 41(1), 51–67.

OPSur (2011). "Inversiones chinas en Argentina: claves del nuevo escenario energético." *Revista Observatorio Petrolero Sur*. August.

PAE (2013). "Programa Pymes Golfo San Jorge. Estudio de caso. Articulación y desarrollo empresario ¿Cómo y cuánto se incrementó el empresariado en las zona del Golfo San Jorge?" *Pan American Energy*, 2013.

Peters, G. P., Andrew, R., and Lennox, J. (2011). Constructing an Environmentally-Extended Multi-Regional Input–Output Table Using the GTAP Database. *Economic Systems Research* 23(2), 131–52.

Ross, M. L. (2013). *The Oil Curse: How Petroleum Wealth Shapes the Development of Nations.* Princeton and Oxford: Princeton University Press.

Strecker Downs, E., Mesic, R., Kelley, C. T. J., Bowie, C. J., Buchan, G. and Levaux, H. P. (2000). "China's Quest for Energy Security." Rand Corporation.

Tan-Mullins, M. and Mohan, G. (2013). "The Potential of Corporate Environmental Responsibility of Chinese State-Owned Enterprises in Africa." *Environment, Development and Sustainability* 15(2), 265–84.

Urban, F., Mohan, G. and Cook, S. (2013). "China as a New Shaper of International Development: The Environmental Implications." *Environment, Development and Sustainability* 15(2), 257–63.

Wu, K. (2008). "China's Overseas Oil and Gas Investment: Motivations, Strategies, and Global Impact." *Oil, Gas, and Energy Law Intelligence* 6(1), 1–9.

Xu, X. (2007). "Chinese NOC's Overseas Strategies: Background, Comparison and Remarks. The Changing Role of National Oil Companies in International Energy Markets." James A. Baker III Institute for Public Policy and Japan Petroleum Energy Center. Rice University, March.

Yue, L. (2013). "Inversión extranjera directa de China en América Latina." In E. Dussel Peters (coordinator), América Latina y El Caribe – China Economía, Comercio e Inversiones. México, D. F.: Red ALC-China. Unión de Universidades de América Latina y el Caribe.

Zweig, D. and Jianhai, B. (2005). "China's Global Hunt for Energy." *Foreign Affairs* 84(5), 25–38.

Chapter 3

COLOMBIA AND CHINA: SOCIAL AND ENVIRONMENTAL IMPACTS OF TRADE AND FOREIGN DIRECT INVESTMENT

Guillermo Rudas Lleras and Mauricio Cabrera Leal

The impact of China in Colombia is particularly visible in the extractive sector. Colombia's coal sector has grown in the last several years, spurred in part by demand from China, the world's largest coal buyer. Chinese Foreign Direct Investment (FDI) in Colombia is small but it is growing, especially in the petroleum sector.

Extractive industries – particularly coal and oil – are intrinsically prone to negative environmental and social impacts. This is particularly true in Colombia, where extraction sites are located in especially poor areas amid sensitive ecosystems. This chapter explores those impacts in the areas surrounding large-scale coal mining and Chinese oil-drilling operations in Colombia. It finds that coal-mining areas in Colombia have worse health, education and governance outcomes and, specifically, a rise in mortality rates caused by acute respiratory infections compared to the rest of the country.

The petroleum sector, in which China participates through FDI by the state-owned enterprises (SOEs) Sinopec and Sinochem, has its own challenges in this matter. This chapter explores them through a case study of New Grenada Energy Colombia (NGEC), a subsidiary of Sinopec. It finds several areas of particular concern, both in the company's performance and in the oversight by the national environmental licensing body, Autoridad Nacional de Licencias Ambientales (ANLA). First, although NGEC committed to invest USD 500,000 in (legally required) conservation investments in 2008, they have not yet materialized. In early 2014, the Comptroller General of Colombia stated that this failure was in part due to ANLA's lack of monitoring and oversight. Furthermore, NGEC's environmental monitoring reports are significantly incomplete and, although the company is legally obligued to respond to public inquiries on the matter, it refused our requests for information. Finally, ANLA's maintenance of these records – while nominally transparent – leaves much to be desired. Important challenges to obtain these records (including travel to Bogotá, fees and a two-week waiting period) could pose serious obstacles to civil society.

The social aspects of our case study center on company–community dialogue about jobs and infrastructure. Employment decisions in the surrounding area have traditionally been handled by intermediaries, which leaves the company itself unaccountable for its commitments to hire local workers. The national government is addressing this problem through major reforms of labor intermediation, which may help resolve these conflicts.

Finally, the community and company have agreed to changes in the route of a major access road to allow the community to travel to the county seat, but NGEC has refused to carry on these commitments, citing the presence of other oil companies in the region that also use the road.

Several important recommendations emerge from this study. First, while ANLA has made important strides in transparency, there is great room for improvement. The government could raise the standard dramatically by joining the Extractive Industries Transparency Initiative, as Peru has done, which entails free online reports of revenue flows from extractive companies. Secondly, Sinopec could learn from its subsidiaries in Ecuador, which have managed more harmonious community relations by honoring its commitments with them. Finally, we conclude that civil society has an important role in monitoring company performance and pressing for continued improvements in both performance and government oversight.

1. Introduction

Colombia's connection to the world is marked by its high dependence on the extraction of natural resources. Foreign direct investment (FDI) is growing with very limited Chinese presence, nevertheless China has positioned itself as a leading trade partner, demanding significant amounts of oil and coal and offering manufacturing in return, specifically of machinery and equipment.

The dependence on commodities, coupled with little or no local production, creates a precarious place for Colombia in global value chains and limits the benefits it receives from the export sector. Risks are accentuated by the volatility of prices, made highly uncertain by non-renewable resources that, sooner or later, will run out. The benefits that derive from the sector tend to be limited to enclave economies in the regions where it is most active, which have little ability to extend their benefits to the local population – further emphasizing points of conflict. Furthermore, the state's tax and royalty revenue from extraction depends on its ability to negotiate favorable outcomes in the face of significant asymmetry of information and bargaining power. Finally, extraction – especially from open-pit mines – significantly impacts the natural environment and requires strict oversight so that its negative impacts do not end up costing the country more money that it brings in.

Proper management of these risks (which are closely linked with one another) is necessary if this extractive activity is to remain economically sustainable. On the other hand, growing tensions will continue to be an obstacle to this activity, creating conflicts that may end up making these investment initiatives unfeasible.

The effects of mining and hydrocarbons extend well beyond the extractive sector. In fact, non-renewable public resources have a series of interactions with various aspects of the public sphere, especially in a country as complex as Colombia, where there are violent conflicts, a high degree of uncertainty concerning property rights, widespread illicit activities and elevated levels of government co-option by irregular interests (Garay, 2008). All of these take place in the context of a fragile natural environment that is especially sensitive to open-pit extraction, which affects water sources and leads to unpredictable effects regarding their ability to satisfy the needs of those who depend on them.[1]

These tensions have captured the attention of specialists and the general public alike. Some choose to approach the issue from a macroeconomic point of view, centering their analysis on the potential that this activity has to accelerate economic growth by attracting foreign investment. They emphasize that it is possible to avoid the "resource curse" and "Dutch disease."[2] Alternative views have emphasized the complexity of the interaction between extraction and the economy as a whole, focusing on multi-factor interactions that determine economic growth and other factors associated with development.[3] Those

---

1   According to US experts, "surface mining permits are issued despite scientific evidence that mitigation measures cannot compensate for the losses caused by its pervasive and irreversible impacts" (Palmer et al., 2010).

2   See Auty (1993), Cárdenas and Reina (2008), Perry and Olivera (2010), Perry and Palacios (2013), and Martínez and Aguilar (2012 and 2013).

3   See Garay (2013, 2013a, 2014 and 2014a), Saade (2013), Martínez et al. (2013), Fierro (2012), Toro et al. (2012), and Gaitán et al. (2011). Also, see Zarsky and Stanley (2013), Bebbington (2013), and Arellano (2011).

who adopt this view propose moving beyond a growth-centered perspective to incorporate the importance of multiple local conflicts, as recommended by a pioneering study from the World Bank (McMahon and Remy, 2003).

In order for extraction to become socially accepted, the industry must take into account the most vulnerable population. This requires reorienting project design so that populations most affected by wealth-generating projects will be left in the same or better condition than before implementation of the project (Cemea, 1988). Furthermore, in places surrounding populations are vulnerable and highly impoverished, such projects must guarantee that the affected population at least remains sustainably above the poverty line.[1]

In the context of these tensions surrounding Colombia's extractive industry, this chapter analyzes three aspects of the extraction-centered relationship between China and Colombia, which has been based on trade but has significant potential for growth of Chinese FDI in Colombia. First, we describe the primary commercial ties between the two countries in a context of reprimarization of the Colombian economy, where China currently stands among the country's main trading partners. Second, we analyze certain characteristics of the Colombian export sector, using open-pit coal mining as a reference due to the fact that China has occupied an increasingly important role as a buyer of this product in recent years. Moreover, the extraction of coal has generated significant environmental impacts over the years and has created serious social conflicts in places where mining occurs, many of which have yet to be resolved. Third, by using a Chinese oil company located in Colombia as a reference point, we review the way environmental and social challenges are addressed in the area in which it operates. We conclude the analysis by indicating aspects to be considered for the future in regard to relations between the two countries.

The analysis is based on a basic assumption that the negative effects of production – in both the social and environmental spheres – should be managed using the resources of the respective project, assuming all costs without using any resources received by the state from the resulting activity. If this condition is not met, it may be concluded that the project is not economically viable.

2. China in the Context of the Colombian Economy

The relations between China and Colombia are addressed in this section from three perspectives: changes in the sectoral composition of the economy, with a specific acceleration in the positioning of the extractive sector; the growth

---

4   Camilo Gonzáles Posso, director of the Institute for Development and Peace Studies (INDEPAZ), is responsible for this proposal.

of FDI, predominantly concerning investments in oil and mining with little participation from China; and the consolidation of the extractive sector in the flow of goods from Colombia overseas, including to China – a major destination for Colombian raw materials.

In the last thirty years the extractive sector in Colombia has been growing rapidly.[5] Between 1975 and 1984 this sector contributed less than 2 percent to the country's GDP. After a period of rapid growth, it reached a peak of 9 percent in 1999 and stabilized around 8 percent between 2011 and 2013. This growth of the extractive sector occurred during the same period in which commerce and other services were consolidated, increasing as a whole from 54 percent to 58 percent of GDP, with an important increase in financial services (around 20 points). In contrast, during those same years strictly productive sectors (industrial, agricultural and construction) decreased significantly, dropping by an average of 10 percentage points, from around 35 percent in the 1975–1984 period to 25 percent between 2011 and 2013. A combination of factors shifted the economy away from production of goods with high employment (in the case of the agricultural sector) or high value-added (in the case of the manufacturing sector) to capital-intensive extractive sectors with highly volatile value-added. Factors responsible for this shift include: the revaluation of the Colombian peso and the discouragement of high value-added exports; the increase in global demand for commodities and the elevation of their prices; and tax incentives for FDI, specifically in regard to extractive activity.

This reprimarization is accompanied by an accelerated growth in FDI, which is concentrated in oil extraction and mining. According to figures from the central bank (Bank of the Republic of Colombia, or BRC), between 1994 and 2004 investment amounts were in the order of USD 2.5 billion annually. From 2005 onward this number shot up, reaching average annual amounts of more than USD 8 billion between 2005 and 2010, and more than USD 15 billion between 2011 and 2013. This jump was accompanied by a change in sectoral composition: in the early years the concentration was primarily in services, with 55 percent of the total compared with 24 percent in the extractive sector. Starting in 2005, the extractive sector became predominant, increasing on average to more than 51 percent of the total, and to more than 32 percent for the hydrocarbon subsector and 19 percent for all other mining.

What remained relatively stable was the origin of this FDI: between 2010 and 2013, Latin America and the Caribbean (LAC) maintained its leading position with 35 percent of the total, followed by the European Union (21%) and the United States (18%) and, finally, by an insignificant portion from Asia

---

5 For more details, see Rudas (2014).

and China in particular. However, this distribution reported by foreign trade authorities does not reflect the true origin of the investment. While Chile, Mexico and Brazil contribute significantly to the investment coming from LAC (16%, 6%, and 3%, respectively), the majority of it comes from recognized tax havens: 33 percent from Panama, and 36 percent from Bermuda, Anguilla, the Cayman Islands, Barbados and the British Virgin Islands. There is no doubt that the dynamism of these countries is a useful mechanism for eluding tax burdens, if not for clearly illegal activities,[6] given the impossibility of identifying the origin of capital.

One example is investments coming from Canada. While between 2010 and 2011 the official numbers (from the BRC) cite investments from Canada at less than USD 600 million, the *Financial Times'* FDI Intelligence database shows USD 6.4 billion during that period, representing close to one third of the FDI reported in official numbers for these two years (USD 20 billion). This phenomenon may be occurring with China as well, although on a much smaller scale. According to FDI Intelligence, between 2007 and 2012 more than USD 1.8 billion may have been received from China, while the official figures only report USD 35 million during the same period – a difference that illustrates the significance of investments coming from tax havens.

The growth of FDI since 2005 can be explained by the growth in investor confidence inspired by the Uribe administration (2002–2010), which included measures such as the reduction of the income tax base by values between 30 and 40 percent of total annual investments, as well as the elimination of taxes on the remittance of profits earned by foreign companies. In addition, the growth of the extractive sector has been another important factor behind the growth of FDI. Trends in the size and composition of exports (Figure 3.1) show that since the mid-2000s, after a relative stagnation, total exports have grown at a rate consistent with the flows of foreign investment. Similarly, the composition of exports has shifted dramatically toward extraction: in less than ten years the manufacturing industry lost 23 percentage points as a share of total exports, displaced by mining and oil. This sector has also supplanted agriculture, which has been losing importance since the mid-1990s. Agriculture now makes up a mere 5 percent of total exports.

The growth of the extractive sector is partly due to the rise of oil and mineral prices since the beginning of the century, with only a slight downturn during the crisis of 2009. These prices, in turn, incentivized more investments in such commodities. In the case of hydrocarbons, new investments have

---

6 Interbolsa, a large Colombian brokerage firm engaged in illegal transactions in these tax havens, collapsed in 2012: http://www.supersociedades.gov.co/prensa/interbolsa/Documents/SuperSociedades%20ordena%20intervenci%C3%B3n.pdf

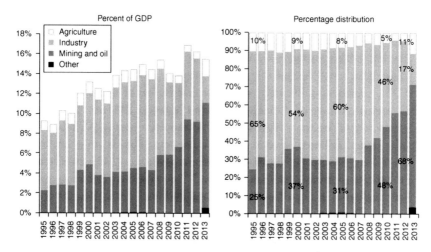

Figure 3.1 Exports by sector, 1995–2013
Source: Authors' calculations based on DANE data.

brought the country close to its goal of producing one million oil barrels a day. This can be seen particularly between 2007 and 2010, when the National Hydrocarbons Agency (Agencia Nacional de Hidrocarburos, or ANH) signed 158 new contracts, 27 in the technical evaluation phase and the rest in exploration production.[7] In contrast, in the case of mining, none of the new investments have resulted in the opening of new mines, but rather have been used to intensify already existing ones and, to a smaller degree, to increase exploration activity. But rather than investor indecision, this situation reflects an underlying institutional crisis that has paralyzed new projects, revealed in the way in which the titling of mining exploration areas has evolved,[8] among other factors (see Box 3.1).

Colombia's foreign trade has also seen important changes in the composition of import origins and export destinations, with China rising to be the second most-important trading partner. Before 2005, the value of exports to China was very low, reaching only as high as 100 million USD (in 2004) and accounting for less than 1 percent of total exports (Dane, 2011). In 2010 the situation began to change, with China receiving 4 percent of the exports from Colombia and ranking fourth among the target countries. In 2013, China reached 9 percent of the total exports and was only surpassed by the United States, which received almost one-third of the total (Table 3.1).

---

7   See www.anh.gov.co
8   See *Non-addressed Environmental Impacts of Mining: Liabilities for the Environment and Society*, in CGR (2012), 145.

Box 3.1 Mining Titles and Institutional Crisis

Mining titles are rights given by the mining authorities to explore and develop subsoil resources, which are state property.* From 1991 to 2004 these rights were distributed at a moderate pace. But beginning in 2005, as FDI accelerated significantly, so did the distribution of mining titles: from an annual average of 170 titles given out between 1991 and 2004, with an average of less than 40,000 annual hectares per year, in 2005 over 400 titles were distributed, covering 150,000 hectares. This began a trend that the Mining Ministry of the first Santos administration (2010–2014) called "the piñata of mining titles in Colombia."** In violation of technical guidelines and without regard to constitutional and legal restrictions for giving out titles in areas of special interest (national parks and parks, indigenous territory, etc.) from 2006 onward titling has shot upward to 830 titles given out for over 530,000 hectares per year. Overall, during the Uribe administration (2002–2010) titles were given out for over 4 million hectares, 4 times more than had been given out over the entire history of the country, under the "first in time, first in right" principle that prioritizes timing over qualifications. The new administration, after a two-year moratorium, reopened the titling application process. In six months 3,400 applications were received for 5.3 million hectares of area, and by the end of that year over 2,000 new titles were given out for 1.4 million hectares. In more recent years a reform process has begun in the regulatory institutions for mining. Following the pattern of the ANH, which oversees state-owned hydrocarbon reserves, the National Mining Agency (ANM) was created in late 2011.*** This new office is charged with overseeing mining resources, seeking to improve on the chaotic situation inherited from before. But over two years after the creation of the ANM, it is still uncertain whether it will be able to rise to the challenge of efficiently carrying out its mission, as evidenced by over 9,000 applications waiting to be reviewed (over 5,000 of which have been waiting over two years) for 8 million hectares.

* Once exploration is complete and before development begins, large-scale mines must also obtain an environmental license from the Environment Ministry in addition to the mining title.
** For more, see Carlos Rodado Noriega's statement from May 30, 2011: http://www.portafolio.co/economia/caos-titulacion-minera-denuncio-ministro-rodado.
*** The ANH was created in 2003, splitting from the SOE Ecopetrol which in addition to extracting, refining and marketing hydrocarbons, also oversaw contract relations with private businesses involved in the sector.
Source: Rudas (2014).

Table 3.1 Exports by destination country, 2006–2013 (percent of GDP)

	2006		2007		2008		2009	
1	USA	5.9%	USA	5.0%	USA	5.8%	USA	5.5%
2	Venezuela	1.7%	Venezuela	2.5%	Venezuela	2.5%	Venezuela	1.7%
3	Ecuador	0.8%	Ecuador	0.6%	Ecuador	0.6%	Netherlands	0.6%
4	Peru	0.4%	Netherlands	0.4%	Peru	0.4%	Ecuador	0.5%
5	Dom. Rep.	0.4%	Peru	0.4%	Chile	0.3%	Switzerland	0.4%
6	Mexico	0.4%	China	0.4%	Netherlands	0.3%	China	0.4%
7	Spain	0.3%	Dominican Rep.	0.3%	Dom. Rep.	0.3%	Peru	0.3%
8	Netherlands	0.3%	Spain	0.3%	UK	0.3%	UK	0.3%
9	Italy	0.3%	Italy	0.3%	Brazil	0.3%	Chile	0.3%
10	China	0.3%	Germany	0.3%	Germany	0.3%	Brazil	0.2%
	Others	4.3%	Others	4.0%	Others	4.4%	Others	3.7%
	Total	**15.0%**	**Total**	**14.5%**	**Total**	**15.4%**	**Total**	**14.0%**

	2010		2011		2012		2013	
1	USA	5.8%	USA	6.5%	USA	5.9%	USA	4.9%
2	Ecuador	0.6%	Netherlands	0.8%	China	0.9%	China	1.3%
3	Netherlands	0.6%	Chile	0.7%	Spain	0.8%	Spain	0.8%
4	China	0.6%	China	0.6%	Venezuela	0.7%	Netherlands	0.6%
5	Venezuela	0.5%	Ecuador	0.6%	Netherlands	0.7%	Venezuela	0.6%
6	Peru	0.4%	Venezuela	0.5%	Chile	0.6%	Ecuador	0.5%
7	Chile	0.4%	Spain	0.5%	Ecuador	0.5%	Brazil	0.4%
8	Brazil	0.4%	Peru	0.4%	Peru	0.4%	Chile	0.4%
9	Switzerland	0.3%	Brazil	0.4%	Brazil	0.3%	Peru	0.3%
10	UK	0.2%	UK	0.4%	UK	0.3%	UK	0.3%
	Others	4.1%	Others	5.8%	Others	5.1%	Others	5.4%
	Total	**13.9%**	**Total**	**17.1%**	**Total**	**16.2%**	**Total**	**15.5%**

Source: Author's calculations based on DANE data.

Imports show a similar trend, as Table 3.2 shows. By the start of the last decade, China had already risen to the fifth-largest source of imports and was closing in on the more important sources (with the exception of the United States, which provided almost a third of the country's imported goods). By the end of the decade, China had established itself as the second-largest source of imports. Reaching a value of USD 8 billion annually – equaling 16 percent of Colombia's total exports – during the last four years of the decade, China surpassed Mexico and gained ground on the United States.

In summary, although China is still not a major source of FDI, the country has quickly established itself as a primary trading partner, surpassed only by the United States. As an export destination, China is an important actor in Colombia's GDP and its generation of foreign exchange, as well as in the channeling of resources to the state. However, because these exports are concentrated in the extractive sector, the many risks that present themselves must be suitably managed if positive returns are to be obtained from this type of activity.

2.1 Colombian extraction and China: Large-scale coal mining and oil extraction

The state's interest in encouraging extractive activity involves mainly income from taxes royalties and attracting FDI. From 2006 to 2010, mining and hydrocarbons together accounted for 28 percent of tax revenues in Colombia. Most of the boom has been due to an increase in the volume of exports, although the considerable profit margins generated by the price boom have also contributed.

If we separate mining from hydrocarbons, we find that hydrocarbons alone represent more than one-third of the value of the country's total exports and contributed close to one-fourth of the central administration's income between 2006 and 2010. In contrast, during the same period minerals contributed little more than 4 percent to total public revenue, despite accounting for more than 20 percent of total export value.[9]

This asymmetry between hydrocarbons and mining in their contributions to public finance can be attributed to a variety of factors. From 2000 to 2010, minerals' share of state revenue was roughly proportionate to their share of GDP. In contrast, hydrocarbons in the same period contributed between four and seven times more to the finances of the central government than to the economy as a whole. Such a situation arises from at least two different conditions. First, the hydrocarbon sector does not only export, but supplies the

---

9   More details in Rudas (2014).

Table 3.2 Imports by origin (annual average, billions of USD)

	1995–1999		2000–2004		2005–2009		2010–2013	
1	USA	4.7	USA	4.3	USA	8.5	USA	13.7
2	Venezuela	1.3	Venezuela	0.9	China	3.1	China	8.5
3	Japan	0.9	Mexico	0.7	Mexico	2.5	Mexico	5.5
4	Germany	0.7	Brazil	0.7	Brazil	2.0	Brazil	2.6
5	Mexico	0.5	China	0.6	Venezuela	1.2	Germany	2.1
6	Brazil	0.5	Japan	0.6	Germany	1.2	Japan	1.4
7	Spain	0.3	Germany	0.6	Japan	1.0	Ecuador	1.0
8	Ecuador	0.3	Ecuador	0.4	Ecuador	0.7	Spain	0.7
9	China	0.2	Spain	0.2	Spain	0.4	Venezuela	0.5
	Others	4.2	Others	4.6	Others	10.0	Others	18.0
	Total	**13.6**	**Total**	**13.6**	**Total**	**30.6**	**Total**	**53.5**

Source: Author's calculations based on DANE data.

internal market with fuel and petrochemicals. In contrast, large-scale mining exports practically raw products, with little or no value added. Second, the government participates directly in the production of hydrocarbons through Ecopetrol, a joint venture that extracts more than a third of the oil in Colombia and operates the country's only refinery.[10] In contrast, since the 1990s the state has not participated directly in the extraction and processing of minerals, completely privatizing previously public mining companies.[11] Finally, there is a significantly more consolidated institutional presence due to the regulation of the ANH, together with Ecopetrol and its research center (the Colombian Petroleum Institute), along with a consolidated business association (the Colombian Petroleum Association) and an influential labor union (Unión Sindical Obrera, or USO). The processes of negotiation are more or less balanced and much more transparent than what prevails in the mining industry.

The rest of this chapter focus more specifically on the social and environmental aspects of two extractive sectors in Colombia. First, it explores trends in large-scale coal mining, in which China is a major importer. Second, it covers oil drilling, in which China is present through FDI projects. Specifically, it develops a case study of the Chinese oil SOEs Sinopec and Sinochem in Colombia.

3. Large-Scale Coal Mining: Social and Environmental Conflicts

After oil, Colombia's second leading export is coal, in which Colombia challenges Russia for third place in world supply. China is by far the primary importer (Table 3.3). This current situation can be traced back to an unsuccessful attempt by the Colombian government to extract coal directly, in association with foreign capital. In 1976, the state enterprise Carbocol was created and tasked with managing the extraction of coal, either on its own or in partnership with private capital. Carbacol signed a contract with Intercor – a subsidiary of Exxon (USA) – to extract coal for 30 years with equal participation of all parties (the Cerrejón project in La Guajira). This agreement was reversed in 2000, when the government sold its share to an

---

10 Colombian citizens own 10.1% of Ecopetrol's shares (Benavides, 2011).
11 Cerro Matoso S. A. was created in 1979, with state ownership, to mine ferronickel. In 1997, the state sold 53% of its share to BHP Billiton (Dávila et al., 2006). Cerrejón was created in 1976 with ownership split equally between the state and Exxon, exporting 49% of Colombian coal between 1994 and 2012. The company was privatized in 2000 (Rudas, 2013).

Table 3.3 Largest exporters and importers of thermal coal, millions of metric tons

A. Top Exporters

	2005	2006	2007	2008	2011	2012
1	AUS 106	AUS 111	IDN 171	IDN 173	IDN 309	IDN 380
2	IDN 89	IDN 104	AUS 112	AUS 115	AUS 144	AUS 159
3	ZAF 72	RUS 82	RUS 85	RUS 86	RUS 110	RUS 116
4	RUS 67	ZAF 68	COL 67	COL 74	COL 75	COL 82
5	CHN 66	COL 60	ZAF 66	ZAF 61	ZAF 72	ZAF 74
6	COL 55	CHN 59	CHN 51	CHN 43	USA 34	USA 51
7	USA 19	USA 20	USA 24	USA 35	KAZ 33	CAN 4
Global Total:	*548*	*593*	*(...)*	*676*	*857*	*963*

B. Top Importers

	2005	2006	2007	2008	2011	2012
1	JPN 114	JPN 114	JPN 105	JPN 128	CHN 146	CHN 218
2	TWN 57	KOR 57	KOR 60	KOR 65	JPN 121	JPN 132
3	KOR 56	TWN 56	TWN 58	TWN 61	KOR 97	IND 123
4	GBR 37	GBR 37	GBR 44	DEU 43	IND 86	KOR 94
5	DEU 31	DEU 31	CHN 33	GBR 42	TWN 62	TWN 56
6	(...)	CHN	DEU 29	CHN 36	DEU 32	GBR 40
7	(...)	IND	IND 22	IND 31	GBR 27	DEU 36
Global Total:	*548*	*593*	*(...)*	*676*	*857*	*963*

Note: No information. AUS: Australia; CHN: China; COL: Colombia; DEU: Germany; GBR: Great Britain; IDN: Indonesia; IND: India; JPN: Japan; KAZ: Kazakhstan; KOR: South Korea; RUS: Russian Federation; TWN: Taiwan; ZAF: South Africa

Source: Author's calculations based on World Coal Association data.

international consortium composed of BHP Billiton (Great Britain), Anglo American (South Africa) and Glencore (Switzerland), the latter partnering with Xstrata (Australia) to form what is now Glencore Xstrata.

The production and export of thermal coal was restricted for many years to Cerrejón. However, midway through the 1990s the company Drummond (USA) initiated new projects in Cesar. Other smaller projects[12] began to appear that ended up combining together under the tutelage of Glencore Xstrata, co-owner of Cerrejón. Others[13] commercialized together with Drummond. In a few years, the extraction of coal in Cesar surpassed that of La Guajira, representing around 60 percent of annual exports in recent years. Colombia exported 40 million tons between 2000 and 2004, and more than 75 million tons in 2011 and 2012.

Colombia's opening to the Chinese market has boosted the current growth of its total exports. Between 2000 and 2010, China imported an annual average of just 15 thousand tons of Colombian coal. In contrast, between 2010 and 2011, Colombia sent China an annual average of more than three *million* tons of coal: 4 percent of total Colombian coal exports. In this context, we will analyze the economic, social, and environmental impacts on the regions where the exportable thermal coal from Colombia is produced: the departments of Cesar and La Guajira.

3.1 Coal and chains of production

Between 2007 and 2012[14] – extractive activity generated a value-added between 3 and 4 million Colombian pesos per resident, followed distantly by the agricultural sector at 300 to 400 thousand pesos per resident. At the beginning of the 1990s, Cesar registered more than 200 thousand hectares of seasonal crops; in 2010 only 25 thousand hectares remained, and there were no significant increases in productivity. Two very important crops (cotton and sorghum) practically disappeared after once occupying close to half of the sown area of the department. With the exception of cacao, which grew from 1000 to 6000 hectares, the permanent crops of peasant farmers receded as well, falling in area by nearly half from the beginning of this period. The only crop that has shown significant momentum is palm oil, a high-growth agro-industrial crop that receives subsidies for agrofuels. In La Guajira the

---

12 Prodeco, La Jagua Coal, United Mining Consortium, and Treasure Coal.
13 *Norcarbón* and Vale Coal Colombia.
14 More details in Rudas (2014).

situation is even more critical, with all of the crops showing a significant reduction.[15]

Moreover, mining has few links to other activities, which affects the local population. Information from financial statements from companies that operate in these areas (Cerrejón in La Guajira and Drummond in Cesar), complemented by detailed information provided by the companies, shows that they have little impact on the local economies: 1–2 percent of their total income is used to purchase local goods, while 35 percent of Cerrejón's income and 47 percent of Drummond's income is spent on foreign purchases. More than 55 percent of their total after-tax profits leaves the country, either for the payment of external suppliers or in remittances.

Furthermore, for these two companies export three-quarters of the country's total coal, government revenue via taxes and royalties represents an average of 51 percent of their total operational profits.[16]

From the perspective of workers' compensation, one of the implications of the decline in agriculture and the lack of industry participation in mining regions has been low job creation. According to figures from DANE, between 2000 and 2011, for every 100 pesos of gross operating surplus generated by agriculture, workers received a wage of 742 pesos; in contrast, in the case of coal mining the ratio was just 23 pesos in wages for every 100 pesos in gross operating surplus (Rudas and Espitia, 2013a). The difference is due in part to the lack of employment generated directly by mining companies or through subcontracting. According to estimates from the University of the Andes (2010, 181), in 2007 all of the mining activity in Cesar employed less than 5,400 workers, of which only 2,700 were native to that department. This is a very low level of employment, especially when viewed in relation to the 35 million tons of coal exported from the region in 2007 – equaling more than 10 percent of the total value of the country's exports and over 1 percent of the total GDP during that year.

3.1.1 Generating wealth amid poverty and environmental damage

Recent studies prove that the regions of Colombia where coal has been extracted for two or three decades show extreme poverty and very little government presence. Although their public authorities have much higher per-capita incomes than other country's municipalities, the living conditions

---

15 Ministry of Agriculture.
16 This figure contrasts with a study contracted by the mining guild, conducted based on a hypothetical company that would give 74.4% of its profits to the state (Ernst and Young, 2012).

of the general population are lower, comparable only to those municipalities with the highest rates of conflict. The populations in the coal mining municipalities of Cesar and La Guajira exhibit similar, or worse, living conditions than what has been recorded in isolated locations of coca cultivation (Rudas and Espitia, 2013a).

Human development indicators for the municipalities of Cesar from where coal is extracted provide evidence for this claim (Figure 3.2). Infant mortality rates – an indicator used to measure health services – are declining, but still remain well above the departmental and national average in almost all cases. Students in their final year almost always score lower than the departmental and national average on the unified exam. The comprehensive municipal performance index (CMPI), which measures various qualitative factors regarding government services, is far lower than the national average in almost all cases (with the exception of just one municipality). Finally, more than half of the population has at least one basic need that has not been met, as compared to the national average of less than 30 percent.

This situation, unacceptable for a region that has been home to one of the primary vehicles for national economic growth for years, is exacerbated by environmental impacts that are far from being responsibly managed. First, open-pit mining affects huge areas of land, as well as surface and underground water. One indicator of the magnitude of this impact is the relationship between exported coal and the waste material that is removed and deposited in the region. Over the course of two decades more than 250 million tons of coal have been extracted from Cesar: an insignificant amount compared with the nearly 5 billion tons of waste material extracted by Drummond and the 7.5 billion tons removed throughout the department.[17] While the companies consider this waste material to be "sterile," its extraction has removed it from an geologically isolated state underground and exposed it to air, light, and water, triggering chemical reactions in the exposed waste, impacting both surface and underground water sources (Fierro and Lopez, 2014).

Another important environmental factor is water use: according to available data, around 178 liters of water may be used per ton of extracted coal.[18] According to this figure, Prodeco, the second-largest producer of coal in Cesar, could be using close to 2 million cubic meters of water per year; and Drummond, the largest company, could be using close to 5 million cubic meters. But while Drummond has authorized an annual volume of more than 35 million cubic meters per year (7 times its current usage), Prodeco only has

---

17 Calculations from CGR (2013) and Drummond (1990).
18 Environmental management plan from Prodeco S. A., cited by the University of the Andes (2010).

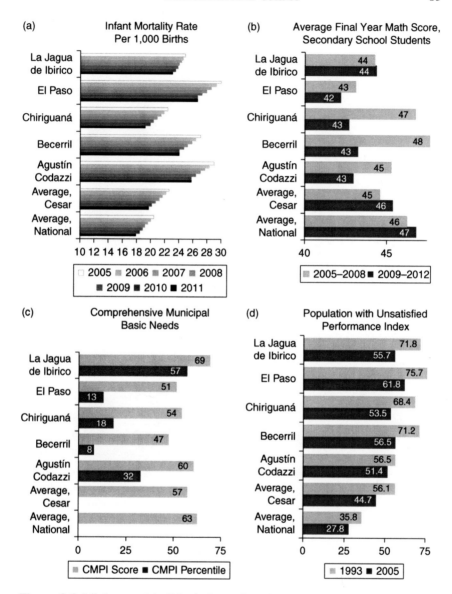

Figure 3.2 Mining municipalities in Cesar: Social and institutional indicators
Source: Author's calculations based on DANE, Instituto Colombiano para el Fomento de la Educación Superior (**ICFES**) and Departamento Nacional de Planeación (**DNP**) data.

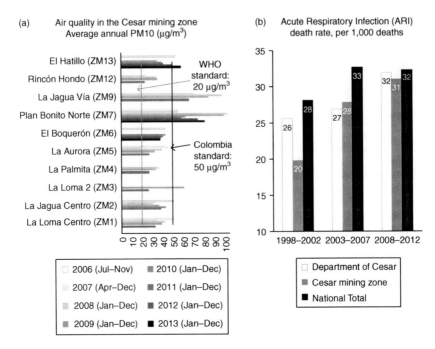

Figure 3.3 Air quality and mortality indicators, Cesar mining areas
Source: Authors' calculations based on the *Red de calidad de aire zona minera de Cesar* (Ministerio de Ambiente and Sisaire-Corpocesar), WHO (2005) and DANE data.

authorization to use 275 thousand cubic meters, barely a fourth of what could actually be used, according to the company's own estimates. Moreover, according to data from regional environmental authorities, in 2011 Drummond paid just 140 dollars for all of the water authorized and used for its mining activities during that year.[19]

Aside from the effects on water, perhaps one of the most troubling issues facing the region is air pollution generated by coal extraction and transportation. The air quality in the mining region of Cesar is dangerous (Figure 3.3). With a few notable exceptions, the majority of record points consistently report concentrations of particulate matter (PM_{10}) within the maximum permissible level in Colombia, but these concentrations also consistently exceed the maximum limit recommended by the World Health Organization (WHO).

This is an especially risky situation, as shown by the few available indicators related to public health. For example, the average death rate for acute respiratory infections (ARIs) in mining towns in the region has risen from 20 for

---

19 *Corpocesar*, report to the Ministry of Environment on water usage rates.

every 1,000 total deaths between 1998 and 2002, to 31 per thousand between 2008 and 2012. At the beginning of the period in question, marked by the emergence of extractive activity, these towns exhibited rates far lower than the departmental average (over 25 per thousand) and the national average (28 per thousand). However, this indicator increased far more rapidly in the mining towns than in the other municipalities in the department and the nation as a whole, equaling these averages by the end of the period. In other words, the death rate in the mining towns increased during this period by 55 percent, far greater than the 15 percent rise estimated by the WHO when PM_{10} levels went from 20 μg/m^3 to 70 μg/m^3 (WHO, 2005, 11).

In 2010 faced with such dangerous levels of particulate matter, the Ministry of the Environment ordered mining companies to relocate the area's residents.[20] The Comptroller General of the Republic deemed this decision to be both late and erroneous, arguing that an environmental license should not have even been issued without first requiring, as a condition preceding the start of operations, the resettlement of these communities. The comptroller also noted, among other aggravating factors, that the mining industry had exacerbated the already precarious living conditions of the region's inhabitants, that the environmental authorities did not promptly punish the companies for failing to fulfill their obligations to the community and that the participation of local actors in the decision-making process regarding relocation was reduced to nothing more than observation (CGR, 2013a). Moreover, postponement of the relocation intensified the conflict. In a guardianship action brought before the Constitutional Court, Drummond was found responsible for adversely affecting the health and privacy of the area's residents,[21] and a ruling was given in favor of the family that filed the lawsuit. Drummond's actions affected 436 families in the region, or more than two thousand people. However, the delay in implementing measures along with the expectation of a resettlement plan created a magnet for the poor, and swelled the number of residents to just shy of one thousand families, or about 4,500 people (CGR, 2013a).

All of these situations, and many others identified in a field study conducted by the University of the Andes (2010) for the Ministry of the Environment, suggest that the benefits that the region's inhabitants have been able to receive do not outweigh the environmental costs, which is aggravated by the poverty of the local population.[22]

---

20 Resolution 970 (20.05. 2010).
21 Ruling T-154 of 2013. See details in Rudas (2013).
22 Applying economic valuation techniques to the environmental impacts of mining, this study concludes that the benefits received by the local population as a result of mining represent only 85% of the costs that the population is burdened with, due to the

4. Oil Extraction: A Case Study of a Chinese Company

Chinese investments in oil extraction in Colombia are small but growing, and are associated with the state enterprises Sinopec and Sinochem. Since 2006, Sinopec has equally shared the Colombian assets of Mansarovar Energy with the Indian state enterprise ONGC Videsh. Furthermore, in 2010 Sinopec purchased fields from US-based Hupecol and created a new company called New Granada Energy Colombia (NGEC). For its part, Sinochem has been extracting oil in Colombia since 2006 via Emerald Energy, a subsidiary of Sinochem Resources UK. Between these three companies, China has gone from producing 14 kbd (thousand barrels per day) of oil in 2009 (2.1% of total national production) to 25.4 kbd in the first semester of 2014 (2.6% of total national production).[23]

For this case study we have chosen to focus on NGEC, which operates primarily in the town of Paz de Ariporo in the department of Casanare, located on the eastern plains of Colombia – a region from which a significant portion of the country's oil is extracted.[24] We start by describing the oil extracting activity in the department of Casanare, emphasizing the peak incidence of oil in the regional economy and in public finances. Next, we describe the primary impacts of this activity in Paz de Ariporo, where NGEC operates. Finally, we present the principal characteristics of this company, as well as the environmental and social impacts of its operation, while considering the most prevalent risks associated with it.

4.1 Oil, economy and public finances in Casanare and Paz de Ariporo

According to figures from the ANH, fifth of the 983 kbd of oil extracted in Colombia (in the first semester of 2014) comes from the 45 thousand square miles of the department of Casanare. The extraction of oil in the region has

---

hidden environmental deterioration that goes uncompensated by mining companies (University of the Andes, 2010).

23 According to ANH figures, Mansarovar currently extracts 38.9 kbd, of which 10.6 correspond to Sinopec, another undetermined amount to the Indian investment, and 17.8 to Ecopetrol, with whom Mansarovar has a partnership contract. NGEC (Sinopec) extracts 8.2 kbd and Emerald (Sinochem) extracts 6.6 kbd.

24 This town was chosen given that more than 90% of NGEC's production occurs here. Interviews were conducted with community leaders and officials from local government entities. Information was requested from entities at the national, regional, and local levels, and field records of the National Environmental Licensing Authority (ANLA) were analyzed. An interview with NGEC was requested, but it was impossible to establish direct contact with the company.

soared since the middle of the 1990s, profoundly transforming the local economy. According to figures from DANE, with an estimated population of 350 thousand in 2014,[25] Casanare was primarily a livestock economy in 1990: 62 percent of the total value-added came from that sector, 8 percent came from agriculture and 12 percent came from oil. Starting in 1995, oil has grown significantly, contributing 84 percent of the regional value-added in the year 2000 (with 3% coming from livestock and 1% coming from agriculture). Even with a downturn in the following years, the extractive sector still contributed 61 percent of the value-added in 2012, with livestock contributing 7 percent and agriculture contributing 3 percent.

These changes are not only due to increased oil extraction, but also to the deterioration, in absolute terms, of the other sectors. In 1990, oil contributed little more than $1,000 of value-added per resident,[26] yet by 1999 it had reached its highest point at more than $17,000. It has since progressively declined, contributing a value of $6,000 in 2012. On the other hand, livestock generated $5,000 per capita at the beginning of this same period, falling to its lowest point in 2003 at less than $325, and slowly recuperating to a value of $750 at the end of the period. The agricultural sector began this period with a value-added between $700 and $1,000 per resident (1990 to 1995), before collapsing to $100 in 2002, and moderately recuperating to a little less than $350 in 2012. Coinciding with one of the first oil booms, between 1994 and 1998 the construction sector – specifically concerning civil projects – exhibited atypical behavior: its value-added per capita grew from less than $300 in 1990 to more than $3,350 in 1998, returning to normal values of less than $500 from 1999 until the end of the period. This reflects important local investments in infrastructure, which were necessary to boost oil activity in the region.

The oil boom also had a positive impact on public finances. A system of royalty distribution was already in effect for the extractive sector in Colombia, meaning that around 85 percent of royalties were paid to the territorial authorities in the departments and municipalities where oil extraction took place. Between 1990 and 1994, before the oil boom in Casanare, the income for the authorities of the region increased in real terms to $180 annually per capita. Between 1995 and 1999 the value grew to $600, increasing between 2003 and 2012 to an annual average of $1,390 – almost eight times that which was recorded at the beginning of the period. Two factors contribute to this result: first, the annual income from royalties increased from less than $100 per resident in the first five years of the period to an average of $760 in the last ten years of the period. However, there also appears to be a dynamic

---

25 74% in 19 county seats and the rest in rural areas.
26 1 USD = 2,321 Colombian pesos from 2005.

effect on the tax on industry and trade, increasing from $6 annually per capita in the first five years to $44 in the last five years of the period.[27] Finally, the dynamism in public finances is reflected in another favorable indicator for the population: the growth of the value-added of educational services, health services, and social security, which practically tripled from less than $180 annually per capita in the first five years that were analyzed (to $520 annually per resident, compared to the national average of $503).

These same trends can be seen in Paz de Ariporo. The annual income per capita of the territorial authorities has more than quintupled between the first and last five years of the period, increasing from $180 to more than $1,450 per capita.

4.2 Environmental impacts of NGEC in Paz de Ariporo

Extracting hydrocarbons in Colombia requires a universal environmental license, granted by the National Environmental Licensing Authority (Autoridad Nacional de Licencias Ambientales, or ANLA). This license establishes general management measures for preventing, mitigating, correcting and finally compensating for the effects identified in the environmental impact study, authorizing the operator to conduct extractive activity in any part of the area covered by the license. Initial extraction is contingent upon the presentation to ANLA of a specific management plan for each site. However, the norm for the extraction of hydrocarbons is such that these specific plans do not need to be evaluated or approved by ANLA, and in fact simply making the presentation is sufficient for gaining the authority's approval.[28] Moreover, the permits for the allocation and use of renewable natural resources are implicitly included in the respective licenses, which are approved by ANLA, which in turn assumes the responsibility of verifying and controlling compliance with the management plans.

When Sinopec purchased four fields in 2010 to create NGEC, this new company began extracting a total of 6.7 kbd of oil. During this period, 75 percent of Sinopec's total capacity was extracted from the two largest fields, located in Paz de Ariporo. The company's total capacity was raised to 9.6 kbd by 2013, 8.7 of which corresponded directly to these two fields, contributing 58 percent of the total oil extracted by all of the companies in Paz de Ariporo.[29] In 2005 and 2007, Hupecol presented the environmental impact

---

27 Figures from the National Planning Department (DNP).
28 Order 2820 of 2010, article 4.
29 According to data from the ANH, two companies (Hupecol and Pacific Stratus Energy) share 25% equally among themselves, while the remaining 17% comes from another 7 companies that operate in the municipality.

studies for the two fields located in Paz de Ariporo (purchased by Sinopec), and obtained the respective licenses by the end of 2008. These licenses took into account the construction and adaptation of exploratory wells, the adaptation and construction of roads, the drilling and testing of production wells and the transportation of oil in tankers, as well as the decommissioning and abandonment of these facilities upon completion of the project.

NGEC's fields are located in the Orinoquía, a special ecosystem of flooded savannas located southeast of the county seat of Paz de Ariporo, accessible by 115 kilometers of unpaved roads. As its name implies, this ecosystem is characterized by frequent floods, evidenced by geological formations such as low, meandering, abandoned riverbeds, dams, and bodies of water both permanent and seasonal. These plains could even be characterized as stable wetland systems "if they are analyzed over long periods of time, according to the behavior of the basin, the course of the river, and the plains, and if we accept the assertion of Alfredo Paolillo and other Venezuelan Orinoquía researchers" (Bank of the West, 2005).[30]

Given the characteristics of the ecosystem, the presence of threatened species of fish and reptiles, and its importance for migratory birds, a study on the Orinoco River basin in Colombia and Venezuela selected – from 19 areas of special interest for the conservation of biodiversity – one of three thousand square kilometers located in Paz de Ariporo. The creation of *Parque de las Hermosas* has been proposed in this region, which would occupy a quarter of the area of the municipality, thus protecting the Orinoquía wetland system that makes up about a third of the municipality's 12,000 square kilometers. This would protect the ecosystem and the ecological functions of the wetlands, which is currently not represented in the country's national park system (Lasso, et al., 2010 and Rincón et al., 2014).

NGEC's fields in Paz de Ariporo are located within this fragile wetland ecosystem, precisely in the La Hermosa basin targeted as the zone for the newly protected area. Despite this close proximity, no mention of it is made in ANLA's environmental monitoring reports, nor are any special actions proposed for the extraction of oil in wetland environments. Furthermore, the construction of 67 kilometers of internal and access roads has been permitted using a method of *lateral loans*, or longitudinal excavations parallel to the roads, in order to construct the embankments.[31] These excavations are between 90

---

30 Alfred Paolillo, Master in Hydraulics and Fluid Power Technology/Technician at the University of Modena and Reggio Emilia (Italy), Hydraulic Test and Application Engineer at Bosch Rexroth.

31 In another project in the Orinoquia floodplain, operated by Ecopetrol, ANLA banned the use of lateral loans due to the high environmental impacts on soil and water flows (ANLA, Resolution 179, February 27, 2014, article 19).

and 100 meters in length and between 9 and 10 meters wide, with a separation of around 6 to 10 meters between each loan area and with location and road levels at 50 centimeters or less in an area of floodplain. Furthermore, all of this has been authorized without consulting any detailed regional hydrologic or hydraulic studies, and without taking the necessary precautions to ensure the normal flow of water in frequently flooded lowlands, such as adequately designed drains, bridges, pontoons and box culverts. Moreover, the development of NGEC's fields has also taken place in floodplains, with the digging of wells and the construction of sites in lowlands that surpass the hydraulic capacity of the systems constructed to drain water in the rainy season. Finally, the high level of ground water must be taken into consideration, which is intensified by the perforations adjacent to the roads and sites made to extract material, as well as the heavy oil tanker traffic that systematically deteriorates the condition of the access roads.[32]

Regarding the impact of these types of roads, a study conducted in the Venezuelan Orinoquía (Rial, et al., 2010) found that by building them in floodplains without the necessary complementary projects, they end up becoming dams that limit the flow of water and reduce the pulse amplitude of floods with gaps between the banks, silting, and sedimentation. This also damages the savanna by limiting or exceeding the supply of nutrients to the floodplain, as well as by enriching certain lentic systems, which contributes to a decline in species richness. However, extreme weather events, such as floods or droughts, becoming more frequent and intense due to climate change (IPCC, 2014) poses the greatest threat to these ecosystems and the population that uses their water – including the fishing sector, the agricultural sector and even the oil sector itself.

In terms of seismic exploration, only environmental licenses are required for the building of roads in Colombia, and only in certain cases. The mining (ANH) and environmental (ANLA) authorities merely require isolated distances between the shot points and houses, bodies of water, and other sensitive areas (Herrera and Cooper, 2010). However, it has been shown that seismic exploration changes the pattern of surface movement of rainwater and runoff, causing surface fissures in the soil and deepening the phreatic stratum, as well as altering the subsoil in the extensive area where the blasts from different seismic programs are located (CGR, 2014). Furthermore, the companies that carry

---

32   During the visit for this study, the rate of traffic was determined at 20 vehicles per hour, 18 of which were associated with oil activities (tankers, dump trucks, pickups, cargo trucks, and tractor trailers with equipment and supplies for oil operations). The companies that use this road are NGEC, Hupecol, Pacific Stratus Energy, Geopark, and Perenco.

out this seismic exploration do not conduct regional hydro-geological studies to evaluate the cumulative impact of the blasts on unconfined and semi-confined shallow aquifers, nor are such studies required by the appropriate authorities.

Given the characteristics of the wetland ecosystem, one of the riskiest situations is water pollution. In Paz de Ariporo, the fluid extracted by NGEC contains 22 percent oil, while the remaining 78 percent is water and basic fluid that must be returned to the natural environment (Mazuera, 2014). To this end, the company utilizes a formation water treatment system prior to dumping the unused fluid. However, many questions arise. For example, the maximum concentration limit for chlorides in the discharged fluid established by the environmental license is 250 mg/L, but in reports supplied by NGEC, ANLA found chlorides in post-treatment formation water in the order of 2,370 mg/L. In turn, ANLA requested information on the quality of the discharged fluid, and consequently obtained NGEC lab results that confirmed levels above the maximum allowed limit.[33] Taking these results into consideration, the environmental authority began an investigative process for exceeding the maximum allowed limit and for failing to provide the required number of samples.[34] Moreover, irregularities in the fluid dumps and inconsistencies in the data have been reported since the very first environmental compliance reports in 2007. However, only in August of 2011 was this alleged irregularity found by the environmental authority, reflecting weakness on its part in exercising adequate control.

Further failures from NGEC and ANLA have mandatory investment commitments unfulfilled and long overdue. Colombian law states that projects that use water must allocate at least 1 percent of the total value of their investment to the recovery, preservation, and protection of the watershed that feeds their water source. The environmental licenses granted to Hupecol (now NGEC) in 2008 established an obligation to allocate USD 650,000 to this end,[35] subject to the presentation of a detailed investment plan to the regional environmental authority (Corporinoquia)[36] within a period of four

---

33 ANLA, Auto 3068 of 2012.

34 ANLA, Notice 4120-E2 35411 to NGEC, August 11, 2014. The investigation has been ongoing since September of 2012, but since then no information has been found in the file regarding any advancement in this process.

35 Exchange rate in 2008: 1 USD = 1,967 Colombian pesos.

36 In Colombia, in addition to the national environmental authority, there are autonomous regional corporations with environmental authority in their respective areas of jurisdiction, as is the case with Corporinoquia in the Orinoco basin. However, with the centralization of the licensing process for these types of projects, these regional authorities carry out very few functions. Control of the investments is one of the few powers they have left.

months. In order to comply this obligation, the company agreed, among others, to an investment of USD 500,000 with Corporinoquia for the purchase of land for environmental protection in the mountains of Zamaricote, located in the piedmont plains northwest of Paz de Ariporo, more than 100 kilometers from the protected area. In November of 2010, upon finding that these investments had not been put into effect, ANLA required NGEC to present an updated program two months later, which was approved in February of 2011. In March of that same year, the company reported that it was compiling information, but due to problems of public order the responsible authority[37] had failed to collect the necessary cadastral information, requesting an extension of the deadline set by ANLA. In July of 2012, the communities in the project area requested that these investments be made in the region affected by the company's activities, and not so far away. In November of 2013 a social/environmental organization sought action against the failure to complete these investments.[38] In the first half of 2014, the Comptroller General of the Republic implemented a special course of action to address the environmental problems in the town of Paz de Ariporo.[39] After reviewing fifty different records, the Comptroller found that the mandatory investments had not been fulfilled due to the failure of ANLA to adequately perform its functions of monitoring and control, which directly affected the basin recovery program. The comptroller did not accept the depositions taken from ANLA on breach of their institutional functions of monitoring and oversight of the mandatory investments of the company in conservation of watersheds, upholding its finding of alleged tax liability on part of the entity (CGR, 2014). To conclude, six years after establishing these mandatory investments, NGEC has not made any of them nor has it presented any specific investment plans. All of this reflects the unwillingness of the company, as well as ANLA's lack of control, despite the sanctions imposed by Corporinoquia on NGEC for its lack of compliance.

---

37 The Agustín Codazzi Geographical Institute (IGAC) is the national entity in charge of cadastral matters.

38 Communication to ANLA directed by the ecological group Mastranto (08.11.3013).

39 Between December of 2013 and March of 2014, a severe drought occurred in the region of Paz de Ariporo where NGEC operates, causing an undetermined number of animals to die (capybaras, turtles, alligators, caimans, and cattle). One hypothesis is that this phenomenon arose from synergistic and cumulative impacts concerning "the high mountain plateaus, where rivers originate that supply Casanare; intensive farming that compacts the soil and hinders the ability of rainfall infiltration and runoff; low moisture retention capacity in the sandy surface; the limited production capacity of the soil; and the use of groundwater from oil sites, all of which makes the area more susceptible to the impacts of climate change" (IGAC, 2014).

4.3 Social impacts of NGEC's operation in Paz de Ariporo

In the 2005 census, the town of Paz de Ariporo registered 18,000 inhabitants in urban areas and 9,000 in rural areas, with a rural population density of 0.63 inhabitants per square kilometer. Of the total population, 925 people were identified as indigenous and 539 as Afro-descendent. However, in the area of influence of NGEC's contracts, the presence of indigenous or Afro-Colombian communities was not reported,[40] acknowledging instead only the *campesino* population. The community in the region is not generally opposed to NGEC or other oil companies. However, daily relations are tense and acts of resistance occur over sensitive subjects, such as the obligation established in the environmental license to hire local workers. The community claims that the companies do not hire sufficient personnel from the region, and it demands that the job requirements be relaxed so that more local people can qualify and that more of them receive job training. The community has noted that, despite the existence of a workforce in the area, outside workers are sometimes hired. For example, the mayor of the municipality of Paz de Ariporo reported that between April 2012 and July 2014 demands on these issues were made by the Association of Technicians and Professionals of Paz de Ariporo, by the local owners of dump trucks and by local communities of Caño Chiquito, Centro Gaitán and Normadía.[41] Furthermore, it has called for improvements in labor welfare conditions and has protested the fact that subcontracting and intermediation companies do not meet its demands regarding working conditions and have on occasion delayed workers' pay. When these tensions are exacerbated, the community applies pressure in the form of strikes, blockades and demonstrations.[42] One particularly inflammatory practice is the chosen method of identifying and presenting local candidates for hire,[43] a responsibility delegated to the long-standing community action boards that are traditionally present in rural areas of Colombia. Complaints have been reported concerning the influence on negotiations of the presidents of these boards,

---

40 The Ministry of the Interior certifies the presence of ethnic communities in the area of interest of these projects.

41 Communication with the authors, October 6, 2014.

42 See the workers' strike (July 2014) http://www.casanare.gov.co/?idcategoria=32662 and the transportation strike (November 2012) http://kratosveeduria.blogspot.com/2012/11/accionar-de-kratos-veeduria-como.html.

43 The oil industry has very little relative ability to generate direct employment: between 2000 and 2011, for every 100 pesos of gross operating surplus generated by this sector, 10 pesos went toward labor remuneration. Compare this with 69 pesos in industry and 742 pesos in agriculture (Rudas and Espitia, 2013a).

alleging that the presidents control the rotation of local personnel and pointing the fact that on occasion they have illegally demanded money for assigning quotas. Regional officials from the Ministry of Labor state that these community complaints have not been formalized for fear of losing the possibility of an employment relationship. However, the president of the Association of Community Action Boards (Asojuntas) has noted that while such situations do occur, they are not widespread. She has further expressed that the internal regulations of these organizations – recognized by law – allow for margins of autonomy when assigning and rotating quotas within their communities. This lax view of autonomy may increase the high risk of assigning quotas based on personal favors, and not in legal way according to the capabilities of potential workers. Conflicts regarding the contracting of local workers are widespread across Colombia's oil zones. In response, the national government has devised a strategy to regulate labor interme- diation,[44] which joins together the National Learning Service (SENA) and the Casanare Family Compensation Fund (Confacasanare) in the region so that these two entities may assume the functions currently carried out by the community action boards. In this regard, the official consulted from the Ministry of Labor of Casanare noted that this has not been well received in the region, given that traditional intermediaries could lose their respon- sibilities. Furthermore, it has been argued that people who are not from the region could put their resumes into the new system, thereby displacing local residents. In this context, a panel was recently formed in the municipality to propose mechanisms to implement the orders in the presidential decree. Another area in which the community has demanded change is the layout of an access road to the NGEC fields. The community pushed for modi- fication of the layout the road, so that it could also serve as a road to con- nect the region with the county seat. The community also demanded that NGEC maintain the road and signed an agreement with the company in that regard. However, according to community leaders, NGEC has either objected to, or delayed, the agreed-upon investment, citing high costs and the presence of other oil companies in the area. This has been a recurring claim in recent years, one that reflects the high sensitivity of the subject as the low willingness of NGEC to comply – and of ANLA in demanding that the company do so. In addition, the community has rejected the construc- tion of a pipeline that would serve the region, apparently out of fear of losing opportunities for the provision of food and housing services, among others, which are provided on the road to oil-tanker drivers.

---

44 Order 2852 of 2013 (December).

4.4 Transparency in the company, the authorities and the community

For this research, we solicited information from NGEC concerning its social and environmental investments, complaints from the communities, ongoing investigations and environmental problems. In Colombia, private entities that manage public resources such as oil are required to meet these requirements and respond to these issues. However, NGEC did not respond to the formal request made for this research and did not agree to participate in a required interview on several occasions. Also, we found no specific information online regarding the company's environmental and social management of its operations in Colombia. ANLA – created in 2011 to assume the licensing and control functions that were once carried out by the Ministry of Environment – has detailed environmental information regarding oil fields. The organization evaluates environmental impact studies and monitors the obligations established by the environmental license. This information is public and, in theory, can be accessed by any citizen. However, while ANLA has an electronic document management system, in order to consult the information it possesses we had to travel to its offices in Bogotá, manually check each record, pay for digital copies, and wait 15 days to receive them. Although ANLA must systematically monitor the obligations of the company, which pays a fixed fee for that very purpose, this usually only happens in response to community complaints.[45] Still, complaints from the community presented in March of 2010 still have not been fully resolved, which speaks to this authority's lack of effectiveness. Some of the functions of the ANH are to assign fields to oil companies, oversee the development of projects and to track community benefit programs – mandatory as of 2011. In 2013 and 2014, the agency tracked NGEC's projects and reported environmental violations to ANLA, without any corrective action being taken by the latter. Furthermore, no monitoring was conducted on the obligations set forth by the community benefits programs. The regional environmental authority Corporinoquia responded to our request for information, and had four professionals participate in an interview. However, the monitoring of oil projects carried out by this corporation is limited to the seismic exploration phase, and it is not responsible for later stages of the process. The information in these records is not available in digital format. The city hall of Paz de Ariporo maintains an office on oil affairs. This office did not respond to the questionnaire we sent, but the person in charge agreed to an interview in which relevant verbal information was provided for this study (but no physical copies of it were allowed). The Ministry of Labor has a regional

---

45 No compliance reports were found between 2012 and 2013, and five instances of information added to or removed from the record were found.

office in Yopal, the capital of the department of Casanare, which has assumed an important role in handling labor disputes. We conducted an interview with the director and another employee, both of whom provided clear and timely information on labor issues related to the area's oil industry. Within the community, the president of Asojuntas facilitated contact with members of the community action board in the area where NGEC operates, with whom discussions and interviews were held. In addition, these members helped us gain access to the oil field's area of operation.

4.5 Final reflections on the activity of NGEC

The overall assessment of the social and environmental management of NGEC does not differ substantially from that of other oil companies in the region, the problems of which are widespread. However, it has been shown that community perception is especially negative toward NGEC, given the company's repeated failure to fulfill its commitments and the manner in which it has impacted sensitive issues affecting these communities. In addition to the inability of the company to fulfill its environmental and social commitments, the environmental authority does not implement monitoring and reporting with the efficiency necessary to ensure the company's compliance with these obligations. These gaps in oversight create an important role for community planning and participation, a role that prioritizes sustainability and permanence over time, makes use of proper knowledge of the ecosystem and the activities that can be developed and is designed in conjunction with municipal, regional and national planning. If such planning is not carried out, oil companies will end up commercializing their relationships with the community, leaving the members to compete for fragmented resources on a circumstantial basis or in situations of immediate urgency, with no long-term viability. The dynamics of negotiation established between oil companies and communities end up blurring the lines of compensation and social investment, which can ignite strikes, demonstrations and blockades. These manifestations are marked by widespread mistrust among the actors, making dialogue and negotiation difficult.

5. Final Conclusions and Recommendations

According to the evidence gathered, as well as the previous reflections, the following general conclusions can be drawn:

• Mining and hydrocarbons currently play a key role in Colombia's economy, and exhibit significant and increasing influence on the composition of the GDP, exports and FDI growth.

- Extractive activity – especially coal mining – has failed to generate the kind of wealth that extends significantly to the population in regions where mining occurs. This dilemma must be addressed by all of the actors involved, especially when it comes to identifying and implementing mechanisms to break the vicious cycle of creating wealth without creating the necessary conditions for overcoming poverty in local contexts.
- There is a structural weakness in Colombia concerning both mining and environmental institutions, which has placed particular mining areas in regions with the most intense social and environmental conflict.
- Whatever the future may hold in Colombia for the development of Chinese FDI (or that of any other country), it is necessary to consider strategies to overcome the level of social and environmental conflict that has been generated so far. This is especially true regarding open-pit coal mining in regions with impoverished populations, as well as small-scale oil drilling in wetland regions – both of which are clear examples of challenges that have yet to be adequately addressed, as we have detailed in this chapter. Taking these issues into consideration is the *sine qua non* for obtaining positive returns on these investments. Failure to do so will create a structural constraint on investment viability.

Finally, the case study in this chapter points to recommendations for improving the situation. There are important roles for NGEC, ANLA and civil society in this regard.

- NGEC could learn from Sinopec's Ecuadorian subsidiaries, which have maintained more positive social and environmental performance records. The simple act of fulfilling previous obligations to the community and to the government would create a drastic improvement in this area.
- ANLA could facilitate greater participation from civil society by continuing to improve transparency. While the government provides important legal guarantees to information, unfortunate obstacles to accessing information still exist. One way to address this could be for Colombia to join the Extractive Industries Transparency Initiative, as Peru has done.
- Civil society can contribute by continuing to press for improvements in both company performance and government oversight.

References

Arellano, J. 2011. *¿Minería sin fronteras? Conflicto y desarrollo en regiones mineras del Perú*. IEP, Instituto de Estudios Peruanos, Lima, Perú.

Auty, R. 1993. *Sustaining Development in Mineral Economies: The Resource Curse Thesis*. London and New York: Routledge.

Banco de Occidente. 2005. *La Orinoquia de Colombia*. I/M Editores, Cali, Colombia.

Bebbington, A. (ed). 2013. *Industria extractivas: conflicto social y dinámicas institucionales en la Región Andina*. Instituto de Estudios Peruanos, IEP. Lima.

Benavides, J. (ed). 2011. *Ecopetrol. Clean Energy for the Future 60 Years*. Villegas Editores, Bogotá.

Cárdenas, M. and M. Reina. 2008. *La minería en Colombia: impacto socioeconómico y fiscal*. Fedesarrollo, Bogotá.

Cemea, M. M. 1988. "Involuntary Resettlement in Development Projects. Policy Guidelines in World Bank-Financed Projects." World Bank Technical Paper Number 80, Washington, DC.

Chaves, F. R., M. A. Rodrigues da Silva, and R. de C. Jimenez (eds). 2011. *Recursos Minerais & Sustentabilidade Territorial. Grandes Minas*. Ministério de Minas e Energia e Centro de Tecnologia Mineral, Brasil.

Contralora General de la República, CGR. 2012. *Informe del Estado de los Recursos Naturales y del Ambiente 2011–2012*. Bogotá.

———. 2013. *Informe de Actuación Especial a PLN del Cesar, Resolución Orgánica 6680 de 2012, Agencia Nacional de Minería*. Bogotá.

———. 2013a. *Evaluación del Proceso de Reasentamiento Poblacional por Minería del Carbón en el Departamento del Cesar*. Actuación Especial, Bogotá.

———. 2014. *Problemática ambiental presentada en el municipio de Paz de Ariporo*. Bogotá.

Dávila, J. C., C. Dávila, A. Jiménez, L. M. Milanés and M. I. Rubio. 2006. *Cerro Matoso S.A. Sustainability of a Mining Company in Latin America's Turbulent Environment (1970–2003)*. Universidad de los Andes, Bogotá.

Departamento Administrativo Nacional de Estadísticas, DANE. 2011. *Exportaciones destinadas a Corea – China – Japón – Singapur, 2000–2010*. En *Boletín Especial de la Dinámica del Comercio Exterior*. Bogotá.

Drummond Ltd. 1990. *Declaratoria de Impacto Ambiental*. Bogotá.

Ernst and Young. 2012. *Análisis comparativo de la participación estatal para las minas de oro y carbón en Colombia*. Bogotá.

Fierro, J. and R. López. 2014. *Aportes a la conceptualización del daño ambiental y del pasivo ambiental por minería*. En: Garay (2014).

Fierro, J. 2012. *Políticas mineras en Colombia*. ILSA, Bogotá.

Gaitán, L., M. Martínez, P. Pérez and F. Velásquez. 2011. *El sector extractivo en Colombia*. Foro Nacional por Colombia, Bogotá.

Galán, L. C. 1982. *Los carbones de El Cerrejón*. La Oveja Negra, Bogotá.

Garay, L. J. (director). 2013, 2013a, 2014 y 2014a. *Minería en Colombia*. Contraloría General de la República, Bogotá (4 volúmenes).

Garay, L. J., E. Salcedo-Albarán, I. de León-Beltrán and B. Guerrero. 2008. *La reconfiguración cooptada del Estado: Más allá de la concepción tradicional de captura económica del Estado*. Fundación Método, Avina y Transparencia por Colombia, Bogotá.

Herrera, Y. and N. Cooper. 2010. *Manual para la adquisición y procesamiento de sísmica terrestre y su aplicación en Colombia*. Universidad Nacional de Colombia, Bogotá.

Instituto Geográfico Agustín Codazzi, IGAC. 2014. *Informe exclusivo: estos serían los 5 pecados de la tragedia ambiental en Casanare*. Comunicado de prensa, Bogotá [www.igac.gov.co/wps/wcm/connect/ef2a84804391398596edf7f9d08ae71d/Estos+son+los+5+pecados. pdf?MOD=AJPERES].

Intergovernmental Panel on Climate Change, IPCC. 2014. *Climate Change 2014: Impacts, Adaptation, and Vulnerability. Summary for Policymakers*. IPCC.

Lasso, C.A., J. Usma, F. Trujillo, and A. Rial (eds). 2010. *Biodiversidad de la cuenca del Orinoco: bases científicas para la identificación de áreas prioritarias para la conservación y uso sostenible de la biodiversidad.* Instituto Humboldt, WWF Colombia, Fundación Omacha, Fundación La Salle de Ciencias Naturales, Universidad Nacional de Colombia y Conservación Internacional Colombia, Bogotá.

Martínez, A. y T. Aguilar. 2012. *Impacto socioeconómico de la minería en Colombia.* Informe para el Sector de Minería a Gran Escala, Fedesarrollo, Bogotá.

————. 2013. *Estudio sobre los impactos socio-económicos del sector minero en Colombia: encadenamientos sectoriales.* Cuadernos de Fedesarrollo, 47, Bogotá.

Martínez, M., J. Peña and F. E. Velásquez. 2013. *El sector extractivo en Colombia 2011–2012.* Foro Nacional por Colombia, Bogotá.

Mazuera, J. 2014. *Operación campos New Granada Energy Corporation Sucursal Colombia.* Bogotá.

McMahon, G. and F. Remy (eds). 2003. *Grandes minas y la comunidad. Efectos socioeconómicos en Latinoamérica, Canadá y España.* Banco Mundial, Bogotá.

Palmer, M. A., E. S. Bernhardt, W. H. Schlesinger, K. N. Eshleman, E. Foufoula-Georgiou, M. S. Hendryx, A. D. Lemly, G. E. Likens, O. L. Loucks, M. E. Power, P. S. White and P. R. Wilcock. 2010. "Mountaintop Mining Consequences," *Science,* vol. 327.

Perry, G. y C. Palacios. 2013. *Emprendimiento alrededor del Sector de la Minería y el Petróleo en Colombia.* Universidad de los Andes, Documentos CEDE no. 13, Bogotá.

Perry, G. y M. Olivera. 2010. *El impacto del petróleo y la minería en el desarrollo regional y local en Colombia.* Fedesarrollo, Bogotá.

Rial, A., C. A. Lasso and J. Ayarzagüena. 2010. *Efectos en la ecología de un humedal de los llanos de Venezuela (cuenca del Orinoco) causados por la construcción de diques.* En Lasso et al. (2010).

Rincón, S., C. Suárez and M. Romero-Ruiz. 2014. *Identificación de sabanas altamente biodiversas basada en la directiva europea de energías renovables.* WWF Colombia, Bogotá.

Rudas, G. and J. E. Espitia, 2013a. "La paradoja de la minería y el desarrollo. Análisis departamental y municipal para el caso de Colombia." En: Garay (2013a).

————. 2013 "Participación del Estado y la sociedad en la renta minera." En: Garay (2013).

Rudas, G. 2013. *Notas sobre el estado de la minería de carbón a gran escala en Colombia.* Foro Nacional Ambiental, Políticas Públicas 40, Bogotá.

————. 2014. *Revisitando el debate sobre renta minera y government take: el carbón a gran escala en Colombia.* En: Garay (2014).

Saade, M. 2013. *Desarrollo minero y conflictos socioambientales: los casos de Colombia, México y el Perú.* Comisión Económica para América Latina y el Caribe (CEPAL), División de Desarrollo Económico. Serie Macroeconomía y Desarrollo, 137. Santiago de Chile.

Toro, C., J. Fierro, S. Coronado and T. Roa (eds). 2012. *Minería, territorio y conflicto en Colombia.* Universidad Nacional de Colombia, Bogotá.

Universidad de Los Andes. 2010. *Valoración económica ambiental en la zona carbonífera del Cesar que comprende los municipios de Becerril, Agustín Codazzi, Chiriguaná, El Paso y La Jagua de Ibirico.* Ministerio de Ambiente, Vivienda y Desarrollo Territorial y Universidad de los Andes, Bogotá.

World Health Organization, WHO. 2005. *WHO Air Quality Guidelines for Particulate Matter, Ozone, Nitrogen Dioxide and Sulfur Dioxide, Global Update 2005, Summary of Risk Assessment.* Geneva, Switzerland.

Zarsky, L. and L. Stanley. 2013. "Can Extractive Industries Promote Sustainable Development? A Net Benefits Framework and a Case Study of the Marlin Mine in Guatemala." *Journal of Environment & Development* 22(2) 131–54.

Chapter 4

A LINE IN THE EQUATORIAL FORESTS: CHINESE INVESTMENT AND THE ENVIRONMENTAL AND SOCIAL IMPACTS OF EXTRACTIVE INDUSTRIES IN ECUADOR

Rebecca Ray and Adam Chimienti

Ecuador's "China boom" encompasses investment, finance and trade and is overwhelmingly concentrated in the oil sector. Ecuador has established a top-level legal framework to limit the social, environmental and economic risks associated with this sector, although this framework is facing increasing pressure from a diverse array of interests. After an examination of the Ecuadoran economy and its general engagement with China, this chapter performs a case study on the experiences of Chinese state-owned Andes Petroleum and PetroOriental, in order to draw lessons for future Chinese investments for the upcoming expansion of Andes Petroleum's concessions into the Ecuadoran Amazon – an expansion that may test both Ecuador's legal framework and Andes's corporate goodwill.

We find that the record of Andes Petroleum and PetroOriental shows they have had relatively positive experiences in Ecuador to date when compared to other domestic and foreign-owned firms in the sector. However, the social and environmental landscapes in the new concession zones are vastly different from where these firms are currently located. Furthermore, this expansion is the first new concession under Ecuador's recent law on prior consultation, and problems have already arisen as to how the law has been applied. How the government, Andes Petroleum and civil society handle this situation will determine whether the Ecuador–China relationship becomes a model of responsible oil production or whether it will betray the vision behind Ecuador's impressive legal framework. Special attention should be paid to transparency and public accountability for all actors involved: government, civil society and the oil companies themselves.

1. Instruction: Ecuador, Oil and the Challenge of Diversification

Oil has been paramount in Ecuador's economy since its discovery there in the 1970s. It quickly displaced bananas as the country's most important export, as Figure 4.1 shows, and has dominated exports ever since. In 2012, petroleum exports represented nearly 60 percent of all exports and over 10 percent of national GDP.

The government of Ecuador has acknowledged publicly that basing the economy on petroleum is not sustainable environmentally, socially or economically, and it has made diversification a major long-term policy priority. The national development plan (Plan Nacional), published early in President Rafael Correa's administration, states that "the existence of oil fields brings opportunities to generate income [...] However, the socio-environmental impacts of this extraction are very high, such as settling protected lands, deforestation, and the resulting habitat degradation, loss of biodiversity, contamination of

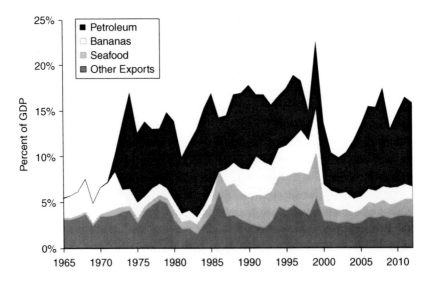

Figure 4.1 Ecuador exports as a share of GDP, by commodity
Source: Authors' analysis based on COMTRADE (SITC, Rev.1).
Note: Seafood includes fish and crustaceans; petroleum includes crude petroleum and petroleum products.

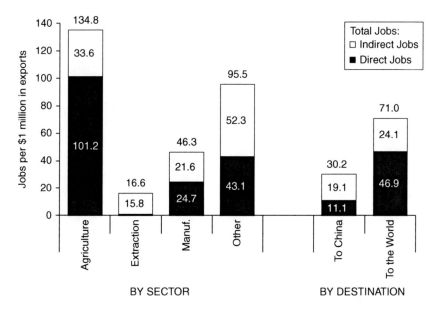

Figure 4.2 Labor intensity of Ecuadorian exports, 2008–2012, by sector and destination
Source: Authors' analysis based on BCE and UN COMTRADE data.
Note: Direct jobs are within a given sector, and indirect jobs are in upstream sectors.

soils and water sources, and others" (SENPLADES, 2009, 460–61, authors' translation).[1]

Socially, oil dependence is problematic for several reasons. First, it is significantly less labor-intensive than other tradable sectors, so every $1 million in extractive exports supports far fewer jobs than the same amount of agricultural or manufacturing exports. Figure 4.2 compares the labor intensity of Ecuador's exports by sector and destination. Based on the Central Bank's most recent input–output tables, it shows both the direct employment and indirect employment (in upstream industries) supported by each $1 million in exports. Extraction supports less than one direct job, and fewer than 20 indirect jobs, for every $1 million in exports. By contrast, manufacturing supports about 25 direct and over 20 indirect jobs, and agriculture supports over 100 direct and over 30 indirect jobs, for the same value of exports. Ecuador's exports to China are heavily concentrated in extraction – much more so than its exports to the rest of the world (more on this below). Consequently, exports to China

---

1 An additional important drawback to Ecuador's dependence on oil is the country's predisposition to earthquakes. For example, in March 1987, two major earthquakes damaged the trans-Andean/Ecuadorian pipeline, severely disrupting the national economy.

support roughly 30 jobs per $1 million, far fewer jobs than exports to the rest of the world.

The government acknowledged the difficulty this employment differential creates for the national job market in Ecuador's Plan Nacional. Since petroleum creates so few jobs, employment has to come from other sectors, and the Plan states that, "slow growth in non-petroleum exports shows the scarcity of options for the creation of good jobs, which has contributed to the deterioration of standards of living, via unemployment, underemployment, precarious employment, and falling real wages" (76). The plan specifically calls for diversifying national production away from oil, by developing local value chains in other sectors such as renewable energy, biotechnology, pharmaceuticals, vehicles, transportation and others (ibid., 393).

Another important obstacle to sustainable oil production in Ecuador is the location of most oil deposits: in the Amazon rainforest, under traditional indigenous lands. The Ecuadorian Amazon is one of the world's most biodiverse areas (more on this below), but it is heavily threatened. From 2005 to 2010, Ecuador's forest cover shrank by 1.9 percent per year, the fastest rate of deforestation in South America and the twelfth-highest rate worldwide. Worse, Ecuador's deforestation has been accelerating, from 1.7 percent per year from 2000 to 2005 and just 1.5 percent per year from 1990 to 2000 (FAO, 2010). Moreover, despite its small size, Ecuador is home to the highest number of endangered species of any country on earth (Berlington, 2010). Not all of the deforestation has been due exclusively to oil fields, but ecological research by Fearnside et al. (2013) and Lovejoy (2014) have concluded that the construction of access roads and railways for these extraction projects are the most important drivers of deforestation. These interrupt animal migration patterns and open the forest to human settlement, large-scale agriculture and logging, which Ecuadorian biologist Hugo Navarrete characterized as "completely unsustainable from every point of view" (*El Comercio*, 2013).

According to the Plan Nacional, indigenous communities comprise a large share of the population in the Amazonian provinces, including half of all children in those provinces (SENPLADES, 143). But oil drilling threatens their access to traditional hunting, fishing and gathering grounds (usually village-adjacent forests, which are not deeded to them and therefore open to exploration). Moreover, contamination from oil spills can make these traditional livelihoods unsafe, poisoning aquifers and downstream waterways. This chapter's case study explains how this contamination has drastically reduced the possibilities for farming and fishing in the northern region of Tarapoa. The consequences can be dire even for the oil companies themselves, which have often faced large-scale protests. As the Plan Nacional states, "the growing problems from environmental degradation – the accelerated loss of natural spaces, constant occupation of indigenous land, and the unequal distribution of the benefits of economic development – have been accompanied by socio-environmental conflicts since the 1970s" (221).

Since the Plan Nacional was published, a series of reforms has mitigated the negative impacts of oil extraction. The largest of these reforms is the Constitution of 2008, the first to recognize the rights of nature itself. In practice, these rights mean that parties can bring legal action on behalf of nature to stop harm to the environment, even if the natural resources at stake are not their private property. The 2010 Citizens Participation Law requires the government to seek communities' free, prior and informed consent before allowing new oil and mining projects; although projects may still advance in the face of local opposition, they must meet higher environmental and social standards if they do. Moreover, Ecuador is a signatory to ILO Convention 169, which commits the government to consider indigenous nations' claims to their traditional lands when planning new extraction projects. Further reforms in 2003 and 2007 require environmental impact assessments (EIAs) for new projects (including plans for prevention, remediation and compensation of contamination) and earmark large shares of oil revenues for local governments in areas affected by the oil industry, to fund public investment projects approved by the central government. Nonetheless, despite these reforms, oil remains the most important export, and the goal of diversification remains an important priority.

Diversification away from reliance on petroleum exports has proven difficult for several reasons. First, Ecuador's use of the US dollar as its national currency means that in practice, its currency faces long-term pressure to become overvalued.[2] As a result, Ecuador's exports are more expensive on the world market than they would otherwise be, which hurts the competitiveness of non-petroleum industries. The Plan Nacional (66) calls the deterioration of competitiveness the "Achilles Heel" of dollarization. Compounding this problem is the "Dutch disease" phenomenon: nations that primarily export raw commodities tend to have overvalued currencies because their exports' prices are determined by the world market rather than by manufacturing costs. The resulting fall in competitiveness in other industries makes it difficult

---

2 Dollarization raises the risk of an overvalued exchange rate because the value of the US dollar is based on the US economy, not the Ecuadorian economy. Currency overvaluation, in turn, can undermine the manufacturing sector and prevent growth or recovery, as had occurred in the United States in the 2000s and Japan in the 1990s. For more on dollarization and an overvalued exchange rate, see Vernengo and Bradbury, 2011. For more on the effects of an overvalued currency on the manufacturing sector, see Palley, 2003.

to escape dependence on those commodities, creating a vicious cycle. As the Plan Nacional states, in an economy "based on [...] extraction and export of commodities, long-term economic growth revolves around external market dynamics, especially the price of oil, and neglects internal demand [...] to the detriment of national production and employment" (SENPLADES, 331, authors' translation). Any effort Ecuador makes to spur investment in non-petroleum sectors is at a significant disadvantage because of this context.

Another obstacle to diversification is that oil represents a significant portion of public revenue. As Figure 4.3 shows, petroleum revenues have represented approximately 20 percent of GDP central government revenues for most of the past decade.

A series of reforms has also boosted devolution of oil revenues to sub-national governments, the Gobiernos Autónomos Decentralizados (GADs) at the province, canton and parish levels. In 2003, the Fondo para el Ecodesarrollo was established, which dedicates $1 per barrel of oil for public investment in the Amazon, under the care of the GADs and the Instituto para el Ecodesarrollo Regional Amazónico (ECORAE). Over the decade since the fund was established, Ecuador has produced nearly 2 billion barrels of oil, distributing the resulting funds to municipalities (58%), provinces (28%), par-ishes (5%) and the ECORAE (9%). The funds come with restrictions: at least 80 percent must be spent on conservation and transportation projects, and the rest is to be spent on public investments approved by the Secretary of

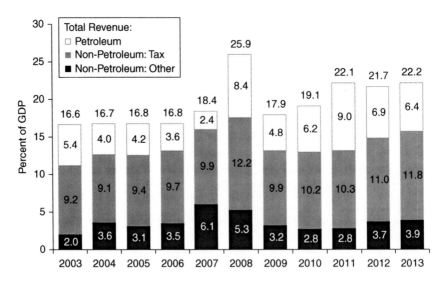

Figure 4.3 Ecuador central government revenue by source, 2005–2013 (% of GDP)
Source: Banco Central del Ecuador (2014).

Hydrocarbons. More recently, the 2010 oil reform law re-directed 12 percent of oil profits (which previously went to the central government) to the GADs in the regions where the drilling takes place, to be used for health and education projects as approved by the appropriate ministry (Asemblea Nacional del Ecuador, 2010b, Art. 94). Because of these devolution schemes, any fall-off in oil production can represent a major disruption in local government finance. So divestment efforts can really only focus on boosting non-petroleum industries in addition to petroleum, rather than shifting resources from one sector to another.

Divestment efforts to date have included microloans with preferential terms, with special attention to the non-petroleum sectors that the government committed to boosting in the Development Plan. From 2007 to 2012, the National Development Bank and the Ministry of Economic and Social Inclusion have issued more than a million small loans totaling nearly $3 billion (about 0.4% of GDP) to individuals and small businesses. (BNF, 2010–2012). Furthermore, the infrastructure and education projects mentioned above provide support for businesses of all sectors and can help support competitiveness in nontraditional industries. As beneficial as these programs may prove to be in the long term, however, they have not proven sufficient to reduce Ecuador's dependence on oil.

Ecuador's attempts to diversify are further complicated by the petroleum-centered relationship between Ecuador and China. Over the last decade China has become an important trading partner and source of investment and finance. However, every aspect of this economic relationship – trade, finance and investment – ties Ecuador more tightly to oil and further complicates the goal of diversification.

2. Ecuador's Burgeoning Relationship with China

Since his election in 2007, President Rafael Correa has facilitated a new type of international engagement for the country. Throughout its history, Ecuador's economy has been primarily dependent on the United States as a source of exports and imports, as well as a primary destination for migrants whose remittances make up a significant portion of GDP. This traditional dependence on the United States has long been a contentious issue for Ecuadorian groups unhappy with perceptions of diminished sovereignty. Lightning rods for this issue have included overwhelming reliance on the United States as an export market, the adoption of the US dollar as official currency and, most recently, a US military base on the Ecuadorian coast. After assuming power, Correa employed several strategies to buffer Ecuador against the volatility of depending on one external partner. These strategies appear to be bearing fruit, as

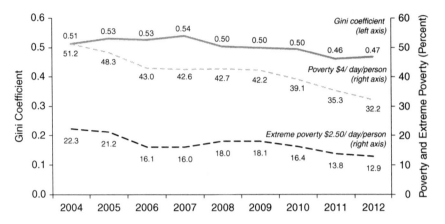

Figure 4.4 Poverty, extreme poverty and inequality
Source: SEDLAC.

Figure 4.4 shows: Ecuadorian poverty and inequality did not rise during the US' recent recession, and since then these have fallen significantly, even as the United States remains mired in a sluggish recovery.

Part of Correa's strategy has involved moving his country away from the United States and toward China. The Ecuadorian leader explained the shift in a speech delivered in 2011 about the two nations' complementarity: "In 2006, 75 percent of our oil was going to the United States […] this year, 50 percent has been committed to China, in exchange for billions of dollars" (*El Telégrafo*, authors' translation). In another example, when Correa's government refused to extend the controversial lease of an Ecuadorian Air Force base to the US military, they turned to China as a potential partner for redeveloping the site. The government made attempts, which ultimately proved unsuccessful, to lease the base to a Chinese firm and to revamp a series of projects related to a transport corridor from Manta to the Brazilian Amazonas capital city of Manaus, with Chinese financing (Narins, 2012). In light of that project's ultimate infeasibility, Chinese interests became more focused on the oil and mining sectors (Bonilla, 2010). In addition, in the last few years China and Ecuador have signed three major treaties, including:

- Treaty on Economic and Technological Cooperation, including an RMB 20 million (about $3 million USD) in Chinese aid to Ecuador.
- Executive Plan of Cooperation in Science and Technology.
- Cooperation document on oil trade finance between PRC Export-Import Bank and PetroEcuador.
- (For more on these deals, see ADB, IADB, and ADBI, 2012).

In many ways, China has become an invaluable economic ally for Ecuador. Ecuador's burgeoning relationship with China has guaranteed it access to financial markets, an investor willing to develop oil fields in a way that benefits Ecuador as well as China, and a partner in generating value added through the Pacífico Refinery. However, each of these aspects of the China–Ecuador relationship further ties Ecuador to oil and limits its ability to diversify production and protect its ecosystems.

2.1 China as a trading partner

China plays only a minor role in Ecuador's export market, buying just 3.5 percent of Ecuador's exports from 2008 to 2012. However, as Figure 4.5 shows, Ecuador's exports to China are much more concentrated in petroleum than Ecuador's exports overall. China did not begin importing petroleum from Ecuador until 2003, but since then petroleum has played an increasingly

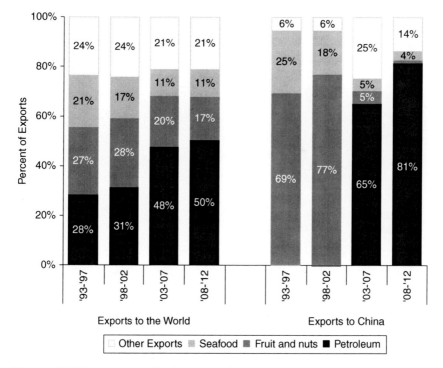

Figure 4.5 Ecuador export basket composition
Source: Authors' analysis based on UN COMTRADE (SITC, Rev. 3).
Note: Seafood includes fish and crustaceans; fruit and nuts exclude oilseeds; petroleum includes crude petroleum and petroleum products.

important role, averaging over 80 percent of Ecuador's exports to China from 2008 to 2012. Although currently China is a relatively small trading partner for Ecuador, it is growing in importance and as it does so, it is increasing petroleum's importance in Ecuador's overall export basket.

Concerning imports, Figure 4.6 shows that the United States still leads in shipments to Ecuador – 25 percent in 2013 – but China is the second most-important source of imports, at 16.7 percent. Notably, from 2000 to 2009 China's gains in the Ecuadorian market have not taken market share from the United States but from smaller, regional partners like Colombia. China has unseated Colombia as the second most-important import source, while the United States continues to grow in importance.

Finally, Ecuador–China trade shows a significant imbalance in composition. Table 4.1 shows the sectors that make up each direction of trade. The heavy concentration in natural resources flowing from Ecuador to China is not matched by China's exports to Ecuador. Instead, they are quite diverse. While the top five product categories made up over 90 percent of Ecuador's exports to China, the top five *imports* from China made up less than one-fourth of the total. In other words, Ecuador's imports from China are diverse and spread over many sectors. Moreover, Ecuador's top five imports from China are all manufactured goods, in contrast with the top exports, which are dominated by natural resources. This imbalance poses two major disadvantages. First, crude petroleum is much more prone to price swings than are manufactured

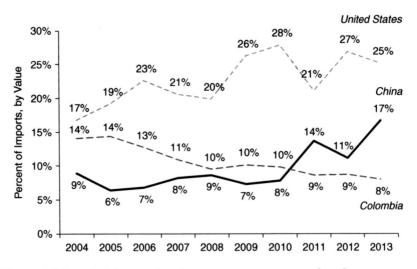

Figure 4.6 Ecuador's imports (top three sources, as a percent of total)
Source: Authors' analysis using UN COMTRADE data.

Table 4.1 Ecuador–China trade: Top five categories each direction, 2008–2012

Ecuador's Exports to China		Ecuador's Imports from China	
Item	Percent	Item	Percent
Crude petroleum oil	81.4	Telecom. equipment and parts	6.4
Metal scrap	3.5	Iron and steel tubes and pipes	5.5
Wood, simply worked	2.4	Bicycles, motorcycles, etc.	3.8
Crustaceans, mollusks, etc.	2.3	Civil engineering equipment	3.6
Animal feed	2.3	Rubber tires, tubes, etc.	3.4
TOTAL, TOP 5	91.9	TOTAL, TOP 5	22.8

Source: Authors' analysis using UN COMTRADE data.

goods, so when oil prices fluctuate worldwide it affects one side of this trading relationship much more than the other, creating instability in the trade balance between the two countries. Secondly, the imbalance leaves Ecuador with low value-added exports, which require little technology and support few well-paying jobs.

2.2 China's and Ecuador's access to international financial markets

China has recently become Ecuador's most important creditor and has seen Ecuador through a prolonged period of limited access to financial markets. In 2008, Ecuador defaulted on two outstanding bonds totalling $3.2 billion dollars, citing irregularities such as having been issued under a dictatorship and without competitive bidding in selecting investment-banking partners (CAIC, 2008). These two bonds amounted to less than half of all public foreign debt, and only about 6 percent of GDP (IMF, 2014). Nonetheless, the default was unusual, because the government did not cite financial hardship but irregularities in the debt itself. Many international analysts and pundits vociferously opposed it, Moody's downgraded Ecuador's debt to Caa3, and Ecuador lost access to its traditional Western creditors (Porzecanski, 2010). This signalled an opportunity for Chinese leaders and investors to diversify their economy's sources of primary commodities through the oil loans described below. On the other hand, Ecuador became unable to seek funding elsewhere, and China's innovative arrangements involving pre-sales of crude oil provided much-needed funds up front.

Since the partial default China has become Ecuador's most important creditor, accounting for over one-third of the nation's total external public

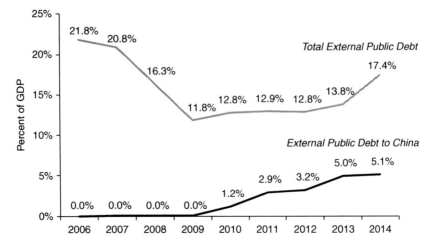

Figure 4.7 Total Ecuadorian debt compared with debt to China (percent of GDP)
Source: Authors' calculations using BCE data.

debt in 2013, as Figure 4.7 shows. Moody's specifically cited Ecuador's ability to secure financing from China as a reason for upgrading its debt to Caa1 in 2012 (Reuters, 2012). In 2014, Ecuador re-entered international finance markets, issuing its first traditional public bond since the partial default (Korby and Jenkins, 2014). As a result, China's share of Ecuador's external public debt fell in 2014. It appears that as of 2014, Ecuador is no longer relying solely on China for new external financing.

Gallagher et al. (2012) explain that China's loans to Ecuador (about 8.5% of Chinese loans to LAC in 2005–2011), constitute a disproportional amount based on its population (2.5% of LAC in 2011) and GDP (1.3% of the region). Moreover, China has signed a series of oil deals with Ecuador in which it prepays for oil shipments, giving both parties predictability in their trade and providing Ecuador with up-front income (Benítez, 2014). SENPLADES subsecretary for planning, Andres Aruaz, emphasized in an interview that the government's ambitious projections depend on this access to finance (Aruaz, 2014).

Most loans from China are directed at the extraction and hydroelectric sectors, as Table 4.2 shows. Ecuador did not receive much Chinese investment until 2009, after the default. Thereafter, China has backed several dams, including both the Coca-Codo Sinclair and the Sopladora projects. These loans have boosted the government's goal of producing some 93.5 percent of its energy needs by the year 2021 via hydroelectric sources (see MEER,

Table 4.2 Loans to Ecuador from Chinese banks and SOEs

Year	Lender	Partner	Quantity (USD$b)	Purpose
Oil-Backed:				
2009	PetroChina	PetroEcuador	1.0	Advance payment for oil
2010	China Dev't Bank	PetroEcuador	1.0	80% discretionary, 20% oil-backed
2011	PetroChina	PetroEcuador	1.0	Advance payment for oil
Other:				
2010	China Ex-Im Bank	Government	1.7	Coca-Codo Sinclair (CCS) dam
2010	China Ex-Im Bank	Government	0.6	Sopladora dam
2011	China Dev't. Bank	Government	2.0	Renewable energy
2012	China Dev't Bank	Government	2.0	Discretionary
2013	China Ex-Im Bank	Government	0.4	Minas-San Francisco dam, highway
2013	Bank of China, Deutsche Bank	Government	0.3	Cañar, Naranjal dams
2014	China Ex-Im Bank	Government	0.5	CCS dam transmission system
2014	Bank of China	Government	0.3	Road construction
TOTAL:			*10.8*	

Source: Gallagher and Myers (2014), Braütigam and Gallagher (2014), verified by Chinese Embassy official.

n.d., 1, 2 for more), but they also carry conditions to use Chinese equipment and contractors.[3] The loans for the hydroelectric projects have the added benefit of providing power for the large-scale Chinese extraction projects in Ecuador.

---

3 As Gallagher et al. (2012) have highlighted, most of China's loans to Ecuador do not have policy conditions, but do have conditions on using the funds to purchase Chinese goods or services.

Loans for oil involve the China Development Bank (CDB), Ecuador and Chinese oil companies, and proceed as follows: the CDB lends money to Ecuador, which in return gives a prescribed amount of oil to China's oil companies.[1] The companies pay for the oil at the current market rate: part of their payment goes to an account at the CDB to repay Ecuador's loan, and the remainder is paid to Ecuador (Gallagher et al., 2012; Sanderson and Forsyth, 2013).

The complicated structure of these loans makes them difficult to compare to traditional loans. However, they have an important advantage in terms of risk management for both China and Ecuador. Most international loans depend on the borrower's continued access to US dollars (or Chinese yuan) for repayment, which can trigger complications for countries with "soft" currencies or with no currency of their own at all, like Ecuador. In this case China and Ecuador avoid that risk, but face two others: the possibility of an unexpected drop in the world oil price (meaning that more barrels of oil would be required to repay the loan) or an unexpected drop in Ecuador's oil output. The short-term nature of these arrangements (usually fewer than eight years, according to Bräutigam and Gallagher, 2014) reduces the risk of a drop in world oil prices (Ecuavisa, 2013). However, technical or community problems could still affect Ecuador's oil production with very little notice or none at all. In practice, this means that ensuring the steady output of oil must be even more of a top national policy priority than it was previously, as important as access to hard currency is for other borrowing countries in Ecuador's position.

2.3 China as a source of investment

Chinese investors have played a crucial role in the development of Ecuadorian oil fields. Overall, China has accounted for only about 4 percent of all greenfield foreign direct investment (GFDI) into Ecuador over the last decade. However, as Figure 4.8 shows, those inflows have been much more heavily concentrated in extraction than overall GFDI inflows. The other category of foreign direct investment, mergers and acquisitions (M&A) shows an even more pronounced difference. China represented nearly half of all M&A inflows into Ecuador from 2003 through 2012, and 100 percent of those inflows went into extraction. In contrast, extraction represented only about 20 percent of M&A inflows into Ecuador from other countries during those years.

---

4 It is important to note that not all oil sold to Chinese oil companies this way is ultimately destined for China. PetroChina, the main purchaser, also ships Ecuadorian crude to California (Schneyer and Mora Perez, 2013).

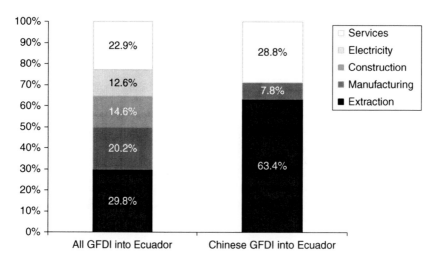

Figure 4.8 Greenfield FDI inflows to Ecuador, by source and sector
Source: Authors' analysis from FDIMarkets.
Note: Extraction includes mining and drilling; electricity includes hydropower and solar; construction includes residential, tourism, and medical facilities.

China has differed from most other sources of oil investment in two important ways. First, Chinese petroleum companies have remained in the country through major oil reforms in 2007 and 2010, each of which increased the state's revenue from oil production. After each round of reforms several other foreign oil companies left the country, including the Brazilian firm Petrobras, the French firm Perenco, and City Oriente, which was registered in Panama. Zach Chen, commercial attaché at the Chinese Embassy in Quito, attributes the perseverance of the Chinese oil companies to a long-term company strategy. The Chinese oil companies in Ecuador, CNPC and Sinopec, are both state-owned enterprises (SOEs) and serve the Chinese government's diplomatic as well as financial interests. Diplomatic relationships take time to build and must be stronger than short-term profit motives.

China has also distinguished itself as an investment partner in its willingness to support downstream industry linkages in Ecuador, rather than solely producing crude petroleum and refining it once it reaches China. As Table 4.3 shows, Ecuador has been a net importer of refined petroleum products over the last decade, even as their net exports of crude petroleum have grown. This arrangement means that Ecuador is losing out on money (because refined petroleum is more expensive than crude), technology and good jobs. Ecuador is addressing this imbalance through the Refineria del Pacifico (RdP), a major refinery project near the Port of Manta that will be the largest infrastructure

Table 4.3 Ecuador's net petroleum exports by type, 1993–2012 (percent of GDP)

	1993–1997	1998–2002	2003–2007	2008–2012
Crude petroleum	5.4%	4.6%	7.4%	8.3%
Refined petroleum products	0.2%	0.2%	−0.3%	−1.1%

Source: Authors' analysis based on UN COMTRADE and BCE data.

undertaking in the country's history when it opens in 2017. The project was in the works for several years as a joint project between Ecuador and Venezuelan oil SOE PDVSA, but it gained new life after China's CNPC acquired a 30 percent stake in 2013. This kind of partnership increases the amount of oil revenue that stays in Ecuador, supports more local employment and allows for technology transfer. So it is not surprising that Ecuador's two partners in this endeavor are two of its closest diplomatic allies: China and Venezuela.

The RdP project is an example of how Chinese investment and finance are interwoven in Ecuador. When CNPC joined as an RdP partner, it brought access to Chinese financing as well as an expectation of the use of Chinese labor and equipment. An interview with an RdP chief engineer revealed that there would be a significant number of Chinese laborers arriving in the coming years to work on the site (RdP, 2014). Venezuela's PDVSA had no such requirements, but could not secure the necessary financing as quickly. Despite the fact that negotiations for the RdP are ongoing and may take a few more years to meet the demands required for such a major investment, with reported costs expected to surpass US$10 billion, the Chinese banks that are financing the bulk of it provide a much faster route toward completion, according to the chief engineer and his colleagues.

3. Case Study: CNPC and Sinopec in Ecuador

The Chinese oil companies mentioned above, CNPC and Sinopec, operate in Ecuador under the names Andes Petroleum and PetroOriental. They are two of the most successful foreign oil companies in Ecuador and have recently won new concessions to increase their presence and production in the country. Nevertheless, their expansion plans face significant obstacles, because the environmental and social contexts of the new concessions are much more fragile than in their current locations. If these challenges are not adequately addressed, this could threaten the viability of the projects altogether. The case study below examines the successful history – and risky future – of CNPC and Sinopec in Ecuador.

3.1 CNPC and Sinopec in Ecuador, 2006–2014

In 2006, CNPC and Sinopec jointly purchased the Ecuadorian assets of Canadian firm Encana, including three oil concessions in the country's eastern provinces of Sucumbios, Pastaza and Orellana, as well as a lead stake (32.3%) in the Heavy Crude Pipeline (Oleoducto de Crudos Pesados, or OCP) project, which was built in 2003 and operated by several MNCs, including Repsol, Perenco and Petrobras. CNPC and Sinopec formed Andes Petroleum to manage Block 62 in the northeastern province of Sucumbios, and PetroOriental to manage Blocks 14 and 17 in Orellana and Pastaza, further to the south. Figure 4.9 shows the locations of these blocks, along with Andes Petroleum's new concessions (discussed below). Both groups are majority-owned (55%) by CNPC, with Sinopec owning the remaining stock.

Andes Petroleum and PetroOriental are among the most important oil producers in Ecuador. Taken together, they account for about one-fourth of Ecuador's total production (ARCH, 2011–2013). Andes alone produces more

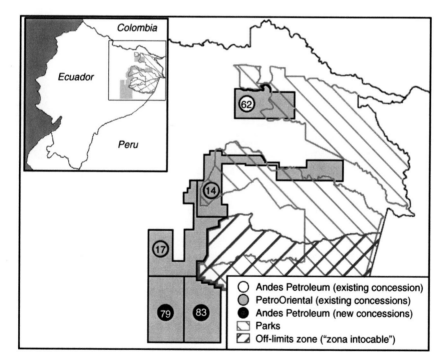

Figure 4.9 Map of Ecuador, with Andes Petroleum and PetroOriental holdings shaded
Source: Adapted from Secretaría de Hidrocarburos.

than any other private producer except for Repsol, and including PetroOriental raises the level even higher than Repsol's.

When CNPC and Sinopec arrived in Ecuador, they inherited Encana's uneasy relationship with community leaders and environmentalists, which was mostly centered on the OCP pipeline. According to Paola Carrera, undersecretary for environmental quality at the Ministry of Environment, the government does not keep databases of firms' environmental or labor performance, but it is possible to track the instances that were severe enough to spur public protest, though CLACSO's "Observatorio Social de América Latina" (OSAL) initiative (Carrera, 2014; CLACSO, 2000–2012). OSAL has documented at least four large-scale strikes during the OCP's construction in 2001 and 2002: two by environmental activists seeking to block the project entirely, one by workers seeking better pay and one by community leaders seeking local jobs and a fund for projects to offset the economic effects of expected environmental damages.

Since arriving in Ecuador, Andes and PetroOriental have maintained more positive relationships with the government and civil society than Encana had. OSAL archives contain zero records of environmental protests that specifically targeted Andes or PetroOriental. In contrast, Repsol was targeted by a weeklong road blockade in 2006 over environmental concerns, and PetroEcuador was the target of large-scale environmental protests in 2006, 2007, 2008 and 2010.

The comparatively peaceful company–community relationship enjoyed by the Chinese oil firms may be partially due to the fact that Andes Petroleum (which produces about three times as much oil as PetroOriental) is located in Sucumbíos, which has been home to large scale agricultural and oil development for decades, including Texaco's original oil fields. Interviews with Undersecretary Carrera and remediation expert Michel Boufadel made it clear that the local aquifer is still so heavily polluted from the remaining Texaco pits that fishing and small-scale agriculture are no longer healthy options for local communities. In a site visit to Texaco's nearby Aquarico 4 well, Boufadel explained that the most toxic components of oil spills are compounds like benzene, which are invisible and quick to dissolve in water and spread throughout the aquifer and downstream waterways. Thus, even after remediation efforts have removed some of the visible effects of these decades-old oil spills, the water used by surrounding communities can still carry powerful toxins, making traditional livelihoods unsafe. According to interviews with Sucumbíos prefect Guido Vargas and local rights activists Jose Fajardo and Ivonne Macias, the region's people and their water supply are still very much negatively affected by Texaco's legacy and by practices they passed on to the state-owned Petroecuador, which also operates nearby (Vargas Ocaña,

2013; Fajardo, 2014; Macias, 2014). Local community leader Javier Piaguaje explained in an interview that members of the local Secoya (also known as Siekopai) and Siona nations must now travel to the nearby Cuyabeno National Park for their hunting and fishing. Since Andes Petroleum does not operate in the park itself, its drilling has not posed any further threat to the quality of life for these tribes (Piaguaje, 2014).

In fact, according to Piaguaje, residents of the local town of San Pablo de Katetsiaya are hopeful that Andes Petroleum will discover oil nearby. Piaguaje was a plaintiff in the now-famous international lawsuit against Chevron for the damage left by Texaco (Chevron acquired Texaco in 2000). However, he explained that at this point, with existing contamination preventing a return to traditional livelihoods, the community's best available option would be for Andes Petroleum to find oil, set up operations, and invest heavily in the town in order to secure local support. Specifically, he mentioned his hope that Andes, in conjunction with the government, would establish a "millennium city" with full public services, like the ones that PetroEcuador has established in nearby Cuyabeno and Pañacocha to win over the local population (Piaguaje, 2014).[5]

However, Andes and PetroOriental have had their share of labor disputes. Early in their presence, they both faced community conflict over local job opportunities. In November 2006, 300 local residents entered, occupied and stopped production at Andes facilities, demanding 400 local jobs. In July 2007 community members, transit workers and municipal staff from the nearby town of Nueva Loja blocked a major road to demand more local jobs and local investment. More serious conflicts involved PetroOriental, in the parish of Dayuma, Orellana. Dayuma crosses several oil blocks, including two major ones: Block 14, operated by PetroOriental, and Block 61, operated by PetroEcuador. Most of the protests focused on PetroEcuador (CLACSO documents 15 different protests, strikes and blockades against PetroEcuador in 2006 and 2007), but PetroOriental also received some attention. In the summer of 2006 and again in 2007, local residents blockaded the road into the PetroOriental facilities twice, demanding more local jobs and the patronage of local transportation providers. After extensive negotiations, an agreement was reached on the provision of a social fund tasked with local job creation and credit programs.

---

5 Other community leaders, cited by Maldonado (2003), have expressed opposition to Andes's expansion in Block 62. However, it is important to note that Maldonado quotes a community leader discussing the voting process that took place in the community prior to the signing of an agreement with Andes to allow for the expansion. As will be discussed in greater detail below, similar votes have been notably absent in the establishment of the new Andes concessions in Blocks 79 and 83.

The issue of local employment has been largely eliminated thanks to the Hydrocarbon Law of 2010, which requires petroleum companies to hire Ecuadorian staff for 95 percent of unskilled positions and 90 percent of administrative and technical positions (Asemblea, 2010b). Furthermore, Chinese Embassy attaché Zach Chen states that Andes and PetroOriental have established English as the primary working language in their Ecuadorian facilities, and only hire workers who speak it fluently. This requirement dramatically limits the pool of potential workers, raising their salaries, reducing turnover and improving morale. However, this policy also has a strong downside: it limits hires from the immediate vicinity, where schools are not able to teach students sufficient English. According to interviews with Shushufindi mayor Édgar Silvestre and human rights advocate Wendy Obando, the requirement contributes to local unemployment and underemployment and will remain so until local schools are able to meet it (Silvestre, 2014; Obando, 2014). So while this problem has been addressed at the national level, it may continue to cause friction with the local community in the future.

Another area of labor relations continued to plague Andes and PetroOriental until recently: profit-sharing with contract workers. Contract work is more limited in Ecuador than in neighboring countries because of a 2008 law that limits subcontracting to "complementary" work such as janitorial and security services. Nonetheless, contract workers must be included in profit-sharing, which Andes Petroleum and PetroOriental neglected to do until a series of lawsuits forced them to make additional payments to a total of 307 former contract workers. At issue was not the companies' willingness to pay – they had originally distributed the correct amount of their profits – but the fact that the original amount was shared among too few workers. As a result, the companies had to pay an additional $16 million to the originally excluded workers (CLACSO, n.d.; Ecuador Inmediato, 2009). Since the oil companies did not benefit financially from skirting the law initially, and since they suffered such extensive financial costs to address the problem later, it is unlikely that their oversight was intentional or that the problem will occur again.

3.2 New concessions in the South-Central Amazon

Andes Petroleum recently won two additional oil concessions, in Blocks 79 and 83 (marked in Figure 4.9 with dark circles). These blocks border the southern end of PetroOriental's current concessions, but they are farther away from Andes's current concession in the northern region of Tarapoa, Sucumbíos. The economy and ecology of the new concessions are quite different from Tarapoa. Moreover, unlike the Tarapoa concession, the new blocks will be greenfield projects. Because of these differences, it seems very unlikely that

Andes will be able to expand its operations with the same positive community and government relations it has enjoyed in the past.

3.2.1 New challenges in the physical and social landscapes of Blocks 79 and 83

The new sites will be greenfield projects just outside of the Yasuní National Park. The prospect of new oil exploration in the Amazon has brought intense criticism from environmental and indigenous groups, including Amazon Watch, the Pachamama Alliance, Acción Ecológica and others (Zuckerman, 2014). Although these new blocks are outside the borders of Yasuní, the area actually boasts a higher level of biodiversity than the park itself. As Figure 4.10 shows, most of the area covered by the new concessions has extremely high biodiversity in four major categories: amphibians, birds, mammals and plants (Bass et al., 2010). In contrast, most of the park has high biodiversity in two or three of those categories. Thus, from a conservation standpoint it is arguably at least as important to treat the ecosystem in blocks 79 and 83 carefully as in the park itself.

Many experts on the Ecuadorian Amazon, such as biologist Santiago Espinosa of the Pontífica Universidad Católica de Ecuador and conservationist Kelly Swing of Boston University and the Universidad San Francisco de Quito, believe that the government currently lacks the institutional capacity to successfully manage the ecosystems near the planned extraction sites

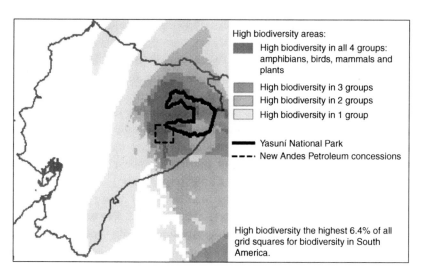

Figure 4.10 High biodiversity areas in Ecuador
Source: Adapted from Bass et al., 2010.

(Espinosa, 2014; Swing, 2013). Federico Auquilla, former vice minister of mines and current advisor to Chinese firms in Ecuador, corroborated this view, although he also expressed confidence that the government will be ready for these responsibilities by the time the new greenfield projects come online (Auquilla, 2014).

Furthermore, the social landscape in blocks 79 and 83 is quite different from the one Andes Petroleum has known in its current concession. First, unlike the northern Tarapoa block, the new southern concessions are entirely covered by traditional indigenous territory. A majority is Sápara territory, with the remainder covered by Kichwa territory. Both groups are classified by UNESCO as having endangered languages; the Sápara language is "critically endangered," with only nine speakers (Moseley 2010). Although the Sápara nation is small (numbering less than 300), its language is one of just two Ecuadorian cultural practices included by UNESCO in the Representative List of Intangible Cultural Heritage of Humanity. By including the language, UNESCO highlighted their "oral culture that is particularly rich as regards their understanding of the natural environment [...] demonstrated by the abundance of their vocabulary for the flora and fauna and by their medicinal practices and knowledge of the medicinal plants of the forest" (UNESCO, 2008). Respecting the rights of this indigenous group, recognized internationally for its vulnerability as well as its cultural importance, will be paramount in Andes's attempt at socially responsible extraction.

In addition, residents in the southern concessions have living standards that are very different from the communities in Andes's northern territory. The new concessions lie within the parish of Montalvo, Pastaza, among the poorest in the country. As Figure 4.11 shows, very few households in Montalvo have even the most basic services. Fewer than 10 percent have electricity in their homes, fewer than 5 percent have indoor running water, and only 1 percent has a sewer hookup or septic tank. These figures place Montalvo in the bottom 3 percent of Ecuador's parishes for running water and the bottom 1 percent for the other two services. The educational situation is equally grim. Only about three-fourths of children attend primary school, and fewer than one in three attend secondary school, putting Montalvo in the bottom 1 percent and 2 percent of parishes nationwide, respectively.

These communities' lower living standards will surely impact Andes's ability to peacefully coexist with them. Past protests directed at Andes and PetroOriental have most commonly demanded jobs and public works (CLACSO, 2000–2012). Specifically, Commercial Attaché Chen reported that Andes has earned its positive community relations in the past by funding the construction of schools and churches. The demand for public works in Montalvo is sure to be much greater than what Andes saw in Tarapoa.

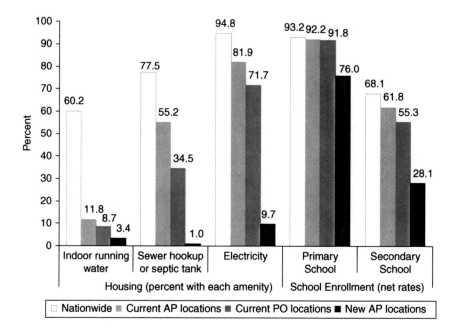

Figure 4.11 Basic service coverage, Ecuador and regions of Ecuador where Andes Petroleum and PetroOriental operate
Source: Authors' analysis of Sistema Nacional de Información (INEC) data.
Notes: Shown are averages of the parishes in each oil concession, weighted by the number of homes or school-age children in each parish. Andes Petroleum's current concession includes the parishes of Aguas Negras and Tarapoa, in Cuyabeno Canton, Sucumbíos. PetroOriental's current concessions include the parishes of Alejandra Labaca, Dayuma, El Edén, Inés Arango and Taracoa, in Orellana Canton, Orellana; and Arajuno, Arajuno Canton, Pastaza. Andes Petroleum's new concessions are in Montalvo, Pastaza Canton, Pastaza.

Finally, communities in the new southern concessions do not have the same decades of experience negotiating with the government and foreign companies as do their northern counterparts. Mario Melo, an Ecuadorian lawyer who has represented indigenous groups in the past, explained that the northern Siekopai nation (who expressed hope for additional petroleum activity) has an exceptional negotiation track record. It would be naïve to expect negotiations in the South to go as smoothly as they have in the North (Melo, 2014).

3.2.2 Addressing the new challenges posed by new landscapes

PetroOriental already has experience working in a delicate ecosystem: Block 14 is located in and around Yasuní (shown in Figure 4.9). However, PetroOriental inherited that concession from Encana. This will be the first time either company has established new concessions anywhere in Ecuador, much less in the Amazon. As of this writing, Andes Petroleum is still negotiating the concession contract with the government. Assuming the negotiations are completed successfully and exploration begins, it will be important for Andes to seriously consider ways to limit its impact.

Clearly, Andes will have to avoid contamination at all costs. Beyond that, however, Andes would do well to make limiting roadways a priority. As mentioned above, ecologists consider access roads from extraction projects to be the single-largest cause of Amazonian deforestation. Biologists Santiago Espinosa and Kelly Swing, who work extensively in Yasuní, claim that roads have already opened inside the park without proper consultation (Espinosa, 2014 and Swing, 2013).

Analysts often point to the nearby Block 16 (which Repsol developed and which, like PetroOriental's Block 14, overlaps Yasuní) as an example of best practices for drilling with limited road construction. Repsol did build a road from their operations to a nearby river, but left it unconnected from the country's highway system to discourage the development of new towns in the park. Instead, equipment and trucks must use barges to reach the road and eventually the oil installations (Bass et al., 2010). In 2012 Repsol sold a 20 percent stake in Block 16 to Tiptop Energy, a subsidiary of Sinopec (one of the two Chinese SOEs that own Andes Petroleum), so Andes has privileged access to the technology used in Repsol's lower-impact methods (Repsol, 2012). However, even the limited use of roads in Block 16 has resulted in continued deforestation around the road, at an annual rate of 0.11 percent. At that rate, by 2063, 50 percent of the forest within 2km of the road will be deforested due to human settlement and forest deterioration (Greenberg et al., 2005). Again, some of the leading biologists working in the Ecuadorian Amazon have consistently argued that roads are the biggest threat and that the Ministry of Environment is not equipped to control accessibility in these remote sections of the forest. Ecuadorian SOE Petroamazonas has also attempted this roadless approach in the past, although a team of Italian researchers from the University of Padua have published reports claiming that it violated its environmental impact assessment (EIA), which promised a "cutting-edge, roadless helicopter-enabled design" (Hill, 2014a).

To truly address road-based deforestation, Andes would need to go beyond Repsol's model and attempt the "offshore-inland" model promoted by former US Secretary of the Interior Bruce Babbitt and the Blue Moon Fund (BMF), in which roads are severely limited or not built at all, and equipment is brought in by helicopter as though the sites were offshore platforms (Tollefson,

2011). Ecologist Kelly Swing reiterated the importance of this approach in an article about oil development in nearby Yasuní:

> [A]ny plan must require that the job genuinely be done in an environmentally sound way. This can be done only if the oil is extracted without new roads, which open the way to so many destructive forces. If roads continue to be built to provide access then, without question, all is lost. Instead, the oil must be extracted using "off-shore" strategies, which are more expensive but do less damage. It goes without saying that any operations would have to include proper maintenance and independent monitoring, but having isolated oil platforms scattered across the landscape has to be better than horizon-to-horizon deforestation. (Swing, 2011)

BMF (2014) and Thomas Lovejoy (2014) point to the successful "offshore-inland" Camisea project in Peru, which has been operating for 10 years and produces over 90 percent of Peru's natural gas (Sanborn and Dammert, 2014). Camisea has been notable for the conservation of forest cover: from 1986 to 2005, the site lost only 43 hectares of forest, or 0.02 percent of the total (Raschio and Contreras, 2013). It should be noted that Andes Petroleum may face a social obstacle in pursuing such a roadless tactic. According to CLACSO (2000–2012), protests against Ecuadorian oil companies have demanded paved roads more frequently than any other form of public-works investment.

However, if Andes Petroleum intends to develop its new concessions in a more environmentally and socially responsible manner, it will have to go beyond the model of Camisea. César Gamboa, of Peru's Derecho Ambeinte y Recursos Naturales, has portrayed Camisea as a first step that nonetheless is lacking in social responsibility (Gamboa et al., 2008; Sanborn and Dammert, 2013; Tollefson, 2011). Gamboa et al. (2008) claim that the Camisea project fell short in two social areas that will be especially important if Andes expands in Ecuador: the prior consultation process with civil society and indigenous groups, and the respect for traditional indigenous lands. The latter concern has brought international condemnation onto the Camisea project, including a demand from the United Nations Committee on the Elimination of Racial Discrimination (CERD) for the "immediate suspension of the planned extractive activities in the [Kugapakori-Nahua-Nanti] Reservation that may threaten the physical and cultural survival of the indigenous peoples and interfere with their enjoying full wellbeing and their economic, social, and cultural rights" (Avtonomov, 2013, authors' translation).

To avoid garnering this kind of international notoriety, Andes will have to genuinely commit to respecting indigenous territory and ensuring a complete and satisfactory prior consultation process. One way to make such a comprehensive and credible commitment would be for Andes to work with the Equitable Origin industry certification program, whose EO100 standard covers a broad array of performance targets, including indigenous peoples' rights as well as biodiversity conservation. The EO100 standard is new, having recently certified its first oil site (Pacific Rubiales, in Colombia), so it offers Andes Petroleum a way to set itself apart as an industry leader.

Unfortunately, problems so far with the prior informed consultation process have already begun to jeopardize Andes's prospects for positive community relations. Ecuador's constitution and international agreements set high standards for community consultation and participation, but they seem to have been circumvented in this case.

Ecuador is one of just 20 signatories to ILO Convention 169, which calls for nations to consult with indigenous groups prior to developing subterranean mineral deposits below tribal hunting, fishing or otherwise traditional territory (ILO, 1989). Article 57 of Ecuador's 2008 constitution also enshrines this requirement, with the added note that if the affected community does not agree to the proposal, the government must follow additional steps detailed in the 2010 Citizen Participation Law, which states that if "a majority opposition emerges in the respective community, the decision to undertake the project or not will be made through a resolution, adequately debated [...], which, in cases where it is decided that the project will be undertaken, must establish parameters that minimize the impact on communities and ecosystems; moreover, it must plan for mitigation, compensation, and damage repair; and where possible, it must include the members of the community in the labor force for the respective projects, in conditions that guarantee human dignity" (Article 83, authors' translation). In sum, the prior consultation process must seek the community's majority approval; if the majority of the community opposes the project, a resolution to proceed in a limited-impact way must be drafted, debated, and approved.

Unfortunately, members of the Sápara nation claim that majority approval was never sought, according to our interviews. Indeed, the Secretaría de Hidrocarburos (SHE), which conducted the consultation, does not claim to have sought it. Instead, SHE reports that the Sápara president at the time, Basilio Mucushigua, signed an agreement allowing oil exploration in exchange for $2.4 million in local public investment (SHE, 2012). This neglect of majority opinion is not surprising, given its omission in Executive Decree 1247, which directed this particular consultation process (Correa, 2012). The decree allows for comments to be submitted either through community meetings or individually at local consultation offices, provided that the offices are extensively advertised through local press, government or community leaders. SHE reports that 16,469 people participated in this consultation process, throughout the 16 blocks that the government hoped to develop. However, Mazabanda (2013) estimates that the indigenous nations whose territories overlap with the oil blocks include 69,114 adults, and that the total adult population of the oil blocks is 141,397. Even if Mazabanda's estimates are significantly overstated, SHE consulted with only a small minority of the affected population. It is worth noting that it is equally likely that SHE's estimates are overstated. SHE includes 10,469 people who participated directly in the consultation process, as well as 6,000 who participated in "socio-environmental management model" workshops, which are outside the scope of Executive Decree 1247; nor does SHE claim to have taken any precautions to avoid double counting those who may be in both groups.[6]

Neither Ruiz nor Ushigua doubts that former Sápara president, Mucushigua, signed an agreement with the SHE. But both insisted that SHE never sought approval from the majority of the Sápara nation, a violation of the 2008 Constitution and the 2010 Citizen Participation Law.

Beyond the consultation process, the potential new oil projects created tremendous conflict in the Sápara nation, complicating Andes's attempts to begin operations smoothly there. Both Ruiz and Ushigua report that when former Sápara president, Mucushigua, was asked about the agreement, he threatened to have anyone who stood in its way killed. Within a week, the 13-year-old son of an opposition community leader was allegedly murdered. Suspecting that Mucushigua was behind the death, the ethnically Sápara majority of the Sápara community met and elected Ruiz as the new president. (Mucushigua is not ethnically Sápara, according to Ruiz, but lived in a Sápara settlement and had been elected president.) Both Ruiz and Ushigua indicate that the community is deeply divided between ethnic Sápara, opposed to the drilling, and other residents who are in the minority but who welcome the oil exploration. Finally, it is unlikely that Andes will be able to win over the Sápara easily. When asked what she would like to say to Andes Petroleum, Ushigua replied: "The indigenous Sápara say to the hydrocarbon companies that we do not want oil exploitation; we want to be left alone[. ...] We ask the big countries to please respect our rights and our life that comes from nature" (Ushigua, 2014, authors' translation). Both the Kichwa and Sápara people have taken this appeal

---

6 Representatives of the Ecuadorian government asked not to be quoted on this matter. An anonymous government source reiterated the government's confidence in the process and asserted that there was full support of indigenous communities for the current oil expansion, even though no vote or poll was taken to establish majority support. This stands in stark contrast to Andes's operations in Block 62, in which a vote was taken prior to the expansion of operations.

internationally, with leaders representing them in the People's Climate March in New York in September 2014. At preparations for the March, Ushigua stated publicly: "We are ready to fight with all the strength of our ancestors against the companies and governments to protect the land from which we came, a land that must remain free from oil exploration" (Zuckerman, 2014).

Finally, Mario Melo, the lawyer for indigenous groups cited above, stressed the importance of respecting the wishes of indigenous groups in the South, who have different goals than their northern counterparts near Andes Petroleum's current concessions:

> I do not doubt that there may be the opportunity to negotiate around further petroleum activity in [Siekopai] territory. But that is not the case for all [indigenous] nations. Indigenous nations and peoples, in their practice of self-determination, may seek out petroleum activity, or not. If they come to agreements that respect their rights and if through those agreements they see greater opportunities, then that is good. There are other communities, such as those in the central-southern Amazon, who are organized and seeking other alternatives for good living[; ...] the problem arises when efforts are made to impose something on them[. ...] It is vital to respect those who say "yes" as well as those who say "no." (Melo, 2014, authors' translation)

3.3 Political fallout from the oil-expansion process

The Correa administration has consistently ranked among the most popular in Latin America, as shown in Figure 4.12. Public support for his Alianza País party, in alliance with environmentalists and indigenous leaders, enabled the writing of the 2008 Constitution. Correa was not the first politician in Ecuador to harness the energy of civil society; the country's indigenous, environmentalist and historically marginalized groups, including campesinos and the Afro-Ecuadorian population, became a significant factor in national politics in the 1980s. Correa, like his predecessor, Lucio Guttierrez, capitalized on the strength of these groups by incorporating their calls for deep reforms and justice. Yet, unlike Guttierrez, who was removed from power after being labelled a lackey for Washington, Correa has maintained a remarkably high favorability rating. However, many of Ecuador's civil-society organizations focused on human, environmental and indigenous people's rights are now opposed to the president. For his part, in 2014, Correa denounced collusion between environmental and indigenous groups and Assembly President Alberto Acosta during the Constitutional Assembly. Specifically pointing to three articles focused on ancestral rights that are under review for possible amendment as of this writing, including Article 57 mentioned above, Correa

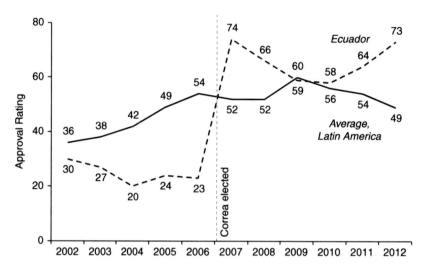

Figure 4.12 Approval ratings, Ecuador and Latin American average, 2002–2012
Source: Latinobarómetro, 2013.
Note: The survey asked respondents "Do you approve or disapprove of the government administration headed by [leader's name]?" (authors' translation).

lamented that his opponents' "incompetence can do more damage than good and it can condemn to poverty the same people that you are trying to help" (*Ecuador Inmediato*, 2014).

Despite Correa's initially astronomic approval ratings, Figure 4.12 also shows that his popularity has been volatile. Correa and other members of his Alianza País party easily won the presidency and maintained strong control of the national assembly in February 2013 (see Neuman, 2013 for more on this election). However, challenges followed and in early 2014 elections the party lost mayoralties in four major cities: Quito, Guayaquil, Cuenca and Manta. Many Ecuadorian pundits connected this loss to Correa's decision to exploit oil in the Ishpingo-Tambococha-Tiputini (ITT) section of Yasuní National Park[7] and to the targeting of indigenous and environmental critics of his policies. Correa has expressed a desire to address the problems behind this "painful" loss, asking his cabinet to resign and implying that there were important lessons to learn (*Economist*, 2014).

---

7 In 2007, Ecuador announced plans to seek funds internationally in exchange for *not* drilling in the Ishpingo-Tambococha-Tiputini section of Yasuní, citing a benefit to the planet (and a cost to Ecuador) of foregoing drilling. This plan, known as the Yasuní-ITT initiative, ultimately failed, and the Spanish oil company Repsol won a concession to drill in the area.

Critics focused especially intensely on two areas: Correa's decision to open the ITT sections of Yasuní National Park to oil exploration, and his perceived favoritism toward Chinese oil investors in the process. Although Ecuadorian SOE PetroAmazonas will ultimately run the ITT concession, a "secret document" allegedly surfaced shortly before the 2014 elections, purporting to show that Ecuador promised China access to those oilfields, as part of a $1 billion loan from the China Development Bank in 2009 (Hill, 2014b). More broadly, sensationalist reports claiming that China now owns all of Ecuador's oil, or that it dictates government policy, often receive considerable attention in national and international press reports (for examples, see Reuters, 2009; Villavicencio, 2013). However, survey results show that Ecuadorians overall have more mixed feelings about their country's relationship with China. According to a 2012 Latin American Public Opinion Project (LAPOP) survey, most Ecuadorians believe that China has a growing influence in their country, although respondents place greater trust in the United States (46.4%) than in China (38.3%). However, respondents appreciate the new relationship with China: 61.1 percent believe China has a positive influence on Ecuador, although that number drops to 56.8 percent for the influence of Chinese businesses specifically (Zechmeister et al., 2012).

After the ITT Initiative failed, Andes Petroleum became a focus of environmental and indigenous-rights protests, even though the ITT concession ultimately went to PetroAmazonas. This is primarily because the ITT concession was auctioned off at the same time as the concessions acquired by Andes, the eleventh round of concession auctions. The auctions themselves drew fierce criticism and protests, which expanded to address all of the new concessions, including Andes Petroleum's. So it is worthwhile to briefly explore the damage done to the alliance between the government and environmentalists and prospects for the future.

The ITT Initiative was popular with the Ecuadorian public, and its failure brought widespread protest. The government that was widely regarded as environmentally conscious now faced broad segments of the Ecuadorian population troubled by the new push for drilling in the ITT. Polls from Quito's *El Comercio* immediately after Correa's decision revealed a strong majority opposed to drilling, although later poll numbers found the population more divided. Moreover, critics noted that by declining to support the initiative, China forfeited an opportunity to prove its commitment to being a partner in Ecuador's stated goal of responsible extraction.

The environmental group Yasunidos reacted to the initiative's failure by attempting to force a referendum on the subject. In May 2014, the Ecuadorian National Electoral Council (CNE) rejected the referendum proposal, ruling that the majority of the signatures Yasunidos collected were fraudulent or otherwise unacceptable. But the environmentalist community held on to its demands, and the struggle gained publicity as a prominent news outlet backed and published an independent analysis by Enrique Mafla, professor of computer science at the Escuela Politécnica Nacional, which called into question the CNE's decision (Mafla, 2014).

The Correa administration's relationship with environmentalists took a further hit during the auction process for the new oil concessions, including Andes Petroleum's new concessions as well as the ITT concession. Yasunidos staged protests during the concession auction, together with representatives of indigenous nations and the Fundación Pachamama, one of the most well-established environmental CSOs in Ecuador. During the protests, the Chilean ambassador to Ecuador and a representative of the Belarusian company, Belorusneft, were assaulted (*El Telégrafo*, 2013). Indigenous representatives claim that the assault was the work of infiltrators, while the minister of the interior accused the protestors of "affecting the public peace" (Alvaro, 2013). Within a week, Pachamama announced that government agents had raided their offices and shut down the organization (Pachamama Alliance, 2013). Regardless of where blame lies for the incidents surrounding the auction, they have seriously damaged the relationship between the government and its erstwhile environmental allies.

Most recently, Ecuadorian civil-society leaders have begun to reach out directly to Chinese firms and banks funding their investments in search of accountability on environmental and social norms. For example, members of Acción Ecológica and rights advocate Paulina Garzón have highlighted various social and environmental policies established by Chinese banks and have worked with transnational partners in Peru and Brazil, while making inroads with Chinese NGOs in addition to their historic cooperation with US and European NGOs, to raise the pressure on Chinese policymakers. Similarly, the Centro de Derechos Económicos y Sociales has produced a manual for Ecuadorian community organizers, informing them of the environmental and social standards that Chinese policy banks expect of the investors and advising them on how to directly contact the banks if projects do not live up to these standards (Hill, 2014c). The existence of this manual could mean that Andes's behavior will receive closer scrutiny in its new concession than it has received in the past, and that perceived misdeeds will be reported back to its funders in China. So it is in the interest of Andes Petroleum as well as the Ecuadorian government to ensure that these new concessions meet the highest standards possible.

This rift between Correa and civil society helps to explain the backlash that Andes Petroleum is facing in its new concessions. It also helps explain why indigenous leaders such as Gloria Ushigua and others have sought audiences internationally, potentially bringing more scrutiny and risk to Andes Petroleum's expansion. It is no exaggeration to say that civil society world-wide is watching Andes Petroleum's expansion. If Andes hopes to continue its track record of peaceful, successful investment in Ecuador, it must take great care in its interactions with environmentalists, indigenous nations, and the Ecuadorian government.

4. Conclusions and Recommendations

China has been an invaluable economic ally to Ecuador over the last several years. This new partnership has ensured Ecuador access to international credit markets after its partial bond default and provided an important source of new investment and trade revenue during the 2009 global downturn. An important caveat is that the relationship's heavy focus on oil production necessarily complicates Ecuador's stated goals of diversifying away from petroleum. Nonetheless, Ecuador has a strong legal framework for the oil industry, including a constitution that recognizes the rights of nature and more specific legislation that requires oil projects to conduct EIAs, consult with the local community, respect indigenous territory, hire Ecuadorian workers and share profits with them and pay substantial taxes to fund public investments in affected communities. This framework, if properly enforced, could be a model for other natural-resource producing countries worldwide.

The upcoming expansion of oil production through new concessions, including those won by Andes Petroleum, is the first major test of Ecuador's social and environmental protections from the oil industry. It is crucial for Ecuador's government and China's oil companies to show their commitment to the protections they have agreed to in the past. But it will not be easy; these concessions are in an area that is extremely important environmentally and completely covered by traditional indigenous territory. A commitment to transparency and public accountability would be a good first step. Ecuador could make progress in those areas by signing on to the Extraction Industry Transparency Initiative (EITI), allowing the public to trace oil revenues from firms to the central government and back to local governments. Andes Petroleum and PetroOriental could also sign onto EITI as a show of good faith, reporting on their taxes, royalties and any additional community spending, as Chinese mining firm Chinalco has done in Peru. Furthermore, Undersecretary Carrera indicated that the Ministry of the Environment has a long-term goal of digitizing records of company environmental behavior and making these records publicly available. Such a move would show the government's commitment to enforcing its laudable legal framework, reward firms that have worked hard to maintain high standards and empower citizens.

Finally, the specific concessions that Andes Petroleum has just won need to be handled with great care. The community consultation process has so far been fraught with protest and caused more division than peace. If Ecuador is to live up to its reputation of valuing its people and ecosystem, it would be wise to consider upholding its commitment to seeking the majority opinion of the local community and taking that opinion into account. In practice, such an approach must include acknowledging that the majority of the local population has not agreed to the project, and then either revisiting the consultation process or initiating the process required by the Citizen Participation Law if there is not majority approval: drafting, debating and approving a development plan that incorporates the highest standards of environmental and social responsibility. Furthermore, the unique biodiversity of the area suggests that all parties could benefit from a serious consideration of an "offshore-inland" approach to any new oil projects in Andes Petroleum's new concessions, which would limit the projects' interference with indigenous communities as well as with the forest itself.

References

ADB, IADB, and ADBI (Asian Development Bank, Inter-American Development Bank, and Asian Development Bank Institute) (2012). "Shaping the Future of the Asia and the Pacific–Latin America and the Caribbean Relationship." http://www.adbi.org/book/2012/05/05/5059.shaping.future.asia.lac.relationship/.

ARCH (Agencia de Regulación y Control Hidrocarburífuro) (2011–2013). "Producción Nacional de Petróleo Fiscalizado: Reportes Históricos." http://www.arch.gob.ec/index.php/descargas/produccion-nacional-petroleo-fiscalizado.html.

Arroyo, María Belén (2014). "Primer revés electoral." *Vistazo*, 12–17.

Aruaz, Andres. Personal interview, 24 January 2014.

Asamblea Nacional del Ecuador (2010a). "Ley Orgánica de Participación Ciudadana." Registro Oficial Suplemento 175, 20 April, 2010. Organization of American States. Accessed 30 August 2014. http://www.oas.org/juridico/PDFs/mesicic4_ecu_org6.pdf.

Asamblea Nacional del Ecuador (2010b). "Ley Reformatoria a la Ley de Hidrocarburos y a la Ley de Régimen Tributario Interno" *Registro Oficial No. 244 – Martes 27 de Julio 2010 Suplemento*.

Auquilla Teran, Carlo Federico. Personal interview, 7 May 2014.

Avtonomov, Alexei. (2013). Letter to Luis Enrique Chávez Basagoitia, Permanent Representative of Peru to the United Nations Office and Other International Organizations in Geneva, 1 March 2013. *United Nations Office of the High Commissioner for Human Rights*. Accessed 30 August 2014. http://www2.ohchr.org/english/bodies/cerd/docs/early_warning/Peru1March2013.pdf.

Bass, Margot, Matt Finer, Clinton Jenkins, et al. (2010). "Global Conservation Significance of Ecuador's Yasuní National Park." PLoS ONE 5(1): e8767. doi:10.1371/journal.pone.0008767.

Benítez, Jeeyla (2014). "Deuda: en 2013 China era financista, ahora es cobrador," *Hoy*, June 22. http://www.hoy.com.ec/noticias-ecuador/deuda-en-2013-china-era-financista-ahora-es-cobrador-608792.html.

Berlington, Meredith (2010). "Infographic: Top 20 Countries with Most Endangered Species," *Mother Nature Network*, 5 March. http://www.mnn.com/earth-matters/animals/stories/infographic-top-20-countries-with-most-endangered-species.

Black, William K. (2012). "The Miraculous Turnaround in Ecuadorian Migration Under President Correa," *Huffington Post*, 19 December. http://www.huffingtonpost.com/william-k-black/the-miraculous-turnaround_b_2329708.html.

BMF (Blue Moon Fund) (2014). "Offshore-Inland." http://www.bluemoonfund.org/wp-content/uploads/2014/07/Blue-moon_8.5x11-1.pdf.

BNF (Banco Nacional de Fomento) (2000–2012). "Estadistica." https://www.bnf.fin.ec/index.php?option=com_joomdoc&view=documents&path=estadisticas&Itemid=56&lang=es.

Bonilla, Omar (2010). "The Manta–Manaos Project: Nature, Capital and Plunder," *The CEECEC Handbook: Ecological Economics from the Bottom-Up*, 2, 7–22.

Boufadel, Michel. Personal interview, 28 July 2014.

Braütigam, Deborah and Kevin Gallagher (2014). "Bartering Globalization: China's Commodity-Backed Finance in Africa and Latin America," *Global Policy* 5:3, September, 346–52.

CAIC (Comisión para la Auditoría Integral del Crédito Público) (2008). *Final Report of the Integral Auditing of the Ecuadorian Debt: Executive Summary*. Quito: Ministry of Economy and Finance. http://www.auditoriadeuda.org.ec/images/stories/documentos/Libro_CAIC_English.pdf.zip.

Carrera, Paola. Personal interview, 25 July 2014.

Chen, Zach. Personal interview, 24 July 2014.

CLACSO (Consejo Latinoamericano de Ciencias Sociales) (2000–2012). "Observatorio Social de América Latina: Cronologías." http://www.clacso.org.ar/institucional/1h.php.

Constitución del Ecuador. Art. LVII, Sec. 7.

Correa, Rafael (2012). "Decreto Ejecutivio 1247." 19 July 2012. Accessed 30 August 2014. http://www.recursosnaturales.gob.ec/wp-content/uploads/downloads/2012/08/PDF-DECRETO_1247-19-JUL-2012.pdf.

Crawford, James, Horacio Grigera Naon and Christopher Thomas, (2006). "Arbitration pursuant to the Canada-Ecuador Bilateral Investment Treaty and the UNCITRAL Rules: EnCana Corporation (Claimant) versus Republic of Ecuador (Respondent) AWARD. London Court of International Arbitration. http:// www.italaw.com/sites/default/files/case-documents/ita0285_0.pdf

Dunning, Thad (2008). *Crude Democracy: Natural Resource Wealth and Political Regimes*. New York: Cambridge University Press.

ECLAC (no date). "CEPALStat: Databases and Statistical Publications." http://estadisticas.cepal.org/cepalstat/WEB_CEPALSTAT/Portada.asp?idioma=i.

Ecuador Inmediato (2009). "Ex Trabajadores de CONAZUL nunca fueron parte de Andes Petroleum, afirman sus autoridades." 26 January 2009. http://www.ecuadorinmediato.com/index.php?module=Noticias&func=news_user_view&id=96467&umt=ex_trabajadores_conazul_nunca_fueron_parte_andes_petroleum_afirman_autoridades.

Ecuador Inmediato (2014). Presidente Correa: "Mayor error cometido en estos años fue permitir que Alberto Acosta sea presidente de la constituyente." 31 August 31 2014. http://www.ecuadorinmediato.com/index.php?module=Noticias&func=news_user_view&id=2818768950

Ecuavisa, 2013. "Fausto Ortiz expuso alternativas económicas para no explotar el ITT," on Ecuavisa, 28 August. http://www.ecuavisa.com/articulo/noticias/contacto-directo/39408-fausto-ortiz-expuso-alternativas-economicas-no-explotar-itt.

El Ciudadano (2014). "People from the Amazon Welcome a New Millennium Community," 16 January. http://www.elciudadano.gob.ec/en/people-from-the-amazon-welcome-a-new-millennium-community/

El Comercio (2013). "En America Latina, Ecuador tiene la mayor tasa de deforestacion," 26 October. http://www.elcomercio.com/sociedad/Ecuador-tasa-mayor-deforestacion-tala-arboles-bosques-America-Latina-Ministerio-Ambiente_3_1018128182.html.

El Telégrafo (2011). "Presidente destaca importancia estratégica de relaciones con China," 6 July. http://www.telegrafo.com.ec/noticias/informacion-general/item/correa-destaca-importancia-estrategica-de-relaciones-con-china.html

El Telégrafo. "Diplomático y empresario extranjeros fueron agredidos en protestas contra ronda petrolera." 30 November 2013. http://www.eltelegrafo.com.ec/noticias/politica/2/diplomatico-y-empresario-extranjeros-fueron-agredidos-en-protestas-contra-ronda-petrolera-video

Espinosa, Santiago. Personal interview, 6 June 2014.

Falconi, Fander (2013). "Ecologismo y la iniciativa Yasuni-ITT," El Telégrafo, 28 August. http://www.telegrafo.com.ec/opinion/columnistas/item/ecologismo-y-la-iniciativa-yasuni-itt.html.

FAO (Food and Agriculture Organization of the United Nations) (2010). "Global Forest Resources Assessment 2010." http://www.fao.org/forestry/fra/fra2010/en/.

Fajardo, Jose 2014. Personal interview, 20 June 2014.

Fearnside, Philp M. et al. (2013). "Amazonian Forest Loss and the Long Reach of China's Influence, *Environment, Development and Sustainability* 15: 325–38, 336.

Gallagher, Kevin, Amos Irwin, and Katherine Koleski, (2012). "The New Banks in Town: Chinese Finance in Latin America." Washington, DC: Inter-American Dialogue. http://ase.tufts.edu/gdae/Pubs/rp/GallagherChineseFinanceLatinAmerica.pdf.

Gallagher, Kevin and Margaret Myers. (2014). "China-Latin America Finance Database." Washington, DC: Inter-American Dialogue. https://www.thedialogue.org/map_list.

Gamboa Balbín, César, Vanessa Cueto La Rosa, and Jimpson Dávila Ordoñez (2008). *¿El Estado Peruano Cumplió con Camisea? Diagnóstico Final Sobre el Cumplimiento de los Compromisos del Perú.* Lima: Derecho Ambiente y Recursos Naturales. http://www.dar.org.pe/archivos/publicacion/39_libro_completo_camisea.pdf.

Greenberg, Jonathan, Shawn Kefauver, Hugh Stimson, et al. (2005). "Survival Analysis of a Neotropical Rainforest Using Multitemporal Satellite Imagery." *Remote Sensing of Environment* 96:2, 202–11, doi: 10.1016/j.rse.2005.02.010.

Hill, David (2014a). "Ecuador: oil company has built 'secret' road deep into Yasuni National Park," *The Ecologist* 6 June. http://www.theecologist.org/News/news_analysis/2426486/ecuador_oil_company_has_built_secret_road_deep_into_yasuni_national_park.html.

Hill, David (2014b). "Ecuador pursued China oil deal while pledging to protect Yasuni, papers show," *The Guardian* 19 February. http://www.theguardian.com/environment/2014/feb/19/ecuador-oil-china-yasuni.

Hill, David (2014c). "What good are China's green policies if its banks don't listen?" *The Guardian* 16 May. http://www.theguardian.com/environment/andes-to-the-amazon/2014/may/16/what-good-chinas-green-policies-banks-dont-listen.

ILO (International Labour Organization) (1989). "Convention 169 – Indigenous and Tribal Peoples Convention, 1989." http://www.ilo.org/dyn/normlex/en/f?p=NOR MLEXPUB:12100:0::NO::P12100_ILO_CODE:C169.

IMF (International Monetary Fund) (2014). "World Economic Outlook Database." Online database, accessed 2 September 2014. http://www.imf.org/external/pubs/ft/weo/2014/01/weodata/index.aspx.

Korby, Brian and Christine Jenkins (2014). "Ecuador Sells $2 Billion in Return to Bond Market." 17 June. http://www.bloomberg.com/news/2014-06-17/ecuador-plans-bond-market-return-today-five-years-after-default.html.

Larrea, Carlos (2006). "Neoliberal Policies and Social Development in Latin America: The Case of Ecuador." Paper presented at the 2006 Congress of Social Sciences and Humanities CERLAC, York University, 2 June.

Latinbarómetro (2013). "Informe 2013." Santiago, Chile. 1 November. http://www.latino-barometro.org/documentos/LATBD_INFORME_LB_2013.pdf.

Laurance, William, Ana Albernaz, Götz Schroth, et al. (2002). "Predictors of Deforestation in the Brazilian Amazon." Journal of Biogeography 29:5–6, 737–48. doi: 10.1046/j.1365-2699.2002.00721.x.

Laurance, William, William Camargo, José Luizão, et al. (2011). "The Fate of Amazonian Forest Fragments: A 32-year Investigation." Biological Conservation 144:1, 56–67. Doi:10.1016/j.biocon.2010.09.021.

Lovejoy, Thomas (2014). "Exploration, Extraction, Remediation." Presentation delivered at the "Achieving equilibrium in the Amazon: Balancing Economic Development, Human Rights and Environmental Justice – Past, Present, and Future" conference hosted by the Ministries of the Environment and Foreign Relations, Quito, Ecuador, 29 July.

Macias, Ivonne. Personal interview, 20 June 2014.

Mafla, Enrique et al. (2014). "Verificación académica independiente: Análisis estadístico de los registros presentados por el Colectivo Yasunidos al CNE," El Universo. http://www.eluniverso.com/sites/default/files/archivos/2014/05/informe_final_verificacion_independiente.pdf.

Maldonado, Adolfo (2013). "Pueblos Indígenas y petroleras: Tres miradas." Quito: Clínica Ambiental. http://www.clinicambiental.org/docs/publicaciones/3historiasweb.pdf.

Mazabanda, Carlos (2013). "Consulta Previa en la Décimo Primera Ronda Petrolera ¿Participación masiva de la ciudadanía?" Amazon Watch. Accessed 30 August 2014. http://amazonwatch.org/assets/files/2013-07-consulta-previa-en-la-11a-ronda.pdf.

Melo, Mario. Personal interview, 27 June 2014.

Moseley, Christopher (ed) (2010). Atlas of the World's Languages in Danger, 3rd edn. Paris, UNESCO Publishing. Online version: http://www.unesco.org/culture/en/endan-geredlanguages/atlas

MEER (Ministerio de Electricidad y Energía Renovable) (no date-1). "Cambio de la Matriz Energética." https://www.celec.gob.ec/index.php?option=com_content&view=articl e&id=91&Itemid=269.

MEER (Ministerio de Electricidad y Energía Renovable) (no date-2). "Proyectos de Generación: Coca-Codo Sinclair." http://www.energia.gob.ec/coca-codo-sinclair/.

Narins, Thomas P. (2012). "China's Eye on Ecuador: What Chinese Trade with Ecuador Reveals about China's Economic Expansion into South America," The Global Studies Journal, 4:2, 300.

Neuman, William (2013). "President Correa Handily Wins Re-election in Ecuador," *The New York Times*, 17 February. http://www.nytimes.com/2013/02/18/world/americas/rafael-correa-wins-re-election-in-ecuador.html.

Obando, Wendy. Personal interview, 19 June 2014.

Observatorio de la Política Fiscal (2007). "Lay Ley 10 para la región amazónica es un cheque en blanco." 2 July. http://www.observatoriofiscal.org/documentos/noticias-de-prensa/el-comercio/700.html.

Palley, Thomas I. (2003) "The Overvalued Dollar and the US Slump," in *Dollar Overvaluation and the World Economy*, eds. C. Fred Bergsten and John Williamson. Washington, DC: Institute for International Economics, 145–63.

Piaguaje, Javier. Personal interview, 18 June 2014.

Porzecanski, Arturo (2010). "When Bad Things Happen to Good Sovereign Debt Contracts: The Case of Ecuador," *Law and Contemporary Problems*, 73: 251, 251–71.

Raschio, Giancarlo and Christian Contreras (2013). "Análisis De Los Impactos Ecológicos del Modelo de Hidrocarburos sin Carreteras." Washington, DC: Ecosystem Services. http://www.spde.org/documentos/publicaciones/Analisis-de-los-Impactos-Ecologicos-del-Modelo-Hidrocarburos-sin-carreteras.pdf.

RdP (Refinería del Pacífico). Site visit and personal interviews. 26 February 2014, Campomento de Aromo, Manta, Ecuador.

Repsol (2012). "Relevant Events." *Quarterly Report 2012Q3*. Accessed 30 August 2014. http://repsol.webfg.com/informesTrimestrales/en/q32012/hechosDestacados.

Reuters (2009). "Oil Hungry China Moves to Strengthen Ecuador t Tes," 13 July. http://www.reuters.com/article/2009/07/13/us-ecuador-china-oil-idUSTRE56C6FF20090713.

Reuters (2012). "Moody's Raises Ecuador to Caa1, Outlook Stable," 13 September. http://www.reuters.com/article/2012/09/13/ecuador-ratings-moodys-idUSL1E8KDKPC20120913.

Ruiz, Klever (2014). Personal interview, 30 August.

Ruiz Giraldo, Carlo (2009). "La eliminación del los fondos petroleros." Quito: FLACSO, March. http://www.flacsoandes.edu.ec/web/imagesFTP/9431.WP_018_CGiraldo_01.pdf.

Sanborn, Cynthia and Juan Luís Dammert (2014). "Caso de Estudio: Perú," in *Las Mejores (y Peores) Prácticas Para la Extracción de Recursos Naturales en América Latina*, Richard André, Ryan Berger, Wilda Escarfuller et al., eds. Americas Society/Council of the Americas. http://www.as-coa.org/sites/default/files/MiningSynthesisReport.pdf.

Sanderson, Henry and Michael Forsyth (2013). *China's Superbank*. Singapore: Bloomberg Press.

Schneyer, Joshua and Nicolas Medina Mora Perez (2013). "A Look at the Traders Behind the China-Ecuador-U.S. Oil Triangle." Reuters, 26 November. http://www.reuters.com/article/2013/11/26/us-china-ecuador-taurus-idUSBRE9AP0I820131126.

SENPLADES (Secretaría Nacional de Planificación y Desarrollo). (2009). *Plan Nacional para el Buen Vivir, 2013–2017*. http://www.buenvivir.gob.ec/documents/10157/26effa35-aaa8-4aec-a11c-be69abd6e40a.

SHE (Secretaría de Hidrocarburos del Ecuador) (2012). "Consulta Previa: Resumen Ejecutivo." http://www.hidrocarburos.gob.ec/wp-content/uploads/downloads/2013/08/resumen_ejecutivo_consulta_previa.pdf.

Silvestre, Edgar. Personal interview, 19 June 2014.

Swing, Kelly. Personal interview, 19 September 2013.

Swing, Kelly (2011). "Day of Reckoning for Ecuador's Biodiversity" *Nature* 496, January, 267.

The Economist (2014). "Ecuador's Local Elections: Local Difficulties," 24 February. http://www.economist.com/blogs/americasview/2014/02/ecuadors-local-elections.

Tollefson, Jeff (2011). "Fighting for the Forest: The Roadless Warrior." *Nature* 480:7375, 22–24. http://www.nature.com/news/fighting-for-the-forest-the-roadless-warrior-1.9494.

UNESCO (United Nations Educational, Scientific, and Cultural Organization) (2008). "Oral Heritage and Cultural Manifestations of the Zápara People." *Intangible Cultural Heritage*. Accessed 30 August 2014. http://www.unesco.org/culture/ich/en/RL/00007.

Ushigua, Gloria (2014). Personal correspondence.

Vargas Ocaña, Guido Gilberto. Personal interview, 30 March 2013.

Vernengo, Matias and Mathew Bradbury (2011). "The Limits to Dollarization in Ecuador: Lessons from Argentina." *Journal of World-Systems Research* XVII: 2, 447–62. http://www.jwsr.org/wp-content/uploads/2013/02/Vernengo_Bradbury-vol17n2.pdf.

Villavicencio, Fernando (2013). *Ecuador: Made in China*. Miami: InterAmerican Institute for Democracy.

Widener, Patricia (2011). *Oil Injustice: Resisting and Conceding a Pipeline in Ecuador*. Lanham, MD: Rowman and Littlefield Publishers.

Zechmeister, Elizabeth J. et al. (2012) "China in Latin America: Public Impressions and Policy Implications," LAPOP, Vanderbilt University.

Zuckerman, Adam (2014). "Voices from Ecuador Echo in New York," Amazon Watch. 20 September. http://amazonwatch.org/news/2014/0920-voices-from-ecuador-echo-in-new-york.

Part III

CHINA'S AND LATIN AMERICA'S MINING SECTORS

Chapter 5

AN ASSESSMENT OF THE ENVIRONMENTAL AND SOCIAL IMPACTS OF CHINESE TRADE AND FDI IN BOLIVIA

Alejandra Saravia López and Adam Rua Quiroga

China has become an important partner for Bolivia, both diplomatically and economically. These two aspects of the relationship overlap frequently, as China and Bolivia have signed over 400 cooperation, aid and loan agreements. In terms of investment, China has been a small but fast-growing partner, currently active in Bolivia's mining sector and set to be Bolivia's main partner in developing its lithium reserves. Bolivia's exports to China have been concentrated in minerals, while imports have been concentrated in manufactured capital and consumer goods. Despite high prices for metals, Bolivia has experienced a significant trade deficit with China. Because of their high concentration in the mining sector, exports to China have put pressure on Bolivia's water supplies.

After exploring the relationship on an aggregate level, this chapter turns to case-study evidence in the tin-mining sector, with the participation of the Chinese firm Jungie Mining. Our research reveals that Chinese tin mining is associated with water pollution and conflicts over water use. Moreover, the case of Jungie indicates that there is a lack of capacity and/or willingness to enforce and upgrade existing environmental laws on the part of the Bolivian government.

Despite the fact that Jungie Mining is in an early stage, the firm's activities have already been suspended due to water pollution in surrounding communities, and it has already clashed with local communities over water rights. This is exacerbated by the lack of action on the part of the Bolivian government, which allowed the firm to operate for four years without obtaining an environmental license and has set a troublesome example by delaying construction of pollution-remediation infrastructure in publicly run mining operations.

The social aspects of our case study are more positive. Jungie has actively engaged in community-consultation processes and has respected their outcomes. This has ensured that ore-processing facilities are located in communities that want them and away from those that do not. In addition, the firm is operating through a joint venture with a local cooperative. Such an arrangement could bring new technology to the cooperative sector and ensure that the local population benefits from mining.

Bolivia's relationship with China is set to deepen through the development of local lithium reserves. This prospect brings great opportunities for the national economy, but our case study on tin highlights areas of deep concern. To address these areas and prevent their repetition in future lithium projects, we recommend:

- Strengthening the enforcement of environmental regulations in all contexts, including international investments and publicly run projects;
- Fostering transparency in public concessions contracts;
- Revisiting the Law on Mining and Metallurgy to ensure that communities and small farms have access to sufficient water for their survival;
- Supplementing the accumulating international reserves with a stabilization fund or sovereign wealth fund, if the appropriate institutional structures can be established.

1. Introduction

China's recent impressive economic growth has had important effects on international trade flows, in terms of both prices and volumes. China is a major exporter of goods (with 11.2% of total world exports), the second largest destination of FDI (with 9% of total inflows), and the third most important foreign investor (with 6% of total flows), according to the Economic Commission for Latin America and the Caribbean (ECLAC, 2012). In addition, China's demand for minerals and raw materials in general has important impacts on international commodity prices (ECLAC, 2012). Thus, China will certainly impact the future of international trade flows for Latin America. It has already directed increasing FDI flows to this region in the last few years.

However, there is more than just economics in the relationship between China and Latin America; there are also environmental and social issues related with this economic link. Empirical studies about this connection for the Chinese trade and FDI are still scarce. It is important to analyze this topic for the Bolivian case, given its particular environmental and economic characteristics. Certainly, during recent decades the Bolivian economy has shown an impressive record of GDP growth, but the country still faces serious environmental and social problems.

The aim of the present study is to analyze the main trends of trade and FDI flows between China and Bolivia, determining their environmental and social impacts. Thus, the study is divided in four parts. The first part briefly describes the trends of Chinese FDI to Latin America. The second part is devoted to analyzing the relationship between Bolivia and China considering the different financial linkages they have to each other, namely loans, donations and FDI, among others. The third part develops the context of the case studies, presenting an overview of the mining sector in Bolivia. The fourth part is the methodological section where two case studies from the mining sector in Bolivia with Chinese participation are evaluated and policy implications are presented. Conclusions are at the end.

2. Chinese Trade and Investment Participation in Latin America

During the last three decades, China has become a strategic international trade partner, having considerably increased its relations with several regions, including Latin America and the Caribbean (LAC), with which China has consolidated businesses links through bilateral agreements characterized by unbalanced commerce between exports and imports (Bittencourt, 2012). According to Balderrama and Martinez (2010), in the 1970s China began to face the difficult task of investing outside its borders. Chinese FDI in LAC increased from USD 200 million in 1975, to USD 916 million at the start of 2000 and to USD 50 billion by the end of the decade (Balderrama and Martinez, 2010; Nacht, 2013).

However, China is deepening its relationship with LAC not only through the market mechanisms of trade, loans and investment, but also through cooperation. China has a solid development strategy characterized by multipolarism, multilateralism, non-interference, soft power, pragmatism, collaboration and persuasion.

It has already been established that during the 2000s, the investment relations of Asian countries in LAC prioritize the extractive sector in its investments (petroleum, gas, mining), and to a lesser extent other productive sectors. It is a relationship characterized not only by partnership but also, in most cases, by competition in the international markets of goods and services (Correa and Gonzales, 2006). In general, Chinese FDI continues to support the production of primary commodities in the economy (returning to the model of exporting of natural resources) of LAC, mainly due to the high profitability of raw materials extraction, with environmental and social impacts that are denounced from different sectors, and with limitations in regulation and human rights oversight. As a special case, Irwin and Gallagher (2013), observe that the Chinese mining companies are often portrayed as predators regarding environmental and labor norms compared to other companies, which is a threat for LAC.

2.1 Chinese investment in the Bolivian economy

During the early 1990s, after series of reforms inspired by a neoliberal model were enacted in Bolivia, economic policy began to improve and expand international insertion, reducing transaction costs, timelines and risks related to the movement of capital (Rojas and Nina, 2001).

2.1.1 Flows of foreign direct investment in Bolivia

According to Figure 5.1, during the period 2000–2013 FDI to Bolivia shows a fluctuating behavior, recording for the year 2004 USD 448.4 million, the lowest amount during the period, reaching a recovery in 2008 due to the increase in the price of raw materials that generated greater FDI injection, falling in 2009 and returning to growth through 2013, when it reached USD 1,520 million.

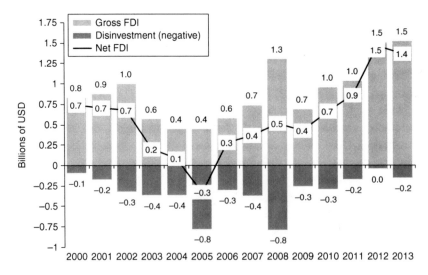

Figure 5.1 Bolivia: Gross foreign direct investment flows
Source: Author's elaboration based on INE, BCB and United Nations data.

2.1.2 Origin of foreign direct investment

Disaggregating by country shows that the primary revenue source of FDI from 2000 to 2008 was the United States (with 46% of the total), several countries in Europe (with 28% of the total) and several South American countries (with 17%). China's FDI in Bolivia represents only 0.09 percent of the total (Figure 5.2).

The share of China's FDI in the Bolivian economy as seen in Figure 5.3 is quite sporadic with small financial sums. During the year 2000 the first Chinese FDI in Bolivia was recorded, with a value of USD 45 million. During the period 2001–2003 no more Chinese FDI in Bolivia were registered.

China's FDI presence in the Bolivian economy did not return until 2004, with a share of USD 30 million accounting for 0.007 percent of the total FDI, down by 33 percent from the figure recorded in 2000. However, from 2005 to 2008, Chinese FDI in Bolivia increased gradually, reaching a peak of USD 2.8 million in 2006, which represented 0.5 percent of total FDI for that year, then decreasing by 38 percent for 2008, to USD 1.8 million. From 2009 to 2013, FDI flows came mainly from Spain (24%), Brazil (19%), Sweden (12%), United Kingdom (7%) and the United States (6%).

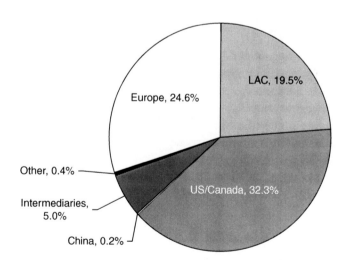

Figure 5.2 Bolivia FDI, according to country of origin, 1999–2008
Source: Authors' calculations based on INE data.
Note: Intermediaries include common pass-through countries, including the Dutch Antilles, the Bahamas, Barbados, Bermuda, the British Virgin Islands, the Cayman Islands, Liechtenstein and Luxembourg. "Other" includes multilateral organizations.

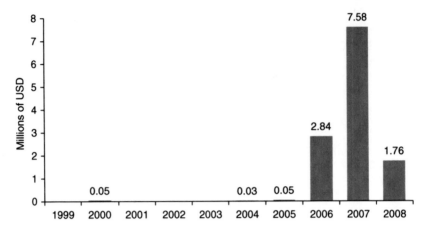

Figure 5.3 Chinese FDI in Bolivia, 1999–2008
Source: Authors' calculations, using INE data 2000–2008.

2.1.3 Destination of FDI in Bolivia

Overall FDI flows have been concentrated in the following sectors: oil, mining and manufacturing, as shown in Figure 5.4. In the five years from 2008 to 2012, FDI into hydrocarbons represented an average of 39 percent of the cumulative total during that period, mining 24 percent, and manufacturing 14 percent.

Beginning in 2000 FDI has been concentrated primarily in the hydrocarbons sector, reaching around USD 4.6 billion. On average from 2000 to 2004, FDI to these sectors represented around 46 percent of the total, followed by other services. This trend is mainly due to both sectors having been capitalized and obliged to reinvest, as in other services such as electricity distribution companies transport and communications.

FDI in the mining sector comprises only 4 percent of the total, since prices of minerals did not provide great benefits for investors until recently. However, during the period of 2005 to 2010 this sector began to respond to price increases. In 2012, mining accounted for 14.5 percent of total FDI inflows.

2.1.4 Incentive policies to attract FDI

Bolivia, through reforms, has introduced a number of incentives for investment, such as a single and uniform tariff of 10 percent applied to all imports of consumer goods, and a tariff of 5 percent on imports of capital goods, compensation mechanisms on export taxes (to ensure tax neutrality), free trade zones both for commerce and industries, and an investment law that stipulates

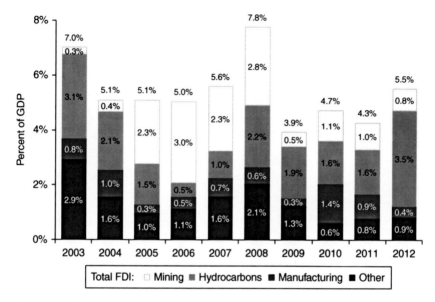

Figure 5.4 Destination of FDI flows in Bolivia, by sector
Source: Authors' calculations using INE and BCB data.
* Production and distribution of electricity, gas and water, construction trade, hotels and restaurants transport storage and communication financial intermediation and others.

equal rights, duties and guarantees to foreign and domestic investors. Bolivian law prohibits discrimination and guarantees freedom of economic activity, provided it does not involve unlawful activity. Other incentives designed to attract FDI include: bilateral agreements to promote and protect investment in the country, economic complementarity agreements and agreements with international guarantee systems.

2.2 Bolivian trade flows with China

Figure 5.5 shows the trade flows between China and Bolivia from 2000 to 2013. In 2013, Bolivia recorded a trade deficit with China of 2.9 percent of GDP (USD 880 million), a decline from the 2012 peak of 3.3 percent of GDP. Recent years' trade deficits with China are due to higher imports of intermediate products for industry and parts and accessories of transport and equipment.

As shown in Figure 5.4, this trend has been recorded since 2000, but until 2005 the gap was much smaller. Since 2009 the deficit has increased substantially. This is mainly because much of the Bolivian exports to China

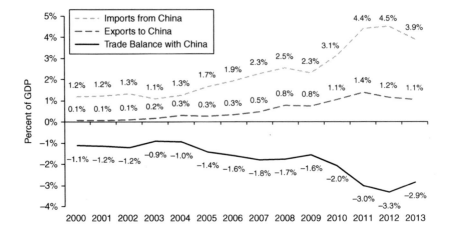

Figure 5.5 Bolivia–China trade balance, 2000–2013
Source: Authors' calculations based on INE, WEO data.
Note: Data are on an FOB basis. China includes Hong Kong, Taiwan and Macao.

are raw mineral materials, while imports from China are mainly manufactures. According to the Central Bank of Bolivia (BCB), between January and November of 2013, Bolivia exported 48 products to China, such as silver ore and concentrates (33% of the total), unwrought unalloyed tin (24%), zinc and its concentrates (16%) and tin and its concentrates (7%). On the other hand, the country bought from China 4,011 products during this period, among which stand out probing and drilling machines (3.5%), motorcycles (3.4%), cell phones (2.8%), and herbicides (1.9%) (INE, 2013).

This trend has major consequences for the manufacturing industry in Bolivia, since over time it is losing its sales position within both the national and international markets. The sale of Chinese manufactured goods has grown exponentially, calling into question the survival of a large number of small and medium-sized enterprises in Bolivia. Another serious threat bears mentioning: remaining stuck in a specialization of primary exports, characterized by very little dynamism.

Moreover, considering the environmental impact of this trend, according to Figure 5.6, Bolivia is exporting to the world products that have an important water footprint, implying a threat to the environment. Bolivian exports to China do not show a different trend from overall exports; the Bolivian water footprint on average was double the water footprint of imports from China, largely because of the trend toward primary goods in the economic relationship with China. Even though the total exports to China do not show a significant jump between 2002 and 2003, in terms of water intensity there is

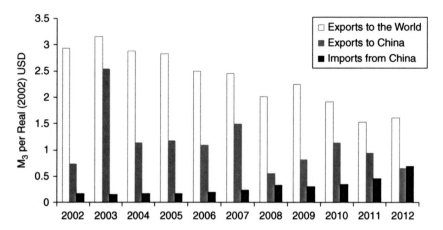

Figure 5.6 Bolivia: Exports according to water average intensity (2002–2012)
Source: Authors' calculations based on Water Footprint Network data.

a notable jump, due to lower export value but higher water use given the nature of Bolivian exports: minerals, leather and textiles. In 2008 the decline in exports' water intensity is not because of lower water use but because of a higher value of Bolivian exports given the increasing prices of raw materials.

Still, China is not considered a key market for Bolivia, as it only represents 2.1 percent of its exports in contrast to Brazil with 31.5 percent, followed by Argentina with 17.7 percent – which can be explained as a result of Bolivian gas sold to Brazil and Argentina (INE, 2013). However, as a supplier to Bolivia, China ranks as the second-largest source of imports with 13.1 percent of the total, after Brazil, which represents 18.4 percent.

2.3 Bolivia's external debt with China

According to data from the Central Bank of Bolivia (BCB), in December 2013, the balance of the debt in Bolivia reached USD 5 billion, an increase of 14.34 percent over December 2012. Over the past 13 years, the debt-to-GDP ratio fell from 53 percent in 2000 to 28 percent in 2006 and to 15 percent in 2012, before rising in 2013 to 17 percent.

Bolivia's bilateral debt to China has been growing since 2001. in small amounts initially, until 2006, when the debt with China was $38.6 million USD (0.3% of GDP), representing an increase of 80 percent in absolute terms or USD 17.2 million over its 2001 level, and in 2010 it reached USD 82.2 million (0.4% of GDP). This trend accelerated during the last few years, reaching USD 430 million (1.5% of GDP) in December 2013, an increase

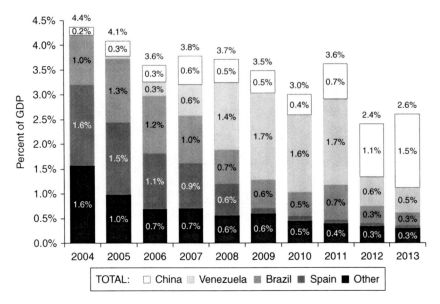

Figure 5.7 Bolivia's bilateral external public debt, 2000–2013
Source: Authors' calculations based on BCB data.

of 423 percent in absolute terms over its 2010 level, as shown in Figure 5.7. By April 2014, China had become the largest bilateral creditor of Bolivia, representing 59 percent of the total of the bilateral debt, according to data from BCB. This growth can be explained by the affinity that the Bolivian government has demonstrated for China, since it has shown support for Bolivia's process of political change.

2.4 Chinese bilateral aid with Bolivia

Relations between Bolivia and China officially began in 1985; following the establishment of bilateral relations, the leaders of both countries have reached agreements to deepen them.

An important area of cooperation is Chinese aid. According to the Chinese embassy in Bolivia, the goal of the funding agency of China is cooperating with all development countries with which China has diplomatic relations, within the following areas: agriculture, water projects, military equipment, health, culture, education, technical cooperation, drilling and environmental protection.

The types of cooperation, all funded by the government of China, are classified as follows:

- Reimbursable Financial Cooperation: these agreements have a term of 10 years with 5 grace years, with a preferential interest rate of 3 percent for loans in renminbi or 15.1 percent for loans in USD, subject to availability by the Chinese government.
- Reimbursable Technical Cooperation: these agreements have a term of 5 years of use, with a 5-year grace period and 10 years of repayment, without any interest or commission.
- Non-Reimbursable Technical Cooperation: these agreements are grants to support human capital, technology and equipment, subject to availability by the Chinese government.

Within this framework, Bolivia has signed more than 400 agreements with China, including economic, technical and agricultural cooperation and financial and telecommunications development, and even assistance in energy, mining, infrastructure and food security issues.

During the last few years, China has also lent equipment to the armed forces of Bolivia for the development of a communications satellite, supported the industrialization of lithium reserves, granted 21 million Yuan (USD 3 million) for the execution of projects of investment and purchase of capital, China-made machinery and other goods. There are agreements of strategic cooperation between the Bolivian and Chinese ministries of agrarian development and agriculture, to deploy tasks for research and transfer in the improvement of agricultural production in Bolivia.

At the financial level, the China Development Bank established a consortium with the Bolivian State Bank Union, a fund involving an initial USD 10 million in capital.

3. The Bolivian Mining Sector

3.1 Division between private and public sectors

The mining industry in Bolivia is structured by two sectors: state-owned and private.

3.1.1 State sector

Before the reforms introduced in 1985, COMIBOL was one of the most important state-owned enterprises in the mining sector supply chain – reforms that decentralized it and restricted its functions to managing joint-venture contracts, leases and services with mining companies or cooperatives (Espinoza, 2010). Since 2006, Bolivia has taken the first steps to recover natural resources.

With S. D. 28901, COMIBOL assumed total control of the mining deposits of the Empresa Minera Huanuni, cancelling the contract with the private company RBG Minera S. A.

In 2007, through Law 3720, COMIBOL was empowered to participate directly in the productive chain through prospecting, exploration, mining, concentration, smelting, refining and commercialization of minerals and metals, as well as managing areas declared to be fiscal reserves, in order to increase the state presence in the mining sector (Sanabria, 2009). Currently, the company performs extractive mining operations, producing 600 to 700 tons per month of tin concentrates whose value is about USD 620 million, and supporting 4,560 jobs.

However, despite COMIBOL's expansion, the institution has presented several cases of corruption, among the most well-known being the case of the Mutún Steel Company, where COMIBOL had hidden information about the price premium on the purchase of land for the concessionary Indian company, Jindal, with a cost to the state of more than USD 2 million (http://www.noticiasfides.net).

3.1.2 Private sector

The structure of the private sector within the Bolivian mining industry consists of two subsectors: medium- and small-scale mining.

Medium-scale mining is organized through the National Association of Medium-Scale Mining (ANMM) involving 14 active companies. The goal of ANMM is to ensure the development of the mining industry and uphold its interests. This sector, unlike small industry, has ample access to financing from the banking system, allowing better technology and other aspects that are critical to minerals operations.

Small-scale mining is divided into two categories: small miners and mining cooperatives. Cooperatives are self-managed units that operate in private areas and leased sites (originally owned and managed by COMIBOL). They are grouped into regional and departmental associations that make up the National Federation of Mining Cooperatives (FENCOMIN). FENCOMIN includes about 635 mining cooperatives that bring together approximately 65,890 members. An important subsector includes producers in arid places, riverbeds and producers of boron in the Salar de Uyuni, which are grouped into Regional Chambers and Department of Mining, which make up the National Mining Chamber (CANALMIN).

Workers of both medium-scale mining and small-scale mining are organized through 42 unions in the Federation of Mine Workers of Bolivia (FSTMB).

3.2 Institutional structure

The Ministry of Mining and Metallurgy is primarily responsible for the definition and implementation of policies and standards that form the framework for the metallurgical mining activities in Bolivia.

The Mining Code establishes the Superintendent of Mines as the highest authority of the administrative jurisdiction mining. The superintendent's powers are: (a) to hear and resolve appeals filed against decisions of the regional superintendents, who are responsible for granting mining concessions on behalf of the state and resolving administrative case opposition under invalidity, expropriation, bondage, resignation and resource recalls; (b) to ensure proper implementation of mining jurisdiction; and (c) to appoint or remove officials of the general superintendence and regional superintendent offices.

3.2.1 Legal framework for mining

Mining activities in Bolivia are regulated by two sets of rules: general and complementary.

Among the general rules, until May 2014 the basic regulation was the Mining Code, established in 1997 (Law 1777). In May 2014, the Bolivian government established the new Law of Mining and Metallurgy 535 with the goal of diversifying investments and supporting the entire supply chain of mining industrialization.

The main changes in Law 535 from the previous law (1777) are as follows:

• Historically, mining law in Bolivia was developed by foreign consultants and established by political imposition, but according to the Bolivian government, the new law is, for the first time, the result of consensus among the representatives of the small, cooperative, private and state-owned mining sectors. In May 2014, at a roll-out event for the new law in the Department of Oruro, Acting President Álvaro García Linera said that this law had the "smell" of the Bolivian worker, after three years of building consensuses between the representatives of the operators of the small, cooperative, private and state mining (ABI, 2014).
• Law 535 prioritizes mining expansion through greater logistical and tax preferences (exemption from payment of all taxes, except royalties) for cooperatives.
• It expands the authority of the Ministry of Mining and Metallurgy over mining and the resolution of mining-related conflicts.
• In order of hierarchy, the state mining sector (COMIBOL) is given priority, followed by local private operators and finally foreign operators.

- Unlike the previous law, under the new law mining concessions are not transferable.
- It establishes that mining activities must fulfill a socioeconomic function and comply with principles of sustainability.

Turning to complementary regulations, the most important is Environmental Law 1333, issued in 1992, which states that mining and extractive operations should be developed with consideration for the comprehensive utilization of raw materials, waste treatment and the safe disposal of tails, tailings and connectors. In addition, during and after operations, firms must plan for the recovery of affected areas in order to reduce and control erosion, stabilize the land and protect water sources. It also sets out that "in each of its operations or mining concessions, dealers or mine operators must have an environmental license for their mining activities" (Art. 2).

The new Constitution of the Plurinational State of Bolivia, established in 2009, is another important aspect of the legal framework. Among its most relevant statements, it provides that:

- Natural resources are directly owned by, and within the indivisible and essential domain of, the Bolivian people and will be for the state to administer in the service of the collective interest. (Art. 349, No. 1, authors' translation)
- The state will assume oversight and management over exploration, extraction, processing, transportation and marketing of strategic natural resources through public, cooperative, or community bodies, which may in turn contract with private companies and form joint ventures. (Art. 351, No. 1, authors' translation)
- The state may enter into partnership with legal entities, be they Bolivian or foreign, for the use of natural resources. It must ensure the reinvestment of profits in the country. (Art. 351, No. 2, authors' translation)
- The use of natural resources in a given territory will be subject to a consultation process with the affected population, called by the state, which will be free, prior and informed. Citizen participation is guaranteed in the process of environmental management and conservation of ecosystems, in agreement with the Constitution and the law. This shall take place in accordance with their own rules and procedures. (Art. 352, authors' translation)

3.2.2 Tax policy framework

The mining sector tax system is established in the Mining Code, and consists of three items: Mining Royalties (MR), the Profit Taxes on Company Profits (IUE) and the windfall tax in addition to IUE (AA-IUE). Another group of taxes includes the Value-Added Tax (IVA), Transactions Tax (IT), and the Specific Consumption Tax (ICE).

Characteristics of the tax law include:

- Mining royalties (MR) are defined according to the type of mineral and prices, and are on average 5 percent on gross sale value. However, for the cooperative mining sector it is reduced to 3 percent – in keeping with the new, more favorable legal framework given to the cooperative sector by the new political constitution of the state, in light of its socioeconomic function. (ERBOL, May 2014)
- Eighty-five percent of MR revenue goes to departmental governments, which must invest at least 10 percent in mining-related prospecting, exploration, industrialization and environmental monitoring. The remaining 15 percent goes to municipal governments.
- The cooperative mining sector is exempt from IUE, IVA, ICE and IT taxes.
- The annual cost per grid for concessions less than 6 years old is USD 25.
- The IUE is 25 percent of annual net profit and is applicable to all companies that extract, produce, benefit, refine and/or commercialize minerals and/or metals.
- The AA-IUE is 12.5 percent of annual net profit. The AA-IUE must be paid for the mining companies that have had windfall profits from price spikes above a certain level, such as USD 400 per troy ounce of gold, USD 5.55 per troy ounce of silver, or USD 2.90 per pound of tin.[1]

MR revenue has grown in recent years, from its 2000 level of about USD 8 million (0.1% of GDP) to USD 168 million in 2011 (0.7% of GDP).

3.2.3 Environmental management

Environmental issues in Bolivia are closely related to mining, which contributes to the continued deterioration of ecosystems, in turn negatively impacting socioeconomic activities (Gutierrez, 2009). According to J. E. Morales (2010), pollution from refineries or steel plants around the discharge becomes contaminated with sulfur, chemical reagents and other organic materials, whose negative effects directly and indirectly impact society and the surrounding ecosystem.

In spite of the legal environmental protections listed above (including Environmental Law No. 1333, which dictates that mining projects must consider treatment factors and possible pollution sources and plan for remediation,

---

1 For the complete list, see http://www.lexivox.org/norms/BO-L-3787.xhtml

and the Mining Code and Mining Law 535, which state that mining activities should adhere to principles of sustainable development), evidence indicates that mining pollution is still rampant. In recent years there have been several studies from various disciplines regarding the environmental impacts of mining in Bolivia. The results show significant environmental liabilities. Some medium-scale mining companies have improved their practices, but not all of them. The cooperatives, which have an overwhelming number of members and exploit thousands of camps, do not practice environmental remediation. Also, according to data in *El Día* (July 2014), there are 450 cooperative mining companies, but of those 80 percent do not have an environmental license and are operating illegally. For its part, the public COMIBOL has not set a strong example in its operation of Huanuni, which had net income of USD 70.4 million through 2009; it has not yet built a tailings dam to address major contamination affecting about 40 communities (Sanabria, 2009; Michard J., 2008; CEDIB, 2012).

One of the merits attributed to royalties from the environmental point of view is that royalties are in fact an "ad valorem" tax on production. Under the assumption that extraction costs increase with the amount that has already been extracted, this type of tax reduces the rate of mineral extraction and its associated pollution externalities. However, the IUE does not have a depletion allowance, and so it does not alter the rate of extraction or associated externalities (Muzondo, 1993).

3.3 The importance of the mining sector in Bolivia

Bolivia is one of the least developed and poorest countries in Latin America: 45 percent of its population lives below the national poverty line, with 21 percent living in extreme poverty (INE, 2011). The numbers are even worse for rural areas, with 61 percent in poverty and 41 percent living in extreme poverty.

Historically, Bolivia has seen a series of resource booms exploited by foreign interests and by a tiny Bolivian elite: silver, then tin, then oil and gas. The real benefits of the wealth taken from the ground went not to the Bolivian people as a whole, but to others. For example, the rise of the silver at the end of the nineteenth century left Bolivia an average of just 4 percent of the value of what was exported from the country. The present case appears to be an extension of this historical trend. State MR and IUE revenues from 1990 to 2005 reached just 2.3 percent of the value of mineral exports. From 2006 to 2010 it rose, but to just 8 percent; from USD 8.686 billion exported, the state received just USD 729.4 million (Diaz,

V. 2011). Moreover, according to ECLAC (2012), in Bolivia, every million dollars invested from FDI supports just one position of direct employment, less than the 2.5 supported in South America overall and the 6.4 supported in the Caribbean. Thus, the adverse effects of FDI concentrated in natural resources exploitation outweigh the benefits in revenue and employment. Such a curious outcome for a country extremely rich in natural resources but poor in terms of the benefits received from them is referred to as a "resource curse" in the literature. A resource curse also implies economic, social and political damage, which is soon joined by environmental destruction, depending on the source of the natural resource and on negative multiplier effects from that destruction.

The mining sector's share of GDP is crucial to the Bolivian economy, as illustrated by Figure 5.8. From 1995 to 2005, the mining sector contributed between 3 and 4.8 percent of Bolivia's GDP, but from 2006 to 2009 it began growing, thanks to higher international prices (INE, 2009). The sector shows a declining trend during recent years, dropping from 9.6 percent in 2011 to 6.3 percent in 2013. This decline reflects a collapse in prices and production due to the global financial crisis. This boom in prices and production is mainly due to the demand for raw materials by emerging economies such as China.

As shown in Table 5.1, mining revenues in the 1990s were very low. However, starting in 2005 this changed, with royalty revenues reaching USD 168 million and tax revenue reaching USD 338.3 million in 2011, due to a favorable trend in international mineral prices.

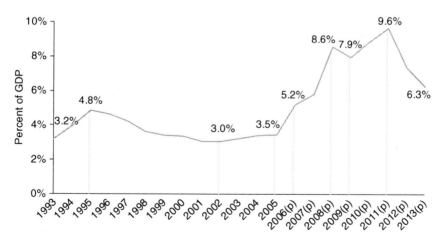

Figure 5.8 Bolivia: Mining as a share of GDP, 2000–2013
Source: Authors' calculations using INE data.

Table 5.1 Bolivian mining royalties and taxes (1990–2011)

	In Millions of USD			As Percent of GDP		
	Royalties	IUE, Other Taxes	Total	Royalties	IUE, Other Taxes	Total
1990	9.5		9.5	0.2%		0.2%
1991	7.5		7.5	0.1%		0.1%
1992	8.1		8.1	0.1%		0.1%
1993	3.5		3.5	0.1%		0.1%
1994	4.6	0.1	4.8	0.1%	0.0%	0.1%
1995	4.9	1.3	6.2	0.1%	0.0%	0.1%
1996	6.2	1.1	7.3	0.1%	0.0%	0.1%
1997	11.0	0.6	11.7	0.1%	0.0%	0.1%
1998	8.5	3.3	11.8	0.1%	0.0%	0.1%
1999	7.4	5.8	13.2	0.1%	0.1%	0.2%
2000	8.0	10.7	18.7	0.1%	0.1%	0.2%
2001	6.7	11.8	18.5	0.1%	0.1%	0.2%
2002	6.3	12.5	18.9	0.1%	0.2%	0.2%
2003	6.2	20.5	26.8	0.1%	0.3%	0.3%
2004	9.9	23.5	33.4	0.1%	0.3%	0.4%
2005	14.3	44.2	58.5	0.1%	0.5%	0.6%
2006	48.0	57.2	105.2	0.4%	0.5%	0.9%
2007	68.7	96.5	165.2	0.5%	0.7%	1.3%
2008	94.1	132.5	226.7	0.6%	0.8%	1.3%
2009	82.6	112.9	195.5	0.5%	0.6%	1.1%
2010 P	120.7	239.4	360.1	0.6%	1.2%	1.8%
2011 P	168.0	338.3	506.3	0.7%	1.4%	2.1%

P: Preliminary estimate.
Source: Statistics of the Ministry of Mining and Metallurgy, IMF WEO database.

Mineral exports, shown in Figure 5.8, have been growing rapidly. Zinc, tin and silver have grown most quickly, in response to higher European demand as well as higher international prices, while gold, copper, lead and antimony recorded major declines. The highest value of exports came in 2011 (14.3% of GDP), as shown in Figure 5.9, as a result of a global boom in raw materials, starting in 2004.

4. Environmental and Social Impacts Assessment of Chinese Funding in the Bolivian Mining Industry

This section evaluates two case studies with Chinese participation, following the net benefits framework developed by Zarsky and Stanley (2013). Both cases are located in the country's southwestern department of Potosí, which has the highest poverty rate (around 85%, UDAPE 2013) and the highest proportionate indigenous population in Bolivia. Potosí is representative of how

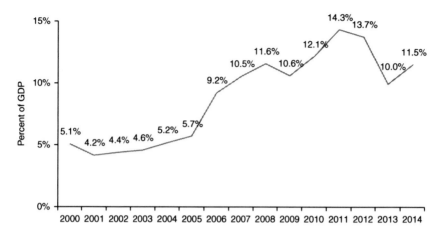

Figure 5.9 Exports of Bolivian minerals
Source: Authors' calculations based on INE data.

the resource booms of the past (in silver and tin) did not bring sustained eco-nomic development to the local population.

3.2 Case study 1: Canutillos mine and processing plant

The northeastern part of the department of Potosi is primarily a mining area. The region has an important number of mining companies, mostly in the cooperative sector. Given the significant increase in international prices of minerals discussed above, the mining sector is growing and, with it, new min-ing companies are emerging.

As mentioned above, under the government of President Evo Morales cooperative mining companies receive preferential treatment. Chinese entre-preneurs have reacted to this situation by undertaking agreements with local mining cooperatives. In this context, in February 2010 a joint venture agreement was signed between the Jungie Mining Industry SRL (Chinese-owned, although currently Bolivian-managed) and the mining cooperative Alto Canutillos, under Resolution 4295TH /2010, with the support of the COMIBOL, with the objective of exploring and developing diverse minerals, but particularly tin in the Canutillos mine. The Alto Canutillos cooperative, consisting of 22 members, submitted a bid to Jungie SRL, seeking a part-ner who could bring technology and financing for their development of the Canutillos mine. Daniel Morales Muruchi, former leader of the Cooperative Minera Alto Canutillos, became Jungie SRL's legal representative, and the company started operations in late December 2012.

The Canutillos mine is located 48 kilometers northeast of Potosí city, in Tacobamba Municipality. Around the mine are located towns of Tacobamba, Colavi, Rodeo, Hahuacari and Ancoma, belonging to Tacobamba municipality, with a total population of 13,205 inhabitants; 61.38 percent of the population live on the margins of poverty, while 32.89 percent live in extreme poverty and just 0.06 percent have their basic needs met (INE 2001). Communities have found their source of income around the mine, and also from agricultural products, such as potatoes, wheat and corn; raising sheep, goats and camelids. Mining in the town of Tacobamba is developed by private companies, including Jungie Mining Industry SRL.

3.2.1 Public consultation

The net benefits approach places paramount importance on individual and collective public consultation with the affected population before the development of a natural resource begins. Furthermore, according to the New Constitution, communities own the territory around where they live. In the case of Jungie SRL, this process appears to have served its purpose, resulting in the company changing its plans and locating its refining plant and tailings dam near a more receptive community.

Accordingly, once the Jungie–Alto Canutillos joint entity was constituted, it conducted surveys in the surrounding communities belonging to the Municipality of Tacobamba before beginning construction of the processing plant and tailings dam necessary for mining. The surveys indicated that the community was not willing to accept the construction of a mineral processing plant and tailings dam, arguing that the construction of this facility would generate pollution.

Therefore, based on the majority decision by the communities living around the mine, neither plant nor the tailings dam was built there. Instead, Jungie SRL. built the minerals processing plant and tailings dam in the Agua Dulce community 5 km from the city of Potosí. The land was donated by the COMIBOL under consultation with the municipality of Villa de Yocalla (specifically, the community of Agua Dulce), which has a population of 10,012 (INE, 2001). It has a very low human development, with an average living standard below the departmental average, a poverty rate of 63 percent, and a subsistence-level economy of the inhabitants. The source of income of the population of the Municipality of Yocalla village is based on agriculture and livestock farming, so land is the fundamental basis of the livelihood of the family unit.

According to the leaders of the community of Agua Dulce, a public consultation was carried out to determine if the population was willing to accept the building of the processing plant in their community. The response was favorable, given that the people had high expectations for job creation and income for the community.

3.2.2 Economic benefits of mine bookbinding treatment plant in Agua Dulce

Jungie SRL has been working on the site since 2010. But according to interviews with officials from Jungie SRL, the company is still in the testing phase and will begin producing in 2015, so it has not yet generated revenue to pay royalties and taxes to the state. Its investment budget includes plans to invest around USD 20 million, of which USD 5.5 million is to be invested in mining equipment, USD 6.5 million in the processing plant, USD 4.3 million in processing equipment and nearly USD 2.1 million in the tailings dam.

The company has a 20-year concession, with an expected annual production capacity of 300,000 tons; the plant has a production capacity of 2,500 tons per day. One of the benefits being generated by the company is employment for members of the cooperative and the community, where about 50 families live (INE, 2001), of which 30 have members working in the mine. Workers at the mine have monthly salaries between USD 250 and 900, with health insurance (but not life insurance), and appropriate work clothing (which is given every three months), according to workers. However, some press reports from the Bolivian Supreme Justice Court (2013–2014)[2] have printed complaints accusing Jungie Mining Industry of abuse and workers' rights violations, such as disregarding rules regarding overtime and nursing breaks.

In sum, the community allowed the company to operate in its territory under certain conditions, including: hiring people living around the plant, primarily in the community of Agua Dulce, building hospitals and schools and other infrastructure to attract commerce to the community. Such an arrangement has local precedent. According to the Civic Committee of Potosí, the large majority of foreign mining companies build roads, schools, hospitals and basic services to gain the community approval required under the New Constitution.

3.2.3 Royalty revenue

Under the joint venture agreement, 7.5 percent of profits go to the cooperative, 12.5 percent go COMIBOL and 80 percent go to Jungie. The joint entity must also pay mining royalties (MR), of which 85 percent goes to the departmental government and 15 percent goes to the municipal governments; the

---

2 See: http//tribunalsupremo.organojudicial.gob.bo/Autos%20Supremos/social/social-II/2014/as201432333b.htmlyhttp://trbunalsupremo.organojudicial.gob.bo/Autos%20Supremos/soaicl/social/2013/as201331540.html

provincial government is minimally required to invest 10 percent in exploration and prospecting; and the Taxes on Company Profits (IUE) levy 25 percent of annual net profit.

3.2.4 Environmental hazards

Even though Jungie Mining SRL started activities in 2010, the company did
not get its environmental license until April 2014. This is an explicit violation
of article 218 in the new mining law, which requires environmental licenses for
all mining activities and projects.

As the company has not entered the operational phase, its environmental
impacts are not yet observable. However, it is expected to have considerable
size and impact, comparable to the publicly run COMIBOL Huanuni mine.
Huanuni is one of the most important in the region, with a net income of
USD 70.4 million between 2006 and 2009. However, it neglected to build a
tailings dam to prevent pollution entering the Huanuni River, which serves 40
communities. This neglect provides a troublesome precedent for mines' water
management in the area, and for the government to enforce its own standards.

Though Jungie SRL plans currently do include a tailings dam, the company has not thus far demonstrated adherence to environmental standards,
as evidenced by its delay in acquiring its environmental license. Furthermore,
although Jungie SRL is still in the testing phase, complaints about pollution
are already emerging. In mid-2014 the residents of Agua Dulce complained
to Potosí authorities about leakage of acidic water from the tailings from the
Jungie SRL into the Jayaj Mayu River, which is essential for farming, ranching
and local community members.

In addition to pollution, one of the biggest impacts will be on water consumption; the company estimates a monthly consumption of 2,465 cubic
meters (651,184 gallons) of water. Although it is still in its testing phase, Jungie
SRL's water use has already damaged local harvests. Felipa Aguirre, one of
the affected people in the town, explains that during this period agricultural
production in the area was almost zero because of a lack of water for irrigation or consumption. Agriculture had to rely on rainwater, and most of the
crops were dry. As of this writing, the company faces trial and its operations
are suspended until remediation is completed.

3.3 Case study 2: Lithium industrialization process
   at the Salar de Uyuni

In the context of these discouraging experiences in the management and use of
mining resources in Bolivia, the country is currently facing a new challenge: it

possesses probably the largest deposits of lithium in the world, which are still unexploited. At the heart of Bolivia's lithium development efforts is a simple goal: to lift people out of poverty by achieving the maximum benefit possible from a natural resource that connects the nation to the cutting edge of global markets. But there is still no clear mechanism to achieve that goal and avoid a new "resource curse."

About 80 percent of the known global lithium reserve base is located in the "Lithium Triangle," an area bordered by the three large South American salt flats: the Salar de Atacama, in Chile, the Salar de Uyuni, in Bolivia, and the Salar del Hombre Muerto, in Argentina. With governments around the globe demanding increased fuel efficiency to reduce their dependence on fossil fuel, private foreign firms are intensively pursuing access to Bolivia's lithium. The US Geological Survey (USGS) estimates Bolivia's lithium reserves to be 5.4 million tons, nearly twice that of Chile. The reserve base is found principally in the Salar de Uyuni, a 3,860-square-mile desert plateau (altiplano) area of the Bolivian Andes located in the department of Potosí, the same department as in the Jungie mining case. Salar de Uyuni is the largest salt flat in the world and the brightest object on the earth's surface visible from space.

3.3.1 Population and economic activity

The Salar de Uyuni basin occupies approximately 61 percent of the Department of Potosí in Bolivia. The 2011 estimated population of the basin was 42,098 people. The most populated towns in the study area are Uyuni and Colcha "K." The most common employment sectors in the basin are quinoa agriculture (only 10% of the land is suitable for agriculture, but the activity occupies 80% of the population) and camelid livestock (which occupies 60% of the land use). The Salar de Uyuni is also one of Bolivia's main tourist centers, attracting some 50,000 visitors a year, as well as being a fragile ecosystem with many indigenous species (Revenga and Kura 2003). Tourism, which provides a living for 23 percent of the population, relies on these untouched landscapes. In addition, a further 12 percent of the population makes a living directly from the salt harvest. Usually land, climate, water and vegetation conditions force the communities to combine these economic activities to cover their basic needs.

3.3.2 The Bolivian lithium industrialization strategy

Bolivia's lithium strategy dates to 1974 when the government, through Supreme Decree (SD) 11674, highlighted the importance of natural resources at the southeast of Bolivia and declared the Uyuni Basin to be a Fiscal Reserve. This status, still in place today, gives the Bolivian state ownership of the Salar and the legal right to exploit and administer all of the natural resources within the reserve's boundaries. Legislation in 2008 (SD 29496) declared the development of natural resources from the Salar de Uyuni to be a national priority, with the specific goal of supporting economic and social development in Potosí. In the same vein, COMIBOL created then the National Directorate of Evaporitic Resources (renamed in 2010 as the National Management Committee for Evaporitic Resources, GNRE). This body will manage around USD 5.7 million for natural resources development at the Salar de Uyuni. Within GNRE a scientific advisory committee was created, bringing together experts from universities, private companies and governments to share knowledge without having to commit to any long-term partnerships.

Since 2006, foreign corporations and governments, including Brazil, Canada, Japanese automakers and the French electric car manufacturer, Bolloré, have lobbied the Bolivian government for access to the lithium resources. Bolivia's current diplomatic tensions with Washington have left American companies on the sidelines as other foreign enterprises continue to actively negotiate lithium deals in Bolivia.

Box 5.1 Bolivian Lithium Industrialization Strategy

The strategy consists of three phases:

Phase 1: Pilot Plants

Development of infrastructure, installation and setup of the state pilot plants for lithium carbonate (LCE) and potassium chloride:

- The pilot LCE plant, located in Llipi, was initiated in September 2012 and opened in February 2013, with a projected capacity of 40 tons per month.
- Infrastructure was built for 30 pieces of equipment in 2,600 square meters.
- 2,000 km of roads were built between Llipi and the evaporation pools.
- Production of LCE is now being concentrated for future sales and, in particular, for the pilot plant of lithium ion batteries in La Palca.

Phase 2: Industrial Production

Industrial Plants design:

- Financing will be provided by the Bolivian Central Bank (BCB).
- Evaporation pools will be built.
- The lithium industrial plant was expected to produce 40,000 to 60,000 tons per year of LCE starting in 2014 (COMIBOL, 2008; La Razón, 2009).

Phase 3: Production of Ion Lithium Batteries (with LCE as a main ingredient)

- Training, experimentation and production of lithium ion batteries and other lithium products, performed by qualified Bolivian workers trained in China and elsewhere (21 workers as of this writing).
- Completed: Purchasing of turnkey technology.
- Contract with the Chinese firm Lin Yi Dake Trade Co. Ltda. to buy a pilot plant for lithium ion batteries, to be installed at La Palca in an area of 1,600 square meters. This contract was signed in May 2012, with 10 technicians working in the installation.
- Production capacity of the pilot plant: 1,200 Ah/day.
- Expected production: 1,000 cellphone batteries per day, 40 batteries for use in electric vehicles.
- Total cost: USD 3.7 million.
- Job creation expected: 35 direct and 100 indirect jobs.
- Partnership or association with foreign enterprises will be sought in order to generate technology transfer.
- January 2014: Inauguration of Pilot Plant of Batteries in La Palca.

Source: Authors' elaboration based on 2012, 2013 reports from GNRE.

3.3 The net benefits approach applied to the Bolivian lithium industrialization process

3.3.1 Local acceptance of the lithium industrialization process

The main towns involved in the lithium industrialization process are the ones bordering the Uyuni Salt Lake: Colcha-K, Uyuni, Tahua and Llipi. Their high poverty rates are the worst in the department of Potosí: in

LLica and Tahua, 89 percent and 99.7 percent of population living in poverty, respectively, according to the unsatisfied basic needs method (CNPV, 2001).

This context has promoted a mixed reaction to lithium development. Some groups and communities in the region openly support lithium development as an opportunity for increased income and development. But there are also important local groups with serious objections to such development. Quinoa producers and tourism operators have expressed concern about supposed benefits that the Bolivian government has promised from lithium, claiming that the benefits are irrelevant to local needs and could easily damage the three key activities in the region – agriculture, cattle ranching and tourism (Ströbele-Gregor, 2013). Moreover, many different international actors have tried to exploit the Salar de Uyuni's mineral riches in the past. But each time, local communities have mobilized to fight what they see as giveaway by corrupt political interests. One of the foreign players forced out of the Salar (by the communities and by a proposed new national tax on the company) was Bolivia's first serious foreign lithium suitor, the US company, Food Machinery Chemical (FMC), formerly known as Lithco.

In this context, and after conducting surveys in the surrounding towns and interviewing key actors (such as the Comite Civico and local authorities) our conclusion is that the willingness to accept the project in the area is very low, for two main reasons: first, potential negative social, economic and environmental impacts; and secondly, the reluctance for foreign investors' participation given the history of exploitation of national natural resources.

3.3.2 Economic benefits

According to Meridian Research Group (MRG) estimates, the concentration of lithium varies widely across the Salar, so production would be concentrated in small areas. The MRG report finds that the structure of the Salar de Uyuni is very different to the Salar de Atacama (Chile), that the quality of lithium available per unit surface is much lower and that a correspondingly greater area of the Salar would have to be exploited for an equivalent lithium production (Meridian Research Group, 2008).

The report concludes that, considering the real grade and distribution of lithium in the Uyuni, its lithium might not be a particularly attractive resource and that the real exploitable reserve could be only approximately 300,000 tons rather than the estimated millions. Moreover, the available methods for mining could be highly environmentally damaging.

3.3.3 Royalties and taxes

Enormous expectations have been generated regarding possible future profits, together with demands for their redistribution. However, neither the Bolivian government nor the Chinese company has reported on the income from the pilot plants. It is also important to highlight that the yearly contribution of the mining sector to the public revenues has already increased significantly between 2006 and 2011, from 0.9 to 2.1 percent of GDP (Ministry of Mining, 2013).

The positive impact of lithium development on human well-being is mainly due to employment opportunities and the general contribution to economic activity in the municipality and the country. However, with regard to the former point, it should be noted that the workforce available in the municipalities is mainly unskilled, so the potential for their participation in mining activities is uncertain. At the pilot plant of ion lithium batteries installed by the Chinese company Lin Yi Dake in La Palca, currently 21 qualified Bolivian professionals work in diverse areas; GNRE estimates that the projected activities at this plant will support 35 direct and around 100 indirect jobs.

At this stage, there are no documented plans for investments by either the private enterprise or the Bolivian government. It is also well known that with regard to the exploitation of lithium reserves in Potosí, the history of resource conflict in Bolivia indicates strongly that the potential for conflict is indeed major. The local indigenous population and the mine workers in Potosí are well organized but are looking for short-term rewards.

3.3.4 Environmental risk

Serious potential environmental problems stemming from lithium mining in Bolivia cannot be ignored. Bolivia's ecologically fragile Salar de Uyuni could become an environmental disaster if sufficient precautions are not taken. Also, lithium development could seriously damage three main activities – agriculture, cattle ranching and tourism. There is already information that in southwest Potosí, the legally protected Eduardo Avaroa Reserve has already been contaminated by evaporitic resource operations (Aguilar, 2009).

Many Bolivian and international environmental organizations question the adequacy of Bolivia's environmental strategy for lithium development in southwest Potosí. The effects of lithium production on the ecosystem, apart from the destruction of natural habitat, would come primarily in the form of water use (due to the creation of evaporation pools) and pollution of water and air by the chemical processing of the lithium. The water reserves of the Salar de Uyuni are classified as nonrenewable, as the groundwater regenerates only extremely slowly. Moreover, there is already a shortage of water in the region today (Aguilar, 2009; Hollender and Shultz, 2010).

Already, there is clear evidence of the competition for water in southwest Potosí between mining operations and crop irrigation (Aguilar, 2009). Another competing force is the tourism industry, although its water demands have not been directly analyzed. Even more alarmingly, there are 90 active mining concessions around the Salar that already rely on the region's water resources. The most exploitative of these concessions is the San Cristobal Mine, concentrated on extracting tin, silver and zinc; which will be a certain competitor for fresh water and salt water from the Rio Grande.

In the face of all of these risks, the Chinese company Lin Yi Dake has not published any measures or plans to confront environmental deterioration. Thus, after describing the main components of the net benefits approach, the results show that the lithium industrialization process does not meet the standard of weak sustainability; the expected social and economic benefits are low and unlikely to outweigh social and environmental costs.

4. Policy Recommendations

Currently, the Bolivian economy is currently very dynamic and in good health. Especially noteworthy is that the Net International Reserves (NIR) of the country amounted to USD 14.43 billion in December 2013. For 2012, the last year for which the World Bank has this data, Bolivian reserves amounted to 14.6 months of national imports (placing Bolivia in sixth place worldwide) and 201.5 percent of national debt (placing it in eighth place worldwide). The IMF, ECLAC and World Bank, among others praise the strong economic performance of the country.

Certainly the Bolivian economy has benefited from high world fuel prices, mainly through exports of natural gas to Brazil and Argentina. Moreover, the increase in the price of raw material exports allowed the income of the public sector to increase significantly. At the same time, Bolivia's policy of income redistribution has also been relevant, since it ensures that these benefits are broadly shared through an improvement of the minimum wage and social programs that have an impact on poverty reduction. FDI flows seem to continue coming to Bolivia given the confidence created by the economic scenario. However, the weak institutional framework is still a deep and remaining problem.

For example, in relation with the important NIR, they certainly provide economic and financial stabilization to the country, support the confidence in its currency, guarantee its imports, prevent external imbalances and maintain the trust to honor the external debt. But why not create a stabilization fund to manage these important natural resources' revenues as done in Chile or Norway? That is a recurrent suggestion, but the mechanisms of savings, spending or even determining which entities will be responsible for its management are not easy to define. Overall, the lack of an institutional framework in the country is the main problem. Indeed, having strong public institutions would allow the state to earn a reputation of credibility for its management of fiscal policy and to guarantee successful management of the stabilization fund. However, Bolivia is not institutionally ready for such a step. In this weak institutional context, the presence of increasing Chinese trade flows and investments imply opportunities but also important threats and challenges for the country.

Overall, the growth of China's exports and its uneven commercial relationship with Bolivia create threats to Bolivian industries such as textiles and footwear, which face stiff competition. Bolivia should apply preventive measures, protecting its products, but also applying proactive measures, such as the promotion of production; imitating some policies of China, such as creating the conditions for greater FDI and promoting productivity to defend the spaces of the domestic market.

Turning now to Chinese investment in Bolivia, this FDI is highly concentrated in natural-resource-intensive sectors – hydrocarbons, mining, transport and basic services – with scarce labor requirements and domestic input demand. In this aspect Chinese FDI is not much different from general trends of FDI inflows into Bolivia in further promoting the deindustrialization of the economy mainly due to the high profitability that the development of raw materials offers today, despite the environmental and social impacts and the limitations in oversight and enforcement of human and worker rights. The Canutillos Mine study case illustrates this clearly: even though the Chinese company, Jungie SRL, just recently started activities, it has already faced recurring environmental and social troubles.

One of the most basic truths of the resource curse is the prospect that when a government suddenly has a great deal of financial resources, there is no guarantee that the people will end up any better off. To those allied with the nation's leaders, new revenues become an incentive for corruption and unsustainable exploitation of natural resources. Bolivia, unfortunately, is still an example of this, especially concerning the potentially devastating impact that mining activities may have on the region's environment. This is a concern that the Bolivian government is not treating seriously; environmental issues are taking a back seat to political alliances such as those with the cooperative mining sector, which is exempt from most of the taxes and has a bad record on environmental issues. The recent contamination of Pilcomayo River by mining operators in Potosí (including Jungie) shows that the government does not have the institutional capacity or the political will to monitor these activities.

Our case study of Jungie, still in its testing stage, already shows significant environmental problems. First the mine's high water demand threatens the natural and human future of the surroundings. Moreover, if industrial-scale mining is the objective, the result will likely be permanent, contaminated tailings that threaten local soil and water quality. The environmental impact of mining also affects the local socioeconomic activities in the production areas through negative effects on the productive activity of local communities near mining operations. Canutillos, one of the oldest mining locations in Potosí, is still one of the poorest and more environmentally degraded towns.

How can we improve environmental outcomes from FDI and Chinese FDI in the mining sector? In particular:

- A national incentive-based mining policy for environmental protection.
- A participatory process to identify and formulate measures for production improvement and environmental mitigation.
- An environmental adjustment program adapted to the socioeconomic reality of small-scale mining, including pilot projects of design, construction and operation of dams.
- Promotion of sustainable technologies, raising environmental awareness through transparency of the results of environmental diagnosis studies and the communication of environmental regulations.

On the other hand, Chinese FDI also represents an opportunity for the Bolivian economy. Three factors explain why the government gives special prominence to China as a potential investor. First, the government identifies ideologically, economically and socially with China, in its process of economic transition, especially since Bolivia changed its economic and social policy under President Evo Morales. Secondly, the Bolivian government considers China to be a country that not only invests but also transmits knowledge, training Bolivians in the productive processes. Finally, Bolivia looks to China as a potential market enabling the economy to diversify its production.

Once again, a strong and transparent institutional framework is the key to driving Chinese FDI towards a more diversified economy, through technology transfer and training of human capital, which means requiring generation of value-added as a prerequisite for any FDI. Moreover, solid and transparent institutions are crucial to guarantee that FDI does not threaten the environment.

Thus, to promote a better long-term outcome for the Chinese FDI and promote a better environmental outcome of mining activities, Bolivia needs to work on:

- Anti-corruption measures and good governance in the mining sector.
- Ensuring a conflict-sensitive approach to mineral development.
- Building bilateral and multilateral clean technology cooperation. For example, in Bolivia, the Center for the Promotion of Sustainable Technologies has proposed the introduction of processes and technologies for cleaner production, which not only allows mining operations to improve its environmental performance, but also to gain savings in material, water and energy, resulting in a double benefit.
- Learning from the experience with stabilization funds in Chile, Colombia, and Norway.
- Adopting an integrated approach: given the complexity of the socio-environmental problem of mining in Bolivia, a more comprehensive approach is needed, to analyze and confront the problem under a framework of integrated watershed management, since one of the main environmental problems of mining activity is water pollution.

Turning to the tax regime for mining, there are important flaws, such as the bias in favor of the mining cooperative sector, based on political alliances, which has achieved clear preferences, such as extensive tax exemption, institutional support, and recently in the new mining law, preferential concessions. These advantages recognize the sector for its social function, but it paradoxically turns out to be the least productive, and in environmental terms the most polluting, given the precarious nature of its technology. Thus, this system of preferences should be reconsidered, and must be based on the incentives for best practices in terms of production, tax payments, and environmental performance.

The new Law of Mining and Metallurgy marks an important setback in environmental policy in Bolivia. It has caused great concern in the population, with the main criticisms as follows:

- The law was debated by mining stakeholders and approved by the Plurinational Legislative Assembly without considering the participation of the rest of civil society – indigenous peoples of the lowlands in particular – even though mineral resources are the property of the Bolivian people as a whole, and the mining industry's impacts are concentrated on indigenous communities.
- The law puts preferential rights for miners over individual and collective rights of indigenous peoples and of all the Bolivian people, towns, rivers, lagoons, irrigation systems of drinking water which are means of livelihoods of communities and protected areas. Furthermore, the law expands mining from its traditional territory in Potosí, Oruro and in general the highlands to

include lowlands, indigenous territories and natural parks, without considering the adverse effects on the environment. (Tejada, 2012)

- The law allows for the use of surface water and groundwater for mining operators and does not specify the replacement of the water used, nor does it refer to plants for wastewater treatment. So the coming generations run the risk of not having access to water.
- The law does not establish either civil or criminal sanctions for mining operators who contaminate and/or produce environmental damage.

For all of these reasons, we recommend that the Law of Mining and Metallurgy be revisited and reformed.

5. Conclusions

Even though Chinese participation in the Bolivian economy is still marginal compared with other trading partners, it must be highlighted that during the last years China has shown an impressive presence in the country in terms of exports and also as a creditor. Moreover, the government considers China one of the most important and strategic allies for the next government period. Relations with China are in general geared toward trade and FDI in raw materials and agriculture, which implies damage to the environment. In this sense, China is not a very different partner in comparison to the trading partners with whom Bolivia has had relationships in the present.

FDI produces economic benefits in the recipient countries because it can provide capital, currency exchange and technology and improve the possibilities of access to foreign markets; but also it has impacts on the type of development financed through their flows.

Bolivia still faces deep institutional problems; the country does not have an industrial or investment promotion strategy consistent and in line with the national limitations and restrictions – objectives, policies, programs, actions and perspectives of clearly defined results.

The country is currently recognized by its sound economic management expressed in increasing GDP growth rates. However, this good economic performance is mainly the result of the high international prices of raw materials. China has been decisive in this outcome given its significant demand. Thus, Bolivia must take advantage of this temporal event and put in place suitable measures, such as the creation of a stabilization fund, and the design of policies towards economic diversification, like building human capital and promoting competitive, emerging labor-intensive sectors.

Related to the stabilization fund, its management will require policies and regulations that go beyond a political cycle. More complex is how to regulate the use of the fund to avoid bad management. The challenge Bolivia faces is once more the lack of institutional maturity and an independent management of governmental power.

The case studies analyzed show that Chinese FDI, which is concentrated in raw materials, minerals and lithium, has not fulfilled environmental regulations. However, as Bolivia has a weak institutional framework, the government also has a joint responsibility in this outcome. The government system in place to protect the environment is inadequate at best. Public institutions, such as Bolivia's Ministry of the Environment and Water, which are responsible for ensuring compliance with environmental requirements, clearly lack the capacity or authority to intervene in an effective way.

With regard the mining sector, one major environmental problem that mining activities under the present Bolivian context could cause is a major water crisis. The south of Potosí, where the Canutillos mine is located, already suffers from a serious water shortage, impacting agriculture and drinking water. Foreign entrepreneurs can easily take advantage of the weak institutional framework and develop unsustainable mining activities. So Bolivia is operating under the framework of short-term economic rewards and long-term environmental costs.

Finally, the recently enacted Law of Mining and Metallurgy marks a major setback in oversight of the environment and the harmful effects of mining activities, as it greatly relaxes the possibility of expansion and mining without prior environmental and social considerations. This new framework could deepen the attraction of FDI into mining given the economic benefits that these companies could obtain. However, the result for the country might be detrimental to the environment and livelihoods of surrounding towns, which leads us to conclude that even the weak sustainability criterion would not be achieved.

References

ABI. Retrieved May 28, 2014, from http://www.abi.bo/abi/.

Aguilar, R. (2009). Estimating the Opportunity Cost of Lithium Extraction in the Salar de Uyuni, Bolivia. Masters Thesis. Nicholas School of the Environment of Duke University.

Arroyo, M., Squeo, F., Armesto, J., Villagran, C. et al. (1988). "Effects of Aridity on Plant Diversity in the Northern Chilean Andes: Results of a Natural Experiment." *Annals of the Missouri Botanical Garden*, 75, 55–78.

Balderrama, R. and Martinez, S. (2010). "China, América Latina y el Caribe: El Doble Filo de una Relación Positiva." UNISCI Discussion Paper.

Banco Central de Bolivia. (2012). "Análisis de la Evolución del Sector Externo 2012." Retrieved February 4, 2014, from http://www.bcb.gob.bo/webdocs/publicaciones/externo%20diciembre%202012/analisis.pdf

Bittencourt, G. (2012). El Impacto de China en América Latina Comercio e Inversiones. Uruguay: Red de MERCOSUR de Investigaciones Económicas.

Caputi, M., Moreira, A., Gomes, M. et al. (2012). "Desempeño de las exportaciones de China y Brasil hacia América Latina 1994–2009." En: Revista de la Cepal, 106, April.

CEDIB (2012). Agua y Minería en Bolivia, CEDIB, Cochabamba.

COMIBOL-Corporación Minera de Bolivia (National Mining Department) (2008). COMIBOL Annual Report. www.comibol.gov.bo/comibol.html

COMIBOL-Corporación Minera de Bolivia (National Mining Department) and Dirección Nacional de Recursos Evaporíticos. (2009). Press Releases: www.evaporiticosbolivia.org/indexi.php?Modulo=NotasPrensa&Opcion=LstGeneral

CNPV (2001). Censo Nacional de Población y Vivienda, 2001. INE. La Paz.

Conservation International. (2007) "Tropical Andes. Biodiversity Hotspots." http://www.biodiversityhotspots.org/xp/hotspots/andes/Pages/default.aspx

Correa, G. and Gonzales, J. (2006). La inversiónextranjeradirecta: Chinacomocompetidory socioestratégico. En Nueva Sociedad 203.

Diario La Patria (2009). COD pide Investigación minuciosa en denuncias de corrupción del Mutún. Diario La Patria, October 5, 2009. Sección Nacional. Oruro – Bolivia. http://www.lapatriaenlinea.com/index.php/somos-noticias.html?t=cod-pide-investigacion-minuciosa-en-denuncias-de-corrupcion-del-mutun&nota=3749

Diario El Día (2014). Según estudios sobre la actividad de las 1600 cooperativas del país 80% de las cooperativas evade licencia ambiental. Diario El Día, November 9, 2014. Sección Portafolio. Santa Cruz – Bolivia. http://www.eldia.com.bo/index.php?cat=357&pla=3&id_articulo=158697

Diaz, V. (2011). La Minería bajo el dominio de las Transnacionales. Equipo CEDIB. Cochabamba.

Dussel, P. E. (2012). "Chinese FDI Latin American: Does Ownership Matter?" Working Group on Development and Environment in the Americas.

ECLAC (2012). La Inversión Extranjera Directa en 2012. Comisión Económica para América Latina y el Caribe (CEPAL), Santiago.

ERBOL. (2014). Ley Minera crea casta privilegiada "las cooperativas," Villegas y Gandarillas analizan a fondo, May 25, 2014. ERBOL Digital. Sección Economía. http://www.erbol.com.bo/noticia/economia/25052014/ley_minera_crea_casta_privilegiada_las_cooperativas

Fearnside, Philip M., Figueiredo, Adriano M. R. and Bonjour, Sandra C. M. (2013). "Amazonian Forest Loss and the Long Reach of China's Influence." Environment, Development and Sustainability 15(2): 325–38.

Gallagher, Kevin and Porzecanski, Robert (2010). The Dragon in the Room: China and the Future of Latin American Industrialization. Stanford University Press.

Gallagher, Kevin, Irwin, A. and Koleski, K. (2012). The New Banks in Town: Chinese Finance in Latin America. Inter-American Dialogue Report.

GNRE (2013). Memoria Institucional 2012–2013. Gerencia Nacional de Recursos Evaporiticos. La Paz.

Gutierrez, R. (2009) Contaminación Minera en Oruro y Potosí. LIDEMA – PIEB. La Paz.

Hollender, R. and Schultz, J. (2010). Bolivia y su Litio. Centro para la Democracia. Cochabamba. Bolivia.

Irwin, A. and Gallagher, K. (2013). "Chinese Mining in Latin America: A Comparative Perspective." Journal of Environment and Development, 22(2), 207–234.

INE (1990–2013). Instituto Nacional de Estadística. Bolivia.www.ine.gob.bo. Recuperado el Febrero de 2014: http://www.ine.gob.bo/

Laufer, R. (2010). "Presente y Perspectivas de la asociación "estratégica" China-América Latina. Presented at the 22nd Jornadas de Historia Económica – Asociación Argentina de Historia Económica. Universidad Nacional de Rio Cuarto. Río Cuarto, September 21–24, 2010.

Meridian Research Group (2008). "The trouble with Lithium 2." Les Legers. France.

Michard, J. (2008). Cooperativas Mineras en Bolivia. Centro de Documentación e Información Bolivia, CEDIB, Cochabamba.

Ministerio de Minería y Metalurgia (2013). Memoria Institucional 2013. Gobierno de Bolivia. La Paz.

Morales, J. E. (2010). *Minería Boliviana.* La Paz: Plural Editores.

Muzondo, T. (1993). "Mineral Taxation, Market Failure and the Environment," IMF Staff Papers, vol. 40, no. 1.

Nacht, P. A. (2013). El Dragón en América Latina: las relaciones económica-comerciales y los riesgo de la región. ÍCONOS.

PDM Colcha-K (2009–2013). Plan de Desarrollo Municipal Colcha "K." AMDEPO.

PDM LLica (2007–2011). Plan de Desarrollo Municipal de LLica.MedicusMundi.

PDM Uyuni (2008–2012). Plan de Desarrollo Municipal de Uyuni. Gobierno Municipal de Uyuni.

Revenga, C. and Kura, Y. (2003). "Status and Trends of Biodiversity of Inland Water Ecosystems." Secretariat of the Convention on Biological Diversity, Montreal, Technical Series no. 11.

Ribera, M. (2011). Análisis General del caso Uyuni-Litio (Minería), COCOON NEBE PROJECT-LIDEMA, La Paz.

Rojas, F. and Nina, O. (2001). Atractivo de Bolivia a los Inversionistas Extranjeros. Documentos de Trabajo. Proyecto Andino de Competitividad, CAF, La Paz.

Sanabria, M. (2009). El Sector Minero. Tomo II, Diagnósticos Sectoriales, Unidad de Análisis de Políticas Sociales y Económicas. Área Macrosectorial. La Paz.

Strobele-Gregor, J. (2013). El proyecto estatal del litio en Bolivia. Revista Nueva Sociedad # 244. Marzo-Abril 2013.

Tejada A. (2012). Minería en las Tierras Bajas de Bolivia. CEDIB, Cochabamba.

Tribunal Supremo de Justicia (2013–2014). http://tribunalsupremo.organojudicial. gob.bo/Autos%20Supremos/social/social-II/2014/as201432333b.html. http:// tribunalsupremo.organojudicial.gob.bo/Autos%20Supremos/social/social/2013/ as201331540.html.

World Resources Institute. (2005). *World Resources 2005: The Wealth of the Poor.* Washington DC: World Resources Institute, United Nations Development Programme, United Nations Environment Programme, World Bank. Available at: http://www.wri.org/ sites/default/files/pdf/wrr05_lores.pdf

Yue, L. (2013). Inversión extranjera directa de China en América Latina.

Zarsky, L. and Stanley, L. (2013). "Can Extractive Industries Promote Sustainable Development? A Net Benefits Framework and a Case Study of the Marlin Mine in Guatemala." *Journal of Environment and Development* 22(2) 131–54.

UDAPE (2013) Dossier de Estadísticas 2013. Unidad de Análisis de Políticas Económicas, La Paz. www.worldlithium.com/An_Abundance_of_Lithium_1_files/An%20Abun dance%20of%20Lithium.pdf

World Development Indicators. databank.worldbank.org.

Chapter 6

CHINESE INVESTMENT IN PERU'S MINING INDUSTRY: BLESSING OR CURSE?

Cynthia Sanborn and Victoria Chonn Ching

Peru's trade and investment relationship with China is overwhelmingly concentrated in the mining sector. Peru is well-positioned to oversee a positive mining-based relationship with China, having recently taken several important steps to increase transparency and accountability in this sector. Peru has been a regional leader in this aspect – for example, by both joining the Extraction Industry Transparency Initiative (EITI) and becoming the first Latin American government to incorporate ILO Resolution 169 into domestic legislation. In 2014, Chinese mining firms demonstrated their own commitment to these standards by joining the EITI program in Peru.

Overall, there is no one Chinese way of doing business in Peru. Chinese mining firms do not appear to be either the best or worst in the country, but their experiences have been emblematic of the challenges that all foreign investors face. In the instances we have found where Chinese firms have failed to meet environmental and social responsibility standards, responsibility must be shared between missteps on the part of firms as well as the reluctance or inability on the part of the government to enforce these standards. However, there are important, positive signs that Chinese investors and Peruvian regulators are willing to work together to improve this record. For example, after the recent acid water spill at the Chinese-run Toromocho mine, regulators stepped in immediately and shut down production until the firm addressed the problem, which took only a few days. Furthermore, after the incident the Association of Chinese Companies in Peru asked the Ministry of the Environment (MINAM) for training on local environmental regulations. That

The authors thank Tania Ramirez and Veronica Hurtado, who provided considerable research assistance on this chapter.

type of training for foreign investors could provide yet another opportunity for Peru to lead the region in its proactive framework for mining.

Two other important recommendations emerge from our findings. First, the EITI program could be substantially enhanced by including local governments. EITI reporting is a powerful tool for citizen empowerment, but it is incomplete without the inclusion of local government, which receives 50 percent of mining tax revenue. Second, while mining firms must meet higher labor standards than other firms, the sector has a history of circumventing these protections through the use of subcontractor labor, contributing to conflict between the firms, labor and the surrounding communities. One way of addressing this problem may be to extend mining-sector labor protections to include contract workers, eliminating the financial incentive for offering informal work.

1. Introduction

Peru has been one of Latin America's most important economic success stories over the last decade, by achieving sustained growth under political democracy, cutting poverty in half and producing an expanding new middle class. These results have been driven in large part by global demand for the minerals and other primary commodities that Peru exports, as well as by sound macroeconomic policymaking and a strong commitment to international trade. Expanding relations with China, while not the whole story, has been an important chapter.

In recent years, copper, iron, gold and other minerals have accounted for around 60 percent of total Peruvian exports, 25 percent of total Foreign Direct Investment (FDI) and 15 percent of total tax revenues. While investors from more than thirty countries are involved in Peru's mining industry, China has become the leading market for these resources, and Chinese demand for them is credited with helping Peru weather the financial crisis of 2008. Peru is considered the leading location for Chinese mineral investment in Latin America, and Chinese firms hold around 30 percent of the country's total mining investment portfolio. Chinese firms also have an important presence in Peru's hydrocarbons and commercial fishing sectors ("Las inversiones chinas" 2014; Sanborn 2014).

Although economic relations with China are seen by many in Peru as a blessing, the global rush for resources has revived concerns about the "resource curse," the risks of excessive dependence on primary commodity exports, and the structural challenges to achieving a more diversified and productive economy. As Chinese demand for minerals and oil appears to be higher than the world average, some argue that this contributes to reinforcing this pattern. At the same time, the main motivation behind Peru's aggressive pursuit of free-trade agreements (FTAs) with the United States, China and 16 other countries, as well as diverse multilateral trade agreements and alliances, has been to diversify the country's trade and investment opportunities (Sanborn and Yong 2014). The evidence to date is mixed.

Dependency on mineral exports has also raised new concerns about the social and environmental implications of large-scale extractive activity. For some, the advantages of attracting Chinese investment have been tempered by concerns over the ability of Chinese-owned firms to comply with global standards in such areas as revenue transparency and environmental and labor policies (Kotschwar, Moran et al., 2011; Friedman, 2006). The mining industry within China has had severe problems with safety and environmental regulations as well, and Chinese companies have not practiced the kind of transparency that many in Latin America have come to demand, nor have they been active participants to date in voluntary efforts and initiatives. However, analysts have also argued that the key issue is not whether a company is Chinese, or of any other nationality, but rather the willingness and capacity of host countries to regulate them adequately (Irwin and Gallagher, 2013; Gonzalez Vicente, 2012).

These issues are put to the test in Peru today. Peru has taken important steps to establish new standards for the extractive industries, and to use the abundant revenues that they generate to advance various development goals (Arellano-Yanguas 2011). Peru joined the Extractive Industries Transparency Initiative (EITI) in 2007 and in 2011 became the first country in the Americas to be declared compliant within that framework. In 2008 Peru established a new Ministry of the Environment, which has vied with the Ministry of Energy and Mines (MINEM) to oversee the extractive industries. In 2011, the Humala administration became the first in Latin America to create domestic legislation to implement ILO Convention 169, guaranteeing the right of indigenous and tribal peoples to prior consultation on major public policies that affect their lives, including the granting of concessions and permits for extractive activity.

But as global prices fluctuate and took a downturn after 2012, the drive to increase mineral production in Peru has tended to conflict with efforts at effective environmental and social regulation. Government initiatives in this area have been hampered by institutional weaknesses, conflicts of interest and strong resistance from investors. There have been numerous and often violent disputes between companies and communities over land and water rights, revenues and environmental contamination, including high-profile cases that have engaged national and transnational activists and the international media. Such conflicts pose potential challenges and delays for all firms, including Chinese investors new to the country.

In this context, it is important to examine Chinese involvement in the Peruvian mining sector, and ask:

- Does it matter if China is a major market for Peruvian minerals? Is Chinese demand different from that of Peru's other trading partners, as a driver of primary commodity dependency or of the social and environmental risks this may pose?
- Does Chinese investment in Peru's mining industries have social or environmental ramifications that are significantly different from that of other investments?
- Do Chinese mining companies comply with Peruvian laws and regulations to a lesser or greater extent than others? Are different standards applied to them?
- Have Chinese firms reacted differently than their industry peers to conflict over such issues as land and water rights or environmental contamination?

In order to address these questions, we examine the Chinese presence at three levels:

1. At the macro level, we examine data on Peruvian trade and investment relations with China in the last decade to assess the extent to which recent trends reinforce or modify this country's primary commodity dependency.
2. At the meso level, we examine some of the main policies aimed at regulating the extractive industries in Peru and improving their impact on development, asking about the extent to which Chinese firms have been engaged in or influenced by them.
3. At the micro level, we briefly examine three cases of Chinese firms operating in Peru today, using the "net benefits" framework proposed by Zarsky and Stanley (2013).

This chapter presents findings at all three levels and ends with initial conclusions regarding the current and potential impact of the Chinese presence in this case.

2. Peruvian–Chinese Relations: The Macro Picture

China has had a major social and cultural presence in Peru for more than 160 years. Starting in the mid-nineteenth century, when some hundred thousand Chinese men were brought to Peru as indentured agricultural workers, relations between China and Peru have gradually expanded (Lausent-Herrera, 2011). In the twentieth and twenty-first centuries, larger waves of Chinese immigrants came to the country along with a growing influx of Chinese goods and enterprises. Today, Peru has the largest ethnic Chinese population in Latin America.

Diplomatic ties with the People's Republic of China can be traced to 1971, but for years these relations mainly focused on economic and technical cooperation. Direct Chinese investment in Peru began in 1992, when the state-owned Shougang Group bought the state-owned iron-ore company, Empresa Minera de Hierro del Peru (Hierro Peru). In 1993, SAPET, a subsidiary of the China National Petroleum Company (CNPC) purchased state-owned assets in the Peruvian oil industry. Yet 15 years would pass before more significant Chinese investments would flow towards the Andes.

The bilateral relationship began to accelerate after 2004, when Peru granted market economy status to China, and in 2008 it entered a new phase, when both countries established a "strategic partnership," leading to the Peru–China Free Trade Agreement (FTA) in 2009. By 2011, China replaced the United States as Peru's main trading partner. That same year, the Association of Chinese Enterprises was formed, with 43 members and support from the Chinese embassy. By 2014 the association had 61 members, and some one hundred and twenty Chinese firms were legally registered to operate in Peru – in mining and energy, telecommunications, machinery, agriculture, construction and commerce ("Las inversiones chinas" 2014).

Peru's relations with China took a new leap forward in 2013, when the two nations' leaders celebrated their "comprehensive strategic partnership" by signing 11 bilateral accords aimed to optimize trade and strengthen cooperation in agriculture, infrastructure, minerals and social development. In November of that year, the first Chinese bank, Industrial and Commercial Bank of China (ICBC) was authorized to operate in Peru. Also, the China Fishery Group purchased shares in a major Peruvian fishing firm, giving it a quarter of the country's commercial fishing quota and turning it into the world's largest producer of fishmeal,[1] while CNPC announced its purchase of the Peruvian holdings of Petrobras, the Brazilian oil giant, giving Chinese firms control of around 40 percent of Peru's hydrocarbon production. In December, President Humala inaugurated the *Toromocho* copper project, operated by the Aluminum Corporation of China (Chinalco), which promises to increase total copper production by 20 percent and help Peru meet its dream of surpassing Chile as the world's leading producer of that metal ("Chinalco eleva" 2013). This was followed in 2014 by the announcement that MMG

---

1 In 2016, however, China Fishery Group filed for bankruptcy and was looking to sell its Peruvian assets (Yong 2016).

(backed by China Minmetals) would purchase Las Bambas, another copper mega-project, and consider Peru as its hub for regional expansion ("Glencore Xstrata Sells Las Bambas" 2014).

2.1 Trade and investment: A summary

China has been Peru's most important trading partner in recent years, representing its single-largest export market and second-largest source of imports after the United States. Total exports to China more than quadrupled as a share of Peru's GDP between 1995 and 2012, from 0.8 percent of GDP in 1995 to 4.1 percent in 2012. In contrast, Peruvian exports to the world as a whole doubled as a share of Peru's GDP over the same period. In 2013 China bought USD 7.3 billion worth of Peruvian goods, or 17.7 percent of total export value from Peru.

Peruvian exports to China remain largely primary goods, with four products – copper, iron, lead and fishmeal – comprising the lion's share of the total, and largely explaining the positive overall trade balance through 2012. The relative share of these goods has changed, however, since the 1990s. In 1997, nearly 80 percent of Peruvian exports to China came from the fishery sector, while around 16 percent was minerals and oil. By 2004 fishery exports had fallen to 36 percent, and by 2013 the shares were reversed from 2004: fisheries accounted for 13 percent of exports to China in value, and mineral and oil products together were 87 percent (CAPECHI 2014). Indeed, in 2013 China was the main market for Peru's mineral exports, at 26.5 percent of the total, followed by Switzerland with 13 percent.

Meanwhile, imports from China to Peru have increased more than those from any other country (Aquino 2013). From 1993 to 2012, Peru's imports from China grew more than tenfold relative to the size of the economy (from 0.3% to 4.1% of GDP), far outpacing overall exports, which roughly doubled as a share of Peru's GDP in the same period. Although Chinese imports compete with local producers in sectors such as footwear, textiles and garments and metal products, in which the trade balance remains negative, this has not exactly led to "deindustrialization." The overall effect of an expanded market and better access to competitive intermediate goods, for example, appears to have outweighed the negative effects of Chinese imports on specific sectors (Cardenas and Gavilano 2013).

The FTA that Peru has signed with China has also been important. It covers merchandise, services and investment, allowing 83.5 percent of Peruvian exports to enter China with zero tariffs and providing some protection for Peruvian products most vulnerable to Chinese competition, such as textiles (Gonzalez Vigil 2012).

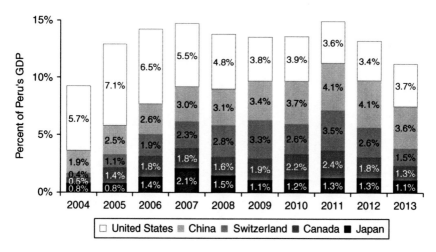

Figure 6.1 Peru's exports destinations, 2004–2013
Source: Authors' calculations based on UN Comtrade, IMF WEO data.

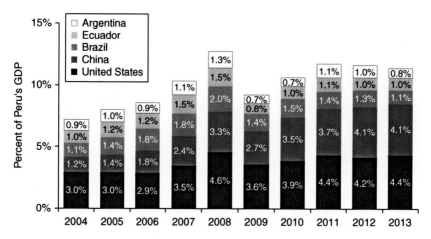

Figure 6.2 Top five sources of Peruvian imports, 2004–2013
Source: Authors' calculations based on UN Comtrade, IMF WEO data.

In summary, China today is the primary market for Peruvian exports, which consist mostly of primary or related commodities. Chinese demand for these products is higher than world demand, while promotion of primary exports – especially minerals – remains a high priority for the Peruvian government, as well as attracting foreign investment to this sector – Chinese or otherwise.

In regard to investment, Peru ranked second only to Brazil in overall Chinese FDI in Latin America from 1990 to 2012, and by 2014 Peru had

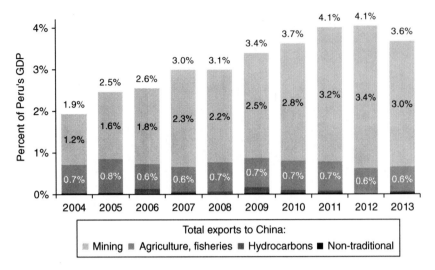

Figure 6.3 Peru's exports to China, 2004–2012, by sector, as a percent of Peru's GDP (FOB)
Source: Authors' calculations based on UN Comtrade, IMF WEO data.

captured nearly half of all projected Chinese investment in the region (Chen and Perez 2013; Capechi 2014). For 2014 alone, the Peru-China Chamber of Commerce (Capechi) predicted as much as USD 12 billion in new Chinese investment.[2] As shown in Table 6.1, this is concentrated in three primary sectors – mining, fishing and hydrocarbons – and most comes from SOEs managed by the central or local governments.

However, in comparison to other sources of investment in Peru, the actual stock of Chinese FDI in Peru remains low. Although it is difficult to trace the total amount of FDI coming from China into Latin America because of tax havens, Peruvian authorities estimate this at just USD 1.8 billion in 2013: 48 percent in minerals, 40 percent in fisheries and 10 percent in finance (Capechi, 2014). China was the seventeenth-largest investor in Peru by nationality in 2013, while Spain was first with 19 percent, followed by the United Kingdom and the United States (Proinversión, 2014). In mining, however, China is the largest single investor, and it now holds an estimated 30 percent of the total projected portfolio.

The main attraction of Chinese FDI in Peru remains the size of projected investments, especially in mining, and the ability of Chinese firms to commit resources over the longer term. Although Chinese SOEs purchased two

---

2 In September 2014, the Peru-China Chamber of Commerce estimated total projected Chinese investment in Peru as USD 9.27 billion for the prior 12 months, or 48% of the regional total of USD 19.3 billion (Capechi, 2014).

older state-owned mining companies in Peru in the early 1990s, more significant investment did not take place until this century. The majority of Chinese mineral investment is concentrated in copper and iron, and since 2007 this has involved primarily greenfield projects obtained through the takeover of Western-owned junior firms.

While Chinese investors have shown interest in other sectors of the Peruvian economy, interviews with businesspeople and diplomats from both countries suggest that there are numerous obstacles for foreign investors in Peru. Some of these are related to Peru's regulatory requirements for all investors, like obtaining work and family visas, translating and officiating documents, and obtaining various permits for operation. Tender processes for infrastructure investments also tend to be complicated. More specific obstacles stem from lack of compatibility between the Chinese and Peruvian tax and legal frameworks and financial systems. These become harder to resolve when there is a lack of professionals on both sides with appropriate language and cultural skills.

At a higher level, although policymakers have been successful at negotiating FTAs and other accords, Peru to date has not had a clear strategy for following up on these opportunities. The state has done relatively little to accompany, finance or otherwise support private entrepreneurs in this process, and cultivation of ties with foreign investors and political allies is mostly driven by private companies and individuals, with little assistance from government, such that opportunities for better negotiation and deals can be lost (Wise 2012).

Chinese investors also find that they may have to communicate – and negotiate – with a large number of other parties after winning a concession and complying with the initial central government rules and regulations. These may include popularly elected regional and municipal authorities, indigenous communities, nongovernmental organizations (NGOs) and diverse media, as well as local bankers and business competitors. Such a diversity of actors is normal in a volatile democracy like Peru's and successful investors have learned over time how to respond to them. Chinese businesspeople and diplomats may be less experienced at multi-stakeholder relations than their Western counterparts, and less accustomed to demands for accountability from non-state actors. However, as our research and other recent studies of Chinese investment in the mining sector suggest, they are learning quickly.

3. Extractive Governance Reforms and Chinese Engagement

Latin America today accounts for nearly a third of total world mineral investment, and a growing share of this is expected to come from Chinese-owned firms, which own or participate in at least thirty-five major projects across South and Central America. Policymakers are concerned not only with

Table 6.1 Main Chinese investments in Peru

Year	Investor	Partners	Project	Sector
1992	Shougang Corporation/ Shougang Hierro Perú S.A.A		Marcona	Mining
1993–1994	China National Petroleum Corporation (CNPC)/ SAPET		Lot VI/VII (Talara, Piura)	Energy; oil and gas
2002	Tiens Group/ Tianshi Perú SAC.			Manufacturing
2005	China National Petroleum Corp. (CNPC)/ SAPET		Lot 111 (Madre de Dios)	Energy; oil and gas
2007	Aluminum Corporation of China (Chinalco)/ Minera Chinalco Perú S.A		Toromocho	Mining
2007	Zijin Mining Group/ Rio Blanco Copper S.A.	Zijin (45%), Tongling Nonferrous (35%), Xiamen C&D (20%)	Rio Blanco	Mining
2007	Beijing Rich Gold/ Jintong Mining		Llama TY01	Mining (Exploration)
2008	China Minmetals Corp.-Jiangxi Copper Corp. / Lumina Copper S.A.C.^^	Minmetals (60%), Jiangxi Copper (40%)	Galeno	Mining
2008	Junefields Company Limited/ Junefield Group		Cercana	Mining
2009	Shougang Corporation/ Shougang Hierro Perú S.A.A		Marcona Expansion	Mining
2009	Nanjinzhao Group/ Jinzhao Mining Peru S.A.		Pampa del Pongo	Mining
2010	Bank of China	Bank of China, Interbank	China Desk Perú	Financial
2010	Industrial and Commercial Bank of China (ICBC)/ ICBC Peru Bank~			Financial
2011	Minera Shouxin Peru	Baiyin Nonferrous Group (51%), Shougang (49%)	Proyecto Explotación Relaves	Tailings

Year	Company	Ownership	Asset	Sector
2012	China National Petroleum Corporation (CNPC)/ SAPET	CNPC (45%) Pluspetrol Norte S.A. (55%)	Lot 1AB (Olaya, Loreto)	Energy, oil and gas
2012	China National Petroleum Corporation (CNPC)/ SAPET	CNPC (27%), Pluspetrol Norte S.A. (73%)	Lot 8 (Trompeteros, Yanayacu, Loreto)	Energy, oil and gas
2013	China National Petroleum Corporation (CNPC)/ PetroChina*		Lot X (Talara), Lot 58 (Camisea)	Energy, oil and gas
2013	China National Petroleum Corporation (CNPC)/ PetroChina*	CNPC (46.16%), Repsol (53.84%)	Lot 57 (Camisea)	Energy, oil and gas
2013	Pacific Andes International Holdings Ltd. /China Fishery Group			Fishery
2014	MMG Ltd.	MMG Ltd. (62.5%), Guoxin Investment Corp. (22.5%), CITIC Metal (15%)	Las Bambas	Mining

Source: Authors' elaboration based on information from various sources, including American Heritage Foundation, ITC calculations based on UN Comtrade statistics, ProInversion, MINEM, Sanborn and Yong, Irwin and Gallagher.

avoiding the negative macroeconomic effects of excessive dependency on mineral exports, but also with issues of revenue transparency and distribution, with achieving adequate environmental and labor standards in the industry and with having companies practice good community relations and corporate social responsibility. The overall objectives are to obtain net benefits from the extractive industries and improve their impact on longer-term development.

In recent years Peru has been something of a laboratory for extractive industry reforms. Yet, while a number of agencies at the national and subnational levels are making efforts to apply global standards, others – including the powerful ministries of Economy and Finance (MEF) and Energy and Mines (MINEM) – are primarily concerned with bringing new projects on line and accelerating production, which leads to efforts to weaken enforcement of laws and regulations that could hinder this effort. On the corporate side, Peru is host to virtually all of the major multinationals involved in the International Council on Minerals and Mining (ICMM), EITI and other industry-led corporate social responsibility (CSR) initiatives, but many local business leaders tend to see these reforms as "trabas" or obstacles to investment, and engage in passive or aggressive resistance.

China has also undergone major efforts at industrial and environmental reform over the past decade. This includes new regulations and guidelines that seek to promote corporate governance and CSR (Global Witness 2013, Tan-Mullins 2012). Yet, although there is increased awareness in China of what is required of firms to comply with global standards, Chinese authorities are still lacking in implementation and enforcement. According to some experts, for some Chinese corporate and political leaders, issues of transparency and accountability are not necessarily considered part of CSR practices (Tan-Mullins 2012: 13). As they go overseas, leaders of Chinese firms understand the need to fulfill the expectations of local governments and communities and contribute to local development, yet they may remain hesitant to open up to the media or civil society groups, or to share what they consider sensitive information (Global Witness 2013, Sanborn and Torres 2009).

In this section we examine selected areas of extractive industry reform in Peru, focusing on how Chinese firms are engaged in or influenced by them, and whether Peruvian policymakers apply them any differently to the Chinese because of the size and value of the investments they bring. Alternatively, are they monitored more closely than others? Of course, an alternative hypothesis is that all firms doing business in this country must meet the same regulations. Such questions are rarely asked about firms of other nationalities in this region, but have been the focus of recent research on the Chinese from both sides of the Pacific (see Torres and Sanborn 2009; Gonzalez Vicente 2013; Irwin and Gallagher 2013, Guo Jie 2014). A summary of our findings in this section can be found in Table 6.2.

Table 6.2 Extractive governance reforms and Chinese engagement

Areas of Extractive Industry Policy	Subareas	Description	Comparison of Cases
Revenue Transparency and Distribution	**Revenue Transparency**	Voluntary or mandatory efforts to make companies more accountable to the citizens and governments as well as shareholders. Since 2005, Peru has participated in the Extractive Industries Transparency Initiative (EITI) and was the first country in the Americas to become compliant in 2011.	Almost all major mining and oil companies in Peru participate in EITI. Until 2014, the only two Chinese companies that paid significant taxes were Shougang Hierro Peru and CNPC (SAPET), but they did not participate in EITI. However, both confirmed participation for the IV EITI Peru report (still in process in 2014). Lumina Copper (China Minmetals) participates.
	Revenue Distribution	Efforts to ensure that revenues generated are used to promote development goals. Since 2003, Peru redistributes 50% of income taxes paid by mining firms to subnational governments where extractive activity is located.	Shougang makes significant contribution to tax revenues in Marcona, Ica. Chinalco, based in Junín, will not be paying income taxes for several years.

(*continued*)

Table 6.2 Continued

Areas of Extractive Industry Policy	Subareas	Description	Comparison of Cases
Voluntary Social Investment		Private firms in Peru are motivated to intervene directly in areas where they operate, through social programs and community relations initiatives. The Peruvian government promotes this in several ways: required social funds as part of concession contracts, voluntary giving related to overall profits ("Programa Minero de Solidaridad con el Pueblo," PMSP), and tax deductions for investment in social programs and public works ("Obras por Impuestos").	**(a) Programa Minero de Solidaridad con el Pueblo, PMSP** Of all major contributors, non-Chinese firms have higher spending rates. Shougang is the only Chinese participant. Neither Shougang nor other firms are very transparent about what they spent. (Grupo Propuesta Ciudadana 2011). **(b) Other social investment** Shougang inherited the commitment to provide housing and services to the city of Marcona. Chinalco created a new "company town," Nueva Morococha. **(c) Obras por Impuestos** Fourteen mining firms engaged in this program. The only Chinese firm participating is Chinalco, in alliance with two Peruvian companies.

Corporate Guilds and Multi-stakeholder Fora	Corporate Guilds	Sectorial and national business associations have political clout, and engage with government and civil society (i.e., National Mining Society).	Chinese firms are not active in National Mining Society. Many Western multinationals are also not active. Chinese firms are active in the Association of Chinese Companies in Peru. The only Chinese-owned firm to attend GDM events for more than one year is Lumina Copper (China Minmetals).
	Multi-stakeholder Forum	Grupo de Dialogo Minero (GDM), founded in 2000, is a multi-stakeholder forum for dialogue and conflict mediation. It involves representatives from companies, government, NGOs, community and indigenous organizations.	
	Specific Cases	Peruvian authorities have established multi-stakeholder "mesas" or roundtables, to manage social conflicts.	Chinalco: "Mesa de Dialogo para el Proceso de Reasentamiento Poblacional de Morococha," organized to support the relocation process of the 5,000 residents of the town. Shougang: "Mesa de Dialogo para el Desarrollo del Distrito de Marcona," created in June 2013 to negotiate agreements on various urban development issues.

(continued)

Table 6.2 Continued

Areas of Extractive Industry Policy	Subareas	Description	Comparison or Cases
Labor	**Labor rules and Regulations**	Wages and benefits for mineworkers on payrolls of the larger firms in Peru are above national average, with a special labor regime that includes profit sharing. However, companies may try to bypass labor unions and rights by subcontracting large numbers of workers off payroll.	Few Chinese firms in Peru have large labor forces. Hiring of tertiary workers appears less prevalent among Chinese (Shougang, Chinalco) than other firms. Shougang places in the middle range in regards to compliance with Peruvian safety and labor standards, but it has a higher rate of strikes and labor protests. Chinalco is apparently paying wages above the market average compared to other mining firms in the central highlands.
	Local Hiring	Demand for local employment is widespread among communities adjacent to mining projects, and most companies commit to this.	Chinese firms vary in their hiring policies in Peru, but most seem to offer some degree of local hires and/or training programs. Shougang' case is different since Marcona is a company town.

Environmental rules and Regulations

Ministry of Energy and Mines approves EIAs, but since 2008, the Ministry of Environment (through OEFA) monitors compliance and penalizes infractions.

Four Chinese firms have received warnings or sanctions: Lumina Copper, Rio Blanco Copper, Shougang and Chinalco. But overall Chinese firms have fewer environmental sanctions than other firms.

Shougang has had 10 infractions cited by OEFA (MINAM) in the last 10 years, but the fines are higher than bigger firms like Antamina and Yanacocha.

In 2014, OEFA ordered Chinalco to halt activities at the recently inaugurated mine due to acid wastewater runoff. Company responded quickly.

3.1 Revenue transparency and distribution

As numerous experts on the resource curse have stressed, greater transparency on the part of companies and governments is the first step in making both more accountable to citizens and shareholders and to ensuring that the revenues generated by the extractive industries are used to promote the longer-term development needs of the societies in which they operate (Karl, 2006).

China still does not have a strong system of regulation of information disclosure by its companies operating abroad. Although there are government agencies that authorize and supervise overseas investments, such as the Ministry of Commerce (MOFCOM), the State-owned Assets Supervision and Administration Commission of the State Council (SASAC), the National Development and Reform Commission (NDRC) and the China Development Bank (CDB), the policies that influence operations of Chinese firms overseas are usually too general to have strong effect, and the data reported by these firms back home varies considerably (Global Witness, 2013; Lin, 2012).

Meanwhile, in Peru individual and corporate taxpayers can protect the confidentiality of what they pay to the state in taxes, through what is called "reserva tributaria" – an equivalent to tax secrecy. This means that the Superintendencia Nacional de Aduanas y de Administración Tributaria (SUNAT), the agency responsible for tax collection, cannot reveal information regarding what companies tribute unless they have explicit permission from the firms. However, companies with annual earnings of over 3,000 UIT or tax units[3] are required to declare these to the Superintendency of the Stock Market, which makes this information publicly available. Starting in the early 2000s Peru has developed numerous other mandatory mechanisms to promote transparency in the corporate sector (see Grupo Propuesta Ciudadana, 2013).

Since 2005, Peru has also been a participating country in the EITI, a global initiative that involves meeting common standards for reporting taxes and other payments made to governments by companies in the mining and hydrocarbons industries. The idea is to prevent significant tax evasion or irregular payments, and demonstrate to citizens the real fiscal contributions made by these industries. Peru was the first country in the Americas to become compliant with these standards. Furthermore, Peruvians successfully lobbied EITI International to include a new standard involving transparency in subnational government revenues, to begin with the fourth national EITI Peru report in 2014.

---

3 For 2014, 1 UIT has a value of S/. 3,800 (Nuevos Soles) or around USD 1,300, so this applies to firms with more than USD 4 million in annual earnings (virtually all medium and large mining companies).

Although the EITI is voluntary, the majority of leading producers and tax-payers in the mining and hydrocarbon sectors participate, including all of the ICMM members operating in Peru (EITI Peru, 2013). How do the Chinese compare? Given the recent nature of most Chinese mining investments, there are only two Chinese companies that pay significant taxes in Peru; Shougang Hierro Peru and CNPC (SAPET). Neither of them participated in the first three EITI Peru reports, covering taxes paid in 2004–2007, 2008–2010 and 2011–2012. Because they were among the few major firms absent from this initiative, this marked their notable difference from other multinationals and contributed to their reputation for lack of transparency. However, this situation began to change in 2013.

According to Chinese executives in Peru, the absence of their firms from EITI Peru was due to the lack of authorization from their mother companies in China. Since 2011, the Humala Administration assigned permanent staff from MINEM to work with a tripartite EITI commission, involving representatives from industry and civil society, and to encourage executives of non-participating companies to join.[4] In 2012 one Chinese-owned firm, Lumina Copper, participated in the second report, and in 2013 the others began to express interest. In 2014, representatives of Shougang and CNPC (SAPET) announced their commitment to participate in the fourth EITI report.

Because Lumina's main Peruvian project is not yet in operation, their involvement is symbolic. However, now that the owner of Lumina, China Minmetals, is also the majority owner of MMG, which purchased the Las Bambas copper project in Apurimac, the firm has announced plans to be more actively involved in this initiative.

Regarding revenue distribution, since 2003, 50 percent of all income taxes paid by mining firms to the central government are redistributed to the regional, provincial and municipal governments in which their extractive activity is located. This is called the "mining canon," and in some parts of the country it means that enormous revenues are in the hands of mayors, regional presidents and others who could invest in much-needed infrastructure and services for their communities. Many of these communities are extremely poor, rural and indigenous.

Does this income provide net benefits for communities where mines are located? This is a hotly debated issue in Peru, and the answer varies. While there have been success stories in such regions as Moquegua and Arequipa, there are also regions such as Cajamarca and Huancavelica, where these

---

4 Cynthia Sanborn has been involved in this commission since 2007: http://eitiperu. minem.gob.pe/

revenue flows have had little positive impact, while mining has brought high environmental and social costs, suggesting a form of "subnational resource curse" (Arellano-Yanguas, 2011). The relevant question here, however, is whether the presence of Chinese firms in certain regions of Peru has a significant impact on tax revenues and on the ability to invest those revenues in promoting development goals.

In the mining sector, there is only one Chinese firm that is fully operating and paying significant taxes: Shougang Hierro Peru based in the district of Marcona, in the region of Ica. As it happens, Ica is one of the most economically dynamic regions in Peru, with socioeconomic indicators above the national average and close to full employment. This is due not just to mining, but also to the presence of commercial agriculture, fishing and tourism. Within Ica, Marcona also has the best social and economic record, and Shougang is the largest taxpayer as well as employer: around 70 percent of the town's adult population works for Shougang or depends on someone who does. According to the Ministry of the Economy, since 2006 over 50 percent of the monetary transfers that Marcona receives comes from the mining canon.

The company itself claims that as of late 2012, it has provided an estimated USD 967 million in tax payments and other contributions, and that between 2004 and 2012 it contributed USD 74.75 million (Shougang 2013; Kong Aimin 2014). In an interview with the authors, Shougang's General Manager, Kong Aimin, stressed that although the company complies with its tax obligations, how that revenue is redistributed and used depends on the priorities of local authorities.

Although Chinalco inaugurated its Toromocho mine in December 2013, it has suffered setbacks in the original timetable and will not be paying income taxes for several years. Furthermore, the region of Junín – where the mine is located – is a longtime mining area, and within the same province other companies have been operating and paying taxes for years, so the specific contribution from this one will be challenging to separate out.

3.2 Voluntary social investment

Although tax revenues from the extractive industries have been abundant in recent years, Peruvian governments have had considerable difficulty investing these revenues in ways that address basic needs and sustainable development goals. Given this situation, private firms have been motivated to intervene directly, through numerous social programs and community relations initiatives. A recent World Bank study identified some forty foundations, NGOs, trusts and social funds created by the mining industry in Peru in recent years (World Bank, 2010).

Peruvian governments have actively promoted this corporate social invest-ment, by requiring the creation of social funds as part of initial concession contracts, and through legislation and tax incentives to encourage voluntary giving. The Programa Minero de Solidaridad con el Pueblo (PMSP), which ran from 2006 to 2011, was the result of a negotiation between mining indus-try leaders and the Alan García administration. It involved 40 companies that signed agreements to "voluntarily" invest 3.75 percent of their profits in social infrastructure and development programs in their areas of influence, in lieu of a windfall profits tax, which García had promised voters in his presidential campaign. Under President Humala, this program was halted and the tax rate on mining was raised modestly; however, the Obras por Impuestos (Public Works for Taxes) program offers tax benefits for investment in social programs and public works.

Shougang was the only Chinese company eligible to participate in the PMSP. From 2007 to 2011, according to MINEM (2012), Shougang des-ignated about S/. 33.5 million (USD 12 million) to the program, although only an estimated S/. 13.5 million (USD 4.8 million) was spent when the program closed. This is considerably less than the top contributors in the same period, such as Antamina (S/. 775 million destined, S/. 631 million spent) and Yanacocha (S/. 268.5 million destined, S/. 207.5 million spent). Because the amount committed is related to overall profits, it is not fair to compare Shougang's net contribution with that of larger companies in the sector. But if we examine their relative capacity to spend what they committed to, over 2007–2011, Antamina had the highest completion rate (81.4%), followed by Yanacocha (77.3%), while Shougang was farther behind (40%).

Shougang's PMSP contribution was channeled through a nonprofit created by the company in 2007, Asociacion Civil del Hierro: Progreso y Desarrollo. According to the company, this association has invested close to S/. 19.17 mil-lion (USD 6.89 million) in education, health and other projects. However, in a ranking of how transparent mining companies were in PMSP in 2011, this association was ranked 32 out of 39 ("No se cumplió" 2011). Other compa-nies with similarly low transparency were Cerro Verde (a US-owned firm), Xstrata Tintaya and Minsur. So while Shougang has not been transparent about what it has spent, it is not the only firm in that position.

This relatively modest level of investment in the PMSP does not take into account the ongoing commitment that Shougang has to provide services for the town of Marcona, including water and electricity as well as housing for its workers (around 2,000 homes). Unlike most new mining projects in Peru, Marcona had been a "company town" well before Shougang purchased the operation, and the Chinese investors were expected to pick up the tab. According to a recent Shougang publication and interviews with company staff, between 2007 and 2012 the company invested USD 39 million in services and infrastructure for its workers and Marcona as a whole, including maintenance and improvement of housing, water and sewage systems, streetlights, roads and public transportation and recreation. They also claim to have invested over USD 13 million in expanding the nearby highway, built homes and provided services for local school teachers and fishermen, and donated another USD 11.5 million for various social activities in Marcona, Ica and Northern Arequipa (Shougang, 2013).[5]

Ironically, the most recent Chinese mining investment in Peru, Toromocho, also involves investment in what might be called a twenty-first century company town. As part of its investment commitment, and to make way for the mine, Chinalco agreed to relocating the 5,000 residents of Morococha six kilometers away and creating a new city for them. Although this process has not been without controversy, the level and complexity of investment proposed was unprecedented in Peruvian mining history (Sanborn and Chonn 2014). And while Chinalco does not yet pay income taxes, in March 2014 it established a consortium with two Peruvian firms, Volcan and Ferreyros, to implement social infrastructure projects under the Obras por Impuestos program (Volcan, Ferreyros and Chinalco, 2014). These projects would include improved access to drinking water, sewage, and water treatment for the residents of the district of Yauli, in Junín.

3.3 Corporate guilds and multi-stakeholder fora

Although five Chinese firms are formally members of the Sociedad Nacional de Mineria, Petroleo y Energia (SNMPE), the main corporate guild for the industry, they have little active involvement in this group. Yet, according to some testimonies the major Western multinationals also have low participation in this organization, which they see as dominated by older Peruvian firms, and which tends to play a conservative role in Peruvian politics. Representatives of the larger multinationals may defend their interests by addressing MINEM or other government agencies directly rather than working through guild channels, and in this sense the Chinese may be no different. However, Chinese mining companies do participate actively in the Association of Chinese Companies in Peru, and two of their executives are on the board of directors (whose president, Gong Bencai, is vice president of CNPC for Latin America).

---

5 This data is based on a company publication received in 2014. In 20 years of operation, Shougang claims to have invested USD 1 billion in renovation of the mine, plant and related infrastructure, including environmental remediation, and another USD 1 billion in local purchases, and to have created 4,200 direct or indirect jobs (Shougang 2013).

The Grupo de Dialogo Minero (GDM) is a multi-stakeholder forum for dialogue and conflict mediation that was founded in 2000 and involves representatives from companies, government, NGOs, community and indigenous organizations. According to annual reports, the only Chinese-owned firm to attend GDM events for more than one year is Lumina Copper. For the participating firms, it has allowed them to get to know other actors, although the effect of participation on the evolution of social conflicts is questionable.

The low profile of Chinese firms in such fora has reinforced their negative image among some sectors engaged with this industry and has encouraged the perception that they are not transparent in other ways. Chinese companies in Peru have also stood out for their reticence to address the media or invest in ambitious communications programs. This lack of participation and seeming disinterest has also generated some hostility toward Chinese investors in general.

More recently, Peruvian authorities have encouraged Chinese firms to participate in multi-stakeholder *mesas* or roundtables, organized by the Oficina Nacional de Dialogue y Sostenabilidad (ONDS), an agency within the Presidencia del Consejo de Ministrios (PCM) tasked with managing social conflicts. In theory there are two types of *mesa*: the *mesa de diálogo*, aimed at conflict resolution, and the *mesa de desarrollo*, aimed at assessing local needs and delivering services and social programs, in theory to prevent conflict. In practice, their objectives overlap.

Both Chinalco and Shougang have been involved in such efforts. In the case of Chinalco, the Mesa de Diálogo para el Proceso de Reasentamiento Poblacional de Morococha was organized in 2010 and put into action in 2013, to support the relocation of the 5,000 residents of the town. In the case of Shougang, the Mesa de Diálogo para el Desarrollo del Distrito de Marcona was created in June 2013, with the involvement of national and local authorities and representatives of the company. Meeting regularly for over a year, the participants negotiated agreements regarding various urban development issues, including land-use planning and the construction of a new shipping terminal. (Marcona Digital, 2014).

3.4 Labor rules and regulations

The situation of mineworkers in Peru varies considerably depending on the size and nature of the firm and project. Overall, the bonanza experienced by the sector in recent years has meant better wages and working conditions for formal sector workers on the payrolls of the larger firms (Sanborn and Dammert 2013). Mineworkers also enjoy a special labor regime compared to other formal sector laborers, including a higher minimum wage, more stringent health and security requirements, a social security fund covered by companies and annual profit-sharing requirements (MINTRA, 2014; MINEM, 2013).

The principal complaints made by mineworkers' unions tend to involve noncompliance with these legal requirements, or the tendency of firms to subcontract large numbers of workers through tertiary "services" that do not provide full benefits. In theory, companies are only authorized to hire through such intermediaries for activities that are temporary or complementary to regular operations, such as construction or food service provision. However, by 2013 such subcontracts represented 67.4 percent of total direct employment in mining, and labor leaders charged that they were being used to bypass union rights (MINEM Empleo Minería, 2013).

Critics of Chinese firms operating overseas often claim that they have less respect for free labor unions, or a greater tendency to violate workers' rights. In some countries they have also been criticized for bringing in large numbers of Chinese workers instead of hiring locally. In Peru, however, there are still few Chinese firms operating with significant labor forces, and no Chinese company is hiring large numbers of Chinese nationals.

Shougang has the largest work force among Chinese firms in Peru, employing 4,200 people including 2,000 direct hires, just 20 to 40 of whom are Chinese (Kong Aimin, 2014). Irwin and Gallagher (2013) examine government data from 1993 to 2006 and place this company in the middle, among industry peers, for compliance with labor standards. The authors argue that the total pay and benefits received by Shougang workers are among the highest in the industry, including a larger than average number of workers on regular payroll and participating in profit-sharing. This is also the only mining firm in Peru that continues to provide housing for all of its employees as well as basic services to the community in which they live.

So why does Shougang have the highest number of strikes and days lost over union disputes in Peru's mining sector? Authors' interviews with union leaders suggest that the main disagreements involve a dual salary scale that applies a less favorable regime to newer workers. Another point of contention is the company's failure to provide a safer working environment. Outdated machinery, apparently more common in Shougang than the industry average in the firm's early years, have contributed to workplace accidents. For their part, company officials argue that they inherited a highly politicized union leadership that is unwilling to recognize major new investments the company has made in the mine and plant in recent years (Kong Aimin 2014).

Most other Chinese mining firms still have few workers on payroll. Chinalco began operations in late 2013, and by mid-2014 company sources claimed 1,247 direct hires out of a total 2,500 that they expect to have in place when fully operational. Only six employees at that time were Chinese (Barrenechea,

2014). Initial observations and interviews with staff from rival firms suggest that Chinalco is paying wages above the market average for skilled labor.

Mining is a high-risk activity, but firms should take measures to reduce accidents and protect their workers. Since 2011 the Ministry of Energy and Mines has published annual fatal accident rates by firm, with totals of 42 to 52 per year. In these four years, Shougang had two fatalities, one in 2012 and the other in 2014. Chinalco had three, one in 2011 and two in 2013. In contrast, Buenaventura reported three to four fatalities per year and Southern Peru Copper (part of Grupo Mexico) had two or three per year. The majority of fatal accidents involve older Peruvian firms (MINEM 2013).

In general, there is high demand for skilled workers in the Peruvian mining industry, and it would be hard for any major company to systematically violate labor law laws or pay low wages without losing their workforce. However, there is a tendency among some firms to hire tertiary workers to avoid granting union rights and full benefits. So far, this practice seems less prevalent among the Chinese companies in Peru (Irwin and Gallagher, 2013).

One of the most frequent demands by communities where mining operations take place in Peru is for local hiring. Companies are often pressured to hire workers from adjacent areas, and this is a key issue when negotiating exploration or construction permits. Some companies include explicit promises of local hiring in contracts or in published agreements with community leaders. In the mining industry overall, MINEM reported that in 2012 around 53 percent of employees were members of local communities, 46 percent from other regions, and just 0.26 percent foreigners (MINEM Empleo Minería, 2013). While Peru does not demand a specific percentage of local hires, mining companies are expected to promote local employment, including workers' training programs, and to report such efforts to the Ministry.

Shougang officials claim that 70 percent of the population of the city of Marcona depends economically on the company (Kong Aimin 2014). This is an exceptional case as Marcona has been a company town since the 1950s. Chinalco has not published local employment numbers, but has reported investing considerable sums in 2012–2013 in temporary hiring for remediation, construction and other tasks, and is expected to give preference to locals in the longer-term hiring process, although the lack of people with appropriate technical and physical qualifications makes this a challenge. Chinalco is investing in scholarships and training programs for local residents in order to increase prospects for hiring.

In 2010, Lumina Copper signed a "social accord" and a series of agreements with the adjacent community of La Encañada, Cajamarca, in which the company agreed to designate 90 percent of all non-skilled jobs to local residents (MINEM, 2010). However, the project has been stalled since 2013. In the Las Bambas project in Apurimac, the new Chinese owner (MMG) agreed to honor a prior commitment to provide at least one job per family in the local community ("MMG: Sin Comunidades" 2014).

In sum, mining company officials in Peru agree that it is necessary to establish and maintain good relationships with local residents for the successful operation of their projects, and that local hiring plays an important role. Community leaders are also becoming more aware of their negotiating powers and demanding training and hiring in these operations. Although there is still limited evidence on Chinese hiring policies in Peru, to date they appear to be making as much effort as other firms in the sector to meet these expectations.

3.5 Environmental rules and regulations

Since the mining industry was privatized in the early 1990s, authorities have struggled to establish a viable legal framework for regulating the environmental impact of this inherently risky activity.[6] Primary responsibility for such regulation lies with the central government, and until 2008 it was the task of MINEM to review and approve the environmental impact assessments (EIA) presented by investors. This meant that the ministry acted as judge and jury, since it is also responsible for promoting new mining investment. In 2008, however, the Ministry of the Environment (MINAM) was created, with nationwide authority to manage environmental plans and oversee environmental regulatory compliance. Tensions between the two ministries have been constant, with the Ministry of Economy and Finance often siding with the MINEM.

Although the MINAM began with a modest staff and budget, it has enjoyed broad legitimacy and considerable international development assistance. Within the ministry, the Office of Environmental Assessment and Control (OEFA) is responsible for monitoring the environmental conduct of firms in the mining, energy, fishing and industrial sectors, and for applying sanctions where appropriate. In 2012 the government also announced the creation of a National Service of Environmental Certification for Sustainable Investments (SENACE), tasked with reviewing and approving EIAs for high-risk projects. However, by mid-2014 the agency was not yet functioning, and its implementation was seen by some in the administration as an obstacle to new investment.

What has been the response of Chinese firms to environmental regulation in Peru? For the most part, it has been compliance rather than contestation

---

6 Specific regulations include the Environment Code of 1990, the Law to Promote Investments in the Mining Sector of 1991 (Legislative Decree 708) and the General Law of Mining in 1992.

and, overall, Chinese firms have had fewer environmental sanctions than many others in Peru.

As mentioned, Shougang invested in a fully operating state-owned company that had already fallen below global standards for worker safety and environmental safeguards, and the Chinese owners delayed in investing in technology to reduce these risks. Irwin and Gallagher argue, however, that through 2006 Shougang's performance was around average for the industry in Peru. More recent data from OSINERGMIN and OEFA, covering 2007–June 2014 (Table 6.3), suggest the situation remains roughly the same: the amount paid by Shougang in fines for environmental infractions has been less than Doe Run, Volcan or Buenaventura, but higher than Yanacocha or Antamina. In total, the firms that have had to pay the most for infractions are not Chinese, but of US or Peruvian origin.

More recent Chinese-owned projects are not comparable due to the shorter time frame; for example, Rio Blanco was halted in the exploration stage. In March 2014, however, in what is considered by environmental authorities as an emblematic case, the OEFA ordered Chinalco to halt activities at its recently inaugurated Toromocho mine, after inspectors detected a runoff of acid wastewater into two nearby lakes ("OEFA ordena" 2014). Apparently, unusually high rainfall caused an overflow before adequate drainage was built. Given the expectations riding on this project, this was a dramatic move by MINAM and a blow to the company's public relations efforts. Yet the company's response was rapid, the structure was reinforced, and a few days later OEFA authorized Chinalco to resume operations ("Chinalco resumes" 2014). As a result of this incident, the Association of Chinese Companies in Peru asked MINAM to organize informational meetings for all of their members to explain Peru's environmental regulations to newcomers.

4. Case Studies – Learning from the Details

So is there a "Chinese way" of doing business in Latin American mining? If so, can we draw conclusions about the net benefits or costs of the Chinese presence in this sector? Based on the Peruvian experiences analyzed so far, the short answer to both questions is, no. Diverse Chinese firms operate in this region, most are SOEs associated with different levels of government in China, and some of them are based on private capital. The policies of the Chinese government and state banks towards their overseas companies are also evolving, and some may receive more support than others. Rather than generalizing at this stage, therefore, it is important to analyze more closely the nature and operations of each firm and project. The following section focuses

Table 6.3 Environmental fines on mining firms in Peru, 2007–2014, by regulatory agency

	By Agency (UIT)[a]		Total: Real (2014) Value		
	OSINERGMIN	OEFA	UITs	Soles (UIT=3800)	USD (2.87 soles)
Doe Run	865	10,133	10,998	41,791,374	14,561,454
Volcán	1,287	5,746	7,033	26,723,880	9,311,456
Buenaventura	530	1,012	1,542	5,858,042	2,041,130
Shougang	213	1,004	1,217	4,626,234	1,611,928
Minera Yanacocha	268	381	649	2,467,036	859,594
Milpo	190	406	596	2,263,698	788,745
Antamina	14	359	373	1,419,110	494,463
Rio Blanco (Zijin)	100	0	100	380,000	132,404
Chinalco	0	71	71	270,256	94,166

Source: Organismo Supervisor de la Inversión en Energía y Minería- OSINERGMIN. Gerencia de Fiscalización Minera. (http://www.osinergmin.gob.pe/newweb/pages/Publico/1514_.htm?6423). Organismo de Evaluación y Fiscalización Ambiental- OEFA. Dirección de Fiscalización, Sanción y Aplicación de Incentivos. Registro de Actos Administrativos. (http://publico.oefa.gob.pe/sifam/faces/page/fiscalizacion/registroInfractor/principal.xhtml). Superintendencia Nacional de Aduanas y Administración Tributaria (SUNAT). (http://www.sunat.gob.pe/indicestasas/uit.html)

[a] UIT (*Unidad Impositiva Tributaria*) is a tax unit that serves as a benchmark to determine tax obligations and penalties under law. Its amount varies from year to year and is established by decree, according to macroeconomic calculations made by the Peruvian tax authority, SUNAT.

on three cases that represent this diversity of situations: Shougang (Marcona), Chinalco (Toromocho) and Zijin Mining Group (Rio Blanco).

4.1 Shougang: Starting off on the wrong foot

Marcona was the first Chinese mine in South America, and is currently the largest iron-ore operation in Peru. It is located in the Ica region, several hours south of Lima, and involves a mine and smelter initially founded in the 1950s by the US-based Marcona Mining Company. In 1975, Marcona was expropriated by Peru's military government and became Empresa Minera de Hierro del Peru (Hierro Peru). In 1992 it was sold by the Fujimori administration to the Shougang Group, a state-owned conglomerate in Beijing whose chairman had close ties to the highest echelons of power and considerable autonomy to operate overseas. Seeking to turn Shougang into China's leading steel producer, company officials paid USD 120 million for Marcona; more than Peru expected to receive at the time and a price analysts thought was too high.[7]

At the time of purchase Hierro Peru had significant economic losses, an aging labor force and a politicized union. Marcona, a former mining camp, had also seen better days. The concession included not only the mine and processing plant, but also rights to use of surface lands, on which the entire town had been built. In preparation for the sale, the Peruvian government fired half of the work force, but apparently left the unemployed in company housing. According to several sources, when Shougang arrived it evicted them and brought in Chinese workers to take their place. Facing violent protests, the foreign workers were quickly sent back home. In this sense Shougang had already started on the wrong foot, provoking conflict with both its remaining labor force and the surrounding community.[8]

Today, Shougang Hierro Peru is still the sole iron producer in Peru. With two decades under Chinese management, it has become highly profitable. In 2011 it produced more than seven million tons of iron ore and recorded a 50 percent growth in its net profits, and revenue increased another 21.26 percent in 2013. Since 2007 the company also embarked on a series of investments

---

7 This transaction was later scrutinized by anti-corruption investigators in China and Perú. In 1995, Shougang chair, Zhou Guanwu, was forced to resign and his son, Zhou Beifang, given a suspended death sentence on corruption charges related to Shougang operations. http://articles.latimes.com/1995-02-21/news/mn-34483_1_hong-kong-companies In 2001, a Peruvian congressional commission investigated alleged corruption by Fujimori government officials in this sale, but no charges were brought.

8 For more on this history, see Gonzalez Vicente (2012) and Irwin and Gallagher (2013). Company officials interviewed for this project say that 171 workers were brought from China for one year only.

to increase production capacity and safety, including the purchase of new machinery and plants, an expansion plan and a project to process tailings. All of this is estimated to require a USD 1.3 billion investment ("Mineros de Shougang," 2012; Shougang, 2013; Kong Aimin, 2014).

Yet Shougang also remains one of the most-criticized foreign mining firms in Peru. In part this is due to reneging on its original investment commitment and postponing plans to modernize the mine. The company had agreed to invest USD 150 million over 1992–1995, but apparently the political and financial problems in the parent company in China during this period made it impossible to comply (Nolan, 2001; Gonzalez Vicent, 2012, Irwin and Gallagher, 2013). According to Shougang's general manager, their request to extend the time period for this commitment was denied by the government, even while others were approved, and instead they were fined for noncompliance (Kong Aimin, 2014).

Privatization in the 1990s had come with the promise of improved conditions for workers, but the company efforts on that score during the first decade of operations were limited. The main priority was reviving production, and with debts and with limited cash back home, Shougang executives took a hardline approach to union negotiations, leading to frequent strikes and protests that grabbed media attention. This backfired politically, as the Hierro Peru workers were leaders in the national miner workers' confederation, with allies in media and politics. Even as things improved for the firm, labor relations remained difficult to manage, and the union tends to stage annual strikes as part of negotiations. In 2013 and 2014, the company continued to have labor troubles and poor relations with the community as a whole.

Shougang has also been criticized for its noncompliance with some environmental regulations, and has had conflicts with the surrounding community over the provision of water and electricity. Before Shougang's arrival, Hierro Peru provided water and electricity without charge to Marcona. Although this was not included in the privatization package, apparently local authorities were unwilling or unable to assume these responsibilities and Shougang found itself continuing to provide these services to Marcona. Today this is done through a contract with the municipality, though problems with access and distribution are often attributed to the firm. Local fishermen in Marcona also have longstanding complaints regarding the environmental impact of Shougang's mining activities.

For many Peruvians and the international media, Shougang represents the negative stereotype of a Chinese company that lowers standards in the race to feed the demand for ore. But is this really the case? The mine has been operating since the 1950s and the town surrounding the mine continues to depend heavily on its operation. Living standards in Marcona are relatively high by Peruvian standards, and the poverty rate is relatively low. Yet many community members have fond memories of the old company town with a benevolent US owner providing housing and all basic services. Some older workers also miss the days when the state was the owner and the union was more powerful. Although the Marcona mine has been in Chinese hands for years, its owners have not won over the hearts and minds of their neighbors.

How different is this from other, older, operating mining firms in Peru? As discussed in section 2, our research confirms Irwin and Gallagher's prior observations that, objectively, Shougang has not performed significantly worse in terms of labor standards or environmental impact than its Peruvian or international counterparts. From 1996 to 2006, Shougang apparently spent USD 12.7 million to build a new tailings deposit, reduce dust and gases and protect against oil spills (Irwin and Gallager, 2012). In 2007, the company completed the construction of a plant for the town's wastewater treatment although, according to Shougang officials, it did not start operating until 2013 due to the lack of prepared personnel within Marcona city hall. By 2012, the company had spent 77 percent of what it had committed in the original Program of Environmental Compliance and Management (PAMA).

One conclusion to be drawn from this is not that Chinese firms have especially low standards, but rather that Peruvian authorities have been weak in enforcement of norms with virtually all operating firms. Shougang also inherited a more difficult situation than most, and one that is not comparable to greenfield projects without prior constraints. But this does not explain the persistent conflicts the firm has generated locally, the delays in adhering to the EITI process, absence from the Grupo de Dialogo Minero, or reticence to invest more time and resources in improving community and public relations. For some observers, these problems can be attributed to cultural and political differences between Peruvian and Chinese managers, the idea being that the Chinese do not know how to deal with free trade unions, a free press or local democracy. Chinese enterprises overseas do need to learn how to negotiate with workers and local communities and to develop a serious management team for doing businesses abroad (矿企海外遇阻 2012; 秘铁 2013).

Yet, more recent cases suggest that Shougang's problems may have more to do with the company rather than its general Chinese origins. Shougang Corporation has been facing an increasing number of challenges in an industry with more and ever-fiercer competition, and appears to be trailing behind other more modern Chinese mining firms. Whether it is at home or overseas, the group will require better strategies to adapt to different economic, political and environmental demands.

Shougang's relationship with the Peruvian state is also distinct from others, including other Chinese firms. The company had a good initial relationship with the Fujimori administration, but that relationship soured by the late 1990s. Under Toledo (2001–2006), congressional investigations into the privatizations of the 1990s included scrutiny of the Shougang deal, and company officials were suspected of corruption; however, the charges were eventually dropped. Members of congress from Ica have been closer to the union than the company and remain critical of Shougang's operations, and company officials claim they are subjected to far more scrutiny than other firms.

In mid-2013 a Mesa de Diálogo para el Desarrollo was installed in Marcona, convened by the ONDS-PCM, with the purpose of bringing together representatives from the Regional Government of Ica, the Municipality of Marcona, and local civil society, including artisanal fishermen, to discuss local development issues ("Shougang mesa diálogo" 2013). Although this involves public-sector coordination, a representative of the firm has been asked to join the process. In September 2013, the participating institutions agreed on a plan to address the population's main concerns, and as of mid-2014 they were working on a master plan for urban development (MINEM Proyecto Marcona).

Meanwhile, Chinese companies moving into Peru in the past decade have explicitly tried to learn from the mistakes of their predecessors, including not only Shougang but also Western-owned firms. En route to becoming truly global firms, a number of Chinese companies are making efforts to act with social responsibility, and to be perceived as doing so. The leading example in Peru so far is Chinalco.

4.2 Chinalco: Holding to a new standard?

The Aluminum Corporation of China (Chinalco) is an SOE founded in Beijing in 2001 after the merger of a group of aluminum companies as part of China's efforts to consolidate and restructure its industry. Today it is one of the world's largest aluminum producers. In 2007, Chinalco acquired the Canadian junior firm Peru Copper, Inc., obtaining the Toromocho project, an open-pit copper mine and processing plant in the Junín region of central Peru. (Sanborn and Chonn, 2014).

According to media reports, Chinalco has invested over USD 3 billion in this project, making it one of the top 20 copper projects in the world ("中铝秘鲁" 2014; "Toromocho solo produjo" 2014). Built over a six-year period, it is expected to have an operating lifespan of 32 years and to provide almost 18 percent of China's total copper supply, as well as helping Peru to increase its copper production by 20 percent.[9] The project also involves a limestone

---

9   By September 2014, the company had reduced its short-term production figures by 56%, due to delays caused by various factors, including a shortage of adequate power supply, problems with its equipment and community-relations challenges. See "Toromocho solo produjo" (2014).

quarry, concentrator, conveyer belt and tailings dump. It is expected to generate close to USD 7.5 billion in income tax revenues, USD 760 million in royalties, and USD 3.8 billion locally through the mining canon, as well as 2,500 direct jobs during the production period and 7,500 indirect jobs over the project lifespan. Located in a high-altitude historic mining region, this project stands out for its promise to use state-of-the art construction, invest in an acid water treatment plant for the area, and undertake a complex process of relocation of the nearby town of Morococha.

In this case, aware of Shougang's problems, Chinalco executives explicitly aimed to establish this as a socially and environmentally responsible company that would comply with global standards. The first CEO of Minera Chinalco Peru, Gerald Wolfe, had previously run Antamina, considered a global model for "new" mining and CSR. The current CEO, Huang Shanfu, has retained a management team and workforce that are primarily Peruvian. Indeed, since the Shougang protests in the early 1990s, no subsequent Chinese mining company in Peru has tried to bring its own labor force. Chinalco also retained the community-relations consultants originally hired by Peru Copper – Social Capital Group (SCG) – and worked with them to conduct the relocation. Putting this commitment into practice, however, has been challenging for Chinalco from the start.

By objective standards, the old town of Morococha is a bleak site. Originally built as mining camp, it is run down, with communal latrines and a limited water supply. The majority of residents were renters who lived in overcrowded and dilapidated buildings while working in mines nearby. At the edge of town sits a toxic tailings dump around which, until recently, the local children played (Sanborn and Chonn, 2014). Yet, moving is always hard, and Chinalco initially encountered resistance, led by the town's mayor and an influential group of property owners. The relocation of the population of the old town was a project that the former holders of this concession had already begun to negotiate with the population of Morococha before the sale to Chinalco in 2007. According to interviews with representatives from SCG, the relocation was initially going to take place with the help of the Peruvian government, but after Chinalco became the owner of the project, it was decided that the company would assume this responsibility.

By late 2013, after prolonged negotiation, the majority of Morococha residents had agreed to relocate. For the minority that resisted, the main concern appeared to be the desire to negotiate a better deal with the company. At this point, however, the Peruvian government issued a controversial Declaration of Emergency, with an evacuation order to be complied with by February 2014 (INDECI, 2013). The argument was that the area is unfit for occupation due to severe environmental contamination, mudslides and seismic risk – a situation that has been in place for decades. Temporary tents were installed for housing those who would not be considered beneficiaries of Chinalco in the new town, and electricity was interrupted in old Morococha. This action was viewed as the government's forceful attempt to make the remaining people leave (Servindi, 2014). While Chinalco repeatedly emphasized that it would not use force in the relocation, the presence of a small group of holdouts remained a challenge for the company (Cárdenas y de la Torre 2016).

Other challenges emerged around conditions in the new town and nearby communities. Nueva Morococha is a city created by a law approved by Congress in September 2013. All of the families relocated there by Chinalco were offered their own home, with running water, a modern sewage system, and – most importantly – property titles. However, the granting of such titles by the state was delayed, and the company remained the legal owner of the town until late 2015, causing persistent tension. Employment was another source of discontent. Some residents of the new town received employment offers in Toromocho, while others work in other nearby mines or seek new forms of income generation, which are still uncertain. Unlike the old town, Nueva Morococha (also called Carhuacoto) is somewhat farther away from Peru's busy Central Highway, causing complaints of a decline in business for local entrepreneurs, who used to sell to local miners from projects in the area. In the Environmental Impact Assessment (EIA) for Toromocho, Chinalco mentioned that it would promote local employment. However, no explicit agreements were made, and instead a dialogue process, supervised by the PCM, is being arranged to reach an agreement ("convenio marco unificado").

Meanwhile, in September 2014 Chinalco faced conflict with the community of Pachachaca, where they plan to locate the limestone quarry (an element necessary for processing the copper). Around 500 people, including community members and supporters, blocked the central highway to prevent access to the plant while demanding that the company honor alleged commitments made, including promises of jobs to community members, purchase of local products and respect for the environment.[10]

In sum, although Toromocho is a relatively new operation, it has produced both important benefits and significant challenges, for Peru and for its Chinese owners. For starters, it raised the bar for community relocations by prioritizing dialogue and consensus-building rather than sheer use of force, and by the scale and complexity of investment in building a new town (PCM–ONDS 2014). Chinalco initially offered better wages and benefits than the industry

---

10 http://elcomercio.pe/peru/junin/oroya-pobladores-rechazan-construccion-planta-chinalco-noticia-1755693

average, and its financial backing appeared unparalleled even by other Chinese firms operating in this region.

However, whether its operations will fulfill the promise of meeting the highest social and environmental standards in the industry remains to be seen. While the initial relocation process was largely consensual, the larger challenge remains of longer term coexistence between the company and the relocated residents. Toromocho also suffered an early setback on the environmental front, when the OEFA ordered temporary suspension of its operations after heavy rains led to acid water runoffs into two local lakes (OEFA 2014). Although this was an accident, and the company quickly complied with authorities to fix the problem, this incident – as well as the conflicts with neighboring communities – further increased the global scrutiny of this operation and others that follow.

4.3 Zijin Mining Group: Not getting off the starting block

Both Shougang and Chinalco are engaged with populations whose residents have long worked in or around mines and do not challenge the presence of mining operations per se. However, many new concessions in Peru involve territories belonging to peasants and indigenous communities, who make their living from agriculture, follow communal forms of governance and are resistant to hosting large-scale mining operations.

To compare the social impact of Chinese-owned mining operations with those of other national origins, we have included one such case: the Rio Blanco copper and molybdenum project in Piura, on the Peru–Ecuador border. This project would involve a major investment and an enormous engineering feat since the future mine is in a remote, high mountain area, and the minerals would be sent to the Pacific coast through an extensive pipeline. Investors in this project must build the mine, the pipeline and their own port facility.

Since 2007, this project has been in the hands of a consortium of Chinese investors led by Zijin Mining Group (with a 45% stake), followed by Tongling Nonferrous Metals (with 35%), and Xiamen C&D Inc (with 20%). This joint venture allowed them to purchase the British junior Monterrico Metals Plc, the parent company of Rio Blanco Copper S. A. in Peru. For reasons that later became evident, the consortium was the only bidder for this project.

This case is interesting for several reasons. First, even before its sale to the Zijin-led group, Rio Blanco was a high-priority project for the Peruvian government. Both presidents Toledo and Garcia gave special authorization to the investors to hold the concession because Peru's constitution does not allow foreigners to operate within 50 km. of Peru's border unless there are reasons of national urgency (Sanborn and Torres, 2009). The project was marketed to Chinese investors by former British and Peruvian diplomats with a stake in the outcome. Subsequently, during a state visit to China, President Garcia promised the CEO of Zijin and other investors that his administration would smooth the way legally and socially for this project.

At the same time, the project was resisted from the start by the peasant communities in its area of influence: Yanta (Ayabaca), and Segunda and Cajas (Huancabamba). Community leaders claim the agreement for use of the surface land was fraudulent, and they have consistently expressed their opposition to the mine. Although the mine site is remote, the communities have important social and political allies in their struggle to drive out investors, including other communities in the region and along the path of the proposed pipeline, members of the local Catholic Church, peasant self-defense leagues (rondas campesinas), national and global NGOs and British MPs, who sent a delegation to the site in 2006 (Peru Support Group 2007). A referendum, or consulta popular, was held by local leaders in 2007, in which 98.3 percent of residents voted against the development of mining in the region. Yet, the results were contested at the time by the regional government of Piura, and rejected by the Garcia administration.

A third factor is that the project is in an area that has not historically had mining operations and has at least two fragile ecosystems, raising significant environmental concerns. Virtually all of the groups that oppose it also have other sources of income and do not perceive a copper mine as bringing net benefits. Resistance to the project turned to violent confrontations resulting in the deaths of seven people between 2005 and 2009. In August of 2005 a group of 32 community leaders was detained and tortured by security guards and police, allegedly hired by the firm. In 2009 the case reached global public opinion and a lawsuit against the firm was presented in British courts, resulting in a freeze of company assets. In July 2011, Monterrico Metals – now in Chinese hands – agreed to indemnify the community leaders involved in this case.

The level of social opposition to this project helps explain why no other major investors were willing to bid on it. Yet when Zijin Consortium became the new owner in April 2007, their staff was apparently unaware of the extent of local resistance, or believed that government authorities in Peru would really smooth the way. If they were not purposefully misled, they at the least did not conduct due diligence. Furthermore, they retained the same community relations staff as the prior owners, who tried to continue with exploration activities despite widespread opposition. This produced more violent conflict and soon forced the consortium to suspend development of the project altogether.

At one stage, Rio Blanco staff tried to shift strategy and engage one of Peru's most powerful private economic groups as a minority shareholder in exchange for helping move the project along (Sanborn and Torres 2009). Rio Blanco directors also promised to invest USD 80 million in development projects in the area. However, locals accused them of using a corporate-sponsored NGO to harass anti-mining activists, and of launching a smear campaign charging the peasants involved with covering for drug traffickers ("Afirman que ONG" 2009). This campaign backfired, and the alliance with local economic brokers also expired. A new regional president elected in 2010 agreed to respect the will of the locals and defined the project as "nonviable" for the foreseeable future ("Javier Atkins," 2013).

In 2012–2014, the Zijin Consortium tried to reopen dialogue with the communities and prepare the EIA required to construct the mine. In April 2013, a group of Chinese men was detained by community leaders as they tried to visit the site. According to a subsequent communiqué by the company, they were potential investors interested in joining the project, but Rio Blanco agreed to desist with site visits as a condition for their release (Cooperacción, 2013). Since then Zijin reconstituted its local staff, secured new political allies and hired the same community relations firm that works with Chinalco, but as of 2016 community resistance remained strong.

By most assessments, the Rio Blanco project does not appear to offer net benefits to Peru, or to the Piura region where it would be based, even though the central government continues to list it among the top 25 priority projects. It does not have the consent of those who own the land nor the "social license" needed from the various communities that would be affected along the pipeline route. This situation is not unique to Zijin, however, and indeed there are numerous cases of non-Chinese mining companies with concessions on lands belonging to peasant communities that do not want mining, or that fear the negative environmental and social impacts it may bring.

5. Conclusions

There is no doubt that the relationship with China is fundamental for Peru today, as for most of Latin America. China is Peru's number one trading partner, the leading investor in the mining sector, and an increasingly important presence in hydrocarbons and commercial fisheries as well.

Whether expanding ties with China will help or hinder countries like Peru in their efforts to sustain growth and raise living standards for their populations remains a subject of intense debate. In the Peruvian case, there are deep historical ties with China, which have facilitated the relations being forged today. At the same time, since the 1990s all Peruvian governments have maintained a strong emphasis on free trade and private initiative and have been giving high priority to the extractive industries, especially mining, as a driver for growth. Hence, the promotion of foreign investment in primary sectors has gone hand in hand with the opening of new channels of interaction with numerous Western, Eastern and Southern partners. Trade with China – but also with the rest of the world – contributed to Peru's booming economy over the last decade, and to its ability to weather the effects of global financial crisis.

A closer analysis of the dynamics of Peru's relationship with China suggests that although this tends to reinforce Peru's overall position as a mineral exporter, the country has not experienced significant deindustrialization. Although the relations are highly asymmetrical and not all sectors of the economy have benefitted, the net effect of expanded markets and access to lower-priced intermediate goods appears to be positive for Peruvian industry. Meanwhile, new investment from China has allowed Peru to develop large-scale mineral projects with important spinoffs in other sectors of the economy, even amidst a context of global uncertainty.

What about the impact of Chinese firms "on the ground"? Some analysts claim that the differences between Chinese and other transnational mining firms today are not that significant. Others have argued that the key issue is not whether a company is Chinese, or of any other nationality, but rather the willingness and capacity of host countries to regulate them adequately. Based on the case studies undertaken for this project, and reports by other researchers, there is no clear "Chinese way" of doing business in Peru's mining sector. Although Chinese firms may have some factors in common – especially the SOEs – on the ground they may differ as much from each other as from other companies in this sector.

In several cases, neither the Chinese investors nor their country's diplomats conducted due diligence on the social conditions they would face, and Peruvian authorities were not forthcoming about these conditions, either. This was true with the investments made by Shougang in the early 1990s, but also with Zijin and the Rio Blanco project in 2007. In all three cases, company staff – either Chinese, or Peruvians they hired – also made mistakes in engaging with unions, communities and local elected officials in Peru's volatile democracy. Although the Chinese government had a strong interest in making these investments work, their overseers may have initially been too inexperienced, or too far away, to guide such efforts.

Nonetheless, what we are observing today are processes of learning on the part of Chinese investors and their political allies. This includes learning from other firms in the industry and hiring better managers and consultants to guide them through the process. There are also increased efforts by both Chinese and Peruvian government authorities to help these firms develop major projects, which for the most part are not different from the support received by other investors in this industry.

At present, the most widely watched cases of Chinese mining investment in South America are the Toromocho mine in Junín and the Las Bambas project in Apurímac, purchased in 2014 by MMG (China Minmetals). In both cases, Chinese SOEs committed to building state-of-the art mining operations and moving entire communities to new quarters, where living conditions were expected to improve. This has not been done before in Peru, and is apparently rare in China as well. For China, and for Peru, a lot is riding on showing the world that both sides are serious about complying with global standards. Only time will tell if this is the case.

References

Newspaper references

(2009) "Shougang Announced in 2009 that It Would Invest USD 1,200 Million in the Expansion of Its Marcona Mine." *Andina*. http://www.andina.com.pe/espanol/Noticia.aspx?id=DqTqn/8OzyE=#.UxzTzVzePwI

(2009) "Afirman que ONG Integrando incita a la violencia en Huancabamba." *La República*. http://www.larepublica.pe/19-11-2009/afirman-que-ong-integrando-incita-la-violencia-en-huancabamba

(2011). "No se cumplió con presentar informes del aporte minero." *El Comercio*. http://elcomercio.pe/impresa/notas/no-se-cumplio-presentar-informes-aporte-minero/20110904/1269611

(2012). "矿企海外遇阻" (*kuang qi haiwai yuzu*). 今日中国. http://www.chinatoday.com.cn/ctchinese/economy/article/2012-07/30/content_475262.htm

(2013)."JavierAtkins:'RíoBlancoesunproyectoirrealizableparaestageneración'." *LaRepública*. http://www.larepublica.pe/27-04-2013/javier-atkins-rio-blanco-es-un-proyecto-irrealizable-para-esta-generacion

(2013). "Chinalco eleva en 20% meta de producción anual de cobre en proyecto en Perú. *Latinominería*. http://www.latinomineria.com/2013/06/chinalco-eleva-en-20-meta-de-produccion-anual-de-cobre-en-proyecto-en-peru/

(2013). "Peru's agro-exports to China grew 8.7 times in post-FTA period." *Andina*. http://www.andina.com.pe/ingles/noticia-perus-agroexports-to-china-grew-87-times-in-postfta-period-461881.aspx

(2013). "Shougang Hierro instaló mesa de diálogo en Marcona." *Mining Press*. http://www.miningpress.com.pe/nota/123798/shougang-hierro-instalo-mesa-de-dialogo-en-marcona

(2013). "秘铁: 首钢的整合之痛" (*mi tie: Shougang de zhenhe zhi tong*). 中国企业报. http://finance.sina.com.cn/roll/20130917/025216779430.shtml

(2013). "China's Copper Mine Starts Production in Peru." China.org. http://www.china.org.cn/business/2013-12/13/content_30888050.htm

(2014). "中铝秘鲁项目投运 为中国海外最大铜矿" (*zhong lu bilu xiangmu touyun wei zhongguo haiwai zuida tong kuang*). Xinhua. http://news.xinhuanet.com/energy/2013-12/12/c_125846135.htm

(2013). "Chinese Outward Foreign Direct Investment." *ChinaGoAbroad*. http://www.chinagoabroad.com/en/commentary/chinese-outward-foreign-direct-investment

(2014). "中铝秘鲁项目为有色企业"走出去"提供经验" (*zhonglu bilu xiangmu wei youse qiye zou chuqu tigong jingyan*). 长江有色金属网. http://finance.sina.com.cn/money/future/20140110/085017909364.shtml

(2014). "Las inversiones chinas en Perú sumarán US$12 mil millones." *La Republica.* http://www.larepublica.pe/13-08-2014/las-inversiones-chinas-en-peru-sumaran-us-12-mil-millones

(2014). "Murió un trabajador tras explosión en planta de Shougang." *El Comercio.* http://elcomercio.pe/peru/ica/murio-trabajador-explosion-planta-shougang-noticia-1704161

(2014). "Restablecen servicio de energía eléctrica en Morococha antigua." *Servindi.* http://servindi.org/actualidad/102497.

(2014) "Iglesia pide a Presidente Ollanta solucionar problema de vivienda en Morococha," *Servindi*, 28 de febrero http://servindi.org/actualidad/102209

(2014). "Empresas chinas son los nuevos actores de la minería peruana." El Comercio. http://elcomercio.pe/economia/peru/empresas-chinas-son-nuevos-actores-mineria-peruana-noticia-1722993

(2014). "Volcan, Ferreryros y Chinalco se consorcian para ejecutar Obras por Impuestos en Junín." *Gestión.* http://gestion.pe/economia/volcan-ferreyros-y-chinalco-se-consorcian-ejecutar-obras-impuestos-junin-2092179

(2014). "OEFA ordena a Minera Chinalco Perú S.A. detener aquellas actividades causantes de vertimientos en lagunas de Junín." OEFA. http://www.oefa.gob.pe/noticias-institucionales/el-oefa-ordena-a-minera-chinalco-peru-s-a-detener-aquellas-actividades-causantes-de-vertimientos-en-lagunas-de-junin

(2014). El OEFA consta que Minera Chinalco Perú S.A. cumplió con detener la descarga de efluentes que vertían hacia dos lagunas de Junín." OEFA. http://www.oefa.gob.pe/noticias-institucionales/oefa-constata-chinalco-cumplio

(2014). "Informe técnico reunión de la mesa de diálogo por el desarrollo de Marcona y la PCM." Marcona Digital. http://marconadigitalnoticias.blogspot.com/2014/06/informe-tecnico-reunion-de-la-mesa-de.html

(2014) "Glencore Xstrata Sells Las Bambas Mine to Chinese Consortium," *Wall Street Journal.* http://online.wsj.com/news/articles/SB10001424052702303887804579499722419173960

(2014). "Peru captó casi la mitad de las inversiones chinas en la región," *El Comercio*, Portafolio, 2 de septiembre, B1.

(2014) "Toromocho solo produjo 31 mil toneladas de cobre a Julio," *El Comercio*, Portafolio, 9 de septiembre, p. B4.

Articles, books and bulletins

Aquino, Carlos (2013). "China and Peru Relations after 41 Years of Diplomatic Links and Three Years of a FTA," http://asiapacifico-carlos.blogspot.com/2013/03/china-and-peru-relations-after-41-years_6404.html

Arellano-Yanguas, Javier (2011). *¿Minería sin fronteras? Conflicto y desarrollo en regiones mineras del Perú*, Lima: IEP.

Arzobispado de Huancayo (2014), "Arzobispo propone a presidente Ollanta solución a problema de vivienda en Morococha," Bulletin, May 8, 2014. http://www.arzobispadodehuancayo.org/?idt=7&id=1088&web=boletines

Capechi (2014). "Comercio con China." http://www.capechi.org.pe/_5_1.html

Cárdenas, Carolina and Giuliano Gavilano (2013). "El Efecto de las Importaciones Provenientes de China en los Salarios Reales: Una Aproximación Microeconómica para el Caso Peruano entre los Años 2007 y 2010." Investigación Económica 2. Lima: Universidad del Pacífico, 2013.

Cárdenas, Gerardo y Karen de la Torre (2016). "Nueva Morococha: Las consecuencias del reasentamiento," MONGABAY, July 28, 2016. https://es.mongabay.com/2016/07/nueva-morococha-las-consecuencias-del-reasentamiento/

Chen, Taotao and Miguel Pérez Ludeña (2013). "China Foreign Direct Investment in Latin America and the Caribbean: China-Latin America Cross-Council Taskforce." Working document prepared for the Summit on the Global Agenda World Economic Forum, Abu Dhabi, November 18–20, 2013. Economic Commission for Latin America and the Caribbean (ECLAC). http://www.eclac.org/cgi-bin/getProd.asp?xml=%20/publicaciones/xml/1/51551/P51551.xml&xsl=/tpl-i/p9f.xsl%20&base=/tpl-i/top-bottom.xslt

"Cientos de familias en la oscuridad total por proyecto minero Toromocho," Servindi, February 21, 2014. http://www.servindi.org/actualidad/101661

Congreso de la República del Perú. "La Privatización de la Empresa Shougang Hierro Perú S. A. A." (Resumen de Caso). Lima, Perú. http://www.congreso.gob.pe/comisiones/2002/CIDEF/resumenes/privatiza/hierro.pdf

CooperAcción (2013). "Piura: Resumen informativo Abril 2013." http://www.cooperaccion.org.pe/OBSERVATORIO/piura_abril13.html

Friedman, Thomas (2006). "Red China or Green?," New York Times, June 30, 2006. http://www.nytimes.com/2006/06/30/opinion/30friedman.html?_r=2&

Gestión (2014). "MMG: Sin las comunidades locales, será muy difícil operar en Las Bambas." June 2. http://gestion.pe/economia/mmg-sin-comunidades-locales-muy-dificil-operar-bambas-2099003

Glave, Manuel and Juana Kuramoto (2007). "La minería peruana: lo que sabemos y lo que aún nos falta saber." En: Investigación, políticas y desarrollo en el Perú. Lima: GRADE. Available at: http://biblioteca.clacso.edu.ar/Peru/grade/20100513021350/InvPolitDesarr-4.pdf

Global Witness and Syntao (2013). "Transparency Matters: Disclosure of Payments to Governments by Chinese Extractive Companies." January 2013. Reports available at http://www.globalwitness.org/transparencymatters

Gonzalez Vicente, Rubén (2012). "The Political Economy of Sino-Peruvian Relations: A New Dependency?" Journal of Current Chinese Affairs 41, 1: 97–131.

Gonzalez Vigil, Fernando (2012). "Relaciones de comercio e inversión del Perú con el Asia – Pacífico." In Instituto de Estudios Internacionales (IDEI) (ed.), "Veinte años de Política Exterior Peruana" (1991–2011). (209–41) Lima: PUCP.

Grupo Propuesta Ciudadana (2011). El Programa Minero de Solidaridad con el Pueblo. Ranking de transparencia de las empresas mineras. Cuarta evaluación. Lima: USAID.

Grupo Propuesta Ciudadana (2013). "Transparencia y Rendición de Cuentas." First Edition, November 2013. Lima. Available at: http://www.propuestaciudadana.org.pe/sites/default/files/Transparencia%20y%20Rendici%C3%B3n%20de%20Cuentas%20-%20XXI%20Ciclo%20Formaci%C3%B3n.pdf

Guo Jie (2014), "Too Big to Fail? China's Economic Presence in Latin America," en Zhongguo Guoji Zhanlüe Pinglun 2014 (China International Strategy Review 2014), Beijing: Shijie Zhishi Chubanshe, July, 160–177.

Indeci (2014). Peligro de movimiento en masa en el distrito de Morococha – Junin. Reporte de Peligro no. 202. 27/2/2014. http://www.indeci.gob.pe/objetos/alerta/NTgy/20140227233200.pdf

"Informe de Conflictos Piura." (2014). Available through Todo sobre Río Blanco. http://www.todosobrerioblanco.com/adjuntos/PrimerInformeObservatorioConflictosPIURA.pdf

"Informe de diferencias, controversias y conflictos sociales: Casos emblemáticos – Morococha y Espinar," Willaqniki No. 15, February 2014, published by the Presidencia del Consejo de Ministros – Oficina Nacional de Diálogo y Sostenibilidad (PCM – ONDS). http://onds.pcm.gob.pe/wp-content/uploads/2014/02/WILLAQNIKI_15.pdf

"Informe técnico reunión de la mesa de diálogo por el desarrollo de Marcona y la PCM," Marcona Digital, June 23, 2014. http://marconadigitalnoticias.blogspot.com/2014/06/informe-tecnico-reunion-de-la-mesa-de.html

Instituto Nacional de Defensa Civil, INDECI (2013). "Declaratorias de estado de emergencia a nivel nacional 2013–2014." Last updated: December 2013. http://sinpad.indeci.gob.pe/UploadPortalSINPAD/CONSOLIDADO%20DEE%202013–2014%20EC%2021.01.14.pdf

Instituto Nacional de Estadística e Informática, INEI (2014). "Evolución de las Exportaciones e Importaciones." Informe Técnico no. 2, February.

Irwin, Amos and Kevin Gallagher (2013). "Chinese Mining Investment in Latin America. A Comparative Perspective." *Journal of Environment and Development* 22, 2: 207–34.

Karl, Terry Lynn (2006). "Ensuring Fairness: The Case for a Transparent Fiscal Social Contract." http://policydialogue.org/publications/working_papers/ensuring_fairness_the_case_for_a_transparent_fiscal_social_contract/)

Kotschwar, B., T. Moran et al. (2011). "Do Chinese Mining Companies Exploit More?," *Americas Quarterly*. http://www.americasquarterly.org/do-chinese-mining-companies-exploit-more.

La República. (2012). "Mineros de Shougang anuncian huelga indefinida para la primera quincena de setiembre," September 8, http://www.larepublica.pe/08-09-2012/mineros-de-shougang-anuncian-huelga-indefinida-para-la-primera-quincena-de-setiembre

Lin, Li-Wen (2012). "Corporate Social Responsibility in China: Window Dressing or Structural Change?" *Berkeley Journal of International Studies* 28(1): 9–10.

Ministerio de Energía y Minas, MINEM (2013). "Empleo en Minería" in the Anuario de Minería 2013. Section available at http://www.minem.gob.pe/minem/archivos/file/Mineria/PUBLICACIONES/ANUARIOS/2013/05EMPLEO.pdf

Ministerio de Energía y Minas, MINEM (2013). "Cartera Estimada de Proyectos Mineros." Last version used: January 2014.

Ministerio de Energía y Minas, MINEM. (2015). "Proyecto Minero Marcona." http://www.minem.gob.pe/minem/archivos/PROYECTO%20MINERO%20MARCONA(4).pdf

Nolan, Peter (2001). *China and the Global Economy. National Champions, Industrial Policy and the Big Business Revolution.* New York: Palgrave.

OEFA (2014). "OEFA ordena a Minera Chinalco Perú S.A. detener aquellas actividades causantes de vertimientos en lagunas de Junín," March 28. http://www.oefa.gob.pe/noticias-institucionales/el-oefa-ordena-a-minera-chinalco-peru-s-a-detener-aquellas-actividades-causantes-de-vertimientos-en-lagunas-de-junin

PCM (2014). http://onds.pcm.gob.pe/wp-content/uploads/2014/02/WILLAQNIKI_15.pdf

Peru Support Group (2007), *Minería y desarrollo en el Perú: Con especial referencia al proyecto Río Blanco, Piura.* Lima: Oxfam, IEP, CIPCA.

ProInversión (2014). Estadísticas de Inversión Extranjera. Lima: ProInversión. http://www.investinperu.pe/modulos/JER/PlantillaStandard.aspx?are=0&prf=0&jer=5652&sec=1

Sanborn, Cynthia (2014). "De la serpiente al caballo: balance de las relaciones Peru–China," *Ideele*, no. 236. http://revistaideele.com/ideele/content/de-la-serpiente-al-caballo-balance-de-las-relaciones-per%C3%BA-china

Sanborn, Cynthia and Víctor Torres (2009). *La economía china y las industrias extractivas: desafíos para el Perú.* Lima: Fondo Editorial de la Universidad del Pacífico y CooperAcción.

Sanborn, Cynthia and Juan Luis Dammert (2013). "Extracción de recursos naturales, desarrollo económico e inclusión social: Peru." *Americas Quarterly Special Report.* Available at: http://www.as-coa.org/sites/default/files/MiningReportPeru2013.pdf

Sanborn, Cynthia and Alexis Yong (2014), "Peru's Economic Boom and the Asian Connection," in Cynthia Arnson and Jorge Heine, eds., *Reaching Across the Pacific: Latin America and Asia in the New Century.* Woodrow Wilson International Center for Scholars, Washington, DC; Wilson Center.

Sanborn, Cynthia and Victoria Chonn Ching (2014). "Making Ways for Mines: Chinese Investment in Peru." *ReVista, the Harvard Review of Latin America,* Winter, vol. 13, no. 2, published by the David Rockefeller Center for Latin American Studies, Harvard University.

Shougang Hierro Peru (2013). Shougang Hierro Perú S. A. A. (Memoria, 2013).

SPDA (2014). "SPDA organizó conversatorio sobre la implementación, funciones e importancia del SENACE," Actualidad Ambiental, 22 August. http://www.actualidadambiental.pe/?p=24684

Superintentencia de Administración Tributaria, SUNAT. (2016). "Unidad Impositiva Tributaria – UIT." Available at http://www.sunat.gob.pe/indicestasas/uit.html.

Tan-Mullins (2012). "China: Gradual Change. Increasing Transparency and Accountability in the Extractive Industries." Transparency Accountability Initiative, May. Available at http://www.transparency-initiative.org/reports/emerging-economies-ta-extractive-industries

Wise, Carol (2012). "Tratados de libre comercio al estilo chino: los TLC Chile-China y Peru-China, in Apuntes: Revista de Ciencias Sociales, no. 71, vol. 39, Second Semester, July–December.

World Bank (2010). "Mining Foundations, Trust and Funds," A Sourcebook, June. http://siteresources.worldbank.org/EXTOGMC/Resources/Sourcebook_Full_Report.pdf

Xinhua (2014). "Chinalco Resumes Copper Mining in Peru," April 15. http://news.xinhuanet.com/english/china/2014-04/15/c_133264538.htm

Yong, David (2016). "China Fisheries Bankruptcy Bid Deepens Bond Pain on Peru Concern," Bloomberg, July 26. http://www.bloomberg.com/news/articles/2016-07-26/china-fishery-s-bankruptcy-bid-deepens-bond-pain-on-peru-concern

Zarksy, Lyuba and Leonardo Stanley (2013). "Can Extractive Industries Promote Sustainable Development? A Net Benefits Framework and a Case Study of the Marlin Mine in Guatemala." *Journal of Environment Development* 22(2): 131–154.

Websites

Agencia de Promoción de la Inversión Privada (Pro Inversión). http://www.proinversion.gob.pe/

Asociación Civil del Hierro, Shougang Hierro. http://www.shougang.com.pe/achierro.htm

Asociación de Empresas Chinas en el Perú. http://asociacionchina.net/directorio/

Cámara de Comercio Peruano China (CAPECHI). http://www.capechi.org.pe/
Extractive Industries Transparency Initiative (EITI), Peru. http://eitiperu.minem.gob.pe/
Grupo de Diálogo, Minería y Desarrollo Sostenible. http://www.grupodedialogo.org.pe/
Minera   Chinalco   Perú   S.A.   http://chinalco.piensamasalla.com/es/producci%
    C3%B3n-y-beneficios
Ministerio de Desarrollo e Inclusión Social (MIDIS) – Dirección General de Seguimiento
    y Evaluación. http://www.midis.gob.pe/mapas/infomidis/
Oficina Nacional de Diálogo y Sostenibilad (ONDS) de la Presidencia del Concejo de
    Ministros (PCM). http://onds.pcm.gob.pe/objetivos-y-funciones/
Organismo de Evaluación y Fiscalización Ambiental (OEFA). http://www.oefa.gob.pe/
Sociedad Nacional de Minería, Petróleo y Energía (SNMPE). http://www.snmpe.org.pe/
    quienes-somos-snmpe/asociados/mineria.html
Superintendencia del Mercado de Valores (SMV). http://www.smv.gob.pe/Frm_
    VerArticulo.aspx?data=BB59C7F473A6A3A7364E3D611A6E59708F2EC053FD3A
    D4533881D5B48E6C9458CAFA3A

Interviews

Kong Aimin, general manager, Shougang Hierro Peru S. A. A., with the presence of trans-
    lator Kit Yi Ho. May 19, 2014. Lima, Peru.
Alvaro Barranechea, Gerente de Asuntos Corporativos, Minera Chinalco Peru S. A.
    Personal communication via electronic correspondence. April 2, April 23 and June
    2, 2014.
Alan Dabbs, Silvia Matos and team, Social Capital Group, January 21, 2014. Lima, Peru.
Richard Graeme, senior vice president and general manager; Jing Zhao, public relations
    manager, and Jessica Morales, government relations manager. Lumina Copper. March
    19, 2013.
Inhabitants of Nueva Morococha (names withheld on request). January 24, 2014. Nueva
    Morococha, Peru.
Inhabitants of the original Morococha (names withheld on request). January 25, 2014.
    Morococha, Peru.
Silvia Matos, consultant from Social Capital Group, January 8, 2013. Lima, Peru.
Delia Morales Cuti, directora de supervisión, OEFA. Personal communication via elec-
    tronic correspondence. April 3, 2014.
Marcial Salomé Ponce, mayor of Morococha. January 24, 2014. Nueva Morococha, Peru.
Rubén Villasante, Social Capital Group, January 23, 2014. Nueva Morococha, Peru.

Part IV

CHINA'S AND LATIN AMERICA'S AGRICULTURAL SECTORS

Chapter 7

CHINA'S INFLUENCE ON DEFORESTATION IN BRAZILIAN AMAZONIA: A GROWING FORCE IN THE STATE OF MATO GROSSO

Philip M. Fearnside and Adriano M. R. Figueiredo

China influences deforestation in Brazilian Amazonia in a variety of ways, including the direct influence of Chinese enterprises. We examine these issues and present data on the growth of China's role in Brazil's soy and beef sectors, which are major drivers of deforestation in the country's Amazon region. We concentrate on the state of Mato Grosso, where soy and beef production are dominant forces and where China is the principal destination for exports. China also purchases other commodities from Brazilian Amazonia, such as iron ore and timber. Chinese financing is increasingly influencing and accelerating infrastructure development projects such as a planned railway that would connect Mato Grosso to ports on the Amazon River in order to facilitate soy exports.

We find that increases in Brazil's exports to China are significantly, positively associated with increasing deforestation rates. Nevertheless, deforestation has been declining in recent years, thanks to improved regulation, including a powerful new measure that disqualifies any operation with environmental irregularities from benefiting from public loans. However, the future of this policy is not secure. The influx of money from the booming Chinese export market is reshaping the Brazilian political landscape. The "ruralist" voting block representing large landowners has used its newfound influence to push for relaxing environmental regulation. If Brazil is to consolidate its gains against deforestation, especially during an agricultural export boom, it will need to hold fast to its regulatory progress and resist the call to sacrifice long-term conservation goals for short-term export revenue.

1. Introduction

As a country with vast natural resources, including agricultural land, timber, hydroelectric capacity and mineral deposits, Brazil is a logical source of imports to supply China's burgeoning demand. Brazil is also a logical destination for Chinese investment, particularly in the extraction or production of commodities and the transport infrastructure needed to facilitate export. Brazil's political stability and openness to foreign investment, combined with the financial power provided by China's strong economy, translate into the impressive growth and scale of China's presence in Brazil. China has become Brazil's largest trading partner and the greatest source of export surplus from agricultural goods (USD 85 billion in 2011), contributing to Brazil's economic growth and to reducing the country's vulnerability to external economic crises (da Nóbrega, 2012). It should, therefore, not come as a surprise that China exerts multiple influences on events in Brazil, often to the detriment of Amazon forest.

Brazil's state of Mato Grosso (Figures 7.1 and 7.2) is one of the main targets for Chinese investment and is the source of much of a major Brazilian export: soybeans. Mato Grosso is twice the size of the US state of California and is one of the most important agricultural areas in South America and in the world. In the 2012–2013 agricultural year Mato Grosso's estimated production was 23.5 million tons of soybeans (29% of Brazil's production), with 7 million hectares planted and a productivity of 2,959 Kg/ha (Brazil, IBGE, 2013). Improvements in transport infrastructure are expected to allow a much larger area to be planted with soy, especially in the northern part of the state. Chinese land purchases in Mato Grosso have been mostly for soy, but they also include some areas for cotton production.

2. Brazil's Exports to China and the World

Brazil's exports to the world, including China, increased dramatically over the 2003–2008 period. The annual mean growth rate of Brazilian exports in the 1990–2002 period was 5.6 percent, but the annual rate jumped to 22 percent for the 2003–2008 period (Bittencourt et al., 2012, 102). The global economic downturn then led to a fall in total Brazilian exports in 2009, but economic recovery was followed by a new export record in 2010. Exports bound for China grew much faster than the trend for Brazilian exports in general: over the 2000–2008 period exports to China grew at an average annual rate of

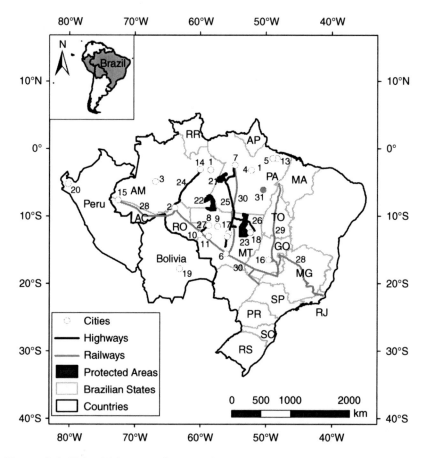

Figure 7.1 Cities, highways, railways and protected areas mentioned in the text (created by Marcelo dos Santos)

Cities: 1 = Itacoatiara, 2 = Porto Velho, 3 = Carauarí, 4 = Altamira, 5= Barcarena, 6 = Cuiabá, 7 = Santarém, 8 = Juína, 9 = Porto dos Gaúchos, 10 = Vilhena, 11 = Sapezal, 12 = Lucas do Rio Verde, 13 = Belém, 14 = Manaus, 15 = Cruzeiro do Sul, 16 = Anápolis, 17 = Sorriso, 18 = Querência, 19 = Santa Cruz, 20 = Piura. *Protected areas:* 21 = Amazonia National Park, 22 = Juruena National Park, 23 = Xingu Indigenous Park. *Highways:* 24 = BR-319, 25 = BR-163, 26 = MT-322, 27 = MT-319. *Railways:* 28 = Transcontinental Railway, 29 = North-South Railway, 39 = Ferronorte Railway. *Other:* 31 = Carajás Mine. *Brazilian states:* AC = Acre, AM = Amazonas, AP = Amapá, GO = Goiás, MA = Maranhão, MG = Minas Gerais, MT = Mato Grosso, PA = Pará, PR =Paraná, RJ = Rio de Janeiro, RO = Rondônia, RR = Roraima, RS = Rio Grande do Sul, SC = Santa Catarina, SP = São Paulo, TO = Tocantins.

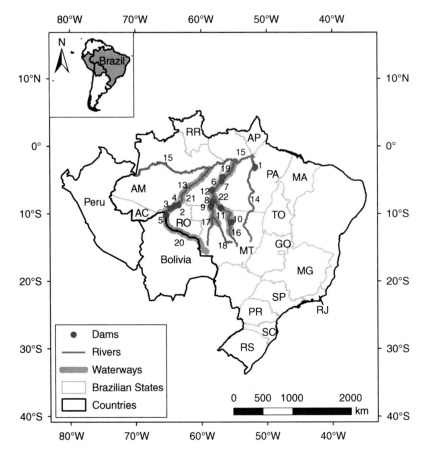

Figure 7.2 Dams, rivers and waterways mentioned in the text (created by Marcelo dos Santos)

Dams: 1 = Belo Monte Dam, 2 = Samuel Dam. 3 = Jirau Dam, 4 = Santo Antônio Dam, 5 = Guajará Mirim (Cachoeira Riberão) Dam, 6 = São Luiz do Tapajós Dam, 7 = Jatobá Dam, 8 = São Simão Alto Dam, 9 = Salto Augusto Baixo Dam, 10 = Sinop Dam, 11 = São Manoel Dam, 12 = Chacorão Dam. ***Rivers:*** 13 = Madeira River, 14 = Xingu River, 15 = Amazon River, 16 = Teles Pires River, 17 = Juruena River. 18 = Arinos River, 19 = Tapajós River. ***Waterways:*** 20 = Guaporé Waterway, 21 = Madeira Waterway, 22 = Tapajós Waterway. ***Brazilian states:*** AC = Acre, AM = Amazonas, AP = Amapá, GO = Goiás, MA = Maranhão, MG = Minas Gerais, MT = Mato Grosso, PA = Pará, PR = Paraná, RJ = Rio de Janeiro, RO = Rondônia, RR = Roraima, RS = Rio Grande do Sul, SC = Santa Catarina, SP = São Paulo, TO = Tocantins.

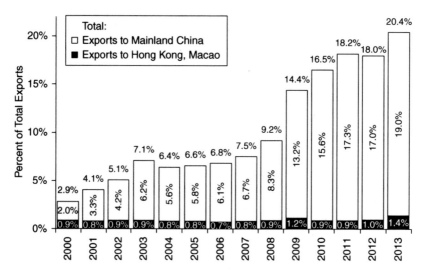

Figure 7.3 Brazil's exports to China as a share of all Brazilian exports, 2000–2013
Source: UN Comtrade (2014).

40.4 percent. They even grew by 23.1 percent in 2009 when Brazil's total exports fell by 22.2 percent (Bittencourt et al., 2012, 103). The percentage of Brazil's exports represented by China grew from only 2 percent (or 2.9% including Hong Kong and Macao) in 2000 to 19 percent (or 20.4% including Hong Kong and Macao) in 2013, making China Brazil's number one individual market, as shown in Figure 7.3 (UN Comtrade, 2014). This percentage doubled in the 2008–2012 period. The increased exports to China were mirrored by decreases in exports to the United States and the European Union.

The nature of what was being exported also changed, with primary commodities increasing from 38.9 percent in 2000 to 44.9 percent in 2008 and 51.0 percent in 2009, when China became dominant (Bittencourt et al., 2012, 106). The increasing role of China is an important factor in this shift. In 2000, Brazil accounted for 27 percent of Latin America's primary and resource-based products (PRBP) exports to China, but that share grew to 48 percent in 2012, after a peak of 51 percent in 2011, as shown in Figure 7.4 (UN Comtrade, 2014). For soybeans and other seeds this percentage grew from 39 percent in 2000 to 79 percent in 2012, after a peak of 83 percent in 2009 (SITC Revision 3, 222). For iron ore and iron concentrate the percentage each year was always between 87 and 91 percent (SITC Revision 3, 281). For crude petroleum, after some variation in the 2000–2003 period, the percentage stabilized between 59 and 65 percent after 2007 (SITC Revision 3, 333). All of these products have significant impact on the environment. Unfortunately,

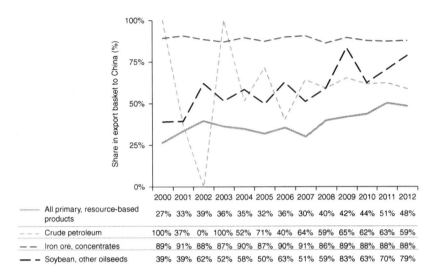

	2000	2001	2002	2003	2004	2005	2006	2007	2008	2009	2010	2011	2012
.... All primary, resource-based products	27%	33%	39%	36%	35%	32%	36%	30%	40%	42%	44%	51%	48%
– – – Crude petroleum	100%	37%	0%	100%	52%	71%	40%	64%	59%	65%	62%	63%	59%
— — Iron ore, concentrates	89%	91%	88%	87%	90%	87%	90%	91%	86%	89%	88%	88%	88%
— – Soybean, other oilseeds	39%	39%	62%	52%	58%	50%	63%	51%	59%	83%	63%	70%	79%

Figure 7.4 Share of Brazil in 2000–2012 Latin American exports to China, by type
Source: UN Comtrade (2014).
Notes: Commodities are defined using SITC Rev.3. Soybeans and other seeds corre-
spond to 222, iron ore and concentrates to 281, and crude petroleum to 333.

cross-national studies indicate that export of primary commodities is associated with the least gains in indicators of human well-being in the exporting
countries (Carmignani and Avom, 2010).

3. China and Deforestation in the State of Mato Grosso

Some of the main drivers of Amazon deforestation include roads, agribusiness development (cattle pasture, soybean production, logging and agro-
industrial expansion), fire and mining (Brown, 2004; Fearnside, 2005a,
2008a). Hargrave and Kis-Katos (2011) analyzed the economic causes of
deforestation in the Brazilian Amazon with a regression method. They investigated the deforested area using the theoretical model of Angelsen (1999),
who argued that deforestation can be explained by the expected profits from
land use, but that liberalization and macroeconomic issues may also be relevant. Angelsen and Kaimowitz (1999) showed that agricultural and forestry
exports may lead to more deforestation. In general, the literature points to
such deforestation causes as the area of soybeans harvested, the area of cattle pastures, the prices of these commodities, roads, population density, cattle
herd size, geographical variables related to climate and soil, rural credit policies and economic growth (Morton et al., 2006; Barona et al., 2010; Martins
and Pereira, 2012). Hargrave and Kis-Katos (2011) estimated deforestation as

a function of these possible causes for each municipality (county) in the Legal Amazon (this 5-million km^2 administrative region includes the states of Acre, Amapá, Amazonas, Maranhão, Mato Grosso, Pará, Rondônia, Roraima and Tocantins). They show soybean prices and environmental fines to be factors influencing deforestation. Their findings, however, did not explicitly take into account the exports to China as the main consumer of Amazonian soybeans. An econometric study of deforestation in Mato Grosso using municipality-level data from 2001 to 2010 shows the strong role of soy, beef and wood exports (Moreira, 2013). Moreira (2013) did not separate exports to China from those bound for other destinations, but as the largest purchaser of these commodities, particularly for soybeans, China's role is clear. Even before the recent surge of exports to China, Nepstad et al. (2006) argued that China's demand for Brazilian soybeans has stimulated production, and also deforestation, in Mato Grosso, the biggest Brazilian producer.

We concentrate our attention on Mato Grosso, where the effect of soybeans is paramount, rather than timber, beef and minerals (which are also exported to China). Soybeans are a major force in clearing of the *cerrado* (central-Brazilian savanna) and in Amazonian deforestation, both in areas that are climatically and topographically appropriate for planting soy and in areas that are not good for soy but where deforesters gain access using soy-related transportation infrastructure (Fearnside, 2001a, 2007). The expansion of soy into pasture areas in Mato Grosso also leads to displaced deforestation for cattle in Pará, the state bordering Mato Grosso to the north (Arima et al., 2011). In addition to its impact on deforestation, the migration of ranchers to Pará and the expansion of pasture there can exacerbate land-tenure conflicts, usually at the expense of small farmers and traditional peoples (e.g., Fearnside, 2001b).

The rapid rise in exports of products such soy and beef to China has consequences for Amazonian deforestation that, while they may appear obvious, are nevertheless complex to quantify and interpret. This direct impact of commodity exports is only the tip of the iceberg of Chinese influence on Amazonia. Money earned from this trade is strengthening Brazilian agribusiness interests, with profound effects on domestic politics that are reflected in legislative and administrative changes weakening environmental protection. Impacts can also be expected from Chinese financing under negotiation for infrastructure, such as a railway linking the state of Mato Grosso to a port on the Amazon River. Mato Grosso is a major focus of expansion of soy, cotton and intensified cattle production. Chinese purchases of land for agriculture and timber imply an increasing direct role in commodity production. Other impacts come from exports from mining and from the processing of minerals, especially the demands for charcoal for pig-iron smelters and for electricity from hydroelectric dams for aluminum smelters.

4. Brazil's Exports to China

4.1 Interpreting export data

Data on exports by product, origin and destination (for quantities as well as value in US dollars) are provided by the Aliceweb system (Online Information System for Analysis of Foreign Trade) of the Brazilian Ministry of Development, Industry and Foreign Trade (MDIC). Chinese demand for Brazilian exports reached approximately USD 30 billion in 2010, having increased tremendously since 2000, with annual geometric rates from 2000 to 2010 of about 44 percent for non-agricultural products and 34 percent for agricultural products in values FOB.[1] Exports from the Legal Amazon to China have also increased at an impressive rate of 52 percent yearly from 2000 to 2010, increasing from USD 104 million in 2000 to USD 6631 million in 2010 (research data based on Brazil, MDIC, 2012).

Exports to China from the Brazilian Legal Amazon rose from an average of 13 percent of total Brazilian exports to China in the 2000–2004 period to an average of 23 percent in the 2005–2010 period. The change occurred abruptly from 14.6 percent in 2004 to 23.3 percent in 2005 and then kept stable. Almost half of the change in the 2004–2005 period can be attributed to FOB price increases, but for the 2009–2010 period (when FOB prices were lower) the physical quantities explain most of the increase in value (research data based on Brazil, MDIC, 2012).

An interesting point to observe is that the share of export value represented by a soybean composite (soy grain, soy oil and other vegetable oil) decreased from a high of 66.3 percent in 2003 to 34.4 percent in 2010, with an average of 47.7 percent over the last five years. Iron and manganese now represent a large share of Brazilian exports to China, reaching 63.1 percent in 2010 (49.8% as a 5-year average). In 2010 about 83 percent of the Legal Amazon's exports were from the states of Pará (52% – iron) and Mato Grosso (31% – soybeans). The share of iron plus soybeans in these two states decreased from 79 percent in 2006 to 72 percent in 2008, but then rebounded to high levels: 89 percent in 2009 and 83 percent in 2010 (research data based on Brazil, MDIC, 2012).

Figure 7.5 graphs the exports of soybeans from Mato Grosso and of iron from Pará. The impressive increase is apparent. The value of iron from Pará and of soybeans from Mato Grosso totaled USD 5.5 billion in 2010 (research data based on Brazil, MDIC, 2012).

---

1   "Free on board," or the value at the port of shipment net of all domestic transportation and loading costs.

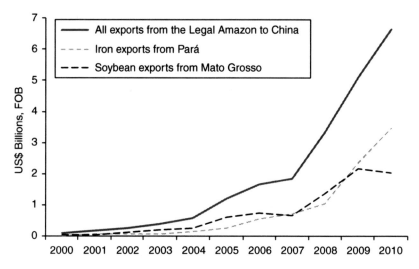

Figure 7.5 Value of exports, soybeans from Mato Grosso and iron from Pará
Source: Brazil, MDIC (2013).
Note: Values are shown in USD, on an FOB basis.

4.2 Interpreting deforestation data

Data on the area planted in soybeans and the size of the cattle herd were
obtained from the Brazilian Institute of Geography and Statistics (IBGE).
Data on area deforested in the Brazilian Amazon are available from the
Prodes project of the National Institute for Space Research (Brazil, INPE,
2013). The database reports deforested area in hectares at the municipal level
for 2000–2010. Note that these data only report the clearing of forest, not
the clearing of *cerrado* (central Brazilian savanna) that represents much of the
soybean area in the state of Mato Grosso. We note that in the past there have
been significant problems with Brazilian deforestation data (e.g., Fearnside,
1997a), but that transparency and reporting have been greatly improved for
the years covered in our quantitative analysis.

Looking at deforestation in the Legal Amazon and comparing it to exports
to China, to soybean-planted area and to cattle herd size, Figure 7.6 exhibits
an interesting behavior. In Figure 7.6, based on Brazil, INPE (2013) deforestation data and on Brazil, IBGE (2012) agricultural data, the cumulative area
may give a misleading interpretation because this area is not the increase in
deforestation. Cumulative deforested area clearly has a positive relationship
with area of soybeans, size of the cattle herd and value of exports, but for
each year there is a different value for exports and soybean area, while the
deforested area is a cumulative value. One point to be observed is that recent

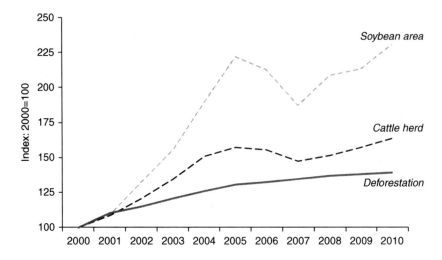

Figure 7.6 Cumulative area of deforestation (km²), soybean-planted area (ha), cattle herd (head) in the Brazilian Legal Amazon, 2000–2010
Sources: Brazil, INPE (2013); Brazil, MDIC (2013). Data normalized to year 2000 = 100.

expansion of soybeans in Mato Grosso is taking place in preexisting pastures that represent areas deforested at some time in the past. The advance of soybeans into pasture areas in Mato Grosso has long been believed to displace ranching activity into forest areas such as those in Pará, contributing to deforestation there (Fearnside, 2001a; Fargione et al., 2008). Recently this effect has been demonstrated statistically (Arima et al., 2011). Brazilian diplomats currently deny this effect, and in March 2014 they were successful in getting mention of it deleted from the summary for policy makers of the Fifth Assessment Report of the Intergovernmental Panel on Climate Change (Garcia, 2014).

In Figure 7.7, increase in deforested area is depicted for each state in the Legal Amazon using Brazil, INPE (2013) data. It can be observed that the deforestation rate has declined since 2001, staying below 10,000 km² in 2009–2010. The state of Pará had the largest increase in deforested area (almost 3,400 km²), or 52.6 percent of the total increase in 2010. Mato Grosso was an important state up to 2008 with a rapid expansion in agriculture and cattle raising, but there was a significant reduction in 2009–2010: Mato Grosso accounted for only 12 percent of the total increase in 2010.

Data from Brazil, INPE (2013) and Brazil, MDIC (2012) exhibit a strict positive relationship between cumulative deforestation and the Legal Amazon's exports, with a high correlation (0.82). A different pattern is seen if the increase in deforestation is plotted against the value of exports. This shows an inverted relationship with a negative correlation of -0.72 with total exports (Figure 7.8).

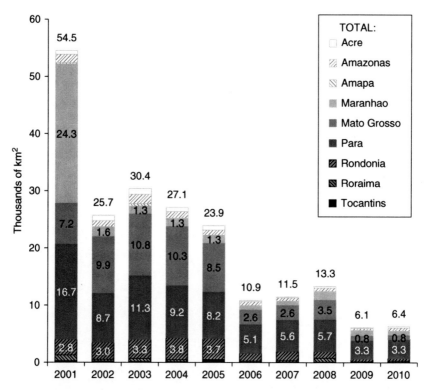

Figure 7.7 Annual increase in deforested area (km²) in each state in the Brazilian Legal Amazon, 2001–2010
Source: Brazil, INPE (2013).

Looking at the data in this way, exports to China are not a driving force of deforestation directly, and more detailed observation is needed. Soy is a major product in total exports to China, but what is its relationship to the increase in deforestation? Figure 7.6 indicates a pattern associating cumulative deforestation with soybean area and cattle herd size. Figure 7.9 shows the increase in deforestation against these two variables using Brazil, INPE (2013) and Brazil, IBGE (2012) data.

According to Figure 7.9, the increase in deforested area is accompanied by increases in either the cattle herd or the soybean area. However, the regression line had non-significant parameters and the correlations with the increase in deforestation were only 0.3 for soybeans and 0.5 for cattle. On the other hand, there is a strong positive correlation (0.85) between the differences in soybean area and in cattle herd size. The same pattern was found by Marta and Figueiredo (2008). A regression was performed for the entire Legal Amazon,

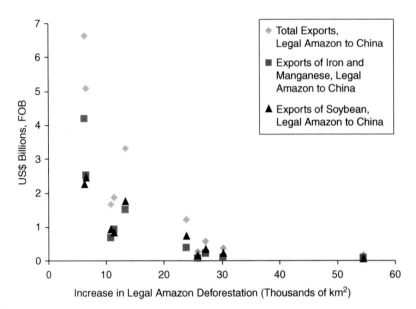

Figure 7.8 Increase in deforested area (km²) in the Brazilian Legal Amazon against the value of exports to China, 2001–2010
Sources: Brazil, INPE (2013); Brazil, MDIC (2013).

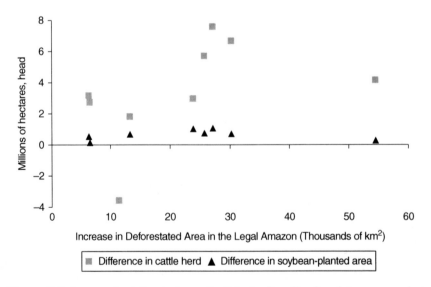

Figure 7.9 Increase in deforested area (km²) in the Brazilian Legal Amazon against the difference in soybean-planted area and in cattle herd size, 2001–2010
Sources: Brazil, IBGE (2012); Brazil, MDIC (2013).

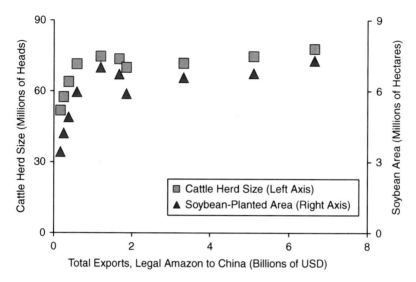

Figure 7.10 Total exports from the Brazilian Legal Amazon to China against the soybean-planted area and cattle herd, 2001–2010
Sources: Brazil, IBGE (2012); Brazil, MDIC (2013).
Notes: Total exports from the Legal Amazon to China in FOB USD billion. Soybean-planted area in 10^3 hectares. Cattle herd in millions of head.

aggregating the data from the nine states in the region. The deforestation process is quite complex, leading us to use a systems approach.[2] This approach allowed us to relate explanatory variables to both a deforestation equation and an exports equation. Here we will discuss some results of this system.

Deforestation rates throughout Brazilian Amazonia have declined substantially since 2004, with a statistically significant negative trend. The decline through 2008 is explained by falling international prices of soy and beef in the 2004–2006 period, together with a worsening exchange rate of the Brazilian real against other currencies from the point of view of exporters, but deforestation continued to decline after 2008 despite a recovery in commodity prices (Assunção et al., 2012).

Figure 7.10 shows the relation of exports to soybeans and cattle according to Brazil, MDIC (2012) and Brazil, IBGE (2012) data. The two dispersion plots in Figure 7.8 present essentially the same information: a positive correlation between the exports to China and the sizes of the herd and the crop. The correlation is 0.69 for soybean area and 0.67 for cattle herd.

---

2   The details for the system of equations as well as its results are provided in the Technical Appendix.

The idea is that soybeans are planted in already-existing cattle pastures (Marta and Figueiredo, 2008). The soybeans are then exported, and there is a kind of learning process where exports lead to an effect on the next period's exports. The preceding period's exports and cattle herd size, as well as current soybean-planted area, soybean price and beef price, explained the change in deforestation in the current period.

On the other side, the soybean plantations are occupying previous pastures. The persistence of cattle herds occupying land is a restriction on soybean cultivation and exports. The land-use shift from old degraded pasture into soybean cropping can have, in some way, a positive effect on exports. The problem is that expansion in soybean area leads to increase in deforestation. Increasing cattle herd size also has a statistical impact on the increase in deforestation, similar to other studies that have found a strong effect of cattle herd size on deforestation (e.g., Alencar et al., 2004; Kaimowitz et al., 2004; Arima et al., 2005). Nevertheless, increasing the herd size appeared to reduce exports to China, and this reduction would lead to a decrease in deforestation.

Two factors can help explain the relationship between cattle and deforestation in Mato Grosso. First, is the recent spread of techniques for improving pasture productivity (or pasture stocking), particularly in Mato Grosso, as well as the growth of feedlots. Feedlot holding capacity in Mato Grosso grew from 668,000 head in 2009 to 883,000 in 2014; interviews with ranchers conducted by the Mato Grosso state government indicate a dramatic surge of intention to hold cattle in feedlots in the northern part of the state, where plans for this practice doubled from 2013 to 2014 (IMEA, 2014). These feedlot meats are mainly for high-quality beef exports. Although our analysis is at the level of the Legal Amazon for all variables, the effect of intensification would probably be substantially less important in other Amazonian states, such as Pará.

A second factor is that China only recently permitted the importation of Brazilian beef. Until that point, the increase in herds represented a restriction on products that could be exported to China, namely soy, leading to more deforestation for pasture. For example, reducing soybean exports would lead to pasture and herd increases. Prices of soybeans and beef also impact deforestation rates, with soybean price as a direct effect and beef price having an indirect negative effect on deforestation rates. Now that China has authorized imports of Brazilian beef, it is expected to exert pressure on the Brazilian beef market, competing with the Brazilian soybean exports.

Even though states like Mato Grosso and Pará exhibited increases in cattle herd size after 2010, the herd in 2010 was about the same size as in 2005 for Pará and Mato Grosso. The herd remained constant over the 2005–2008 period and had remarkable increases of more than 5 percent annually in 2009 and 2010. Mato Grosso had small increases in deforestation in 2009

and 2010, although it was one of the states with the largest increases in deforestation between 2000 and 2008, clearing land for herd expansion in the
following years.

The relations of soybeans and cattle to deforestation over the 2000–2010
period were complicated by other factors that influenced the deforestation
process to differing degrees in each year. The efforts of environmental authorities to control illegal deforestation through inspections and fines have varied
substantially (Nepstad et al., 2014). Increased efforts to control deforestation
appear to have had a significant effect from 2008 onwards, whereas before
2008 deforestation rates track soy and beef prices closely (Barreto et al., 2011;
Assunção et al., 2012). In addition, the periods immediately preceding elections are normally characterized by deforestation increases both as a result of
political pressure to relax environmental enforcement (especially at the state
level) and as a result of anticipation by deforesters that election results will
bring relaxed enforcement and/or amnesties forgiving past violations (see
Fearnside, 2003).

A key change that occurred in 2008 was a decision by Brazil's Central
Bank that no public bank loans could be given to operations with environmental irregularities reported by agencies such as IBAMA (BACEN Resolution
3.545/2008). Unlike fines given by IBAMA and other agencies, which can be
circumvented with a seemingly endless sequence of appeals, the restriction
on bank loans has real teeth and an immediate effect. The credit restriction
greatly increases the impact of the environmental inspection programs, even
if the programs themselves do not change substantially in scale, and even in
the face of the inability of agencies like IBAMA to collect most of the fines.
This recent change in bank policy was not included in our model, and its effect
remains as a suggestion for further study. Increased exports were possible at a
time of decreasing deforestation due to rising per-hectare soy yields, clearing
in non-forest vegetation types (i.e., *cerrado*), and soy expansion in former cattle
pastures (the indirect effects of which would be displaced beyond the borders
of Mato Grosso to increase pasture in Pará).

4.3 Other commodities exported from Brazilian Amazonia

4.3.1 Timber

China has cut almost all of its natural forests and, despite large-scale plantations of fast-growing trees, the country has a tremendous demand for timber such as that from Brazil's Amazon forest. Unlike European and North
American markets, China is willing to buy wood from almost any species
of tropical tree. An example of this occurred when timber was sold prior to

the 1988 flooding of the Samuel Dam in the state of Rondônia (Fearnside, 2005b). Export of raw logs from Brazil has been prohibited since 1965, but an exception was opened to allow logs from Samuel to be exported (Nogueira, 1988). From 1987 through 1989, a continuous chain of barges arrived in the Amazon River port of Itacoatiara with logs for loading on ships, and one ship loaded with logs departed for China every two weeks during this period. The exception, opened for the relatively small Samuel reservoir area, had allowed logs to be illegally exported from vast areas in western Amazonia.

Chinese companies purchased several bankrupt sawmills in Manaus in 1996, thereby gaining the forestland holdings of the sawmill companies. Land purchases by China and Malaysia together in the state of Amazonas totaled 4.5 million hectares (*Amazonas em Tempo*, 1996). Most of the forestland bought by Chinese companies was in the municipality of Carauarí. A major increase in logging activity was expected at the time, but this did not occur (presumably because of the substantial bureaucratic barriers to obtaining approval of forestry-management plans). Other countries have been satisfying most of the world's demand for tropical timber, including the demands of China. However, Brazil has by far the largest stock of remaining tropical forest, and the pressure of this demand is bound to focus on the country once available stocks elsewhere are exhausted (Fearnside, 1989a).

4.3.2 Alumina, aluminum and iron

Chinese companies have interests in alumina (Al_2O_3: the precursor of primary aluminum) in Barcarena, Pará, where Alumina Brasil-China (ABC) and Aluminum Corporation of China Limited (Chalco) have a joint venture with the Brazilian mining company Vale (Vale, 2009). The power demand for this electricity-intensive industry contributes to Brazil's push for a massive increase in building hydroelectric dams in Amazonia over the next decade. Brazil's 2011–2020 ten-year energy-expansion plan (Brazil, MME, 2011) calls for 30 large dams to be built in the Legal Amazon by 2020, a rate of one dam every four months. The Chinese–Brazilian alumina plant will be an important beneficiary of the Belo Monte Dam on the Xingu River, near Altamira, Pará. Belo Monte has environmental and social impacts that extend far beyond the areas that will be directly flooded, and the dam is likely to justify much larger upstream reservoirs to regulate the river's flow (Fearnside, 2006). The dam has functioned as a "spearhead" in creating precedents that weaken Brazil's environmental licensing system and prepare the way for the many dams proposed under the energy-expansion plan (Fearnside, 2012). In February 2014 a consortium led by Chinese State Grid won the bidding for the R$5 billion (USD 2 billion) contract to build the transmission line for Belo Monte. The expansion of Amazonian dams also receives a boost from China's equipment sales, as in the case of the turbines from Dong Fang Electric Corporation International and Dong Fang Electric Machinery for the Jirau Dam on the Madeira River. The influence of both Brazil and China in expanding carbon credit for hydro-electric projects under the Kyoto Protocol's Clean Development Mechanism has further increased the profitability of dams (Fearnside, 2013a, b).

Iron from Brazil is now largely exported to China (Soares, 2012) (and previously shown in the introduction of this chapter). The Chinese market has eclipsed the European purchasers who dominated exports from the Carajás Mine, in Pará, when the mine was opened in the 1980s. Processing of part of the ore for export as pig iron consumes charcoal, providing a longstanding source of pressure on the forests of eastern Amazonia and a challenge to environmental and labor authorities (Fearnside, 1989b). The environmental and social impacts of charcoal production made European iron imports from Amazonia a target for criticism from non-governmental organizations (e.g., Sutton, 1994), but this is no longer evident now that exports have shifted to China. Brazil's export of iron alloys, although representing far smaller quantities than iron in the form of ore or pig iron, is the fastest-growing category of exports to China, tripling from 4,000 to 12,000 tons between 2013 and 2014 (CEBC, 2014). Producing iron alloys consumes a tremendous amount of electricity and creates a miniscule amount of employment in Brazil: 1.1 jobs per GWh of electricity consumed, or even less than primary aluminum, which creates only 1.5 jobs per GWh (Bermann and Martins, 2000, 90; Fearnside, 2016a).

5. China and Political Shifts in Brazil

The political influence of the "ruralist" voting block that represents large landholders in Brazil's National Congress has increased markedly due to the large amounts of money entering the country from the export of soybeans, China being the number-one source of these earnings. The shift of Brazil's economy towards agricultural commodity exports (strengthening the influence of large landowners) and away from manufacturing (weakening the influence of industrialists and labor unions) is affecting virtually every aspect of Brazil's politics (e.g., ISA, 2014). Effects include the positions of the previous and current presidential administrations on environmental issues (Fearnside, 2016b; Santilli, 2014; Smeraldi, 2014). The ruralist block is currently trying to revert the Brazilian Central Bank's resolution blocking loans for agriculture and ranching from the Banco do Brasil (BB), Caixa Econômica Federal (CEF) and Banco da Amazônia (BASA) for properties with pending fines for environmental violations.

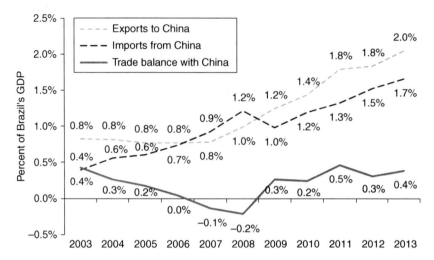

Figure 7.11 Brazil's trade balance with China
Source: Authors' calculations based on UN COMTRADE data.

China's influence on this transition extends beyond the boost to ruralist influence from soy income: China's exports of cheap manufactured goods to Brazilian manufacturers' former export markets has cut deeply into Brazil's exports from this sector, and China's direct export of manufactured goods to Brazil further displaces Brazilian manufacturing and reduces the political influence of this sector within the country. Brazil has maintained an approximate balance in terms of monetary value between exports to and imports from China (Figure 7.11). This balance may be influenced by trade negotiations between the two countries in which the Chinese interest in maximizing its exports could help explain the close parallel between the increasing monetary flows in the two directions. Unlike countries that have little domestic manufacturing to lose, the effect in Brazil is significant. The increasing exports of agricultural commodities and imports of manufactured goods contribute to a shift in political influence in Brazil from the manufacturing to the agribusiness sectors, with consequences for environmental policies.

6. Financing from China

Another issue is the effect of Chinese finance in Latin America. China is a new and growing source of funding with less environmental restrictions, lower interest rates and different size loans (Gallagher et al., 2012).

Official data regarding foreign direct investment (FDI) in Brazil are found in the census from the Brazilian Central Bank (Brazil, BCB, 2014).

The Chinese stock of FDI in Brazil (in capital shares and immediate investor) changed from USD 582 million in 2010 to USD 1,093 million in 2012. From the perspective of the final investor, who occupies the top of the control chain, this FDI stock in capital shares went from USD 7,874 million to USD 10,226 million in the same period (Brazil's total FDI stock is USD 617,384 million for all source countries). This 2012 value is divided by sector as: extractive industries (82.3%); manufacturing (1.3%); trade and repair of vehicles (2.6%); and other (13.9%).

Most Chinese loans are for the oil, iron, steel, energy and telecom sectors. From 2007 to 2012, the China Brazil Business Council (CBBC) "recorded a total of 60 announced Chinese investment projects for a total of USD 68.5 billion" (CBBC, 2013), of which 54 were in the 2010–2012 period and 47 were partially or completely state-funded. Regarding the investment motivation, 57 percent were resource seeking, but from 2011–2012 market-oriented investments dominated. The Chinese investment project is distributed among 14 Brazilian sectors, as shown in Figure 7.12.

The Chinese investment is highly concentrated in the three states of the Southeast macro-region: São Paulo (27% – banking, telecom, automotive and electronics), Minas Gerais (18% – machinery and equipment) and Rio de

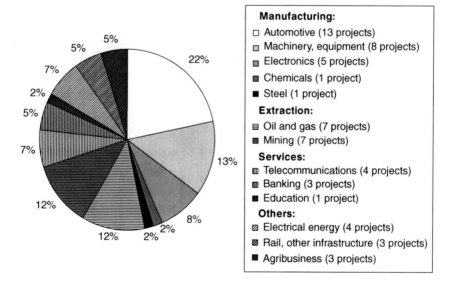

Figure 7.12 Chinese investment projects by sector (number of projects), from 2007 to June 2012
Source: CBBC (2013, 14).

Janeiro (17% – electrical energy, oil and gas) (Figure 7.13). Mato Grosso and Amazonas account for 5 percent each.

The official website of the state of Mato Grosso reports that the China Development Bank Corporation (CDBC) intends to finance the China Railway Engineering Corporation (CREC) which, together with the Asian Trade and Investments (ATI, a holding in Hong Kong), is interested in building and operating an 1,800-km railroad between Cuiabá (Mato Grosso) and Santarém (a port city on the Amazon River); the railway (EF-170) would cut through Amazonia beside the BR-163 Highway (Mato Grosso, 2012; Bland, 2013; CBBC, 2013). The China National Machinery Import and Export Corporation (CMC) would be among the partners, according to *Business News Americas* (2011). CREC staff also met with the governor of Mato Grosso, who led a delegation to China to negotiate support for the planned railway (Lucatelli, 2012).

The Cuiabá- Santarém railway (Ferronorte) has long figured in Brazilian development plans (see Laurance et al., 2001), but the high cost has kept it from being built until now. This railway has appeared in Brazilian government plans since the 1990s (See Fearnside, 2002a), but the project did not rise to the top of the priority list until China's interest in providing a USD 10 billion loan to finance it became clear in 2012. Chinese financing could remove this barrier (Maisonnave, 2012).

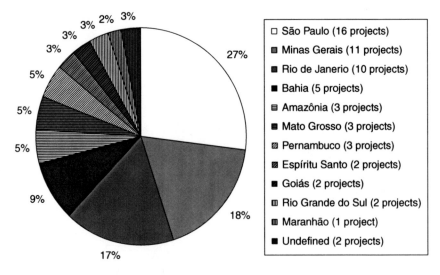

Figure 7.13 Chinese investment projects by state (number of projects)
Source: CBBC (2013, 15).

Another project, the "Transcontinental Railway" (EF-354), is planned to link to the North–South Railway at Anapolis, Goiás, cutting across the entire state of Mato Grosso from East to West. It would connect Lucas do Rio Verde (a major soy production area in central Mato Grosso) to Porto Velho, Rondônia, which is already connected to a deep-water port on the Amazon River via the Madeira waterway. The railway project, which is led by VALEC (a Brazilian government-owned company under the Ministry of Transportation), would subsequently continue on from Porto Velho to Peruvian ports on the Pacific (VALEC, 2014). Just the Brazilian portion of the route totals 4,400 km, including a connection of this railway from Mato Grosso to the Atlantic. The president of the China Brazil Business Council has suggested that Chinese firms have "funds to finance partnerships with Brazilian construction companies" that would be "strategic" in completing the rail connection from Lucas do Rio Verde to the Atlantic (Amaral, 2014).

These major infrastructure development projects are intended to facilitate trade and save on logistical costs, improving and having more efficient export corridors in Brazil. The railway can be expected to stimulate substantial soy expansion in Mato Grosso. *Soybean and Corn Advisor* (2012) reports "The [Cuiabá–Santarém] railroad alone could save soybean producers in the state R$2 billion annually in reduced transportation costs."

It should be remembered that major construction projects such as these very frequently involve corruption, with significant effects on decision-making in the Brazilian government. An example is provided by revelations regarding the ongoing construction of Brazil's North–South Railway, with recent revelations being just the latest in a series of scandals since construction began in 1986 (Mello & Amora, 2012). Options for improved regulation of this process include the establishment of a system of railway use permits that would be sold through auctions organized by the Brazilian government.

7. Global Investments for Chinese Demand

Chinese investments in Brazil, such as the planned soy railway from Mato Grosso to the Amazon River, are not the only way that China's market influences infrastructure and deforestation in Amazonia. Multinational (as well as Brazilian) corporations are also investing with the intent of supplying Chinese markets. For example, Bunge, a multinational soy company currently responsible for 25 percent of Brazil's production, opened a USD 700 million soy port in Barcarena, at the mouth of the Amazon River, in April 2014. The company expects its exports from Brazil to double in the next 10 years, mainly as exports to China, and considers Brazil to be the only producer country capable of responding to China's expected increase in demand in the coming years (Freitas, 2014). In the future, the soy to be exported from Barcarena is expected to arrive from Mato Grosso by barge via the planned Tapajós Waterway. This waterway would convert the Tapajós River in Pará, and its tributaries in Mato Grosso (the Teles Pires and Juruena Rivers) into navigable *hidrovias* to bring soy to the Amazon River from the northern part of the state of Mato Grosso. The waterway is a high priority in the "transport axis" of Brazil's current five-year development plan, the second "Program for the Acceleration of Growth" (PAC-2). Land use in the northern part of Mato Grosso is currently dominated by cattle pasture, but the reduced cost of transportation would lead to the area being converted to soy. The Tapajós waterway is controversial because it depends on a series of hydroelectric dams and locks being built to allow barges to pass a number of formidable rapids. Part of Amazonia National Park has already been degazetted to make way for the São Luiz de Tapajós reservoir (e.g., WWF Brasil, 2012). The São Luiz de Tapajós and Jatobá reservoirs would flood land of the Munduruku tribe that has not yet been officially designated as "indigenous land" (Lourenço, 2014). The government plans to remove part of the Juruena National Park to make way for the São Simão Alto and Salto Augusto Baixo Dams on the Juruena River (WWF Brasil, 2014). Most controversial is the Chacorão Dam, which would flood 18,721 ha of the Munduruku Indigenous Land. This dam does not appear in Brazil's current ten-year plan for energy expansion (Brazil, MME, 2013) and in the "energy axis" of PAC-2, but it is a key part of the waterway plan (Brazil, MT, 2010) and it appears in the viability study for the Tapajós Dams (CNEC, 2014; Fearnside, 2015a,b).

The branch of the Tapajós waterway on the Juruena River would connect roads to bring soy from the central-western portion of the state, including Sapezal – location of the 44,500-ha property that serves as headquarters of the A. Maggi Group, which has 20 properties spread throughout Mato Grosso (e.g., Ondei, 2012). Blairo Maggi, known as the "soy king" in Brazil, is an influential senator and past governor of Mato Grosso; in 2005 he was presented with the Greenpeace "golden chainsaw award" (Greenpeace, 2005). The Juruena River branch of the waterway would begin at a new port in Juina on the Juruena River and at Porto dos Gaúchos on the Arinos River, a Juruena tributary. Soy would reach these ports via roads from the South, including a new road (MT-319) to connect Juina to Vilhena, in eastern Rondônia, bisecting two indigenous areas (Macrologística, 2011).

Blairo Maggi also has an 80,800 ha property in Querência, in northwestern Mato Grosso. This would export soy via the BR-163 (Cuiabá-Santarém) Highway that is planned for reconstruction under PAC-2. This soy export corridor is expected to have strong impacts on deforestation other than that caused by expansion of soy plantations (Fearnside, 2007). The Maggi plantation in Querência would be linked to the BR-163 via the MT-322 (former BR-080) Highway. Reconstruction of this East–West road bisecting the Xingu Indigenous Park is resisted by indigenous peoples; the Mato Grosso state government released a statement that an agreement had been reached to allow construction (Martins, 2014), but the indigenous groups involved are emphatic that no such agreement was made (Mayalu Kokometi Waurá Txucarramãe, pers. com., 2014). A. Maggi is Brazil's largest soy company. The multinationals Cargill, Bunge and Archer Daniels Midland (ADM) are also present in the portion of Mato Grosso to be served by the BR-163 connection through Pará.

Another branch of the Tapajós waterway would extend up the Teles Pires River to Sorriso; this requires a series of five dams, two of which (Sinop and São Manoel) are already under construction. The São Manoel Dam is located adjacent to an indigenous area and has already provoked conflicts with the Kayabi tribe (ISA, 2013).

Yet another area of Mato Grosso that is expected to be converted from pasture to soy is the southwestern corner of the state. This area would be opened for soy export by the planned Guaporé waterway that would connect with the Madeira River waterway once locks are installed in the recently built Santo Antônio and Jirau Dams, plus one additional planned dam (Guajará Mirim, also known as Cachoeira Riberão) (Fearnside, 2014). Soy would be transported by barge to Maggi's soy terminal and deep-water port at Itacoatiara, on the Amazon River near the confluence with the Madeira. As with all of Brazil's major soy facilities, China is the main destination for exports.

An intriguing possible change in China's future soy imports has been raised by reported discussions within China of banning genetically modified organisms (GMOs). Were this to occur, Brazil would experience the negative consequences of excessive dependence on a single trading partner. However, China might find an immediate switch to non-GMO imports difficult to implement quickly, given the scale of the country's demand for imported soy. Were Brazil to attempt to convert its soy back to non-GMO varieties, the effort and expense needed to obtain uncontaminated harvests would be substantial. Ironically, Brazil was one of the last major soy-producing countries to make the switch to GMOs. Even Maggi himself opposed the switch when Europe was the major importer of Brazilian soy and the price of non-GMO soy was higher than that for GMO soy by an amount that made non-GMO soy the more profitable option (see Fearnside, 2001a). The price differential subsequently diminished, and GMOs were made legal in Brazil in 2003 (Decree 4680) over the objections of the Ministry of the Environment. Since concern over risks of GMO technology is greatest among European consumers, Brazil's switch to GMO

Table 7.1 Chinese land purchases in Brazil in progress in January 2012

Company	Area	Investment	Purpose
1. Chongquin Grain Group China	100,000 ha, with option to expand to 200,000 ha	USD 879 million, much of this from the CDB	Soybeans
2. Pengxin Group China	200,000 ha		Cotton, soybeans

Source: GRAIN (2012).

soy undoubtedly contributed to the replacement of Europe by China as the main destination for Brazilian exports.

8. Land Purchases by China

Currently land purchased directly by foreigners is limited to a maximum of 50 rural modules (making the limit 5,000 ha in most of the Amazon region). The Brazilian government is planning to lower this limit with the express purpose of inhibiting land purchases by China (Reuters, 2011). Among other effects, the Brazilian government believes that a spate of recent Chinese land purchases is an important factor in a sharp rise in land prices in the country (*Latin American Herald Tribune*, 2012). However, the rising price of soy is also a factor (Agrimoney.com, 2011). Chinese land purchases in Brazil in progress in January 2012 are shown in Table 7.1.

The China National Agricultural Development Group Corporation, the Pengxin Group China and the Chongqing Grain Group have announced acquisitions of land (GRAIN, 2012; Raimundo and Azevedo, 2011). This is part of the strategy connected with the railroad project cited above, with a joint venture including the Chinese Chongqing Huapont Pharm. Co. Ltd. (a Chinese pesticide industry), the Brazilian Agricultural Cooperative Consortium (which includes 16 cooperatives of grain producers from different states) and Chinatex Corporation, which is a large Chinese state-owned company engaged in producing, trading and integrated service of textiles and edible oils (Cintra, 2013).

This is undoubtedly very incomplete, since the Brazilian government stopped tracking foreign land purchases in 1994 and only resumed collection of this information in April 2012. Restrictions on outright purchases by foreigners are not likely to halt the trend to increasing control of land from abroad because Brazil's 1988 Constitution changed the definition of "Brazilian" companies: rather than requiring a majority of the capital to be Brazilian, companies can be classified as "Brazilian" merely by having a headquarters in Brazil.

Moreover, the lower house of the National Congress is currently debating the question of land acquisition by foreigners and a number of influential deputies have proposed changes in the law in order to relax existing restrictions (Brazil, Agência Câmara de Notícias, 2012).

9. China's Impact on "Sustainable Development"

The changes driven by China's commodity purchases from and investments in Brazil's Amazon region, including the state of Mato Grosso, have a significant impact on the set of concerns grouped under the rubric of "sustainable development." The term sustainable development implies that what is happening is "development," meaning a change in a direction seen as improving human well-being (not to be confused with "growth," or increase in the throughput of matter and energy – or their proxy in terms of money [e.g., Daly and Cobb, 1989]). The adjective "sustainable" implies that these benefits will last for a very long time, theoretically indefinitely. The widely used description of sustainable development from the World Council on Environment and Development's 1987 *Bruntland Report* allows the current generation's actions to be considered "sustainable" if future generations, which are presumably wealthier and more technologically advanced, are capable of coping with the environmental and social losses provoked by the current generation's activities (WCED, 1987). This allows the current generation's activities to be considered "sustainable" even if these activities destroy their bases of support, as by exhausting a nonrenewable resource such as a mineral deposit or by destroying a potentially renewable one such as a forest or a fishery.

Deforestation destroys a potentially renewable resource, eliminates indigenous and traditional cultures that predominated in the area (clearing only takes place at some time after expelling the traditional inhabitants) and provokes losses of environmental services such as maintaining biodiversity, carbon storage and water cycling (Fearnside, 2008b). Throughout most of Brazilian Amazonia, deforestation has been for low-value cattle pastures that are ephemeral and that support only a few people after the initial clearing activity has passed (Fearnside, 1986, 2002b). Soil and other limits constrain this activity (Fearnside, 1997b, 1998), but land speculation, land-tenure establishment, money laundering, fiscal incentives and a variety of other "ulterior" motives have driven clearing for pasture even in agronomically unpromising locations (Fearnside, 2005a; Carrero and Fearnside, 2011). Recent dramatic increases in beef prices and the opening of export options by elimination of foot-and-mouth disease have added a significant economic force to the previous drivers for pasture: beef that a decade ago could only be exported in canned form is now shipped abroad frozen or even as live cattle. Is the conversion of Amazon forest to cattle pasture "sustainable development"? Various indicators suggest that it is neither sustainable nor development (Fearnside, 1979, 1989c).

Particularly in the state of Mato Grosso, soybeans have replaced tropical forest with a land use that can generate much more financial return than do either cattle pasture or management of the original forest. Soy cultivation is entirely mechanized and generates relatively little employment per hectare. Those who own or are employed in the soy plantations enjoy substantially higher incomes than most Brazilians. Soy production centers in Mato Grosso have some of the highest human-development indices in Brazil, the municipality of Sorriso having become famous by being ranked number one among Brazil's 5,570 municipalities (*Folha de São Paulo*, 2005). Most of the individuals involved in soy cultivation are relatively recent arrivals from other parts of Brazil, especially the states of Rio Grande do Sul, Santa Catarina and Paraná, rather than the descendants of the population that inhabited Mato Grosso before these areas were converted to soy.

The physical sustainability of soy cultivation depends on the purchase (in some cases including importing from other countries) of inputs such as fertilizer, lime, pesticides and herbicides. The financial viability of supplying, for example, soil nutrients from distant sources once the initial stocks are depleted depends on the costs relative to those in other potential production areas. An example of potential loss of competitive viability is provided by soy in Bolivian Amazonia, where older plantations in the Santa Cruz area have progressively been abandoned in favor of moving farther north into the rainforest portion of the country (Barber et al., 1996; Fearnside, 2001a). Phosphorus is a nonrenewable resource that is limiting in Amazonian soils and for which global resources are expected to be depleted well before the end of the current century (United States, CEQ and Department of State, 1980). Brazil is not particularly well endowed with phosphate deposits (de Lima et al., 1976; Beisiegel and de Souza, 1986). The supply of phosphorous could be significantly altered by plans of the Peruvian government to build a railway connecting the phosphate-rich area of Piura, located on the Pacific coast in the north of Peru, with Cruzeiro do Sul in the Brazilian state of Acre; this is one of several plans for a rail connection from Brazil to a Pacific port in Peru, with soy export to China being the main justification (Dourojeanni, 2013). Brazil's planned "transcontinental railway" would connect Mato Grosso to this railhead (Marquina, 2013).

So, is converting tropical forest (or former tropical forest that first is converted to cattle pasture) into soy plantations "sustainable development"? Different parties would respond differently to this question, depending on whether they are economic winners or losers as a result of the transformation to soy. Those concerned with the environment are likely to conclude that encouraging soybeans is not a wise development path (Fearnside, 2001a, 2008c).

Expansion of soybeans is different from many types of development in terms of "net benefits" *sensu* Zarsky and Stanley (2013). Projects such as establishment of a mine have major environmental and social impacts in surrounding communities, plus gains from employment opportunities and from the monetary flows derived from wages and procurement. In such cases, interviews with community members and meetings held in the area can reveal strong dissatisfaction among affected people, indicating a net impact. The Marlin mine case in Guatemala studied by Zarsky and Stanley (2013) offers a clear example. In the case of soy plantations in Mato Grosso, however, only the winners remain in the area. The losers have sold their land or been otherwise expelled, and are now spread across frontiers elsewhere in Amazonia.

Successive waves of displacement have taken place before reaching the soy plantation stage. First the indigenous peoples were displaced (or killed), followed by occupation either by small farmers or by ranchers. The ranchers may either follow a first wave of small farmers or, alternatively, may obtain the land directly without its passing through the small-farmer phase. Logging is also a major activity that may occur in forested land held by actors of any size from small farmers to large ranchers. Timber may be bought or stolen, including logs taken from unclaimed land (or from indigenous areas and conservation units). Logging is a temporary and unsustainable phase, and most loggers move on to other frontiers after exhausting the resource (Lentini et al., 2011). Finally, the land is bought by soy farmers. Extreme income concentration has repeatedly been the result of conversion of land to soybeans throughout Latin America (Kaimowitz et al., 1999). The net balance and the apportionment of blame for the various environmental and social impacts is therefore complicated. Once established, soy farmers continue to clear the remaining forest despite the widely believed myth that they only plant in degraded cattle pasture and thus provide an economic boom at no environmental cost (e.g., Macedo et al., 2012).

10. Conclusions

The estimates confirmed the effect of soybean-planted area in increasing exports to China and in increasing deforestation, even though deforestation rates were lower in 2010 than in 2000, and the general downward trend continued through 2012. Exports to China from the Brazilian Legal Amazon were also significant in explaining the increase in deforestation.

The cattle herd size also had a significant relation to increases in deforestation, but the relationship of cattle to soybean-planted area is strong and positive. Therefore, the change in land use from pasture to soybean cropping (unless it occurs in degraded areas) may lead to more deforestation. The increase in cattle would, however, lead to more pasture and deforestation associated with opening new areas. The recent authorization of Chinese beef imports may lead to additional deforestation.

Chinese purchases of agricultural and forestland, and Chinese imports of commodities such as timber and aluminum also cause environmental impacts in Amazonia. Chinese financing and investment in Amazonian infrastructure such as railways and mineral processing facilities have additional impacts.

Brazil's ability and willingness to mitigate the risks of soy-led expansion has been very limited. This is in part due to a newly emboldened ruralist class that has benefited from the boom.

11. Acknowledgments

The first author thanks Conselho Nacional do Desenvolvimento Científico e Tecnológico (CNPq: Proc. 304020/2010–9, 610042/2009-2, 575853/2008-5), and Instituto Nacional de Pesquisas da Amazônia (INPA: PRJ13.03). We also thank Boston University for financial support. Much of this discussion is adapted from Fearnside et al. (2013). Two reviewers and the editors provided helpful comments.

References

Agrimoney.com. 2011. Soybeans' strength boosts Brazil's farmland prices. 7 November 2011. http://www.agrimoney.com/news/news.php?id=3352.

Alencar, A.; Nepstad, D. C.; McGrath, D.; Moutinho, P.; Pacheco, P.; Diaz, M. del C. V.; Soares-Filho, B. 2004. *Desmatamento na Amazônia: Indo além da Emergência Crônica*. Belém, Pará, Brazil: Instituto de Pesquisa Ambiental da Amazônia (IPAM). Available at: http://www.ipam.org.br/biblioteca/livro/Desmatamento-na-Amazonia-Indo-Alem-da-Emergencia-Cronica-/319.

Amaral, S. 2014. O novo momento das relações Brasil-China. *Folha de São Paulo*, 7 July 2014, A-3.

Amazonas em Tempo [Manaus]. 1996. Madeireiras asiáticas são multadas em R$91 mil. 2 August 1996, A-5.

Angelsen, A. 1999. Agricultural expansion and deforestation: Modeling the impact of population, market forces and property rights. *Journal of Development Economics*, 58(1), 185–218.

Angelsen, A. and Kaimowitz, D. 1999. Rethinking the causes of deforestation: Lessons from economic models. *The World Bank Research Observer*, 14(1), 73–98.

Arima, E.; Barreto, P.; Brito, M. 2005. *Pecuária na Amazônia: Tendências e Implicações para a Conservação Ambiental*. Belém, Pará, Brazil: Instituto do Homem e Meio Ambiente da Amazônia (IMAZON), http://www.imazon.org.br/publicacoes/livros/pecuaria-na-amazonia-tendencias-e-implicacoes-para.

Arima, E.Y.; Richards, P.; Walker, R.; Caldas, M. M. 2011. Statistical confirmation of indirect land use change in the Brazilian Amazon. *Environmental Research Letters*, 6: 024010. doi:10.1088/1748-9326/6/2/024010

Assunção, J.; Gandour, C. C.; Rocha, R. 2012. Deforestation Slowdown in the Legal Amazon: Prices or Policies? Climate Policy Initiative (CPI) Working Paper, Rio de Janeiro, RJ, Brazil: Pontífica Universidade Católica (PUC), Available at: http://climatepolicyinitiative.org/publication/deforestation-slowdown-in-the-legal-amazon-prices-or-policie/.

Barber, R. G.; Orellana, M.; Navarro, F.; Diaz, O.; Soruco, M. A. 1996. Effects of conservation and conventional tillage systems after land clearing on soil properties and crop yield in Santa Cruz, Bolivia. *Soil & Tillage Research*, 38(1–2): 133–52.

Barreto, P.; Brandão Jr., A.; Martins, H.; Silva, D.; Souza Jr., C.; Sales, M.; Feitosa, T. 2011. *Risco de Desmatamento Associado à Hidrelétrica de Belo Monte*. Belém, Pará, Brazil: Instituto do Homem e Meio Ambiente da Amazônia (IMAZON). Available at: http://www.imazon.org.br/publicacoes/livros/risco-de-desmatamento-associado-a-hidreletrica-de-belo-monte/at_download/file.

Barona, E.; Ramankutty, N.; Hyman, G.; Coomes, O. T. 2010. The role of pasture and soybean in deforestation of the Brazilian Amazon. *Environmental Research Letters*, 5, 9.

Beisiegel, W. de R.; de Souza, W. O. 1986. Reservas de fosfatos-Panorama nacional e mundial, 55–67. In: Instituto Brasileiro de Fosfato (IBRAFOS) *III Encontro Nacional de Rocha Fosfática, Brasília, 16–18/06/86*. IBRAFOS, Brasília, Brazil.

Bermann, C.; Martins, O.S. 2000. *Sustentabilidade Energética no Brasil: Limites e Possibilidades para uma Estratégia Energética Sustentável e Democrática*. Rio de Janeiro, RJ, Brazil: Projeto Brasil Sustentável e Democrático (Série Cadernos Temáticos No. 1), Federação dos Órgãos para Assistência Social e Educacional (FASE).

Bittencourt, G.; Peters, E. D.; Hiratuka, C.; Castilho, M.; Bianco, C.; Carracela, G.; Cunha, S.; Doneschi, A.; Lorenzi, N. R.; Sarmento, D. M. K.; Sarti, F.; Bazqueet, H. 2012. *El Impacto de China en América Latina: Comércio y Inversiones*. Serie Red Mercosur No. 20, Montevideo, Uruguay: Red Mercosur de Investigaciones Económicas. http://www.redmercosur.org/amenaza-y-oportunidad-china-y-america-latina/publicacion/238/es/.

Bland, D. 2013. China mulls financing multi-billion dollar railway project in Brazil. BNAmericas. 11 November 2013. Available at: http://www.bnamericas.com/news/infrastructure/china-eyes-financing-multi-billion-dollar-railway-project-in-brazil.

Brazil, Agência Câmara de Notícias. 2012. Relatório sobre compra de terras por estrangeiros será votado em 11 de abril. 28 March 2012. Brasília, DF, Brazil: Agência Câmara de Notícias. Available at: http://www2.camara.gov.br/agencia/noticias/agropecuaria/413045-relatorio-sobre-compra-de-terras-por-estrangeiros-sera-votado-em-11-de-abril.html.

Brazil, BCB (Banco Central do Brasil). 2014. Censo de capitais estrangeiros no país – resultados para 2012. Brasília, Brazil: BCB. Available at: http://www.bcb.gov.br/Rex/CensoCE/port/Censo%202013%20ano-base%202012%20-%20resultados.pdf.

Brazil, IBGE (Instituto Brasileiro de Geografia e Estatística). 2012. Sistema IBGE de Recuperação Automática, SIDRA. Rio de Janeiro, Brazil: IBGE. Available at: http://www.sidra.ibge.gov.br/.

Brazil, IBGE (Instituto Brasileiro de Geografia e Estatística). 2013. Levantamento Sistemático da Produção Agrícola: 4ª Estimativa Safra 2013. Rio de Janeiro, RJ, Brazil: IBGE.

Brazil, INPE (Instituto Nacional de Pesquisas Espaciais). 2013. Projeto PRODES: Monitoramento da Floresta Amazônica Brasileira por Satélite. São José dos Campos, São Paulo, Brazil: INPE. Available at: http://www.obt.inpe.br/prodes/.

Brazil, MDIC (Ministério de Desenvolvimento, Indústria e Comércio). 2012. Aliceweb. Brasília, DF, Brazil: SECEX-MDIC. Available at: http://aliceweb2.mdic.gov.br/#.

Brazil, MME (Ministério das Minas e Energia). 2011. *Plano Decenal de Expansão de Energia 2020.* Brasília, DF, Brazil: Empresa de Pesquisa Energética (EPE), MME. Available at: http://www.epe.gov.br/PDEE/20120302_1.pdf.

Brazil, MME (Ministério das Minas e Energia). 2013. *Plano Decenal de Expansão de Energia 2022.* Brasília, DF, Brazil: Empresa de Pesquisa Energética (EPE), MME. http://www.epe.gov.br/PDEE/24102013_2.pdf.

Brazil, MT (Ministério dos Transportes). 2010. Diretrizes da Política Nacional de Transporte Hidroviário. Brasília, DF, Brazil: Secretaria de Política Nacional de Transportes, Ministério dos Transportes. http://www2.transportes.gov.br/Modal/Hidroviario/PNHidroviario.pdf.

Brown, L. 2004. The Brazilian dilemma, 157–76 in: *Outgrowing the Earth: The Food Security Problem in an Age of Falling Water Tables and Rising Temperatures.* New York: Earth Policy Institute and Norton.

Business News Americas. 2011. Chinese groups eye USD 10bn Cuiabá-Santarém rail Project. Available at: http://www.bnamericas.com/news/infrastructure/chinese-groups-eye-us63bn-cuiaba-santarem-rail-project1. 18 July 2011.

Carmignani, F.; Avom, D. 2010. The social development effects of primary commodity export dependence. *Ecological Economics,* 70(2): 317–30.

Carrero, G. C.; Fearnside, P. M. 2011. Forest clearing dynamics and the expansion of land holdings in Apuí, a deforestation hotspot on Brazil's Transamazon Highway. *Ecology and Society,* 16(2): 26. http://www.ecologyandsociety.org/vol16/iss2/art26/.

CBBC (China Brazil Business Council). 2013. *Chinese Investments in Brazil from 2007–2012: A Review of Recent Trends.* Rio de Janeiro, RJ, Brazil: Conselho Empresarial Brasil-China (CEBC). Available at: http://www.chinapda.org.cn/chn/cbkw/acd/P020140127355857998526.pdf.

CEBC (Conselho Empresarial Brasil-China). 2014. Comércio Bilateral Brasil-China. CEBC Informativo No. 21, April 2014. http://www.cebc.org.br/sites/default/files/informativo_no_21._exportacao.pdf.

Cintra, M. R. V. P. 2013. A presença da China na América Latina no século XXI – suas estratégias e o impacto dessa relação para países e setores específicos. (Masters Dissertation in International Political Economics) Rio de Janeiro: Instituto de Economia, Universidade Federal do Rio de Janeiro (UFRJ-IE).

CNEC (Consórcio Nacional dos Engenheiros Consultores). 2014. *Estudo de Viabilidade do AHE São Luiz do Tapajós.* CNEC, São Paulo, SP, Brazil. 11 vols. plus annexes.

Daly, H. E.; Cobb, J. B. 1989. *For the Common Good: Redirecting the Economy toward Community, the Environment and a Sustainable Future.* Boston: Beacon Press.

da Nóbrega, M. 2012. A China, a Embrapa e o passado. *Veja* [São Paulo], 22 February, 20.

de Lima, J. M. G. 1976. *Perfil Analítico dos Fertilizantes Fosfatados.* Ministério das Minas e Energia, Departamento Nacional de Produção Mineral (DNPM) Boletim No. 39. Brasília, DF, Brazil: DNPM.

Dourojeanni, M. 2013. Multiplicação de vias entre Brasil e Peru é cara e desnecessária. *OEco* 13 May 2013. http://www.oeco.org.br/marc-dourojeanni/27170-multiplicacao-de-vias-entre-brasil-e-peru-e-cara-e-desnecessaria.

Fargione, J.; Hill, J.; Tilman, D.; Polasky, S.; Hawthorne, P. 2008. Land clearing and the biofuel carbon debt. *Science,* 319: 1235–38.

Fearnside, P. M. 1979. Cattle yield prediction for the Transamazon Highway of Brazil. *Interciencia*, 4(4): 220–25.

Fearnside, P. M. 1986. *Human Carrying Capacity of the Brazilian Rainforest*. New York: Columbia University Press.

Fearnside, P. M. 1989a. Forest management in Amazonia: The need for new criteria in evaluating development options. *Forest Ecology and Management*, 27(1): 61–79. doi: 10.1016/0378-1127(89)90083-2

Fearnside, P. M. 1989b. The charcoal of Carajás: Pig-iron smelting threatens the forests of Brazil's Eastern Amazon Region. *Ambio*, 18(2): 141–43.

Fearnside, P. M. 1989c. *Ocupação humana de Rondônia: Impactos, limites e planejamento*. Brasília, DF, Brazil: Conselho Nacional de Desenvolvimento Científico e Tecnológico (CNPq).

Fearnside, P. M. 1997a. Monitoring needs to transform Amazonian forest maintenance into a global warming mitigation option. *Mitigation and Adaptation Strategies for Global Change*, 2(2–3): 285–302. doi: 0.1023/B:MITI.0000004483.22797.1b

Fearnside, P. M. 1997b. Limiting factors for development of agriculture and ranching in Brazilian Amazonia. *Revista Brasileira de Biologia*, 57(4): 531–49.

Fearnside, P. M. 1998. Phosphorus and human carrying capacity in Brazilian Amazonia, 94–108. In: J. P. Lynch and J. Deikman (eds) *Phosphorus in Plant Biology: Regulatory Roles in Molecular, Cellular, Organismic, and Ecosystem Processes*. Rockville, MD: American Society of Plant Physiologists.

Fearnside, P. M. 2001a. Soybean cultivation as a threat to the environment in Brazil. *Environmental Conservation*, 28(1): 23–38. doi: 10.1017/S0376892901000030

Fearnside, P. M. 2001b. Land-tenure issues as factors in environmental destruction in Brazilian Amazonia: The case of southern Pará. *World Development*, 29(8): 1361–72. doi: 10.1016/S0305-750X(01)00039-0.

Fearnside, P. M. 2002a. Avança Brasil: Environmental and social consequences of Brazil's planned infrastructure in Amazonia. *Environmental Management*, 30(6), 748–63. doi: 10.1007/s00267-002-2788-2.

Fearnside, P. M. 2002b. Can pasture intensification discourage deforestation in the Amazon and Pantanal regions of Brazil? 299–314. In: C. H. Wood and R. Porro (eds) *Deforestation and Land Use in the Amazon*. Gainesville: University Press of Florida.

Fearnside, P. M. 2003. Deforestation control in Mato Grosso: A new model for slowing the loss of Brazil's Amazon forest. *Ambio*, 32: 343–45.

Fearnside, P. M. 2005a. Deforestation in Brazilian Amazonia: History, rates and consequences. *Conservation Biology*, 19(3): 680–88.

Fearnside, P. M. 2005b. Brazil's Samuel Dam: Lessons for hydroelectric development policy and the environment in Amazonia. *Environmental Management*, 35(1): 1–19.

Fearnside, P. M. 2006. Dams in the Amazon: Belo Monte and Brazil's hydroelectric development of the Xingu River Basin. *Environmental Management*, 38(1): 16–27.

Fearnside, P. M. 2007. Brazil's Cuiabá-Santarém (BR-163) Highway: The environmental cost of paving a soybean corridor through the Amazon. *Environmental Management*, 39(5): 601–14. doi: 10.1007/s00267-006-0149-2

Fearnside, P. M. 2008a. The roles and movements of actors in the deforestation of Brazilian Amazonia, *Ecology and Society*, 13(1): 23. Available at: http://www.ecologyandsociety.org/vol13/iss1/art23/.

Fearnside, P. M. 2008b. Amazon forest maintenance as a source of environmental services. *Anais da Academia Brasileira de Ciências*, 80(1): 101–14. doi: 10.1590/S0001-37652008000100006.

Fearnside, P. M. 2008c. Ameaça da soja. *Scientific American Brasil,* Especial Amazônia (3): 44–51.

Fearnside, P. M. 2012. Belo Monte: A spearhead for Brazil's dam-building attack on Amazonia? GWF Discussion Paper 1210, Global Water Forum, Canberra, Australia. Available at: http://www.globalwaterforum.org/wp-content/uploads/2012/04/Belo-Monte-Dam-A-spearhead-for-Brazils-dam-building-attack-on-Amazonia_-GWF-1210.pdf.

Fearnside, P. M. 2013a. Carbon credit for hydroelectric dams as a source of greenhouse-gas emissions: The example of Brazil's Teles Pires Dam. *Mitigation and Adaptation Strategies for Global Change,* 18(5): 691–99. doi: 10.1007/s11027-012-9382-6.

Fearnside, P. M. 2013b. Credit for climate mitigation by Amazonian dams: Loopholes and impacts illustrated by Brazil's Jirau Hydroelectric Project. *Carbon Management,* 4(6): 681–96. doi: 10.4155/CMT.13.57

Fearnside, P. M. 2014. Impacts of Brazil's Madeira River dams: Unlearned lessons for hydroelectric development in Amazonia. *Environmental Science & Policy,* 38: 164–72 doi: 10.1016/j.envsci.2013.11.004.

Fearnside, P. M. 2015a. Amazon dams and waterways: Brazil's Tapajós Basin plans. *Ambio,* 44(5): 426–39. doi: 10.1007/s13280-015-0642-z.

Fearnside, P. M. 2015b. Brazil's São Luiz do Tapajós Dam: The art of cosmetic environmental impact assessments. *Water Alternatives,* 8(3): 373–96. http://www.water-alternatives.org/index.php/alldoc/articles/vol8/v8issue3/297-a8-3-5/file.

Fearnside, P. M. 2016a. Environmental and social impacts of hydroelectric dams in Brazilian Amazonia: Implications for the aluminum industry. *World Development,* 77: 48–65. doi: 10.1016/j.worlddev.2015.08.015.

Fearnside, P. M. 2016b. Brazilian politics threaten environmental policies. *Science,* 353: 746–48. doi: 10.1126/science.aag0254.

Fearnside, P. M., Figueiredo, A. M. R.; Bonjour, S. C. M. 2013. Amazonian forest loss and the long reach of China's influence. *Environment, Development and Sustainability,* 15(2): 325–38. doi: 10.1007/s10668-012-9412-2.

Folha de São Paulo. 2005. Em Sorriso, estrada divide Daslu e miséria. *Folha de São Paulo,* 19 June 2005, B-4.

Freitas, T. 2014. Exportação de grãos vai dobrar, diz Bunge; para empresa, China manterá demanda. *Folha de São Paulo,* 26 April 2014, B-2.

Gallagher, K. P.; Irwin, A.; Koleski, K. 2012. *The New Banks in Town: Chinese Finance in Latin America.* Washington, DC: Inter-American Dialogue.

Garcia, R. 2014. Impacto do clima será mais amplo, porém mais incerto. *Folha de São Paulo,* 31 March, C-5.

GRAIN. 2012. GRAIN releases data set with over 400 global land grabs. 23 February 2012. http://www.grain.org/article/entries/4479-grain-releases-data-set-with-over-400-global-land-grabs.

Greenpeace. 2005. 'Soya King' wins Golden Chainsaw award. http://www.greenpeace.org/international/en/news/features/soya-king-wins-chainsaw/.

Hargrave, J.; Kis-Katos, K. 2011. Economic causes of deforestation in the Brazilian Amazon: A panel data analysis for the 2000s. Discussion Paper Series No. 17, Freiburg, Germany: University of Freiburg. Available at: http://www.vwl.uni-freiburg.de/iwipol/discussion_papers/DP17_Hargrave_Kis-Katos - Economic Causes of Deforestation in the Brazilian Amazon.pdf.

IMEA (Instituto Matogrossense de Economia Agropecuária). 2014. Primeiro levantamento das intenções de confinamento em 2014. Cuiabá, Mato Grosso, Brazil: IMEA. 9 May 2014. Available at: http://www.imea.com.br/upload/pdf/arquivos/2014_05_1_LEVANTAMENTO_DAS_INTENCOES_DE_CONFINAMENTO_EM_2014.pdf.

ISA (Instituto Socioambiental). 2013. Dilma homologa terra indígena Kayabi (MT/PA) em meio a atritos por causa de hidrelétricas. *Notícias Direto do ISA*, 19 April 2013. http://www.socioambiental.org/pt-br/noticias-socioambientais/dilma-homologa-terra-indigena-kayabi-mtpa-em-meio-a-atritos-por-causa-de[29-Apr-13 17:11:09].

ISA (Instituto Socioambiental). 2014. Ataque de deputado ruralista a índios, quilombolas e gays repercute na imprensa e na internet. *Noticias Socioambientais*, 13 February 2014. http://www.socioambiental.org/pt-br/noticias-socioambientais/ataque-de-deputado-ruralista-a-indios-quilombolas-e-gays-repercute-na-imprensa-e-na-internet.

Kaimowitz, D.; Mertens, B.; Wunder, S.; Pacheco, P. 2004. *Hamburger Connection Fuels Amazon Destruction*. Bogor, Indonesia: Centre for International Forestry Research (CIFOR). Available at: http://www.cifor.org/publications/pdf_files/media/amazon.pdf.

Kaimowitz, D.; Thiele, G.; Pacheco, P. 1999. The effects of structural adjustment policies on deforestation and forest degradation in lowland Bolivia. *World Development*, 27(3): 505–20.

Latin American Herald Tribune. 2012. Brazil limits land sales to foreigners. *Latin American Herald Tribune*, 12 April 2012. http://www.laht.com/article.asp?ArticleId=364278&CategoryId=14090

Laurance, W. F.; Cochrane, M. A.; Bergen, S.; Fearnside, P. M.; Delamônica, P.; Barber, C.; D'Angelo, S.; Fernandes, T. 2001. The future of the Brazilian Amazon. *Science*, 291: 438–39. doi: 10.1126/science.291.5503.438.

Lentini, M.; Veríssimo, A.; Pereira, D. 2011. A Expansão Madeireira na Amazônia. Belém - Pará – Brasil: Instituto do Homem e Meio Ambiente da Amazônia (Imazon). http://www.imazon.org.br/publicacoes/o-estado-da-amazonia/a-expansao-madeireira-na-amazonia-1.

Lourenço, L. 2014. MPF processa União e Funai por demora na demarcação de terra indígena no Pará. *Agência Brasil*, 27 May 2014. Available at: http://amazonia.org.br/2014/05/mpf-processa-uni%c3%a3o-e-funai-por-demora-na-demarca%c3%a7%c3%a3o-de-terra-ind%c3%adgena-no-par%c3%a1/.

Lucatelli, L. 2012. Silval vai à China viabilizar ferrovia que liga MT ao Pará. *MidiaNews*, 20 June 2012. Available at: http://www.midianews.com.br/conteudo.php?sid=2&cid=123569.

Macedo, M. N.; DeFries, R. S.; Morton, D. C.; Stickler, C. M.; Galford, G. L.; Shimabukuro, Y. E. 2012. Decoupling of deforestation and soy production in the southern Amazon during the late 2000s. *Proceedings of the National Academy of Sciences of the USA*, 109: 1341–46. doi.10.1073/pnas.1111374109.

Macrologística. 2011. Projeto Norte Competitivo. Macrologística Consultaria, São Paulo, SP, Brazil. http://www.macrologistica.com.br/images/stories/palestras/Projeto%20Norte%20Competitivo%20-%20Apresentação%20Executiva%20no%20Ministério%20do%20Planejamento%20-%20Agosto%202011.pdf.

Maisonnave, F. 2012. MT negocia financiamento chinês para ferrovia. Banco pode emprestar USD 10 bi, diz governo; contrapartida inclui importação da China. *Folha de São Paulo*, 27 June 2012. http://www1.folha.uol.com.br/fsp/mercado/51212-mt-negocia-financiamento-chines-para-ferrovia.shtml.

Marquina, R. B. 2013. Presidenta Dilma Rousseff impulsará con Humala una conexión ferroviaria bilateral. *Gestión* [Lima], 8 November 2013. http://gestion.pe/politica/presidenta-dilma-rousseff-impulsara-ollanta-humala-conexion-ferroviaria-bilateral-2080586.

Marta, J. M. C.; Figueiredo, A. M. R. 2008. Expansão da soja no cerrado de Mato Grosso: aspectos políticos. *Revista de Política Agrícola*, 15(1): 117–28.

Martins, P. F. S.; Pereira, T. Z. S. 2012. Cattle-raising and public credit in rural settlements in Eastern Amazon. *Ecological Indicators*, 20: 316–23.

Mato Grosso. 2012. Modal ferroviário e a economia de Mato Grosso (Parte I). Available at: http://www.mt.gov.br/conteudo.php?sid=151&cid=73205&parent=0.

Mello, F.; Amora, D. 2012. PF aponta superfaturamento na obra da ferrovia Norte-Sul. *Folha de São Paulo*, 15 July 2012, A-4.

Moreira, L. M. 2013. *A Exportação como Causa do Desmatamento em Mato Grosso: Uma Análise dos Anos 2001 a 2010*. (Masters dissertation in economics), Cuiabá, MT, Brazil: Universidade Federal de Mato Grosso.

Morton, D. C.; DeFries, R. S.; Shimabukuro, Y. E.; Anderson, L. O.; Arai, E.; Espirito-Santo, F. D. B.; Freitas, R.; Morisette, J. 2006. Cropland expansion changes deforestation dynamics in the southern Brazilian Amazon. *Proceedings of the National Academy of Sciences of the USA*, 103(39): 14637–41.

Nepstad, D. C.; McGrath, D.; Stickler, C.; Alencar, A.; Azevedo, A.; Swette, B. Bezerra, T.; DiGiano, M.; Shimada, J.; Seroa da Motta, R.; Armijo, E.; Castello, L.; Brando, P. Hansen, M. C.; McGrath-Horn, M.; Carvalho, O.; Hess, L. 2014. Slowing Amazon deforestation through public policy and interventions in beef and soy supply chains. *Science*, 344: 1118–23. doi: 10.1126/science.1248525

Nepstad, D. C.; Stickler, C. M.; Almeida, O. T. 2006. Globalization of the Amazon soy and beef industries: Opportunities for conservation. *Conservation Biology*, 20(6): 1595–1603.

Nogueira, W. 1988. China importa madeira em toras. *Amazonas em Tempo* [Manaus], 9 March 1988, Caderno 1, 8.

Ondei, V. 2012. O império da família Maggi. *Dinheiro Rural*, No. 93, June 2012. http://revistadinheirorural.terra.com.br/secao/agronegocios/o-imperio-da-familia-maggi.

Raimundo, L. da C.; Azevedo, C. A. L. (eds). 2011. *A emergência da China e suas relações com América Latina e África*. Campinas, SP, Brazil: FACAMP/Embrapa/GSI-PR. Available at: http://geopr1.planalto.gov.br/saei/images/publicacoes/2010–2011/caderno_tematico_a_emergencia_da_china_e_suas_relacoes_com.pdf.

Rajão, R.; Azevedo, A.; Stabile, M. C. C. 2012. Institutional subversion and deforestation: Learning lessons from the system for the environmental licencing of rural properties in Mato Grosso. *Public Administration and Development*, 32: 229–44. doi:10.1002/pad.1620.

Reuters. 2011. Brazil plans stricter land purchase rules. 19 November 2011. http://farmlandgrab.org/post/view/19629.

Santilli, M. 2014. Ruralismo de fronteira. Instituto Socioambiental (ISA), 27 February 2014. Brasília, DF, Brazil: ISA. http://www.socioambiental.org/pt-br/blog/blog-do-ppds/ruralismo-de-fronteira.

Smeraldi, R. 2014. Para sair da estaca zero. *Folha de São Paulo*, 26 February 2014. http://www1.folha.uol.com.br/opiniao/2014/02/1417853-roberto-smeraldi-para-sair-da-estaca-zero.shtml.

Soares, P. 2012. Vale diz que venda à China continua em alta. *Folha de São Paulo*, 14 July 2012, B-4.

Soybean and Corn Advisor Inc. 2012. News, 4 December 2012. Available at: http://www .soybeansandcorn.com/news/Dec4_12-Chinese-Investors-Closer-To-Building-Railroad-in-Mato-Grosso.

Sutton, A. 1994. *Slavery in Brazil–A Link in the Chain of Modernization.* London: Anti-Slavery International.

United States, CEQ (Council on Environmental Quality); Department of State. 1980. *The Global 2000 Report to the President.* New York: Pergamon Press, 3 vols.

UN Comtrade. 2014. New York: United Nations. http://www.columbia.edu/cgi-bin/cul/ resolve?clio4217949.

Vale. 2009. Pará terá refinaria de alumina. 18 January 2009. http://saladeimprensa.vale. com/pt/versao_impressao/prt_detail.asp?tipo=1&id=15686.

VALEC – Engenharia, Construções e Ferrovias S.A. 2014. EF-354 – Ferrovia Transcontinental. Brasília, DF, Brazil: VALEC http://www.valec.gov.br/acoes_pro-gramas/FerroviaTranscontinental.php.

WCED (World Council on Environment and Development). 1987. *Our Common Future.* Oxford: Oxford University Press.

WWF Brasil. 2012. Construção de hidrelétricas ameaça rio Tapajós. 11 February 2012. http://www.wwf.org.br/informacoes/sala_de_imprensa/?30562/construo-de-hidreltricas-ameaa-rio-tapajs.

WWF Brasil. 2014. Hidrelétricas podem alagar parque nacional na Amazônia. *Amazônia*, 5 June 2014. http://amazonia.org.br/2014/06/hidrel%c3%a9tricas-podem-alagar-parque-nacional-na-amaz%c3%b4nia/.

Zarsky, L.; Stanley, L. 2013. Can extractive industries promote sustainable development? A net benefits framework and a case study of the Marlin mine in Guatemala. *The Journal of Environment and Development*, 22(2): 131–54. doi: 10.1177/1070496513483131.

Technical Appendix

The system uses the following variables for the Brazilian Legal Amazon: endogenous variables of deforested area (Defor) and the FOB value of Brazilian exports to China (Export); and exogenous variables of soybean-planted area (SoyArea), cattle herd (Herd), beef price (BeefPrice), soybean price (SoyPrice),[3] and a trend variable (Trend). Previous-year deforestation, SoyArea, previous-year herd, beef and soybean prices and previous-year exports as instruments (the variables used in the first step of the three-stage linear system). All

---

3 Prices from the World Bank Global Economic Monitor (GEM) Commodities price database, available at: http://databank.worldbank.org/data/views/variablesel-ection/selectvariables.aspx?source=Global-Economic-Monitor-%28GEM%29-Commodities. Soybeans price: (US), c.i.f. Rotterdam in $/mt; beef price: meat, beef (Australia/New Zealand), chucks and cow forequarters, frozen boneless, 85% chemical lean, c.i.f. U.S. port (East Coast) in cents/kg.

variables refer to the Legal Amazon from 2002 to 2010 with values expressed as logarithms. The system can then be expressed as (1) for year "t".

$$\text{Dlog(Defor)}_t = \beta_0 + \beta_1 \text{Dlog(Herd)}_{t-1} + \beta_2 \text{Dlog(SoyArea)}_t + \beta_3 \text{Dlog(Export)}_t$$
$$+ \beta_4 \text{Dlog(SoyPrice)}_t + \beta_5 \times \text{Dlog(BeefPrice)}_{t} + \beta_6 \times \text{Trend} + \varepsilon_{1t}$$
$$\text{Log(Export)}_t = \beta_7 + \beta_8 \text{Log(Herd)}_{t-1} + \beta_9 \text{Log(SoyArea)}_t$$
$$+ \beta_{10} \text{Log(Export)}_{t-1} + \varepsilon_{2t} (1)$$

where the variables are as described above and the Dlog operator denotes the first difference between the logarithms, or $\text{Dlog(X}_t) = \log(\text{X}_t) - \log(\text{X}_{t-1})$. This is done to account for the increase in deforested area, as well as the size of the cattle herd, the area in soybeans and prices.

The estimation follows the three-stage least-squares method, where a generalized least-squares estimator is applied to a system of equations (in this case two equations) with a variance-covariance parameter matrix estimated in a previous step (in the first and second stages, the endogenous variables are regressed against instrumental variables and forecasts of endogenous variables are then used to calculate the variance–covariance parameter matrix).

Table 7.2 System estimation for the change in the Brazilian Amazon deforestation and its exports to China, 2002–2010

Variable	Coefficient	Standard Error	t-Statistic	Prob.
Dependent: Change in Deforestation (Dlog(Deforest))				
Intercept	3.375	0.188	17.932	0.000
Dlog(Herd)_{t-1}	0.142	$4.59{*}10^{-3}$	30.949	0.000
Dlog(SoyArea)_t	0.035	$1.84{*}10^{-3}$	19.050	0.000
Dlog(Export)_t	0.014	$1.02{*}10^{-3}$	13.614	0.000
Dlog(SoyPrice)_t	0.043	$1.24{*}10^{-3}$	34.304	0.000
Dlog(BeefPrice)_t	−0.020	$1.11{*}10^{-3}$	−17.830	0.000
Trend	−0.002	$9.36{*}10^{-3}$	−17.982	0.000
Dependent: Exports (Dlog(Export))				
Intercept	9.174	9.096	1.009	0.347[NS]
Log(Herd)_{t-1}	−2.105	0.867	−2.427	0.046*
Log(SoyArea)_t	1.987	0.557	3.596	0.009
Log(Export)_{t-1}	0.910	0.057	16.007	0.000
	Increase in Deforestation		Exports	
R^2	0.9997		0.9912	
Adjusted R^2	0.9986		0.9859	

Source: Research data.

Note: Portmanteau tests confirmed the hypothesis of no residual autocorrelations, as did system residual normality tests. NS= statistically not significant; * = statistically significant at 95% confidence; all other coefficients were significant at the 99% confidence level.

Unfortunately, at this time we do not have data on exports by municipality. Municipal-level data would increase the degrees of freedom in this combination of cross-sectional and time-series data, allowing spatial regression techniques to be applied.

The results of the system estimation, as in Equation 1, are presented in Table 7.2. The system residual Portmanteau tests for autocorrelations showed no autocorrelation at the 90 percent confidence level. There were satisfactory fits in both equations, with most of the parameters significant at the 99 percent confidence level, except the intercept in the second equation.

In the equation for the increase in deforestation, the difference in soybean-planted area as well as the previous year herd exhibited a positive relationship, meaning that the expansion in soybean-planted area or in the herd may increase deforestation. Additionally, increases in exports to China and the world price of soybeans have a statistical association with the increase in deforestation. The beef price, in the other direction, exhibited a negative relationship with the change in deforestation.

In the export equation, the cattle herd size in the previous year reduces exports to China. The current exports are positively related both to soybean-planted area and to exports in the previous year. All of these results may be explained by the fact that most of soybeans in the Legal Amazon are, in fact, exported, and that China is expanding its imports. This functions like a learning-by-doing process, strengthening the trade relationship.

Part V

CHINA'S AND LATIN AMERICA'S MANUFACTURING SECTORS

Chapter 8

CHINESE INCIDENCE ON THE CHILEAN SOLAR POWER SECTOR

Nicola Borregaard, Annie Dufey, Maria Teresa Ruiz-Tagle
and Santiago Sinclair

Over the last decade, China has become an important ally in Chile's goal of diversifying its energy matrix away from fossil fuels. China's overproduction of solar PV panels came at just the right time for Chile, which was looking for new sources of low-emissions electricity after Argentina drastically reduced its gas exports. The resulting relationship between Chile and China is very promising for both parties. Solar power is still nascent in Chile, but growing quickly: as of this writing, over half of new power projects with approved environmental permits are solar.

Chile can maximize the local benefit from this new relationship by encouraging linkages, establishing norms and investing in education. Encouraging linkages can include training local companies to perform related services such as equipment maintenance, which only a few Chilean firms currently provide. Establishing quality norms for imported PV panels can protect the grid from defective or unsafe equipment and would not be prohibitively complicated: Chile could require certification from one of the international bodies or adopt international norms. Finally, the Chilean state should consider investing in education for residential and business consumers of PV panels as well as for potential workers in the industry.

1. Introduction

Chile's power sector is characterized by mainly relying on large power plants based on hydropower and fossil fuels and by long distribution lines. By 2013 installed capacity in Chile was just over 18,000 MW. A key structural change in the Chilean electricity mix occurred in 1998 when low-cost natural gas from Argentina was introduced. However, in 2004 drastic export restrictions from Argentina implied an end to this natural-gas-based expansion and in 2008 the gas valve to Chile was finally completely closed.

This Chilean energy crisis, together with high international oil prices and an unprecedented drought that continues through this writing have triggered a complex situation in the Chilean power sector. The lack of natural gas has been remediated by introducing other imported inputs of more polluting or more expensive sources of energy, such as coal and oil. The carbonization of the electricity mix, together with new investment projects of large hydropower dams located in pristine southern areas of the country, have been the source of criticism from different sectors of society. Citizens' concerns have been reflected in increasing legal actions that have even paralyzed the construction of new power projects.

In this tense scenario, renewable energies could play a vital role in achieving the huge challenge faced by the Chilean power sector: a cleaner, lower-cost and more socially legitimate energy portfolio. At present there are 1,117 MW of non-conventional renewable energy (NCRE) in operation, from which only a small fraction are solar projects. However, it is foreseen that solar power will increase its relevance in the near future. In fact, it is expected that solar PV surpassed 200 MW in operation by the end of 2014, and will continue growing, considering that more than 50 percent of the 10,000 MW of new projects with environmental permits approved in the country are currently solar projects.

On the other hand, the growth of China's large-scale, export-oriented solar industry, fueled by favorable policies in many industrialized governments, together with important Chinese support policies to encourage its overseas trade and investment, has rapidly catapulted China to the top of global solar-cell manufacturing capacity. This significant supply capacity, together with recent efficiency improvements in modules manufacturing, have led to a dramatic fall in global PV prices in recent years, leading to important changes in the global solar industry.

Chilean access to low-cost PV cells and modules from China may open a window of opportunity in terms of contributing to solving the current energy crisis, providing lower cost solutions, curbing carbon emissions and other environmental impacts and reducing social conflicts around energy investments. On the other hand, the existence of significant policy support to China's solar industry is a major issue for Chile to consider if the country decides to promote the development of a national solar industry.

As solar energy has become a crucial element for the future of energy strategies in Chile, and a potentially interesting sector for economic development, Chile has to confront the question of the potential medium- to long-term effects of the Chinese involvement in its domestic industrial development.

This chapter is a first attempt to identify key emerging issues involved with the development of the solar PV industry in Chile and solar PV imports and investment from China. It provides an overview of trade between Chile and China and key insights about the trends in the Chilean electricity-generation sector and determinant policies and regulatory measures. Section 4 examines the emerging solar energy sector in Chile identifying the Chinese influence. Section 5 analyzes Chinese policy towards its solar energy sector. Finally, section 6 draws an analysis of the previous sections and provides key emerging issues and policy implications for Chile.

2. Overview of Trade between Chile and China

2.1 Trade between Chile and China

2.1.1 Imports and exports between Chile and China

Trade relations between Chile and China have been overall positive, wherein China has become one of the four major trade partners for Chile, increasing its trade in the last ten years, as shown in Figure 8.1. Nonetheless, Chilean exports to China have been heavily concentrated in copper, while Chilean imports from China are much more diversified, with an emphasis on machinery, as shown in Figures 8.2 and 8.3. China became the main export destination for Chile in 2009, and has increased its position since 2010.

2.1.2 Trade agreement between Chile and China

As shown in Table 8.1, in October 2006 Chile and China's trade relations reached another stage, as the free trade agreement (FTA) between these

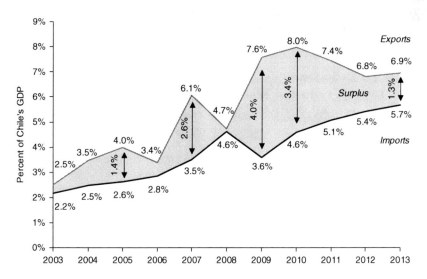

Figure 8.1 Chilean total exports/imports with Mainland China (percent of GDP)
Source: Author's work based on Banco Central Chile (2013), IMF WEO.

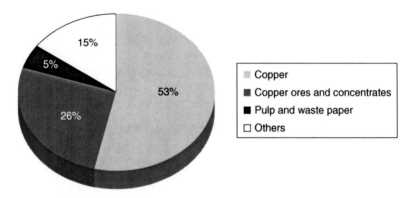

Figure 8.2 Chilean main exports to China (1994–2013)
Source: Author's work based on UN Comtrade (2014).

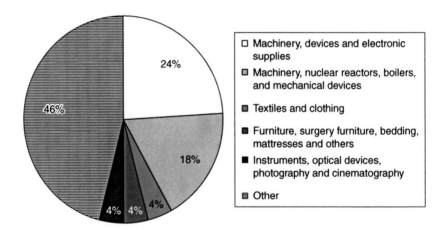

Figure 8.3 Chilean main imports from China in 2012
Source: Dirección General de Relaciones Económicas Internacionales, DIRECON (2014).

nations came into force. This agreement was the first Chinese negotiation of its type with a non-ASEAN country (DIRECON, 2014).

The first results were the reduction of barriers and increment of incentives for the entry of products in both directions. Tariff reductions in January 2013 implied that 1,610 products from Chile and 811 products from China that belong to the "10 year" category had a 10 percent reduction in their tariffs. Up to this date Chilean and Chinese products included in the agreement have had an 80 percent reduction in their tariffs, and by

Table 8.1 The China–Chile free trade agreement progressive negotiation phases

Phase	Trade Agreement	Date
I	Free trade agreement for goods	October 2006
II	Supplementary trade agreement for services	August 2010
III	Supplementary trade agreement for investment	February 2014

Source: Dirección General de Relaciones Económicas Internacionales, DIRECON (2014).

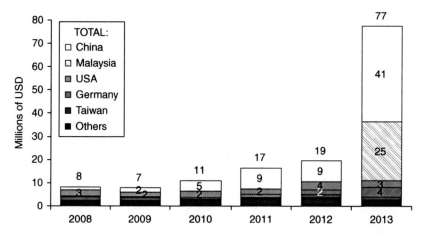

Figure 8.4 Chilean solar PV imports (2008–2013)
Source: Author's work based on Servicio Nacional de Aduanas Chile, 2013

2015 100 percent of these products had zero tariffs, excluding an exception list[1] (DIRECON, 2014).

2.2 Trends in Chile's solar panels trade

Chile's imports of PV panels reached USD 76.9 million by 2013, as shown in Figure 8.4, while there are no registered exports of this product. Imports of PV panels have increased largely between 2008 and 2013. As shown in Table 8.2, China has dramatically increased its participation in Chilean PV imports, growing from 18 percent of the total in 2008 to 53 percent by 2013, becoming the main supplier.

---

1 Solar panels and direct accessories are not considered in the exception list.

Table 8.2 Main origins of Chilean solar PV imports, 2008–2013

	2008	2009	2010	2011	2012	2013
China	18%	26%	42%	54%	45%	53%
USA	33%	23%	22%	15%	18%	4%
Malaysia	0%	0%	0%	0%	0%	33%
Germany	5%	8%	7%	8%	11%	5%
Taiwan	12%	7%	2%	1%	4%	1%
Others	31%	36%	27%	22%	21%	4%
Total:	100%	100%	100%	100%	100%	100%

Source: Author's work based on Servicio Nacional de Aduanas Chile, 2013.

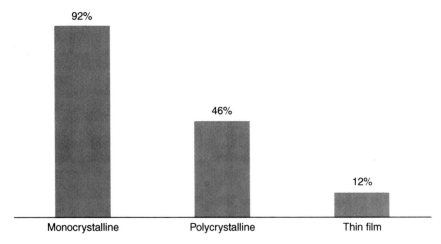

Figure 8.5 Commercialized solar PV technology in Chile
Source: CDT, 2012.

The bulk of the PV panels in the Chilean market have either mono- or polycrystalline silicon technology, as shown in Figure 8.5. Crystalline silicon PV panels are widely manufactured and exported by Chinese companies.

3. The Chilean Energy-Power Sector

3.1 Trends in the power sector

3.1.1 Trends in the power grid

The Chilean electricity grid is divided into three subsectors: generation, transmission and distribution. In total, the electricity sector generated 68,000 GWh in 2013 (CNE, 2013), supplying a demand that has been growing at an annual rate of 4.4 percent over the last 10 years (CNE, 2013).

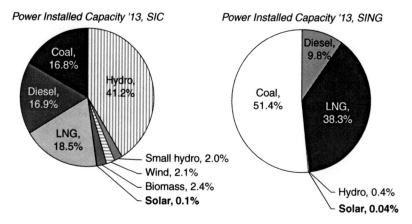

Power Installed Capacity '13, SIC

Power Installed Capacity '13, SING

Figure 8.6 The Chilean electricity portfolio (2013)
Source: Authors' work based on CNE, 2013.

The Chilean electricity market is composed of four subsystems. There are two main interconnected systems: the Central Interconnected Grid (SIC) provides 75 percent of the country's electricity demand and supplies over 90 percent of its population, and the Norte Grande Interconnected Grid (SING), which provides 24 percent of the country's electricity demand and mainly supplies the copper-mining industry. The remaining 1 percent is shared between small subsystems in more isolated areas. Currently, the government is endorsing a project for the interconnection between the SIC and SING subsystems by 2018, arguing that it would provide more security and sustenance to the national electricity grid (EE2030, 2013).

By 2013 the Chilean electricity grid had a total installed capacity of 18,653 MW. As shown in Figure 8.6, the SIC has a combination of different technologies, clearly predominated by hydroelectricity; although it has fallen considerably since 2008. NCRE accounts for 5 percent of the total installed capacity in the SIC. The SING, however, relies almost exclusively on thermal power generation, and only 1 percent is supplied by NCRE.

Most of the inputs used to generate electricity are currently being imported (coal and diesel), with the notable exception of hydroelectricity and biomass. As of this writing, Chile imports 72 percent of its energy needs, while in 1990 it only imported 48 percent (FCH, 2008).

The Chilean energy crisis produced by Argentina's cut of natural gas over the past decade, together with an unprecedented drought that continues at this writing and that has drastically reduced the traditional hydroelectric capacity of the country, have triggered an extremely complex scenario.

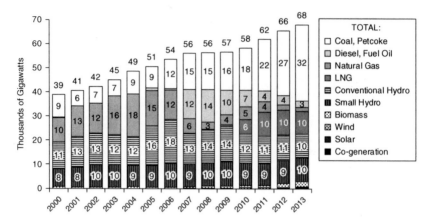

Figure 8.7 Trends of the power generated in the SIC-SING subsystems (GWh)
Source: Author's work based on CNE (2013) and Ministerio de Energía (2010).
Note: The SIC-SING subsystems generated a total power of 68.049 GWh in 2013.

As shown in Figure 8.7, the lack of natural gas has been compensated for by the introduction of other imported sources of energy such as coal and oil, which are more polluting and more expensive than natural gas. The carbonization and higher cost of the electric portfolio, together with the push by large hydropower dams located in southern pristine areas to fill the future energy gap, have been subject to strong criticism from different sectors of the society. Likewise, the current Chilean electric model, which relies almost exclusively on private initiative to define the power portfolio with no real long-term planning, has also been criticized (EE2030, 2013).

Citizens' concern and unrest related to the electric sector is reflected in increasing legal actions or litigation procedures that have led to the halting of the construction of new power projects. At present, more than 75 percent of the megawatts from new projects with their construction permit approved by the environmental authority (SEIA) are paralyzed due to legal or administrative claims against them. They mostly involve large hydroelectric dams or coal-fueled thermo electrical plants located far away from the main consumption centers (EE2030, 2013). At the moment, this phenomenon is the most important factor preventing the development of new power projects, which together with the absence of appropriate measures to address policy bottlenecks, have led to a critical situation in terms of the lack of implementation of new projects for the period 2013–2018. Altogether, it has resulted in a difficult challenge for the Chilean power sector: the need for a cleaner, lower-cost and more socially acceptable energy portfolio.

Under this scenario, NCRE could become a crucial factor to unlock the current energy crossroads. NCRE involves important attributes, including low local and global emissions, the latter being a key tool for advancing with greenhouse gas (GHG) mitigation; it enjoys greater social acceptability and has nearly null operational costs, and therefore lowers marginal costs or spot prices of the system and, in the case of solar and wind projects, are of very rapid implementation.

3.1.2 Trends for non-conventional renewable energies in the power grid

NCRE total installed capacity reached 1,117MW in 2013, which represents 6 percent of the total, and was mainly composed by small hydro, wind and biomass, while solar energy only represented 0.6 percent, as shown in Figure 8.8 and Table 8.3. This indicates that the NCRE quota, established by the Law No. 20,257 and recently modified by the Law 20/25 was achieved.

NCRE is a new but emerging market in Chile, and it shows significant growth prospects, as shown in Figure 8.9. Projects submitted to the Environmental Impact Assessment System (SEIA) in 2013 had a record of a total supply capacity of 17,000 MW of new renewable energy projects, either approved or in progress. These projects corresponded to solar (59%), wind (36%), and small hydro, geothermic, and biomass projects (5%). Nearly all the country's electricity-generation companies are developing or considering

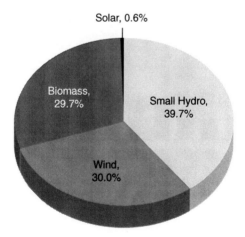

Figure 8.8 Non-conventional renewable energy installed capacity (2013)
Source: Author's work based on CER, 2013.

Table 8.3 Conventional versus NCRE sources in 2013 by system (MW)

Source	SIC	SING	Total
Hydro > 20 MW	5,681.3	-	5,681.3
LNG	2,776.9	2,111.7	4,888.6
Coal	2,394.3	2,099.7	4,494.0
Diesel	2,263.6	378.0	2,641.6
Total Conventional	*13,116.1*	*4,589.4*	*17,705.5*
Hydro < 20 MW	433.8	10.2	444.0
Biomass	332.0		332.0
Wind	335.0		335.0
Solar	2.9	3.8	6.7
Total NCRE	*1,103.7*	*14.0*	*1,117.7*
Total	**14,052.8**	**4,601.0**	**18,653.8**

Source: Author's work based on CDEC SIC and CDEC SING (2013) and CER (2013).
Note: Rows may not add to totals due to rounding.

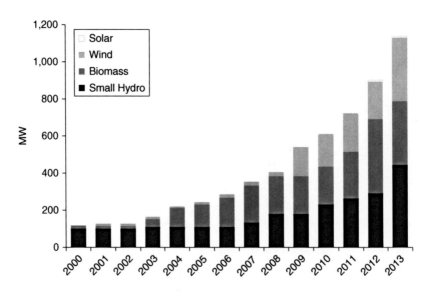

Figure 8.9 NCRE installed capacity in the electricity grid
Source: CER and CNE (2013).

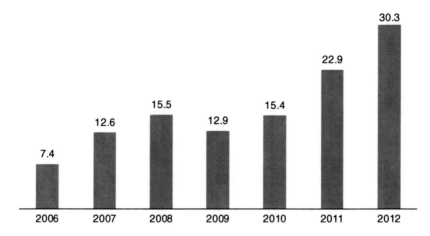

Figure 8.10 Total foreign direct investment (FDI) flow (2006–2012) (billions of USD) *Source*: Foreign Investment Committee (CIE, 2010).

projects of this nature; new companies have already been set up with the sole purpose of starting such initiatives, and a further significant number hope to follow this path in the near future (CER, 2013). This solar trend responds to the incentive of Law 20/25, the reduction of investment costs in solar PV and a deeper knowledge and technological adaptation from developers and citizens.

3.2 Trends in investments and FDI in the energy sector

3.2.1 Investments and FDI in Chile

The privatization of the Chilean electricity companies initiated in the 1980s was the main incentive to attracting private investment into the national electricity sector, completely state-owned and controlled until then. Up until the mid-1990s, private investment was mainly domestic but by the end of the 1990s was largely controlled by foreign companies (Pollitt, 2004).

Total Foreign Direct Investment (FDI) in Chile, through law DL 600[2]; grew rapidly from 2009 to 2012 (as shown in Figure 8.10) and reached USD 81.5 billion over these years. This new investment has been concentrated in mining and services, as shown in Figure 8.11.

---

2   Law No. 600 of 1974 is the instrument by which direct foreign investment enters Chile.

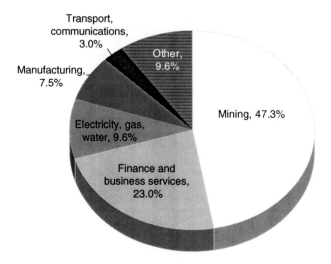

Figure 8.11 FDI in Chile by sector (2009–2012)
Source: Central Bank of Chile (www.bcentral.cl).

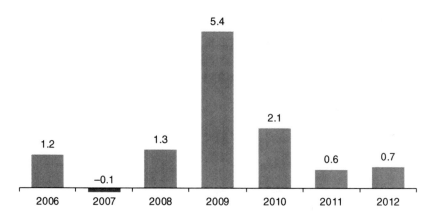

Figure 8.12 FDI in electricity, gas and water (2006–2012) (billions of USD)
Source: Author's work based on Central Bank of Chile (www.bcentral.cl).

3.2.2 Investment and FDI in the energy sector

Foreign and particularly European investments dominate the electricity generation and transmission network today. Spain has been the main source of FDI
in the energy sector in Chile, accounting for over half of the inflow through DL
600 between 1974 and 2010. Spain was followed by the United States (20.4%)
and Canada (16.1%); 82.7 percent of FDI in the energy, gas and water sector
corresponded to multi-region projects, because of its nature (CIE, 2010).

FDI in the sector had great fluctuation during the period 2006–2012,
as shown in Figure 8.12, even reaching negative figures in 2007, due to

disinvestment in the energy sector possibly as a reaction to the strict restrictions towards natural gas imports in that period. However, FDI began to recover, reaching a peak in 2009 when it accounted for over 40 percent, partly explained by investment in the Mejillones and Quinteros natural gas storage plants.

Although there are no official figures about FDI in the NCRE segment, it has also become a pole of attraction for foreign investors. As Box 8.1 suggests, this has been especially true for wind power and small-scale hydroelectric projects and increasingly for solar energy.

Box 8.1 Examples of FDI in NCRE in Chile

- **Endesa Eco:** wind farms Parque Eólico Canela in 2007 (18 MW) and Canela II in 2009 (60 MW), and small-scale hydroelectric project Ojos Aguan in 2008 (9 MW).
- The Spanish Group **Enhol**, wind-power project: Parque Eólico Hualpén (38 MW).
- **Iberdrola**, small-scale hydroelectric plant, Ruca Cura, in the Bio Bio region (4.7 MW).
- In 2004, joint venture between Australian company **Pacific Hydro** and Norwegian company **SN Power (Tinguiririca Energy)**. Two hydropower projects, La Higuera and La Confluencia. The run-of-hydro project La Confluencia (158 MW) was registered under the Clean Development Mechanism (CDM) of the Kyoto Protocol.
- **SN Power** subsidiary Norwind, built the wind farm Parque Eólico El Totoral (46 MW) in 2010.
- **Pacific Hydro** also operates the run-of-river hydropower plants Coya and Pangal (76 MW), and is currently building the Chacaves project (111 MW) in the Alto Cachapoal Valley and Pacific Hydro's first wind farm in Chile, the Punta Sierra Wind Farm, in the Coquimbo Region.
- In 2009, the Irish group **Mainstream Renewable Power** announced a joint venture with the Chilean company **Andes Energy** involving a series of projects for USD 1 billion to generate 481 MW of NCRE. Currently, there are 33 MW operating in the Negrete wind farm and 266 MW approved and beginning construction for solar PV projects and 2,680 MW in development, of which 731 MW are solar PV energy.
- In July 2009 **GTN LA**, the Latin American subsidiary of the German geothermal company GTN, began operations in association with

Fundación Chile and Manvitt (Iceland) for the exploration of geothermal resources in Chile.

- Italian enterprise **Enel**, in conjunction with Chilean state enterprises **ENAP** and **CODELCO**, are developing geothermal explorations and projects for a geothermal plant with a capacity of 50 MW that would produce 375 GWh annually for the SING. Besides, the Chilean generating company Colbún has an alliance with the US company Geoglobal Energy (GGE) to develop geothermal projects.

Solar energy foreign investment in Chile:

- **Solar Pack** (Spain) currently has different ongoing solar PV projects in the I and II regions of Chile with an investment of USD 253.3 million. Of these projects 62 MW are in development and 1 MW operational.
- **Saferay** (Germany) has created a joint venture with Seltec Chile, developing projects under the name SelRay. These projects with an estimated investment of USD 370 million are located in the I and III regions with 186 MW in development and 1.4 MW operationa.
- **Juwi** (Germany) through Kaltemp Chile has an operational 1.08 MW solar PV project in the IV Region, with an investment of USD 3 million.
- **Sun Edison** (United States) has different solar PV proejcts in the I, II, and III regions of Chile, with a total investment of USD 1,148.5 million, which implies 499 MW in development and 2 MW operational.
- **Kraftwerk** (Germany) through Subsole Chile has an operational solar PV project of 0.3 MW with a total investment of USD 1 million.
- **First Solar** (United States) in 2013 acquired the Chilean project developer Solar Chile and is developing projects of 192 MW in the I and III regions of Chile with a total investment of USD 460 million.
- **Andes Mainstream** (Ireland) is developing two solar PV projects: Parque Pedernales with an investment of USD 420 million and an installed capacity of 162 MW in the III Region; and Parque Solar Azapa with an investment of USD 210 million and in installed capacity of 104 MW in the XV Region. Both these plants have received permit approval and will begin construction soon.

Chinese investment in solar PV in Chile:

- **ReneSola**: SelRaywill acquired 29.1 MW of multicrystalline solar modules from the Chinese company ReneSola for the La Huayca II plant. The project will expand the existing 1.4 MW La Hayca I solar PV power plant to a total capacity of 30.5 MW and would be the first large-scale solar project in Chile's SING.

- **Jinko Solar**: The Chinese company supplied the solar PV modules for the operating Andacollo plant. The project in the IV region of Chile has been operational since June 2013, with a capacity of 1.2 MW, providing energy to both the mining company, Dayton Mining, and the Chilean spot energy market through the SIC grid.

- **Sky Solar**: Developers Sky Solar and *Ingenieria y Construccion Sigdo Koppers Chile* (ICSK) with the financial support of the China Development Bank are in an early stage of construction of the Planta Solar FV Arica I. The project has a planned installed capacity of 18 MW. Sky Solar is a Chinese renewable energy asset developer and IPP (Independent Power Producer) with close relations with the Chinese solar PV manufacturers.

- **Powerway**: This Chinese company is participating in the *Esperanza* project of 3 MW ground mounted project in El Salvador, III Region of Chile, with a commercial partnership with the Chilean solar developer RTS Energía Ltda. This project of 23,040 panels will inject electricity to the SIC grid and is equipped with 6,300 PV Powerway high quality ground screws. The group's core business includes electrical design, structural design, product supply, construction services, installation and operation and maintenance.

3.3 Policy framework: Regulations and incentives

Chile was the first country in the world to implement comprehensive reforms to its electricity grid (Pollitt, 2004). The first modifications to the Chilean Electricity Law were made in the early 1980s with the 1982 General Electricity Services Law (also known as DFL1), which is still the main regulatory instrument for the sector. Key modifications to the law resolved the vertical integration problems of the market, separating the electricity generation, transmission and distribution segments, which also allowed the private sector to participate in an area that had been until then 100 percent state-controlled (Pollitt, 2004). Large-scale privatization of the electricity companies began in 1986, and the grid is now 100 percent privately owned.

One of the fundamental principles of the Electricity Law is that resources from investment are administered by the national electricity market based on economic efficiency, with a guarantee of equal treatment for all energy sources. The law establishes two kinds of clients: regulated and unregulated consumers. Generating companies not participating in the above participate in a spot market (described in Table 8.4), where prices correspond to the short-term marginal cost that results from the fluctuating in-the-moment balance between supply and demand.

Table 8.4 Key policy changes relevant for NCRE

Key Policies	Detail
Law N°. 19.940 (2004)	Improves the electricity transmission payment system. It opens the spot market, guaranteeing small-scale plants the right to connect to distribution networks and exempting them from main transmission tolls (full exemption for plants producing less than 9 MW and partial exemption for plants producing 9–20 MW).
Law N°. 20.018 (2005)	Establishes that contracts between regulated consumer and the distributing and generating segment must be through a process of open tendering.
Law N°. 20.257 (2008)	Defines NCRE and seeks to create favorable conditions for investment projects of NCRE. From 2010, all electricity companies of SIC and SING that operate over 200MW installed capacity must obtain 5% of their annual electricity sales from NCRE, or pay a surcharge (this percentage will gradually increase to 10% in 2024).
Law 20/25 (2013)	Increases the target for NCRE from 10% in 2024 to 20% by 2025.
Law N°. 20.571, Net-Metering Law (2012)	Establishes rights for generators with an installed capacity below 100 kWp, to inject their surplus power to the distribution grid and receive compensation. Key points of dispute so far involve: differences between the price that the generators will receive per kWh and the price they will pay to the distributor per kWh.
Promotion and Financing Instruments for NCRE from CORFO and the CNE	Pre-investment program for preliminary NCRE research: supports projects with amounts above USD 400,000 subsidizing pre-investment studies or consultations.

Table 8.4 Continued

Key Policies	Detail
	Pre-investment program for advanced NCRE level: fund from banks and CNE to co-finance part of the costs for basic and specific engineering, electrical connection research, and environmental evaluation research.
	CORFO credit for NCRE: soft loans for investments in NCRE through financing lines of CORFO operating through local banks. The loans are under fixed fee deadlines from 3 to 12 years, and can reach up to USD 5 million per project. There is also another financing line for energy efficiency and NCRE with a maximum amount of USD 15 million, with a deadline of 13 years. A project could apply for both instruments.

Source: Author's work based on Ministerio de Energía (2012); Laws: No. 19.940, No. 20.018 and No. 20.257; and draft laws: No. 20.571 and 20/25.
Note: CORFO: Productive Development Corporation; CNE: National Energy Commission of Chile.

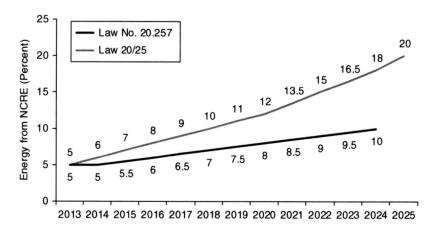

Figure 8.13 NCRE Annual Energy Requirement Modification Law 20/25
Source: Author's work based on ACERA (2013).
Note: Law 20/25 increases the target for NCRE from 10% in 2024 to 20% in 2025.

4. The Emerging Solar Energy Sector in Chile

4.1 Trends in the solar PV sector structure

As shown in Figure 8.14, Chile has exceptional conditions for solar power generation, with among the highest radiation rates in the world, reaching a capacity factor of 31 percent for solar PV technology (NRDC, 2012). Apart from excellent radiation levels, Chile has wide land areas available for future solar PV installations in the North of the country (desert), mainly belonging to the Ministry of National Assets (91%).

Additionally, PV Grid Parity has already been reached in the residential segment, although to different extents in diverse locations of the country (Eclareon, 2013). For instance, in Santiago, Grid Parity is only partial since PV LCOE is only competitive with the rate applicable to excess consumption in winter. However, in Northern Chile, PV LCOE is not only significantly lower than the rate applicable to excess consumption in winter but, for the most competitive quotations, it is also lower than the standard (non-TOU) electric rates. Moreover, considering that the small-scale PV market in Chile is still relatively immature, there are plenty of margins for further price reductions, which could push full grid parity proximity closer.

At present there are 1,117 MW of NCRE in operation, from which only a small fraction (7.5 MW) are solar projects. However, the pipeline of solar projects shows that this proportion is dramatically changing. Figure 8.15 shows that there are 128 MW of solar PV projects in construction (of a total of 686 MW of NCRE in construction), and by the beginning of 2014 it is expected

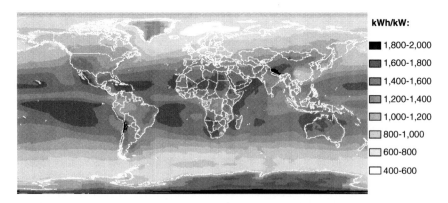

kWh/kW:

■ 1,800-2,000
▨ 1,600-1,800
▨ 1,400-1,600
□ 1,200-1,400
▨ 1,000-1,200
□ 800-1,000
□ 600-800
□ 400-600

Figure 8.14 Global solar radiation
Source: Kawajiri, Kotaro, Takashi Oozeki, and Yutaka Genchi. (2011). "Effect of Temperature on PV Potential in the World." Environmental Science & Technology Volume 45 (Issue 20), 9030–9035.

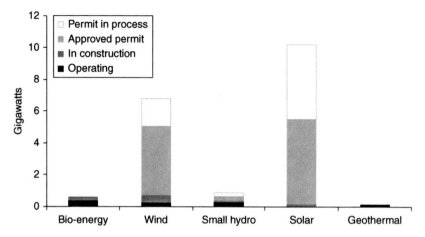

Figure 8.15 State of NCRE projects in 2013 (MW)
Source: Reporte CER (2014).

that solar PV will reach approximately 200 MW in operation. These projects do not only involve small projects of 1 to 2 MW as it has been the case, but also large projects of more than 100 MW.

In the long run, solar prominence in the Chilean power grid will continue growing, considering that more than 50 percent of the 10,000 MW in new projects that have their environmental permit approved already correspond to solar initiatives. This figure is likely to grow even further considering that there are another 5,000 MW of solar projects that have their environmental permits under review.

Key driving forces behind the solar phenomenon are Law 20/25 (which increases the target for NCRE from 10 percent in 2024 to 20 percent in 2025), lower solar PV modules prices, a better understanding and technological acceptability by developers and citizens and a more consolidated foreign market looking for new market opportunities.

4.2 Ownership of the projects, providers and developers

4.2.1 Large-scale solar PV projects

According to SEIA and the Renewable Energy Center (CER), there are a number of operational solar projects in place throughout the northern regions of Chile, and several projects under construction that would be operational in the coming years (CER, 2014). These projects, shown in Table 8.5, are aimed at generating electric power at a larger scale for both the SING and the northern

Table 8.5 Current large PV electricity generating projects

Project Name	Cap. (MW)	Investment (USD million)	Developer	Off-taker	Location (Region)	State
El Águila PV Plant	2.4	7.0	E-CL / SunEdison	Quiborax	XV	Operational
La Huayca I	1.4	2.5	SelRay	Spot SNG	I	Operational
Andacollo	1.3	2.0	Solaire Direct	Dayton Mining	IV	Operational
Tambo Real	1.2	3.0	Kaltemp / Juwi	Spot SIC	IV	Operational
Calama Solar 3	1.0	3.5	Solarpack	Codelco	II	Operational
Subsole	0.3	1.0	Subsole / Kraftwerk	Spot SIC	III	Operational
Amanecer Soar CAP PV Park	100.6	241.0	Sunedison	CAP	III	Construction
Provincia del Tamarugal PV Plant	30.5	-	SelRay	Spot SING	I	Construction
FV Arica I PV PLant	18.0	70.0	Sky Solar	Spot SING	XV	Construction
Pozo Almonte Solar 3	16.0	71.0	Solarpack	Collahuasi	I	Construction
Pozo Almonte Solar 2	9.0	40.0	Solarpack	Collahuasi	I	Construction
El Salvador PV Plant	2.9	-	RTS Energy / Powerway	Spot SIC	III	Construction
Diego de Almagro PV Park	36.0	-	Enel	Spot SIC	III	Construction
PSF Lomas Coloradas	2.4	-	Coener	-	IV	Construction
PSF Pama	2.4	-	Coener	-	IV	Construction

Source: Author's work based on RedSoLAC (2013).
Note: FV: Fotovoltaico

part of the SIC systems, and should be seen as "first initiatives" of larger plants and have linked projects aiming to expand their capacity in the near future.

The developers are generally international enterprises and in many cases they work together with Chilean companies through joint ventures or collaborations. PV projects under construction involve 197 MW, with more than 50 percent of them corresponding to one project: Amanecer Solar CAP, developed by US company SunEdison to provide energy to the national mining company CAP.

Regarding the current role of the Chinese solar PV industry in these projects, they act mostly as manufacturers and suppliers of PV modules and less commonly as project developers or EPC companies (providing engineering, procurement and construction services). Examples of Chinese participation in PV operating projects include the 1.3 MW Andacollo plant with Jinko Solar's PV modules, the 1.2 MW Tambo Real plant with Kaltemp as developer and the Canadian Solar (through its Chinese subsidiary) supplying PV modules, and the 1 MW Calama Solar project developed by Solarpack, which involves Chinese and German PV panels.

Considering the projects that are under construction, the Chinese presence in the form of PV panel suppliers include Yingli Solar, which supplies 100 percent of the PV panels involved in Pozo Almonte (23 MW), and ReneSola, which will supply 7.5 MW of solar PV modules to SelRay's first expansion project to La Huayca and will later provide 21.5 MW once the second stage of this expansion project is approved. Furthermore, the Chinese company ET Solar would also be providing 4.8 MW of solar PV modules to Chilean developers Coener SpA, for the projects PSF Lomas Coloradas and PSF Pama. Lastly, Chinese solar PV project developer Sky Solar, together with the Chilean company Sigdo Koppers, have Arica I, an 18 MW solar PV plant under construction. The involvement of Chinese companies in the Arica I project is projected to be threefold: a Chinese project developer (Sky Solar), possible Chinese PV panel supplier (unidentified) and the project's financial support from the China Development Bank (CDB).

Financial support from CDB is a common practice facilitating Chinese investment abroad. CDB provides credit lines to corporate entities and supports project financing, specifically to acquire and develop overseas power plants. CDB also provides credit to overseas buyers of Chinese solar products and to EPC companies building projects overseas, which can catalyze Chinese investments in the host country. In Chile, in addition to the Arica I project, financial support from CDB has been involved in the wind farm Estancia Negrete, developed by the Irish company Mainstream with technology from the Chinese Goldwind. Moreover, Mainstream is about to start the construction of the 162 MW Parque Pedernales solar plant. The company is currently in the process of selecting the EPC who will be later in charge of selecting the PV panel supplier. According to the company, the fact that Chinese technology comes with access to financial resources through the CDB gives this technology a competitive advantage. Indeed, according to the WRI (2013), it is the access to this capital that has enabled Chinese companies to expand their businesses overseas, without the need for project financing. This makes their investment returns more attractive compared to other developers who have to rely on relatively higher-cost project financing.

More broadly, many solar projects that have been approved or are in the process of obtaining their environmental permits would have some sort of Chinese involvement, either as suppliers of PV modules or, less commonly, as project developers.

According to Table 8.6, the main projects with permits to start construction, and with Chinese involvement, include:

- La Huayca II from SelRay Energias Ltda. will acquire 21.5 MW of multicrystalline solar modules from the Chinese company ReneSola for the second stage of expansion.
- Chinese solar PV project developers Sky Solar plan to install 300 MW of solar PV plants in a period of 3 years with a total investment of USD 1.3 million. This Chinese company has several approved projects, but there is no further information about the construction plans or about the origins of their supplies.
- Andes Mainstream is working with the CDB for financial support of the Parque Pedernales project; this could lead to further involvement of Chinese solar PV companies. The environmental resolution documents (RCA) of Andes Mainstream's Parque Solar Azapa provide information about the possible use of Chinese PV solar modules for this project.

Summing up, China has become a key supplier of solar PV modules to Chile for large-scale projects. However, Chinese incidence in the Chilean PV solar sector goes beyond being a technology supplier; it also plays a role as a contractor (ECP), project developer and as a source of funds for project development.

4.2.2 Commercial-residential scale solar PV sector

The PV market for commercial and residential scale in Chile is still in a very early development stage. Up until 2011 there was a total installed capacity of 904 kilowatts-peak (kWp) for off-grid PV systems, and according to the

Table 8.6 Approved solar PV projects with Chinese involvement

Project Name	Capacity (MW)	Investment (USD million)	Developer	Location (Region)	Status
Diego de Almagro PV Park (Parque Pedernales)	162	420.0	Andes Mainstream	III	Approved
Azapa PV Park	104	210.0	Andes Mainstream	XV	Approved
Solar Sky I	26	78.0	Sky Solar	II	Approved
Solar Sky II	26	78.0	Sky Solar	II	Approved
La Huayca II	21	46.0	SelRay	I	Approved
Planta SF Arica II	15	45.0	Sky Solar	XV	Approved
Planta SF Arica I (expansion)	9	15.4	Sky Solar	XV	Approved

Source. Author's work based on RedSoLAC (2013).

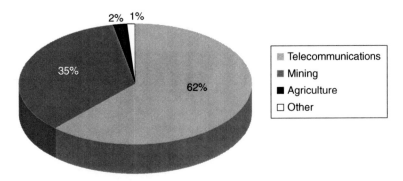

Figure 8.16 Solar PV sector demand
Source: CDT, 2012.

Technological Development Corporation (CDT, 2012), it will approximately reach 2 MW during 2014.

A recent study on the solar PV market in Chile carried out by CDT provides an overview and characterizes the market of commercial and residential solar PV in Chile. The main buyers of solar PV equipment for small-scale systems in Chile are businesses that focus on NCRE system development, services and commercialization; these include solar PV equipment for residential and commercial PV systems. Among the major importing businesses in the small-scale solar PV market in Chile are Solener and Heliplast, which have 30 percent and 22 percent of total installed small-scale solar PV systems in Chile, respectively (CDT, 2012). These businesses develop and commercialize modules mainly for sectors such as telecommunication and mining, as shown in Figure 8.16. There is also a growing demand for smaller systems in the agricultural sector, universities and residences, generally located in the northern regions of the country, which are mostly off-grid systems that do not inject power directly into a grid.

In general, businesses that develop small-scale solar PV module systems in Chile cover the whole value chain, including the supply of cabling and mounting frames. The only exception is the manufacturing of panels, and other equipment such as inverters, which come from foreign companies, such as Kyocera (Japan), Yingli (China), Komaes (China), Sun Tech (China) and Solar Word (Germany). Only a few Chilean companies carry out maintenance and other auxiliary services so far.

The primary imported appliances for the commercial–residential scale solar PV systems in Chile are solar PV panels with monocrystalline modules. As illustrated in Figure 8.17, currently there are no local PV module manufacturing companies. The main importing companies to Chile in 2012, as shown

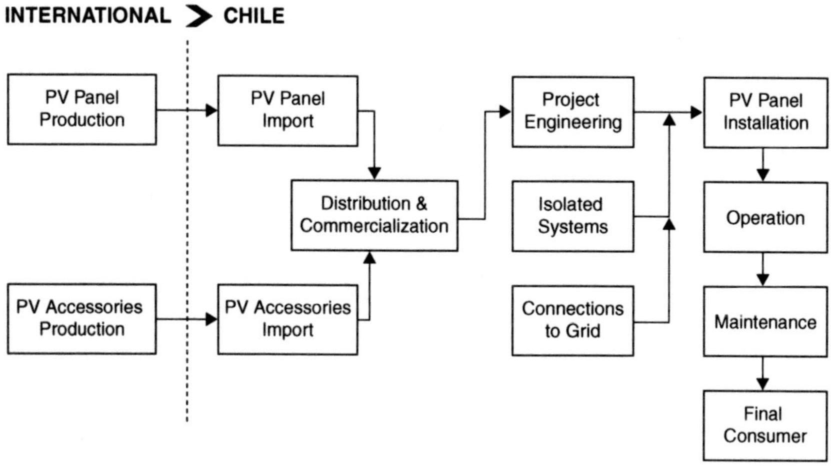

INTERNATIONAL ➤ CHILE

Figure 8.17 Small-scale solar PV value chain in Chile
Source: CDT, 2012.

Table 8.7 Importing solar PV panel companies to Chile in 2012

Solar PV Panel Manufacturers	Country	Import Percent
Kyocera	Japan	35.1
Suntech	China	16.4
SolarWorld	Germany	12.6
Yingli Energy	China	8.4
Sun Wize	USA	2.9
Beijing	China	2.7
Solisto	USA	2.4
Ningbo Komaes Solar	China	2.2
Other	Various	17.3

Source: CDT, 2012.

in Table 8.7, were Kyocera, Suntech, Solarworld and Yingli Energy, representing 72 percent of total solar PV module imports. By 2013, the Chinese presence had reached 53 percent for PV modules.

4.3 Costs of PV solar panels

A key matter regarding Chinese PV solar panels relates to their lower cost in relation to panels from other countries. As shown in Figure 8.18, Chinese silicon PV modules have had a persistently lower price than those from other origins in the German spot market.

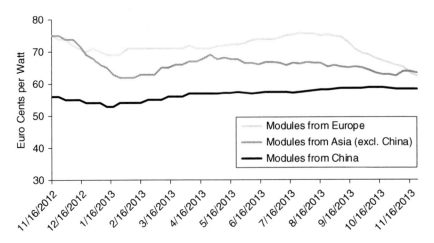

Figure 8.18 German spot market prices for solar PV modules
Source: Author's work based on Photon Module Price index from *Photon International Magazine* (2013).

Table 8.8 Cost of solar PV in Chile

Company	Country	Average Cost per Wp		
		CLP/Wp	**€/Wp**	**USD/Wp**
Komaes	China	858	1.08	1.51
Hareon	China	664	0.84	1.17
SolarWorld	Germany	939	1.18	1.65
Kyocera	Japan	1435	1.81	2.52
Ja Solar	China	788	0.99	1.38
Bosch	Germany	1247	1.57	2.19
Schott	Germany	1159	1.46	2.04
Tianwei	China	695	0.88	1.22
OEM	China	603	0.76	1.06

Source: Author's work based on market costs information from local solar PV commercial distributors (2014).

The costs depicted in Table 8.8 (most common modules available, between 100–250 Wp) are the market average of the main brands found in Chile for a smaller scale commercial–residential client.

The first noticeable matter is the significant amount of PV module alternatives from Chinese origins. In terms of the costs of solar PV modules in the Chilean market, there is a significant difference between Chinese PV modules and those from Germany or Japan. The analysis shows that Chinese modules' prices are between €0,76 and €1,08 per watt, while those from Germany are €1,18–€1,57 per watt and Japanese €1,69–€1,99 per watt.

4.4 Technology and quality standards

There are several relevant international standards for PV technology that support longevity, safety, and related market guarantees of solar PV panels worldwide, from certification laboratories such as TÜV Rheinland PTL or Intertek among others. Among key conditions to make a large-scale PV solar project bankable is that the selected technology complies with specific quality standards and technical guarantees, and that these modules come from tier 1 manufacturers. Generally, in the case of project finance this is reflected in a reduction in the revenue return risk borne by equity investors and, debt servicing risk borne by lenders. Common conditions for long-term energy guarantees from EPC contractors are up to five years. Longer-term guarantees are not commonly available from EPC contractors; however, insurance products that offer longer-term guarantees are available (WSGR, 2012). In terms of module manufacturers, five-plus years term product warranties are quite common. Furthermore, non-compliance with these standards and guarantees is a key barrier to attaining project finance for solar PV projects.

Cases of non-compliance with international standards and guarantees by some Chinese solar PV companies have created controversy so far. The certification laboratory TÜV Rheinland has followed up and publicly listed different solar PV products and companies that make use of unauthorized TÜV labels (see Table 8.9).[3] Even though large global Chinese PV technology companies comply with the main standards, noncompliance is still an issue among many smaller Chinese PV manufacturers, many of which target the Chilean residential and commercial segment. The problem is exacerbated by the fact that there are only a few distributing and NCRE institutions intervening in the selection of the technology, leaving clients unprotected. Although in Chile there is no evidence of activities or products from companies on the TÜV Rheinland blacklist, such as Sungold Solar and G&P New Energy, this is still an issue that needs to be followed.

Currently, there are no national regulations that require certifications or standards for solar PV modules in Chile. Requirements of existing international standards are only regulated by the market. Due to the absence of national regulations, financial institutions play a key role, especially regarding large PV power plants. All major large-scale solar PV projects in Chile

---

3   Complete TÜV Rheinland blacklist (available at: www.tuv.com/en/corporate/business_customers/product_testing_3/blacklist.html)

Table 8.9 Unauthorized labeling of Chinese solar PV panels

Product/Type/Brand	Importer/ Manufacturer	Type of Misuse
Solar Products	Dongguan Changan Hengpu Hardware Products Factory No. 1, West First Street, Xingfa South Road Wusha Liwu Sixth Industrial Zone Chang'an, Dongguan, Guangdong, China	Unauthorized labelling, TÜV Rheinland trademark
Solar Panel SGM-200W	Shenzhen Sungold Solar Co., Ltd. Weentao Industry Park Yingrenshi, Shiyan Town Shenzhen, Guangdong, China	Unauthorized labelling, TÜV Rheinland trademark
Solar Panel GPM-xxx	Zhejiang G&P New Energy Technology Co., Ltd. West Industrial Zone Yongkang, Zhejiang, China	Unauthorized labelling, TÜV Rheinland trademark
Silicon Solar module	Bol Photovoltaic Technology Co., Ltd. Building 4, No. 18 Songshan Road Huimin Street, Jiashan County Jiaxing, Zhejiang, China	Unauthorized labelling, TÜV Rheinland trademark
Solar Panel HPSM-200W	Shenzhen Hopesun Tech. Co., Ltd. C1626, 16/F, Niulanqian Building Minzhi Road, Minzhi Street Bao'an District, Shenzhen, Guangdong, China	Unauthorized labelling, TÜV Rheinland trademark
Solar Panel CNCBxxx, CNCCxxx, CNCK-xxx	Ningbo Zhenhai Geebo Electronics Tech. Co., Ltd. Zhongguang West Road 777# Ningbo City, China	Unauthorized labelling, TÜV Rheinland trademark

Source: Author's work based on TÜV Rheinland blacklist (www.tuv.com/en/corporate/ business_customers/product_testing_3/blacklist.html).

have been supported, until this writing, through multilateral financing institutions, which can take on greater risk in terms of guarantees than local Chilean financing institutions can afford to take at present. Due to the fact that solar PV projects are still in an early stage in Chile, there are questions about the actual role of local financing institutions in how to minimize solar PV project risks regarding financial guarantees. Local banks are developing some ideas to support future solar PV plants, possibly first through pilot projects with a capacity equal to or above 3 MW (a lower MW capacity is not viable under the project finance system used by private banks). These solar PV pilot projects would assist local institutions in understanding more about the guarantees and standards of this sector and could lead to opening up more support to develop future projects. There is also the possibility of a bank association able to finance future large solar projects.

Therefore, there are at least three elements of risk in relying on Chinese manufacturers:

- The bulk of the segment – especially the residential sector – has no information regarding the existence of international standards and guarantees, and thus they do not enforce compliance by the supplier.
- There have been cases where Chinese PV panels and related products have entered markets with unauthorized labels and certifications.[4] As mentioned, above there are many cases of solar PV panels with unauthorized labels being on the TÜV Rheinland blacklist. This list shows many solar PV products from different Chinese companies.[5]
- The current restructuring process of the Chinese solar PV industry (see section 5.3) has led many Chinese producers to struggle for survival with many of them going into bankruptcy, leaving project developers using that technology while uncertain about who will be accountable for the respective quality standards and guarantees.

4.5 Environmental impacts of solar plants

Although it is generally considered that solar PV technology has mostly beneficial impacts on the environment, research also points out several potential impacts that must be taken into account when referring to this technology. The main environmental impacts considered from solar PV technologies are detailed below.

---

4   Information gathered from the interviews.
5   Complete TÜV Rheinland blacklist (available at: www.tuv.com/en/corporate/business_customers/product_testing_3/blacklist.html).

4.5.1 Extensive land use of large-scale solar PV plants

Larger scale solar plants are raising concerns about land degradation, habitat loss and archaeological value. Total land area requirements vary depending on the technology, geography of the site and the intensity of the solar resource. Estimates for solar PV systems need approximately one square kilometer for every 20–30 MW of generated electricity, and the land could have a secondary alternative use (EPA, 2011). A study comparing a solar PV installation to a coal power plant concludes that a 30-year old PV plant is seen to occupy approximately 15 percent less land than a coal power plant of the same age, mainly due to the disposal of solid residues at coal power plants. As the age of the power plant increases, the land-use intensity of PV power becomes considerably smaller than that for coal power (Turney and Fthenaki, 2011). Land-use impacts from large-scale solar systems can be minimized by setting them at lower-quality locations such as brownfields, abandoned mining land, or existing transportation and transmission corridors. Smaller-scale solar PV modules, at homes or commercial buildings, which in most cases can be built on rooftops, have minimal land-use impact.

According to the inventory of operating solar PV plants in Chile, the land use for these types of installations reached 0.03 km² in 2013 with a total capacity of 3.7 MW, and is expected to reach 1.62 km² assuming a total capacity of 200 MW during 2014. Under an scenario where solar PV installations reach 2,033 MW in Chile by 2030, the land use involved would be 28.5 km,² representing around 5 percent of the total land used by both SIC-SING grids (EE2030, 2013).

Most of the PV plants are and will be located in desert, brownfields and unused areas in the North of the country, having a minimal land-use impact. However, the danger of an archeological loss or damage has gained increasing attention recently. This risk has been rising, given the planned growth in this sector – increasingly linked to technology and development from Chinese companies. This creates a need to carry out proper due diligence in solar PV projects in order to avoid or minimize this potential impact.

4.5.2 Life cycle greenhouse gas and other air emissions

Even though there are no global GHG emissions involved in power generation from solar PV technology, there are GHG emissions related to the life cycle of solar PV panels, specifically in the processes of raw material extraction, manufacturing, materials transportation, installation, maintenance and decommissioning and dismantlement (IPCC, 2012). The stage where more emissions are generated is in the upstream processes, such as raw material extraction

Table 8.10 Estimated life cycle GHG and air pollutant emissions

Region	GHG Emissions Associated w/ Fuel Mix (CO_2 eq, g/ kW h)	Technology	GHG Emissions (CO_2 eq, g/kW h)	NO_x (mg/ kW h)	SO_x (mg/ kW h)
Western	484	Multicrystalline	40–50	75–85	125–150
Europe		Multicrystalline	40–50	80–85	140–160
		CdTe	15–25	35–45	50–90
United	678	Multicrystalline	50–60	157–185	350–375
States		Multicrystalline	50–60	180–200	360–390
		CdTe	20–30	75–85	150–175

Source: Environment Canada (2010).

and module manufacturing, reaching between 60–70 percent of the total emissions of solar PV technology (NREL, 2012). Among the solar PV cells with higher GHG emissions are the widely used monocrystalline and polycrystalline silicon technology (IPCC, 2012). According to an analysis comparing life-cycle air emissions of different solar PV technologies, thin-film CdTe technology has the lowest air emissions (CO_2eq, NOx and SOx) of the main solar PV technologies, as shown in Table 8.10 (Environment Canada, 2010).

The total life cycle emissions of GHG (CO_2eq) have been reported to be between 28 and 72.4 g/kWh for crystalline silicon, and 18 to 20 g/kWh for thin-film CdTe (Environment Canada, 2010). This is mainly due to the amount of energy required to manufacture the crystalline silicon panels. The GHG emissions related to the life cycle of the panels would also vary according to the utilized source of energy, as it is different depending on the country and the power grid. However, research indicates a trend towards declining GHG emissions for three types of silicon technologies: monocrystalline, ribbon and polycrystalline (Alsema, 2006). Alsema (2006) predicts that life-cycle GHG emissions could drop to 20 g/kWh for crystalline silicon technologies.

As for Chile, it is estimated that the emission factor related to solar PV technology is 48 tCO_2eq/GWh. These emission levels are lower than those of natural-gas-fitted power plants (IPCC, 2012). Furthermore, PV Insider (2014) research shows that solar PV plants operating in Chile reduced the national GHG emissions by 2.2 million tCO_2eqfor 2013, and it is expected to reduce it by at least an additional 4.4MM tCO_2eq for 2014 (PV Insider, 2014).

In terms of life cycle emissions from solar PV panels, Chile might need to start considering the indirect emissions from the shipment and manufacturing processes of Chinese PV panels. Currently, these PV panels could have a significant carbon footprint due to China's highly carbonized energy grid and large distances transported. Even though this impact is arguable, considering that the benefit of clean energy produced by these panels could be greater than the energy needed to produce them, the PV panel's footprint itself can still be improved with local participation such as storage and assembly.

4.5.3 Hazardous materials in solar PV technology

The PV industry uses some toxic and explosive gases as well as corrosive liquids in its production lines. The presence, amount and type of chemicals used depend on the type of PV cell. In general, many hazardous materials used are applied to clean and to purify the semiconductor surface, such as hydrochloric acid and sulfuric acid (NREL, 2012).

Thin-film PV cells contain many more toxic materials than silicon PV cells, such as gallium arsenide and cadmium-telluride. If not handled and disposed of properly, these materials could pose serious environmental and public health threats (IPCC, 2012).

However, even though hazardous chemicals can be found in solar PV technology, these are in significantly smaller proportions than in other energy sources; for instance, activities for solar PV technology emit 30 times less mercury and 150 times less cadmium than those generated by coal plants (Turney and Fthenaki, 2011). Furthermore, the PV industry has a strong financial incentive to recycle these highly valuable but hazardous components, forcing the use of rigorous control methods that minimize the emission of potentially hazardous elements (IPCC, 2012).

In Chile, most solar panels installed today are silicon crystalline cells, while only a small amount of the PV modules being used are thin film cells (CDT, 2012). Moreover, China's PV industry manufactures mainly silicon technology cells (REN21, 2013). In terms of the environmental impacts of hazardous materials from PV products, the larger use of silicon PV technology in Chile – with most of them coming from China – can be considered a positive aspect as this technology utilizes less hazardous materials in its activities or components.

5. Chinese Global Prominence and Its Solar Energy Policies

As in other renewable energy sectors worldwide, the solar market in China has been developed thanks to ambitious national policies with strong domestic support. China, like many other countries, has sought to promote its renewable energy sector in order to achieve several strategic policy goals, including energy security, a low-emissions development path and an industrial pole that generates high-quality jobs. By its very nature, these policies have important feedback effects on employment and international trade.

5.1 Chinese PV production in a global context

The development of the PV industry in China started at the beginning of the new millennium, growing quickly from 8 percent of the global PV market in 2005 (Zhao et al., 2006) to more than 30 percent in 2012 (REN21, 2013).

In contrast with other NCRE, China's PV industry has predominantly been oriented to the export market, with cell and module manufacturers exporting more than 95 percent of their products (Zhao et al., 2006). This export growth has also been fueled by favorable energy policies among wealthy countries, in particular from countries like Germany, Spain, Italy and the United States and, more recently, also from some emerging markets. In order to support their exports of solar modules and cells, competitive Chinese companies have embraced practically the whole of the solar value chain in these countries, providing manufacturing, engineering, procurement and construction (EPC) services and even developing solar PV plants (Tan, Zhao et al., 2013). China has rapidly vaulted to the top of global solar-cell manufacturing capacity, as shown in Figure 8.19, nine Chinese manufacturers rank among the top 15 global solar PV module manufacturers.

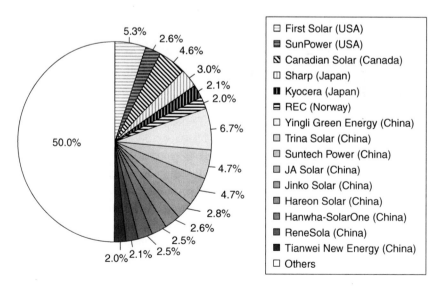

Figure 8.19 Solar PV, top 15 global PV module manufacturers (2012)
Source: REN21 (2013).

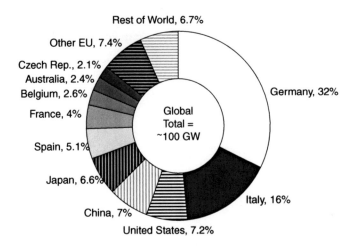

Figure 8.20 Solar PV global installed capacity, top 10 countries (2012)
Source: REN21 (2013).

The strong export orientation of the Chinese solar industry is also reflected by its relatively small solar installed capacity: about 7 GW, or 7 percent of global installed capacity.

However, according to forecasts from REN21 (2013) this global picture is changing, as installed capacity in China is expected to accelerate (REN21, 2013). China plans to add 10 GW of solar capacity each year from 2013 to 15, with a goal of 35 GW of installed solar power capacity by 2015.

REN21 (2013) states that China's aggressive PV sector growth in 2010 and 2011 resulted in excess production capacity and supply. Combined with extreme competition, this drove prices down in 2012, yielding smaller margins for manufacturers and spurring continued industry consolidation. The average price of crystalline silicon solar modules fell by 30 percent or more in 2012, contributing to an 80 percent fall between 2008–2013 (*Bloomberg New Energy Finance*, 2013), while thin film prices dropped about 20 percent in 2012 (REN21, 2013). This situation, together with the global economic crisis, meant that many competitors, especially from Europe and the United States have struggled and even closed down their operations. As a result, main solar PV associations from both the United States and the EU have raised accusations against Chinese manufacturers for unfair trade practices and have brought cases to the WTO, resulting in antidumping measures (see section 5.4).

The economic crisis that led to declining subsidies to the European solar market, the fall in prices of PV modules, driven by the Chinese oversupply, together with trade measures, have caused domestic Chinese solar manufacturers to scale back production, lay off workers, and some even to stop operations completely (Stones and Associates, 2011).[6]

This entire situation has prompted China to change its policies with respect to the solar industry, from one oriented solely toward incentivizing exports, to one with two main goals: to stimulate domestic demand and to push companies to invest in and develop markets overseas.

Even though the main global solar associations from the European Union and the United States complained about the Chinese production, downstream national producers from these countries have seen important benefits from the fall in global prices driven by Chinese production, as many of them use Chinese cells as part of their overall manufacturing processes, especially those in the commercial and residential rooftop segment (Bridges, 2013a)

The recent global crisis, the overproduction of PV panels by China, and the associated fall in PV prices have led to changes in the solar industry. Indeed, while during the past five years the focus of the industry has been on module cost reduction, it is now about reductions in the balance of systems costs. This includes the cost of inverters, hardware, customer acquisition and financing costs. At the same time, this has been leading to the consolidation of the global industry, with no clarity yet about which enterprises will survive. Under this scenario, many Chinese manufacturers who were facing debt and overcapacity have been struggling. The Chinese government, which supported the creation of several manufacturing giants, such as LDK Solar Co. (LDK) and Snitch Power Holdings Co. (STP), is now pushing for the consolidation of the Chinese market to just 10 or 20 major international players.

Forecasts for the industry are optimistic. Bloomberg (2013) argued that after several years of painfully low pricing for manufacturers, prices across the value chain are stabilizing. Deutsche Bank outlooks state that surging domestic demand in China, Japan and the United States may underpin a "second solar gold rush" (Deutsche Bank, 2014). By 2014, annual global solar installed capacity is expected to increase by 46 GW, and by an additional 56 GW in 2015. A key point behind this outlook is the spread of grid parity. As of 2014, solar power was competitive without subsidies in at least 19 markets globally, and Deutsche Bank expects more markets to reach grid parity by 2014, as solar system prices decline further.

5.2 Chinese solar FDI in the world

Declining subsidies in the European solar market, together with trade sanctions, have decreased demand for Chinese solar products. As a result, direct

---

6   For example, Suntech Power announced bankruptcy (Bradsher, 2013).

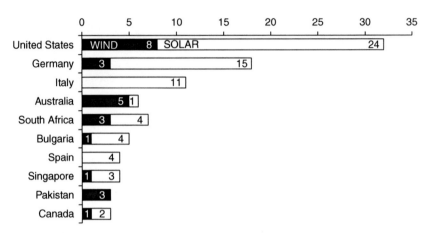

Figure 8.21 Number of China's overseas investments in solar and wind industries in top 10 destination countries (2002–2012)
Source: Tan et al. (2013).

investments overseas are seen as a way of retaining and expanding market share, typically through creating demand for the export of products. As such, China is also increasingly becoming a global force in international clean energy investment. The country has provided at least 124 investments to other countries' solar and wind industries, summing up at least USD 40 billion over the past decade, as shown in Figure 8.21.

As Figure 8.22 shows, more than 90 percent of China's investments in the solar industry were made by companies performing three functions: electricity generation; sales, marketing and support; and manufacturing. Nearly half of the 83 investments were made in new photovoltaic (PV)-based electricity generation plants, either as greenfield investments or through joint ventures.

In a few cases, Chinese solar companies have also invested in ancillary industries in the supply chain, as illustrated in Figure 8.23. In 2008, Suntech Power partially acquired KSL Kuttler in Germany to gain new production technologies and localize production. In 2011, China National Bluestar Company acquired the silicon operations of Norway's Elkem to enhance competitiveness in the industry. Also, notably, while most Chinese companies have been using first-generation crystalline silicon PV cell technology, a few of them acquired US companies to access second-generation thin-film PV cell technologies. China Solar Energy Holdings Ltd. has acquired stakes in two companies: 100 percent in Thin Silicon Inc. and 51 percent in Terra Solar Global Inc.

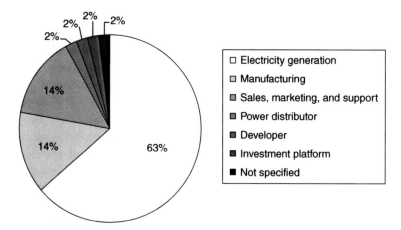

Figure 8.22 Percentage of solar investment by function
Source: Tan et al. (2013).

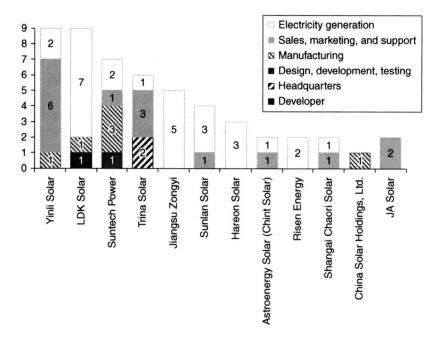

Figure 8.23 Functions of investments by Chinese companies with multiple investments
Source: Tan et al. (2013).

In December 2013, J A Solar opened a sales office in Chile, with the view to supply the South American market. In contrast, relatively smaller companies like L D K Solar, Jiangsu Zongyi, Sunlan Solar and Hareon Solar put most of their overseas investments into building solar power plants worldwide. Thus, it appears that the top solar exporters set up foreign subsidiaries mainly to support the export of their Chinese manufactured products.

Many would see this strategy as a good way to keep Chinese industry competitive in the current round of global consolidation. Forbes (2013) argues that Chinese solar manufacturers that are focused on silicon technologies or newer thin-film entrants can significantly improve their existing technology through acquisitions of innovative or even disruptive technologies from Western countries. Forbes maintains that Chinese manufacturers are also well positioned to bring down production and research costs and accelerate a move towards an era expected in 5–7 years, when solar energy will not require any subsidies to be profitable.

5.3 Chinese policies towards the solar industry

Key factors behind the growing global prominence of China's solar industry include domestic policy incentives in host countries that attract Chinese companies, and Chinese financing from Chinese banks.

China's solar industry relies largely on the international market. This has been enabled by a push from the Chinese government to develop these strategically emerging industries and address the problem of excess capacity, enabling support from China's financial sector through access to abundant and relatively low-cost capital, and measures by host country governments to pull (attract) investments.

As described in Box 8.2, Chinese government has taken several steps to push its renewable industry overseas, with a clear objective to combat domestic oversupply, in recognition of the fact that this industry offers an opportunity for them to compete internationally.

The first direct major policy push for the industry to invest overseas came in September 2009 when the government issued a circular to "curb excess capacity and redundant construction in several industries and promote the healthy development of industries" (State Council, 2009). This, coupled with declining subsidies in Germany, Spain, Italy and other major markets, hit their domestic solar industries, providing an opportunity for Chinese companies to invest in these markets since they were known to accept lower returns. In October 2010, the State Council gave the strategic emerging industries a further impetus to go overseas, targeting seven priority industries, including new energy – nuclear, solar thermal, solar PV, wind, smart grid and biomass (State Council, 2010). A year later, the Ministry of Commerce of the People's

Republic of China (MOFCOM) provided guidelines to the solar industry to acquire key technologies to enhance international cooperation and to build power plants overseas to restructure its exports (MOFCOM, 2011a). Further guidance was expected from the "New Energy Industry Development Plan" that was approved in 2012 (Xie, 2010).

Box 8.2 Chinese Government Programs to Incentivize Overseas Solar Investment

2012:

- 12th Five-Year Plan for the Solar Photovoltaic Industry.
- Draft 12th Five-Year Plan for Renewable Energy Development.
- 12th Five-Year Plan for Strategic Emerging Industries Development.

2011:

Guidelines on Enabling Strategic Emerging Industries to Go Overseas, encouraging renewable energy industries to acquire key technology overseas.

2010:

- Decision of the State Council on Accelerating the Fostering and Development of Strategic Emerging Industries, including solar PV and wind.
- Opinions on Promoting Healthy Development of the Wind Equipment Industry, call for internationalization.
- National Law for Renewable Energy amended, guaranteed electricity generated from renewable sources to be purchased in full amount.

2009:

- Curbing Excess Capacity and Redundant Construction of Several Industries and Promoting Healthy Development of Industries, including wind equipment and polysilicon.
- Notice on Policy to Improve Grid-Connected Power Pricing for Wind Power, set feed-in tariff for wind.

2008:

Renewable Energy Development under the 11th Five-Year Plan published; National Renewable Energy Development Fund established.

2007:

Medium and Long-Term Renewable Energy Development Plan, 2007–2020.

2005:

National Law for Renewable Energy established.

Source: Tan et al. (2013).

During the last few years, China has been prompted to foster market development, as described in Box 8.3. A key policy promoting development of its domestic market is the setting of a national target of sourcing 15 percent of its energy mix from renewables by 2020 and 30–45 percent by 2050.

Box 8.3 Chinese Government Incentive Programs for Developing Its Domestic Solar Market

Program	Structure
Concession for grid-connected solar PV plants	Before setting fixed feed-in tariff, reverse bidding for PV concession was implemented. About 130 MW of projects were approved in 2009; 280 MW in 2010; 500 MW in 2011.
"Golden Sun" demonstration projects	The program is designed to subsidize 50–70% of the initial costs of connected solar PV power plants. First tranche of the program supported 294 projects with total capacity exceeding 632 MW.
Building integrated solar demonstration program	First tranche of the program invested Y1.27 billion to support 111 roof-top solar installation projects with total capacity of 91 MW.
Solar feed-in tariff	Y1-1.15/kWh, paid with renewable energy premium charged on all end users.

Note: All incentives are designed to be streamlined under the National Renewable Energy Development Fund. The fund sources from specialty funding allocated in national budget and renewable energy premium charged on all end users.
Source: Tan et al. (2013).

An additional but interrelated factor enabling the mainstreaming of the solar industry abroad has been access to abundant and relatively low-cost capital provided by Chinese financial institutions, especially the CDB, which has enabled Chinese state-owned enterprises (SOEs), and to a lesser extent privately held solar and wind companies, to invest overseas. Financing has been available through lines of credit to corporate entities and as project financing, specifically to acquire and develop overseas power plants. It has also been available as credit support to overseas buyers who import Chinese wind and solar products and to EPC companies building projects overseas, which can catalyze overseas investments. Access to other available capital allowed Chinese companies to expand their businesses overseas on their balance sheets without the need for project financing, which makes their returns on investments more attractive than European and US market developers. These include the USD 46 billion "green stimulus" package announced in 2009, USD 5.9 billion from the capital markets in 2009 through initial public offerings (IPOs), and Chinese government loan guarantees worth USD 36 billion in 2010.

5.4 Solar PV domestic policies and trade conflicts

Chinese support policies to its national solar industry have been the source of trade conflicts. The most relevant trade disputes against the Chinese solar industry relate to dumping and receiving unfair policy support from the government. Both cases have been raised almost in parallel during the last few years, led by the respective main solar association industries of the European Union and the United States. While main solar associations seek to protect larger domestic manufacturers, downstream producers are against imposing duties on foreign-made cells, as they will raise costs for national producers who use these cells as part of their overall manufacturing processes.

Trade conflicts involving PV panels from China are inserted in an old discussion about the impacts of domestic policy support to renewable energy industry and how countries can best foster the development of renewable energy. Many countries devote policy incentives to their renewable energy industries with the aim of creating new markets and high-quality jobs. Most of these incentives contain measures related to local content requirements or restrictions, which are increasingly used as policy tools to achieve green growth (Kuntze and Moerenhout, 2013). They are controversial due to their protectionist nature and discrimination against foreign producers, which have important consequences on employment and international trade. A crucial element behind current discussion is the cost-effectiveness of local content requirements, the context where they are useful and legality under the trade regimes (Kuntze and Moerenhout, 2013).

6. Key Emerging Issues and Policy Implications for Chile

The Chilean energy crisis has triggered a complex situation for the Chilean power sector. The lack of natural gas has been remediated by introducing other imported inputs: more polluting and more expensive sources of energy, such as coal and oil. The carbonization of the electricity mix, together with the push of new investment projects of large hydropower dams located in southern areas of the country have been the source of criticism from different sectors of society, resulting in legal actions that have contributed to paralyzing the construction of new power projects.

Under this scenario, renewable energies could play a vital role in meeting the challenge faced by the Chilean power sector: a cleaner, lower-cost and more socially legitimate energy portfolio.

Besides the exceptionally high solar radiation conditions and land availability in the desert areas, there are key features behind the recent development of solar power in Chile. From a regulatory angle, Law 20/25 represents a key factor in the development of NCRE. Likewise, the implementation of the Law of Net-metering will play a key role in driving solar power at a residential and commercial scale in Chile. Likewise, the dramatic reduction in the costs of PV technology worldwide implies that in certain areas in northern Chile and under certain conditions of transmission costs, solar energy generation has already reached grid parity.

Solar power may have an important impact on the way energy is generated and used, making it a catalyst for the transformation of the whole of the power industry. Solar energy is not only suitable for large-scale utility projects, but new developments in solar technology at the commercial–residential scale appear increasingly likely to give consumers the option of generating their own power. Moreover, the eminent characteristic of solar power, being its intermittency, constitutes a potential catalyzer for investments in new types of storage technology, smart grids, electric vehicles and other innovations.

Under this positive scenario, Chile might develop its national solar sector to achieve strategic policy goals, including energy security, sustainable development, a low-emissions development path, higher quality of life in rural and urban areas and industrial development based on high-quality jobs. In pursuit of these goals, national policies and regulations involving some selective domestic support will have to be developed and implemented, and existing practices and regulations will have to be analyzed with regard to their effect towards this goal. It is in this context that Chinese involvement in the Chilean solar industry acquires its relevance.

The analyzed evidence suggests that the presence of China in Chile has been threefold so far. First, Chinese companies are relevant players in the pipeline to become project developers. Second, Chinese companies are PV panel suppliers. Third a significant number of projects receive project financing through the CDB.

The first may imply more international presence in the country and a real contribution to comply with the Law 20/25. The second has helped to increase the range of suppliers and to have access to cheaper PV panels. The third element has contributed to financing NCRE projects in Chile, as local financial institutions are still not well developed to support and to finance these types of initiatives. This is a window of opportunity for Chile, but the short-run benefits have to be weighed against the dependence on imported supply, the lost opportunity for industrial development, and quality risk and environmental impacts.

All in all, the Chilean model to maximize benefits related to developing its solar industry should embrace the following pillars:

• Selective industrial policy
• Standards for the solar sector
• Education and capacity building among all stakeholders involved in the solar industry.
• Reduction of existing barriers to solar projects

6.1 Selective industrial policy

Given that Chile is not a solar manufacturer, and given its market-oriented energy policies, it encounters the Chinese policy impacts in a very different way than do other countries with established PV manufacturing bases. In particular, access to low-cost PV cells and modules for the development of solar power plants may open a window of opportunity for Chile and could help in solving the current energy crisis, providing lower-cost solutions, curbing carbon emissions and other environmental impacts and reducing social conflicts around energy investments.

On the other hand, as solar energy becomes a crucial element for the future of energy strategies in Chile and a potentially interesting sector for industrial development, Chile has to confront the question of the potential long-term effects of the Chinese involvement in its domestic industrial development. This development will be influenced by Chile's ability to compete against Chinese solar industry products, which have been subject to significant and highly volatile subsidies. It also involves questions of quality, guarantee and environmental issues around solar technology imported from China, which have to be considered when aiming to create a solid, growing and long-lasting solar market and industry in the country.

Despite the potential for the development of the solar industry, as of this writing Chile has not established a clear and solid solar industrial policy and still lacks a national vision with concrete goals and a strategic action plan to foster solar industry development.

So far, Chile has not proved to be competitive in the manufacturing of solar panels or cells. The maturity reached by the technology at the global level, together with the high costs involved in local production, suggests this is not a viable path. However, industrial development for the solar industry in Chile goes beyond panel or cells production. It involves a wide range of goods and services for which Chile may present development opportunities. In the short term, experts agree that there are immediate opportunities in the production of several goods and services for grid-connected PV projects including: resource measurement; construction of control houses; maintenance of PV panels and the provision of copper wires needed by grid-connected solar projects both for the national and other Latin-American markets. In the longer term, as utility-scale solar projects and the industry itself develop, Chile may become a pole of solar energy exports to neighboring countries. In the residential-rooftop segment main opportunities lie in marketing, installation, and maintenance of solar systems.

In this scenario, policymakers could play an important role in creating the enabling environment, technical capabilities and education across the value chain to foster solar development. This should not only involve capabilities along the value chain but also within the public sector so as to create adequate counterparts in this process. There have been some positive signs with the government taking some steps, however hesitantly and sporadically, towards initiating a more systematic approach, including:

- The creation of the Research Centre for Solar Energy (SERC-Chile) in 2013 with public funding by CONICYT.[7] Its main objectives were to further scientific knowledge and training; to educate, inform and interact with citizens and with those responsible for public policies, regarding the use, importance and potential of solar energy; and to facilitate technological transfer programs through private–public projects, among others.
- Creation of a company-driven International Center of Excellence on Solar Energy and Energy Efficiency, by the French/Belgian group GDF SUEZ-LABORELEC, with the support of Chilean government funds, through CORFO. The main objective is to become a center for research and development for renewable energies that could be a reference for Latin America.

---

7   National Commission for Scientific and Technological Research.

- The Fraunhofer Institute for Solar Energy (ISE) established in 2013, and partially financed by CORFO and the Ministry of Energy. Its main objective is to develop market-oriented solutions in sustainable energies, with a main focus on solar energy.
- Initial studies started in 2014 to foster a cluster of solar energy in northern part of the country promoted by the Ministry of Energy. The studies, to be carried out by the Energy Centre of Universidad de Chile, aim to create a system of collaboration and synergies among various Chilean solar PV industry stakeholders; to assist project developers, financial institutions and consumers in obtaining a deep comprehension of the resource; and to identify the solar technology barriers and opportunities. The cluster should also promote coordination and engagement in agreements for the transmission and distribution of solar energy, and it should permit the development of local expertise in maintenance and complementary services in the solar PV sector.
- Moreover, the new government just released its "Energy Agenda 2014–2017." A key focus of the agenda is to promote a "I&D Program on Solar Energy," which looks to stimulate innovation and selective industrial-based solar developments, including the development of a solar technological road map, a closer collaboration among key stakeholders (government institutions, the above-mentioned centers and the private sector) as well as new tools and financial resources.

In this scenario, Chile could eventually become a platform for the solar market oriented towards both local and other Latin American markets in the near future. Chile could thus seize the opportunity of rapidly developing its solar industry and enjoying second-mover advantages in the industry with respect to the rest of the region.

6.2 Standard setting for the solar sector

Solar industrial development should go hand in hand with the expansion of a national solar market. In this sense, a key issue that Chile has to confront in order to develop a national solar market is the lack of compulsory quality standards for solar panel manufacturing or any formal monitoring of the quality of the PV imports into the country. However, for large-scale projects, where private finance, multilateral institutions, and/or national development banks are involved, due diligence is playing an important role as an indirect form of regulation. In contrast, commercial and residential projects are naturally less regulated, partially due to their lack of knowledge regarding the international quality standards and certifications that are in force in more consolidated markets and the lack of technical capacity to process and to monitor such information.

Even though there are still no signs of the development of a Chilean standard for the solar industry at the moment, the regulators should particularly focus on commercial and residential consumers, who could be more susceptible of being trapped in this market. Therefore, policymakers could start by implementing an information-disclosure program to present information on the international standards in place, the certification processes available, and the reliability of certain firms, in order to empower Chilean solar PV consumers and consolidate a long-lasting solar market in the country. The energy policy plan could eventually consider the adoption of international norms and standards for the domestic market, requesting certification with an international agency and developing norms and standards and promoting the development of Chilean certification agencies, which could provide the necessary guarantees for the consolidation of the solar market in the country.

6.3 Education and capacity-building programs for consumers

Education and empowerment must also reach consumers of solar PV energy. Not only do they need to be aware of the international certification programs, but they also need to be trained about the use and maintenance of the technology. Brand building of solar technology among consumers would improve its acceptability, particularly among those who would like to be differentiated as green consumers. This education process would require a strategic and coordinated approach, such as Foundation, Deployment and Public Exit: Foundation (including a vision set by the national government with stakeholder buy-in and participation); Deployment (including education and capacity building); and Public Exit (including transferring responsibility from public/private to private) (UC Berkeley Haas IBD Team, 2013).

6.4 Reduction of existing barriers to solar projects

According to Escenarios Energéticos,[8] one of the most important barriers facing solar projects in Chile is access to finance. The role of the public sector is fundamental in order to reduce such a barrier and to be able to encourage the proliferation of both small- and large-scale projects. Examples of such policies are: grants or special rates for pilot projects, access to loan guarantees

---

8   "Electricity Generation Projects: preliminary identification of key issues affecting their development" Comité Técnico, Plataforma Escenarios Energéticos Chile 2030, 31 August 2012.

through multi-lateral banks or government funds,[9] cash incentives to earlier adopters, mitigation of soft costs, decoupling, net metering, encouraging of utility cooperation[10] and so forth. Moreover, the public sector could contribute to reducing the upfront costs of solar projects for residents and small business owners by promoting Third Party Ownership (TPO) models that promote solar leases or a Solar Power Purchase Agreement (PPA). The regulator could promote the bundle of individual projects and the aggregation of community demand (group-purchase programs, crowd-funding platform for solar projects) to drive down costs and to achieve scale, and thereby induce financing from banks and other multilateral institutions. Regulators could also introduce mechanisms to reduce financing risk (e.g., loan guarantees) and thus make the solar projects more appealing for banks.

Another important barrier is the economic viability of connecting the solar plants to the grid using the transmission system. Given that solar plants are more efficient in areas of high radiation, this limits their mobility and increases the cost of transmission required to connect solar plants with the national grid. However, the law currently exempts generators of less than 9 MW and NCRE generators of up to 20 MW from transmission fees of using the national grid. Regulators could also encourage the association of solar plants to share a transmission line towards the national grid.

The third main identified barrier is access to terrain for the location of solar plants, due to the ownership of land. If lands are not privately owned they will very often require legal permits from the regulator. In the northern part of the country, the regulator owns about 91 percent of the land, and the Ministry of National Assets has given away, as concessions, 8,300 hectares for NCRE projects so far.

Finally, the issue of environmental impacts of the projects can create barriers to project development. Although solar plants have a low environmental impact over the land compared to other energy sources, and imply a non-exclusive use of the land, there may be some archeological concerns to be considered. Therefore, the role of the regulator in trying to disclose information regarding the legal status of the terrain and in improving the efficiency of permit applications would be essential. Given the high demand for terrain for these types of initiatives, the Ministry of National Assets has introduced a mechanism of allocation of rights in two stages that guarantees that these projects will finally take place.

---

9 Private loans so far could only be available for projects of 3 MW or more, so small-scale projects are definitely out of scope so far.

10 Data sharing to improve grid management and to ensure grid reliability and safety.

All in all, solar energy represents an opportunity for a cleaner and more secure source of energy, which could help to insulate from price volatility in the sector, create exports and diversify economic growth. It could also democratize and diversify energy generation, even contributing to reduce income inequality. Indeed, it currently also represents a market opportunity for solar energy leadership in the Latin American region (UC Berkeley Haas IBD Team, 2013).

References

ACERA. (2013). *La Ley 20/25: una nueva visión para las ERNC en Chile*. Asociación Chilena de Energías Renovables, A.G. on October 14, 2013 in Santiago, Chile.

Alsema, Erik and Mariska J. de Wild-Scholton. (2006). "Environmental Impacts of Crystalline Silicon Photovoltaic Module Production." Presented at the 13th CIRP Conference on Life Cyle Engineering, Leuven, 31 May–2 June 2006.

Banco Central de Chile. (2013). *Importaciones y Exportaciones de bienes*. Available at http://si3.bcentral.cl/ESTADISTICAS/Principal1/Excel/SE/COMEX/excel.html

Bitar, S. (2014). Política Energética 2020. *El Mercurio*, March 6. Available at http://www.elmercurio.com/blogs/2014/03/06/19992/Politica-energetica-2020.aspx

Bloomberg. (2013). Chinese Zombies Emerging After Years of Solar Subsidies. Available at http://www.bloomberg.com/news/articles/2013-09-08/chinese-zombies-emerging-after-years-of-solar-subsidies

Bloomberg New Energy Finance (2013). *Solar Market Update*. April.

Bradsher, K. (2013). Suntech Unit Declares Bankruptcy. *The New York Times*, March 20.

Bridges (2012a). US-China Renewable Energy Row Escalates with Solar Duty Announcement. *Bridges Weekly Trade News Digest* 16, 20.

Bridges (2012b). US Commerce Department Announces Final Duties on Imports of Chinese Solar Cells. *Bridges Weekly Trade News Digest* 16, 34.

Bridges (2013a). European Commission Imposes Duties on Chinese Solar Panels. *Bridges Weekly Trade News Digest* 17, 20.

Bridges (2013b). EU-China Solar Panel Deal in Place; Subsidies Probe to Continue. *Bridges Weekly Trade News Digest* 17, 28.

Bridges (2013 c). China Announces Anti-Subsidy Duties on US Solar-Grade Polysilicon. *Bridges Weekly Trade News Digest* 17, 30.

Bridges (2014a). US Launches New Probe into China, Taiwan Solar Trade Practices. *Bridges Weekly Trade News Digest* 18, 3.

Bridges (2014b). US Launches New WTO Challenge Against India Solar Incentives. *Bridges Weekly Trade News Digest* 18, 5.

CDEC SIC (2013). *Reporte Mensual Energía Eléctrica: Precio SIC*.

CDEC SING (2013). *Reporte Mensual de Sector Eléctrico: Precio SING*. Available at: http://www.systep.cl/documents/estadisticas/Precios%20SING.xlsx

Corporación de Desarrollo Tecnológico. (2012). "Análisis y Caracterización del Mercado Solar FV en Chile." Santiago, Chile. Available at: http://www.construccion-sustentable.cl/?page_id=624&download=166

Centro Nacional de Energías Renovables (CENER) and Fundación Chile. (2013). "First Solar CdTe Photovoltaic Technology: Environmental, Health, and Safety Assessment."

Available at: http://www.firstsolar.com/-/media/Documents/Sustainability/Peer-Reviews/Chile-Peer-Review---Cener_EN.ashx

Centro de Energías Renovables (CER). (2014). *Centro de Energias Renovables. Reporte CER. Febrero 2014.*

Centro de Energías Renovables (CER). (2013). *Centro de Energías Renovables: Reporte CER 2013.*

Comité de Inversiones Extranjeras (CIE). (2010). "Invest in Chile: Opportunities in Energy." Available at: http://www.investchile.gob.cl/wp-content/uploads/2015/08/BROCHURE_Energ%C3%ADa_web.pdf

Comisión Nacional de Energía (CNE). (2013). *Operacion Real por sistema Electrico Nacional 1998–2012.*

Deutsche Bank. (2014). "2014 Outlook: Let the Second Gold Rush Begin." Available at: https://www.deutschebank.nl/nl/docs/Solar_-_2014_Outlook_Let_the_Second_Gold_Rush_Begin.pdf

DIRECON (2014). *Dirección General de Relaciones Económicas Internacionales.* Retrieved 2014, from http://www.direcon.gob.cl/

Eclareon. (2013). *PV Grid Parity Monitor: Residential Sector* Issue 2. Available at: http://www.leonardo-energy.org/sites/leonardo-energy/files/documents-and-links/pv_gpm_2_residential_2013.pdf

Environment and Climate Change Canada. (2010). "Assessment of the Environmental Performance of Solar Photovoltaic Technologies." Available at: http://ec.gc.ca/scitech/B53B14DE-034C-457B-8B2B-39AFCFED04E6/ForContractor_721_Solar_Photovoltaic_Technology_e_09%20FINAL-update%202-s.pdf.

Environmental Protection Agency (EPA). (2011). "Shining Light on a Bright Opportunity: Developing Solar Energy on Abandoned Mine Lands." https://semspub.epa.gov/work/11/176032.pdf

Escenarios Energéticos Chile 2013 (EE2013). (2013). "Visiones y Temas Clave Para la Matriz Eléctrica." Available at: http://www.fch.cl/wp-content/uploads/2013/08/Escenarios_Energeticos_2013.pdf

Flannery, Russel. (2013). "China's Growing Role in the Global Solar Power Industry." *Forbes.* http://www.forbes.com/sites/russellflannery/2013/10/20/chinas-growing-role-in-the-global-solar-power-industry/

Fundación Chile: FCH (2008). *Tendencias Tecnológicas y Oportunidades para Chile en Energías Renovables No Convencionales.*

ICTSD (2013). *Local Content Requirements and The Renewable Energy Industry – A Good Match?* International Centre for Trade and Sustainable Development, Geneva.

International Electrotechnical Commission: IEC (2013). Retrieved from www.iec.ch

Intergovernmental Panel on Climate Change (IPCC). (2012). "Renewable Energy Sources and Climate Change Mitigation." Available at: https://www.ipcc.ch/pdf/special-reports/srren/SRREN_FD_SPM_final.pdf

Kawajiri, Kotaro, Takashi Oozeki and Yutaka Genchi. (2011). "Effect of Temperature on PV Potential in the World." *Environmental Science & Technology* 45, 20: 9030–35.

Kuntze, Jan-Christoph, and Tom Moerenhout. (2013). *Local Content Requirements and the Renewable Energy Industry – A Good Match?* International Centre for Trade and Sustainable Development. www.ictsd.org, Geneva.

Opciones de Mitigación para Enfrentar el Cambio Climático (MAPS Chile). (2012). "Escenarios Referenciales para la Mitigación del Cambio Climático en Chile." http://portal.mma.gob.cl/wp-content/uploads/2014/12/Fase-1-MAPS-Chile.pdf

Ministerio de Energía. (2010). "Antecedentes de la Matriz Energética en Chile." Available at: http://antiguo.minenergia.cl/minwww/opencms/02_Noticias/descargas_noticias/antecedentes_matriz_energetica_010611.pdf

Ministerio del Medio Ambiente. (2012). "Estrategia Nacional de Energía 2012-2013." Available at: http://portal.mma.gob.cl/wp-content/uploads/2014/10/3_Estrategia-Nacional-de-Energia-2012-2030_Energia-para-el-Futuro.pdf

Ministerio del Medio Ambiente (2012). *Informe del Estado del Medio Ambiente* (2da. ed.). Santiago de Chile: MMA.

Ministerio del Medio Ambiente (2011). *Segunda Comunicación Nacional de Chile Ante la Convención Marco de las Naciones Unidas sobre Cambio Climático.* Santiago de Chile: MMA.

Ministry of Commerce of the People's Republic of China: MOFCOM. (2011a). *Guidelines on Enabling Strategic Emerging Industries to Go Overseas.* www.miit.gov.cn.

National Renewable Energy Laboratory (NREL). (2012). "Life Cycle Greenhouse Gas Emissions from Solar Photovoltaics." Available at: http://www.nrel.gov/docs/fy13osti/56487.pdf

Natural Resources Defense Council: NRDC (2012). *El costo nivelado de energía y el futuro de la energía renovable no convencional en Chile: derribando algunos mitos.* Available at http://www.laondaverde.org/laondaverde/international/files/chile-LCOE-report-sp.pdf

Photon International Magazine (2012–2013). *Solar Module Price Index.*

Pike Research (2011). *Photovoltaic Manufacturer Shipments, Capacity & Competitive Analysis 2011/2012.*

Pollitt, M. (2004). *Electricity Reform in Chile: Lessons for Developing Countries.* Cambridge Working Papers in Economics No. 0448.

PV Insider(2014). *Radiografía de la industria fotovoltaica en Chile.* Available at: http://www.pv-insider.com/chile/content.php?utm_source=Energetica%20XXI&utm_medium=eamil%20content&utm_content=email%20content&utm_campaign=Energetica%20XXI%20email%20content

RedSoLAC (2013). *RedSoLAC: Fundación Chile.* Retrieved from www.redsollac.org

Renewable Energy Policy Network for the 21st Century (REN21). (2013). "2103 Global Status Report." Available at: http://www.ren21.net/Portals/0/documents/Resources/GSR/2013/GSR2013_lowres.pdf

Servicio Nacional de Aduanas Chile. (2013). *Servicio Nacional de Aduanas Chile.* Retrieved from www.aduana.cl

State Council (2009). *Curbing Excess Capacity and Redundant Construction of Several Industries and Promoting Healthy Development of Industries.*

State Council. (2010). *Decision of the State Council on Accelerating the Fostering.* Available at: http://en.pkulaw.cn/display.aspx?cgid=139218&lib=law

Stones and Associates (2011). Overview of the Solar Energy Industry and Supply Chain, January. Available at: http://www.thecemc.org/body/Solar-Overview-for-BGA-Final-Jan-2011.pdf

Tan, X., Zhao, Y., Polycarp, C. and Bai., J. (2013). *China's Overseas Investments in the Wind and Solar Industries: Trends and Drivers. Working Paper.* World Resources Institute, Washington, DC.

Turney, D., and Fthenaki, V. (2011). Environmental impacts from the installation and operation of large-scale solar. *Renewable and Sustainable Energy Reviews*, 3261–70.

UC Berkeley Haas IBD Team (2013). The Democratization of Energy: Distributed Solar Energy in Chile. June. Available at: http://docslide.us/documents/the-democratization-of-energy-distributed-solar-energy-in-chile.html

UL (2013). Underwriters Laboratories. www.ul.com.
UN Comtrade (2014). UN Comtrade Database. Retrieved from comtrade.un.org/
Wilson Sonsini Goodrich & Rosati: WSGR (2012). *PV Project Performance Guarantees – Commercial, Legal and Technical Considerations.*
World Bank (2014). *Exports of Goods and Services.* Retrieved from http://data.worldbank.org/indicator/NE.EXP.GNFS.ZS
WRI (2013). *China Invests Billions in International Renewable Energy Projects.* Available at: http://www.wri.org/blog/2013/06/china-invests-billions-international-renewable-energy-projects
Xie, D. (2010). *Industry Development Plan for New Energy Delayed.*
Zhao, Y., Wu, D. and Li, X. (2006). *The Status of Photovoltaic Industry and Market Development in China.* Beijing: Beijing Solar Energy Institute.

Chapter 9

CHINA IN MEXICO: SOME ENVIRONMENTAL AND EMPLOYMENT DECISIONS

Claudia Schatan and Diana Piloyan

This chapter explores the unique characteristics of Mexico's trade with China and investment from China, especially for Mexico's manufacturing sector. In addition, we examine the environmental and social characteristics of these flows, looking specifically at greenhouse gas (GHG) emissions and employment-related impacts for Mexico. Finally, we perform a case study of a Chinese company doing business in Mexico's manufacturing industry.

Mexico is unique relative to the other studies in this project. Mexico has indeed experienced a surge in exports to China, but these still remain very modest as compared to the great flow of imports from China. This phenomenon reflects Mexico's difficulties in competing in the manufacturing sector with China, both at home and abroad, and its still incipient primary goods exports to that country. Moreover, Mexico has thus far not received as extensive foreign direct investment from China as compared to the other countries in the region.

GHG caused by Mexico's exports to China are increasing much faster than Mexico's GHG generated by its total exports. Though there has been some offsetting of these emissions because of technological changes in Mexican export to China in several sectors, the change in export structure toward more polluting sectors (including primary sectors), together with the high rate of growth of these exports, explain this tendency. When looking into manufacturing exports from Mexico to China, the structure or composition effect favors less-polluting sectors, so this has a somewhat compensating effect together with the technology effect. This shows up in our statistical analysis, and in our case study we find a serious effort by a Chinese enterprise to comply with Mexican environmental regulations. Regarding employment, Mexican manufacturing firms, particularly in the textiles and apparel sector, have shed jobs due to competition with China. However, technical innovation in several sectors where there is competition with China has also had an important role in these job losses, especially in more recent years.

In analyzing a group of 36 Chinese manufacturing enterprises in Mexico we can see that, in general, they display varied environmental performances and labor conditions, but they generally comply with Mexican environmental law, which has improved dramatically over recent years (although its enforcement is still weak). Our case study exemplifies the fulfillment of environmental regulations. Of course, these results should be interpreted with caution, as this may not apply equally in sectors where Chinese Outward Foreign Direct Investment (OFDI) is present and expanding in Mexico. Furthermore, both OFDI and exports to China are shifting to include more primary sectors, especially mining. In terms of labor relations, labor law violations appear to be the exception rather than the rule in the Chinese manufacturing enterprises and in our case study, but important cultural differences seem to lead to some incompatibilities between what Chinese firms expect from their workers and what the local Mexican workers' customs are, with some conflictive outcomes.

In moving forward, there are important roles to play for Chinese firms (in adapting to Mexican labor and environmental laws), Mexican authorities (in enforcing those laws) and Mexican labor unions (in ensuring that labor law violations are addressed).

1. Introduction

General trends show that trade between China and Mexico, particularly imports from the former to the latter, has grown enormously over the last two decades as a result of China's entry into the World Trade Organization (WTO) in 2001, the end of the Multifiber International Accord (MIA) in 2005, and various loopholes in Mexican import oversight. This phenomenon has created a significant foreign trade deficit for Mexico with China. Competition has been especially intense in the textile and apparel market. Chinese exports to the United States displaced Mexican ones in this sector during the 2001–2006 period, but overall Mexico has been expanding and gaining US markets again, albeit with a different export structure. These trends in the first half of the 2000s contributed to great tensions between China and Mexico, which only very recently have begun to subside. These phenomena have widely been studied by different researchers (Dussel Peters and Gallagher, 2013; Dussel Peters, 2013, Jenkins and Dussel Peters, 2009, Gallagher and Porzecanski, 2010; Ayala and Villarreal, 2009).

As to Mainland Chinese OFDI, Mexico has received very limited and fluctuating amounts, while its structure is increasingly favoring primary goods sectors, namely mining and, to a lesser extent construction (of infrastructure), while manufacturing has lost importance in the whole.

This chapter is organized as follows: the second section gives a general background on trade between Mexico and China and on Chinese OFDI flowing to the manufacturing sector in Mexico. The third section looks into the environmental effect of Mexican exports to China as well as that of Chinese OFDI in the Mexican manufacturing sector. The fourth section studies the effects on employment and labor conditions of Mexican imports from China, especially in the textiles and apparel industry and that of OFDI in the manufacturing sector in Mexico. The fifth part presents a case study on GDA. Finally, we draw conclusions and propose some public policies for Mexico that might help improve environment and labor conditions as Mexican exports to China and Chinese OFDI in the manufacturing sector expand.

Three caveats are warranted regarding this study, since it is one of nine country studies in Latin America and the Caribbean (LAC) on environmental performance and effects on labor conditions of trade flows and OFDI from China. First, while competition from manufactured Chinese products has had a visible impact in Mexico, especially on employment and labor conditions in some sectors and time periods, neither Mexican exports to China nor Chinese OFDI in Mexico are drivers of environmental or social conditions in Mexico, because in both cases these activities are very limited (in contrast with other LAC countries), albeit growing in the case of exports. Second, this study concentrates mostly on the manufacturing sector, so its focus is rather restricted. Finally, there were great information limitations to carrying out this research, especially regarding Chinese manufacturing firms' emissions, since very few of them generate reports on the subject. Hence, firm environmental behavior was evaluated indirectly, with international indicators, but mostly qualitatively, taking into account their great heterogeneity. The same was true for the labor conditions in Chinese firms in Mexico. More specific information was found for the case study on Golden Dragon Affiliates (GDA). Notwithstanding these difficulties, we consider this study to provide a relevant analytic precedent for a rapidly intensifying relationship between China and Mexico, which requires attention so that it will contribute to improving rather than harming the environmental and labor conditions of the country.

2. Trade between Mexico and China and Chinese OFDI in Mexico

2.1 Mexico–China bilateral trade

There has been a growing trade relationship between Mexico and China, although quite asymmetric since the Mexican trade deficit with China

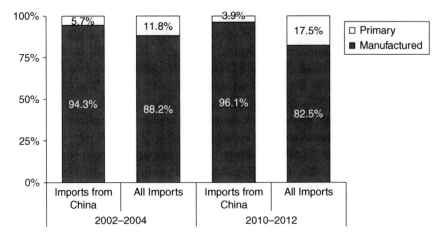

Figure 9.1 Mexican import structure from China and the world
Source: COMTRADE.

increased almost tenfold between 2002 and 2012.[1] Imports from China have risen at a very high speed and it has become the second-largest trading partner for Mexico. Mexico is now the largest importer from China in LAC, accounting for 48 percent of the region's total purchases (Rosales and Kuwayama, 2012). Although exports from Mexico to China are very far from catching up with the inflows of goods, they have also grown very quickly over the last ten years (from USD 0.6 to 5.7 million between 2002 and 2012, according to COMTRADE data), although they accounted for only 2 percent of total Mexican exports in 2013.[2]

Imports from China consist mainly of manufactured goods (Figure 9.1), resembling the Mexican total import structure. However, its export structure to China has changed and is increasingly concentrated in primary goods (predominantly minerals and animal feed), reaching about half of the total exports to China in 2010–2012 (up from 13% in 2002–2004) while almost 80 percent of Mexican exports to the world were still manufactured goods in 2010–2012 (Figure 9.2).[3] Within this overall export tendency at least two exceptions have to be made: Mexico's passenger vehicles, almost nonexistent at the beginning of the 2000s, and telecommunications equipment parts, which gained great importance among exported goods. Within imports, around 85 percent of them are intermediate goods, among which electronic goods are important,

---

1   COMTRADE.
2   Ibid.
3   Ibid.

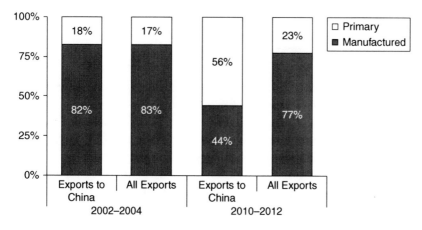

Figure 9.2 Mexican export structure to China and the world
Source: COMTRADE.

especially telecommunications equipment and its parts, confirming Mexico's involvement in the final assembly stage of the global value chain (GVC). Hence, the deep imbalance in this sector with China (Mexican manufacturing exports to China accounted for only 7 percent of the value of manufacturing imports from China of these goods in 2010–2012) is to some extent compensated by Mexican exports to the United States with Chinese inputs. At the same time, the figures for imports of textiles and clothing seem to be underestimated since they explain only around 8 percent of total imports – a surprisingly low figure. In fact, these are reported in an irregular way and have negative consequences for competition in the domestic market.

2.2 Chinese OFDI in Mexico

We will devote more space to Chinese OFDI, and especially to that going to the manufacturing sector in Mexico (section 2.3), than we did to trade between Mexico and China, because of the limited availability of statistical data. The following analysis develops a more qualitative assessment of environmental and social issues.

Mainland China had become the third-largest source of worldwide FDI in 2012 after the United States and Japan, and its importance is rising for developing nations (UNCTAD, 2013). There is evidence that China's government has given wide support to its enterprises to invest abroad, making use of the massive foreign currency reserves, especially through the Going Global Strategy (since 1999). The support given to OFDI by the Chinese government has included financial backing (through ExIm Bank, the National

Development and Reform Commission, China Development Bank and since 2003 commercial banks), logistics help, preferential insurance coverage, and other supports (Dussel Peters, 2012; Dussel Peters 2013; ECLAC, 2010; Lumsden, 2013).[4]

In general, Chinese OFDI is carried out mainly by state-owned enterprises (SOEs) and to a lesser degree by privately owned companies (Dussel Peters, 2012a; CCPIT, 2012; CCPIT, 2013). More specifically, the China Council for the Promotion of International Trade (CCPIT, 2012), categorizes OFDI in three groups, according to its target: (a) state-owned energy and resources enterprises that seek resource access; (b) high-tech companies, especially those in communications and IT industries, that seek greater competitiveness and access to technology; and (c) enterprises with comparative advantages, mainly in textiles and apparel as well as in home appliances, that look for greater access to international markets, while avoiding trade restrictions. Some domestic restrictive elements motivating Chinese enterprises to go abroad include increasing domestic costs, rising market competition in their markets and difficulties with access to talent and capital (CCPIT, 2012).

The performance of Chinese industries in foreign countries is quite different depending on the activity they undertake. Mineral and oil extraction can be done efficiently by Chinese firms abroad and can be securely sold to the Chinese market itself, so it does not entail much risk. As for construction, their knowledge, logistics and technology is advanced and the end product does not need to be marketed. Chinese investment in the manufacturing sector abroad is a different matter: it is a relatively recent phenomenon, and when its initiative comes from enterprises with little or no prior experience investing in countries abroad, there is a risk of being unsuccessful because of lack of marketing networks, of technology access or of cultural misunderstandings that may hinder efficient results.

When dealing with international manufacturing investments, Chinese firms frequently looks for joint ventures, mergers and acquisitions (M&A), or strategic alliances with developed countries' companies because this paves the way for acquiring technology (and transferring it to the home country), market access and even cultural familiarity of the firm with its surroundings (Zhang et al., 2013).[5] So countries like Mexico often receive OFDI of Chinese

---

4   In 2009 and 2010, China ExIm and CDB together lent more to developing countries than the World Bank (Dyer, Anderlini and Sender, 2011; cited by WRI, 2013).

5   Several interviews with different ProMexico and the Economics Secretary officials shared this view.

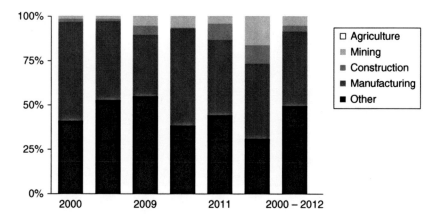

Figure 9.3 Structure of total FDI flows to Mexico
Source: Secretaría de Economía, Mexico.
Note: Sector Classification: NAICS.

manufacturing firms that have already made joint ventures or other forms of relationship with developed countries' enterprises.

Although measuring Chinese OFDI abroad is a controversial issue (ECLAC, 2010; WRI, 2013; Lin, 2013; Dussel Peters, 2012b, Dussel Peters, 2014), by any standard such flow going to Mexico has been very modest. According to Mexican official data the country had received USD 270.5 million between 1999 and the second quarter of 2013 (Economic Secretariat, Mexico). Mexico has attracted less OFDI as compared to that of other large LAC countries, because of its more limited availability of natural resources, the comparatively fewer incentives to foreign investors, as well as the trade and political tensions between China and Mexico, which permeate other activities, although these have been settling.

When comparing Chinese FDI to total FDI going to Mexico during 2000–2012, we can see from Figures 9.3 and 9.4 that the first has recently become considerably more concentrated in mining than total FDI received by Mexico, while almost all FDI went to manufacturing at the beginning of the 2000s (although the amount was insignificant). The FDI profile in Mexico is acquiring that of the Chinese FDI going to South American countries, where mining and other primary goods are very attractive and construction is acquiring relevance (Lin, 2013).

2.3 Present Chinese OFDI in the Mexican manufacturing sector

Mexico should be an interesting destination for Chinese OFDI in manufacturing, because of its proximity to the United States. Producing or assembling

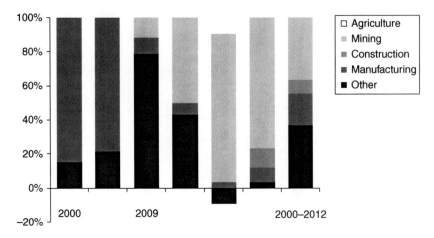

Figure 9.4 Structure of Chinese net OFDI flow to Mexico
Source: Secretaría de Economía, Mexico.
Note: Sector Classification: NAICS.

goods in Mexico to be exported to the United States has become more attractive, as many enterprises in China are starting to experience a rise in production costs in addition to existing transport costs and the time required to ship goods from China to the United States (UNCTAD, 2013; Sirkin, Rose and Zinser, 2012). By investing in Mexico, Chinese producers have the additional advantage of paying lower tariffs because of the North American Free Trade Agreement (NAFTA), and may avoid facing some countervailing duties for unfair trade practices that are charged to them if exporting directly from China. Finally, the bilateral investment treaty (BIT) signed between Mexico and China in 2008[6] provides important legal guarantees for both parties, improving certainty for Chinese OFDI (Berger, 2013).

Yet Chinese OFDI has been very scarce in the manufacturing sector, and there are still very few (mainland) Chinese manufacturing enterprises in Mexico. For this study we were able to identify 36 manufacturing enterprises of this kind. These enterprises are quite diverse: they are in the automobile industry, electronics industry, textiles, apparel and shoe industry; plastic materials, metal products, recycling and products for the construction industry, among others (see Table 9.1).

The nature of investment is also varied. As stated above, a portion of Chinese OFDI has arrived in Mexico through Chinese companies already in joint ventures, especially from developed countries. This is the case of Lenovo, which bought the Personal Computer Department of IBM, and afterwards

---

6   http://www.economia.gob.mx/files/China_actual.pdf

took the strategic decision of setting up its largest firm outside China in Mexico. Others have become Chinese because the mother company has been taken over by Chinese capital elsewhere, such as:

- TCL-Thomson (TCL, with majority Chinese ownership and French enterprise Thomson), merged with the purpose of producing televisions on a large scale and exporting them to the United States through Thomson's trade networks.
- Preh-Joyson (German enterprise Preh, specialized in automotive electronics, bought by Joyson Group, which produced automotive parts, in 2012) built a stronger position in the international market as an automotive supplier group, as they combined the strong market positioning of Preh in Europe and North America and access to the quickly expanding Chinese market through Joyson.[7]
- TK Minth (a joint venture of Chinese Minth and Japanese Tokai Kogyo Co. Ltd. Firms) is another of these cases: the first is an auto parts maker and the second is a plastic and rubber products maker, and TK Minth produces plastic and rubber automobile parts; Minth is favored by Tokai's global resources and strategic partners.[8]
- Foton, a very important Chinese truck and tractor producer at an international level, with one of its 23 subsidiaries in Veracruz, signed a joint-venture agreement with Daimler, a German automobile manufacturer, which will provide improved technology to the former and help diversify the range of products it makes. This will create an opportunity for the assembly of a wider range of trucks in Veracruz, too.[9]

There are a few examples of associations between Chinese and Mexican firms. An important case is Giant Motors de Latinoamérica (fully Mexican capital), which has had a strategic alliance with Faw trucks since 2006 by which the latter provides technology, technical advice and parts for various vehicle models to be produced in Mexico. Such models range from light passenger vehicles to heavy trucks, built with imported parts from China but increasingly including Mexican inputs (Dussel Peters, 2014).

---

7   http://www.prlog.org/12147592-preh-and-joyson-automotive-show-dynamic-growth-in-every-market.html

8   "Minth and Tokai Kogyo Form Auto Parts Joint Venture," in *Plastic News*, January 20, 2012 http://www.plasticsnews.com/article/20120120/NEWS/301209978/minth-and-tokai-kogyo-form-auto-parts-joint-venture

9   http://t21.com.mx/terrestre/2013/06/18/foton-autorizado-vender-camiones-daimler-mexico

There also are investments made by fully Chinese-owned firms in Mexico in industries in which China has a long manufacturing tradition and a mastery of the technology, such as textiles and apparel and steel and metal products. Among the most important are SINATEX S. A. de C. V in Sonora, a yarn producer and now a part of a very large Chinese conglomerate. Another one is Golden Dragon Affiliates, which produces precise copper tubes in Coahuila and also belongs to this category (see case study). One more case worth mentioning is HCP Packaging (packaging of cosmetic products), which established its fifth subsidiary abroad in Tamaulipas, Mexico, in 2009.

Other Chinese firms in Mexico were initially small in size but have grown to be medium size. This is the case of Long S. A. de C. V., which produces bicycles and motorcycles in Mexico City, mainly for the domestic market. Finally, there are those very small Chinese firms that continue being family owned for which little information is available.

One of the manufacturing sectors that would seem very promising, in theory, for Chinese OFDI in Mexico is the automobile (and especially the auto parts) industry, since Mexico has become a very important production and export platform, integrated to the NAFTA value chains and markets. As China needs to expand its industry abroad, Mexico is a promising location. However, the experience of OFDI in the automobile industry has met several challenges in Mexico, and there are better chances that Chinese investment in auto parts will expand before China becomes involved in finished vehicle production. The foreign enterprises that invest in this industry in Mexico have to comply with demanding regulations, such as producing a minimum of 50,000 vehicles a year, although this is not an impediment under certain forms of strategic alliance, as has been shown by Giant Motors (Dussel Peters, 2014). Furthermore, some Chinese automobile enterprises may find it difficult to meet the high quality and environmental standards required by the United States.[10]

In summary, Chinese OFDI in the Mexican manufacturing sector is diverse, although still very limited. The reasons for this are numerous: OFDI flow to Mexico has been inhibited by political tensions among the two nations; the scarce chances for Chinese firms to engage in the kind of joint ventures they are most interested in; the fact that their technology is somewhat behind the most modern required to enter the US market; the government-to-government tensions derived from trade conflicts between the two countries; and the obstacles posed by cultural and linguistic differences between them, among others.

---

10 Interview with ProMexico officials in China.

Table 9.1 Mexican enterprises owned by Mainland China firms or recipients of capital flows from China (1999–2012)

Firm	Activity	State	Emissions (CO$_2$ eq./USD)
Acerotech; S.A. de C.V.	Steel Industry	Nuevo Leon	1.66
Asontech S.A. de C.V.	Valve assembly plant	Baja California	0.53
Carrocerias y Remolques SA de CV	Car metal bodywork, lathe conversions	Baja California	0.39
Dong Fang Apparel; S.A. de C.V.	Apparel assembly	Yucatan	0.53
Fortune Plastic Metal de Mexico; S.A. de C.V.(*)	Recycling of different materials	Chihuahua	n.a.
Fortune Plastic Metal de Mexico; S.A. de C.V.	Recycling of different materials	Tamaulipas	n.a.
Foton	Trucks and agriculture tractors assembly	Veracruz	0.39
Giant Motors Latinoamerica(*)	Light trucks	Hidalgo	0.39
Gdl Yuncheng; S.A. de C.V.	Cylinders for engraving, products for printing enterprises	Jalisco	1.66
Godak-Mex; S. de R.L. de C.V.	Broadwoven fabric mills, cotton (textile assembly)	Baja California	0.78
Golden Dragon Affiliates S. de R.L. de C.V.(*)	Copper tubes	Coahuila	0.91
HCP Packaging USA Inc	Cosmetic Plastics packaging materials and unlaminated film and sheets	Tamaulipas	1.09
Herramientas Cleveland; S.A. de C.V.(*)(**)	Cutting tools and special tools	Mexico City	0.66
Hisense	Production of TVs among other electronic products	Mexico City	0.41

(*continued*)

Table 9.1 Continued

Firm	Activity	State	Emissions (CO$_2$ eq./USD)
Industria Megacinta; S.A. de C.V.	Adhesive tape	Mexico State	1.09
Jincheng Ronda; S.A. de C.V.	Motorcycle production	Tlaxcala	0.34
KBL de México, S. A. de C. V.	Apparel assembly	Guanajuato	0.53
King Cordmex; S.A. de C.V.	Electric cables	Baja California	0.41
Konka	Consumer Electronics	n.a.	0.41
Lenovo[*][**]	Personal computers and iPhones	Nuevo Leon	0.41
Long; S.A. de C.V.	Bicycles and motorcycles	Mexico City	0.34
Mexico Curtain Wall System Engineering; S de RL de CV	Glass and Aluminum walls, doors and windows	Baja California	0.91
New Field de Mexico; S.A. de C.V.	Shoe manufacturing	Guanajuato	0.49
Plastico Gigante de Mexico; S.A. de C.V.[*][**]	Plastic parts for industrial use (molded plastic through injection)	Chihuahua	1.09
Polygroup Industrias Mexico S.A. de C.V.	Parts for Christmas trees and plastic small swimming pools	Chihuahua	1.09
Preh/Joyson	Parts for automobiles' transmission systems (it includes thermal processes)	Nuevo Leon	0.39
Ranboy Sportwear; S.A. de C.V.	Apparel (other exterior textile material clothing)	Baja California	0.53
Reciclamax Mexico; S.A. de C.V.[*]	Recycling firm	Queretaro	n.a.
Rotomex Yuncheng; S.A. de C.V.	Cylinders for engraving.	Mexico State	1.66
Sinatex; S.A. de C.V.	Yarn manufacturing	Sonora	0.78

Table 9.1 Continued

Firm	Activity	State	Emissions (CO$_2$ eq./USD)
Sinterama de Mexico S. A. de C. V.	Yarn made from hard natural fibers	Tlaxcala	0.78
TCL-Thomson	Consumer electronics (TV sets and DVDs)	Chihuahua	0.41
Textiles de Guaymas; S.A. de C.V.	Exterior apparel made from knitted yarn and other products	Sonora	0.53
TK Minth Mexico;S.A. de C.V.	Molded plastics for automobiles	Aguascalientes	1.09
Yuanda Mexico S. A. de C. V.	Glass and metal new construction materials	Baja California	0.91
ZTE	Smart Phones	n.a.	0.41

Source: Secretaría de Economía, Mexico; GTAP/Boston University China-Latin America Project Databases (GHG emissions per dollar produced in 2007); Semarnat/Profepa and own research.

(*) Enterprises that made annual reports for SEMARNAT (Cédula de Operación Anual, COA) on its emissions to the atmosphere, to the water system, and on their hazardous wastes and their disposal.

(**) Enterprises that reported to the Pollutant Release and Transfer Registry (PRTR).

3. Environmental Analysis of Mexican Exports to China and Manufacturing OFDI in Mexico

3.1 Environmental characteristics of Mexican exports to China

This section looks specifically into pollution (GHG) increases resulting from Mexican production for exports to China, and we will compare them to those linked to total exports from Mexico. It also complied with the environmental impact assessment required by SEMARNAT. It distinguishes between emissions changes as a result of the rise in exports (scale effect), as a result of the changing structure of exports during the period under study (composition effect) and as a result of technology innovations (technique effect)[11]. The methodology is described in the technical appendix.

---

11 To calculate the technique effect we used the sectorial GTAP GHG information of emissions for each dollar produced for exports in 2004 and multiplied it by the 2000–2002 average exports sector and did the same for exports in 2007, multiplying it by the 2010–2012 average exports by sector. We calculated what the emissions would have been in 2010–2012 if the increase in exports had generated the same amount of GHG than in 2004. Thus the technique effect is represented by the difference between these two values.

Table 9.2 Scale, composition and technique effects of Mexico's exports (2000–2002 to 2010–2012)

	Exports to China		Exports to the World	
	Total Exports	Mfg. Exports	Total Exports	Mfg. Exports
Change in exports:				
In millions of USD	2,957.4	1,560.5	175,297.8	121,318.0
In percent	1,279.7	773.9	108.5	88.8
Change in export-based GHG emissions:				
In millions of kg CO_2 equivalent	2,286.6	993.8	103,753.9	52,079.2
Scale effect	2,384.6	1,843.7	158,982.4	103,897.8
Composition Effect	912.3	−496.7	36,759.4	−8,555.0
Technique Effect	−1,010.3	−353.2	−91,987.9	−43,263.6
In percent:	1,227.1	689.8	70.8	54.4

Source: GTAP Database and COMTRADE.

Table 9.2 shows that total exports from Mexico to China increased at a much higher rate (1,280%) than manufacturing exports (774%) between 2000–2002 and 2010–2012. This resulted in a change in the exports structure as mentioned before, in favor of primary goods, whose GHG emissions are higher, in general, than most manufacturing activities.

The increase in total Mexican exports to China during this period generated a 1,227 percent rise in GHG emissions, most of which was caused by the scale effect. However, the composition effect also increased total export emissions because the change in their structure favored more polluting sectors. The technique effect had a partially compensating effect on GHG emissions, since these were 31 percent lower than what they would have been without that effect (see Table 9.2). The sectors for which technical change contributed the most to reduce emissions (50% of the total) were primarily the passenger motor vehicles and secondly the telecommunications equipment parts (sectors 781 and 734 of the Comtrade classification). These are the same sectors that had the highest technical offsetting effect for total Mexican exports GHG emissions.

The technique effect had a different behavior if exports to China and those to the world are compared. In both cases, this effect pushed emissions downward, but this impact was less pronounced in exports to China. Technology improvements reduced emissions in exports to China by about 31 percent compared to what they would have been otherwise, but for overall exports, they reduced emissions by 47 percent – nearly half of what they would have been otherwise. This difference is even more pronounced in manufactured

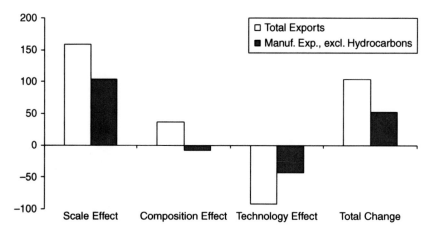

Figure 9.5 Breakdown of Mexican exports to China (emissions, billion kg. CO_2 equivalent)
Source: Table 9.2.

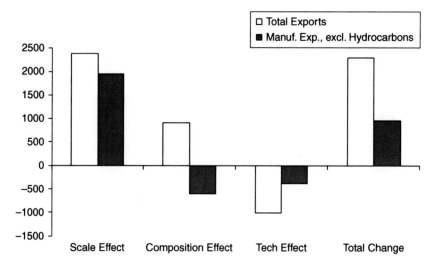

Figure 9.6 Breakdown of Mexican exports to the world (emissions, million kg. CO_2 equivalent)
Source: Table 9.2.

exports. Technology improvements reduced emissions from exports to China by 26 percent, but among overall exports they reduced emissions by 45 percent.

The GHG emissions growth produced by total Mexican exports to the world (Figure 9.6), as in the case of exports from Mexico to China (Figure 9.5), can mostly be attributed to the scale effect. Also, as in the former case, Mexican manufacturing exports emissions to the world expanded at a considerably lower rate than those of total exports to the world.

The composition effect on GHG emissions is somewhat different if Mexican exports to China and those to the world are compared. Such effect has a relatively greater impact on Mexican exports to China than those exports to the world, because of a more pronounced reorientation of Mexican exports to China toward primary goods. In contrast, within the manufacturing sector specifically, the composition effect reduced emissions more among Mexican manufacturing exports to China compared to those from Mexico to the world, indicating that manufacturing exports to China shifted to cleaner industries.

3.2 Environmental characteristics of Chinese manufacturing OFDI in Mexico

Because it is still quite limited, Chinese OFDI has not been an independent driver of environmental change in Mexico, either in primary goods or in the manufacturing industry, but it is an important issue to be studied, especially considering its growing flow.

Until now, Chinese investment in manufacturing in Mexico has not been concentrated in very polluting sectors. From the group of 36 manufacturing enterprises with Chinese capital in Mexico, only four of them had to report their emissions to the Pollutant Release and Transfer Registry (PRTR) (enterprises from environmentally sensitive sectors and large in size have to provide this information) and eight had provided a COA (see Table 9.1).

Regarding GHG emissions of these firms, two thirds of them emit less than 1 kg GHG (of CO_2 equivalent) for each dollar produced (Table 9.1). As a point of comparison, the most polluting sectors in the manufacturing industry are glass and mineral manufacturing, with 2.40 kg GHG per USD, according to the Global Trade Analysis Project (GTAP). Among the 36 companies, the ones that register the highest GHG emissions are a steel producer and two metal products companies, with 1.66 kgs (CO_2 equivalent). GHG emissions are only one aspect of pollution, but soil and water pollution caused by these enterprises may be quite damaging, too (Schatan and Castilleja, 2005). Thirteen of the Chinese firms produce hazardous wastes and three of these have been sanctioned for not complying with environmental regulations regarding hazardous wastes and soil pollution (information provided by Semarnat/Profepa). On the other hand, seven of the Chinese enterprises generated a COA and four provided PRTR environmental emissions accounts (see Table 9.1).

In general, our findings indicate that the environmental behavior of Chinese enterprises in Mexico is quite heterogeneous.

Firstly, as stated above, several of the important Chinese enterprises in Mexico are joint ventures or are acquisitions of third-country companies, and several of these are from developed countries. Hence, it is difficult to ascribe their environmental behavior to a pre-determined Chinese standard. In fact, in such cases, Chinese firms will be following technical and environmental procedures mostly inherited from their European, Japanese or US partners. Furthermore, one of the purposes of these joint ventures is for Chinese firms to be able to master new technologies, which are usually cleaner than obsolete ones.

Second, for those firms that have been fully owned by Chinese capital from the beginning, although the information is limited, there is evidence that some of them comply with local environmental norms (see Golden Dragon Affiliates, GDA, case study). For example, they may be contributing with environmentally groundbreaking products (as is GDA)[12] or may have numerous quality and environmental certifications (as does CP Packaging USA Inc, a cosmetic plastics, packaging materials, unlaminated film and sheet producer, which has ISO 9001 and ISO 14001 certifications).

Third, there are three recycling enterprises among the 36 under study, which have an environmental value for Mexico, since these sorts of firms are still scarce in the country. The potential is much greater for both pet and scrap metal recycling (of which Mexico is also an important exporter to China).

On the less encouraging side of this heterogeneity, the Chinese and Mexican legal and regulatory frameworks for environmental protection are still insufficient for OFDI to have an improved and more uniform environmental performance. China does not have a specific legal framework for corporate social responsibility (CSR) of its OFDI abroad, although there is an increasing awareness that environmental and social transgressions can contribute to the failure of Chinese OFDI projects (WRI, 2013). Still, OFDI can mostly choose to comply or not with the mostly voluntary guidelines provided by governmental institutions.

The greatest oversight over the environmental and social performance of Chinese OFDI seems to come from several Chinese institutions that intervene when financing or approving Chinese OFDI projects. This is the case of the China ExIm Bank, which has the "Guidelines for Environmental and Social Impact Assessments of the China Export and Import Bank's Loan Projects," which, among other things, require investors to perform environmental impact assessments (EIAs) on their projects. Also, the China Banking Regulatory Commission (CBRC) issued the "Green Credit Guidelines" in 2012, which gives guidance on environmental and social risk management for lending both at home and abroad (WRI, 2013). More recently, the Ministry of Commerce

---

12 Golden Dragon won the "Anti-Dumping War" in the US State Intellectual Property Office of the PRC (SIPO), http://english.sipo.gov.cn/news/iprspecial/201309/t20130909_817185.html

People's Republic of China (MOFCOM) has produced the "Guidelines for Environmental Protection in Foreign Investment and Cooperation," which help Chinese investors understand and observe environmental protection policies and regulations of the host country (MOFCOM, 2013)

When looking at the concrete CSR of Chinese OFDI abroad there are signs of very uneven company policies. The CCPIT (2013) report on a wide survey of Chinese firms with investments abroad found that SOEs are stronger and more institutionalized regarding CSR than private firms. A general result of the survey indicates a much higher level of CSR in OFDI operating in the European Union and in the United States than those in developing nations. Therefore, CSR of Chinese enterprises abroad seems to respond to host countries' laws and regulations instead of having its own improved targets in this area, regardless of where they operate (CCPIT, 2013).

On the Mexican side, the country has developed and progressively improved its legal and regulatory framework for the protection of its environment, which makes it increasingly difficult for domestic and foreign investors to undertake activities that overtly violate the law.

The institutional setting for designing and enforcing the environmental policy is the Secretaría del Medio Ambiente y Recursos Naturales (SEMARNAT) and Procuraduría Federal de Protección al Ambiente (PROFEPA, linked to SEMARNAT). According to the information provided by PROFEPA, in June 2013 it had 69,124 sources of pollution under its surveillance. There also are several Mexican Official Norms and other rules that have been enacted during the last 20 years, meant to curb pollution of manufacturing sectors. The fact that Mexico has joined important international and regional agreements has also improved its environmental standards. By becoming a part of NAFTA, which includes an Environmental Side Agreement (ESA) with tools that offer cooperation among the three countries and a dispute settlement agreement, Mexico has received support both to improve its environmental standards and to enforce them, as well as to advance its capacity in many aspects of environmental protection.

Other initiatives by the Commission for Environmental Cooperation of NAFTA (CEC) include the Sound Management of Chemicals (SMOC), which aims at phasing out the use of specific substances through the North American Regional Action Plans (NARAPs). Two of these are meant to eliminate or reduce considerably the use of mercury and another will also try to do so with lead (CEC). All these measures impose limits on certain pollutant emissions for all producers, including Chinese ones, and have a positive environmental influence on the production process of some activities.

Therefore, Chinese OFDI coming to Mexico has had to comply with the rules, standards and international environmental agreements signed by

Mexico, especially if the final destination of its goods is the United States, and even if these products are to stay in the domestic market. However, Mexico still faces many corruption problems and capacity limitations that are an obstacle in the surveillance of environmental behavior by economic actors. Hence, with weak Chinese environment policies for their companies abroad, and still somewhat weak enforcement in Mexico, there is much to be done to ensure an efficient policy for Chinese and all FDI coming into Mexico.

4. Employment Effects of Trade with China and OFDI in Mexico

4.1 Employment effects of trade between Mexico and China

The accelerated growth of Chinese exports to Mexico, described above, has probably had a negative impact on overall employment in the country, especially in the first half of the 2000s. However, at an aggregate level there are no precise estimates on job losses from this cause, nor an econometric model that demonstrates a clear link between the import growth from China and employment in Mexico (Dussel Peters, 2009). However, at a disaggregated level there is much more evidence that this has happened, especially in the textiles and apparel industry (and to a lesser extent, this has also occurred in the steel and machinery industries, among others). Hence, we will concentrate in the textile-apparel sector to illustrate the employment effects of Chinese competition on Mexico. Such phenomena, as is well known, comes in two forms at least: the direct competition of Chinese imports in the Mexican markets, and the one posed by China to Mexico in the US market.

The textiles and apparel industry has lost prominence in total manufacturing industry employment in Mexico, from roughly 18 percent in 2000 to 15 percent in 2003 and 11 percent in 2012. During this period, within the aggregate sector of textile inputs, textiles and apparel, the greatest number of jobs were lost in textile inputs and apparel. It must be noted that apparel had its greatest jobs loss after 2004 (with the elimination of the MIA), but employment was still falling in all textile and apparel subsectors between 2007 and 2012 (INEGI, 2000, 2009, and 2013).

The surge penetration of Chinese textiles, and especially apparel, into the Mexican markets occurred through legal, but mostly illegal channels since the international opening up to China. It was estimated that, in 2007, 65 percent of domestic consumption of textiles and apparel in Mexico was satisfied by illegal imports, especially from China (Dussel Peters, 2007b; interview with CANAINTEX, 2013). In fact, the surge in imports from China occurred notwithstanding the agreement Mexico and China signed when the latter country joined the WTO – an agreement that granted Mexico a six-year transition period for phasing out its compensatory tariffs on Chinese products and a further three-year trade remedy agreement.[13] Hence, the avalanche of these products was to a great extent the result of the irregular imports based on false declarations of goods descriptions and origins to avoid duties, as well as entry of Chinese exports to Mexico with US labels and other forms of disguising mechanisms.[14] These Chinese imports have hit the whole yarn-textile-apparel value chain in Mexico, so this industry has not only been reduced in size but also has become more shallow, with fewer economic interrelationships and, hence, engaging less employment at all stages of production (Dussel Peters and Gallagher, 2013).

Direct competition of Chinese textile and apparel goods in the Mexican market is only part of the problem faced by this industry, since the challenge they have had in the US market, where there has been fierce competition from China, has been also important.

The signing of NAFTA (1993) allowed Mexico to be very successful in some goods exports to the United States, among which textile and apparel (including footwear) was a prominent sector, contributing to this sector's employment expansion from 497,454 to 703,102 between 1994 and 1999. But over the following years the industry lost about 260,000 jobs, mostly in the apparel industry (INEGI, 2000; 2009; and 2013). There is little doubt that there is a role of Chinese competition in these job losses, but to what extent this is so is a matter of debate.

According to Dussel Peters and Gallagher (2013), between 2000 and 2009 52 percent of Mexican manufacturing exports to the United States were under direct Chinese threat (i.e., China's market share in the US export market was expanding while Mexico's country's share was shrinking). They found 53 sectors in which both Mexico was threatened in the United States and the United States was under threat in Mexico: 17 of them were in yarn, textile and apparel (including leather products). Although the authors do not analyze employment, we can infer that there were negative effects on this variable. There are few studies that estimate the impact of Mexican exports displacement by Chinese exports to the United States on employment in Mexico. Ayala and Villarreal (2009) find that such displacement occurred mostly in four Harmonized System sectors (three in textiles and apparel and one in

---

13 Over these three years, anti-dumping duties on China would be partly replaced by transitional duties, and finally these would be eliminated by December 2011.
14 A. Vazquez, H. López-Portillo, V. Vázquez-Bravo; "How Far is Mexico Willing to Go to Protect Itself from China?" International Law Office, http://www.internationallawoffice.com/newsletters/detail.aspx?g=ccc3e33e-221a-44dd-abba-00290b32c6ca

non-electrical machinery and equipment). According to their study, the period in which the contraction of employment was the greatest (-6.5% a year), Chinese displacement of Mexican exports to the US market explains one-third of such loss, while the rest is the result of other factors, mainly of technical change.

The apparel sector is not only the sector hardest hit by job losses, but also among the sectors with the weakest collective bargaining, lowest trade union affiliation of workers and greatest informal working arrangements. So it is unsurprising that labor conditions in this sector also had a setback. This sector has traditionally had lower salaries, on average, than most other manufacturing sectors, as well as more vulnerable labor conditions. Between 1995 and 2000, when there was a great expansion of exports to the United States because of NAFTA and the peso devaluation, conditions improved somewhat (including a greater number of written contracts and more benefits offered to workers). But after 2001 conditions have worsened for most enterprises – predominantly medium and small size – contracts became shorter and included very few or no worker benefits (Guadarrama Olivera et al., 2012).

Lastly, modern technology has borne an increasing responsibility for job losses and limited job creation in the textile–apparel sector and therefore has also been responsible for the deteriorating working conditions, especially in the apparel segment. In fact, technological innovation has widely been introduced in these sectors in China, Mexico and internationally, partly as a result of intensifying competition since the early 2000s (Duran and Pellandra, 2013; Watkins, 2013; INEGI, 2013).

4.2 Employment effects of Chinese OFDI on the manufacturing sector in Mexico

There is considerable fear in Mexico that Chinese firms will bring in Chinese workers, who may displace Mexican employees by working for lower wages and weaker rights compared to local workers, thus deepening the present employment scarcity and harming labor conditions. However, Chinese firms display the same heterogeneity in this aspect as in the environmental behavior described above. Social aspects of Chinese firms in Mexico are frequently inherited from businesses acquired by Chinese capital or from those with which they have joint ventures. This is not a rule, however, because there has been at least one case of a joint Chinese and US capital firm where irregularities were spotted: the apparel firm KBL de México, S. A. de C. V. in Guanajuato, where the Immigration Office made a verification visit in 2006 and discovered 61 isolated Chinese workers, with 14-hour workdays and with their immigration documents held by the enterprise.[15]

Purely Chinese-owned firms seem to have a comparatively greater proportion of Chinese workers. This is the case of SINATEX S. A. de C. V., in which almost one-fifth of workers are Chinese. In another common scenario, there may be a greater presence of Chinese workers in the initial stage of the firm's operation, after which most of them return to China, and a much smaller group remains (as in GDA, for example). Finally, sometimes Mexican workers may not have access to all their potential rights, such as those belonging to a trade union (as is the case of SINATEX), but this is not true in other enterprises (see case study, section 5).

From a number of personal interviews with public-sector officials, private-sector and Chinese representatives, it seems that the need for Chinese employees in manufacturing Chinese enterprises in Mexico stems not so much from the possibility of paying them lower wages but because they can understand each other better, are used to the organization of Chinese firms and culturally and linguistically they have greater synergies than with the Mexican personnel. As was mentioned above, one of the big obstacles for Chinese firms to successfully carry out manufacturing investments comes from the cultural complications. Also, a massive immigration of Chinese workers into this sector seems impossible because of the rule that only 10 percent of workers in any enterprise can be foreign, as well as the lengthy procedures necessary for Chinese citizens to obtain the Mexican work permits (although the new migration law has eased the process somewhat).

Information on social and labor standards in the Chinese manufacturing enterprises in Mexico is difficult to access. However, it is very telling that the CCPIT (2013) survey of more than a thousand Chinese enterprises shows that the greatest threats that they face in the European Union and in the United States were labor disputes. As with environmental performance, these firms must comply with host-country standards as long as workers have ways of expressing their complaints and there also are enforcement mechanisms. On the other hand, if such standards are poor, firms may not aim at higher ones solely from their own convictions. Unlike environmental legislation, however, firms in many sectors have much stronger capacity to implement Mexican labor regulations than environmental ones. This capacity, however, is uneven in the textile–apparel industry, as the textile industry has stronger legislation and trade unions than the apparel industry.

---

15 El Sol de Salmanca, *Se deterioran las instalaciones de la KBL de México*, http://www.oem. com.mx/elsoldesalamanca/notas/n2131938.htm, 04/07/2011.

5. Case Study on Golden Dragon Affiliates S., de R. L. de C. V. (GDA), Monclova, Coahuila

5.1 The Golden Dragon Group

5.1.1 General characteristics and background

GDA belongs to Golden Dragon Precise Copper Tube Group Inc. (GDG) – which is among the largest manufacturers of precise copper tubes in the world. It was set up in 1988 in China as a state-owned enterprise (SOE) and in 1994 it was privatized. It has six plants in different provinces in China; the most important is the Xinxiang Facility, with 1,700 employees and a capacity to produce 100,000 metric tons (MT) of copper tubes a year. It has one plant outside China – in Monclova, Coahuila, Mexico – and is building a second one in Alabama.

GDG was attracted to invest in Mexico by its closeness to the US market and also the benefits offered by this country: they were exempted from paying payroll taxes for one year; they offered one-year scholarships for the first workers hired to study; and the government provided the land for them to construct and also helped in the construction process itself.

This firm produces several kinds of tubes: smooth tubes, IGT (inner grooved tubes), pancake coils, fin tubes,[16] solar tubes, and RF (radio frequency) tubes. These tubes have a very wide range of applications: air conditioning and refrigeration equipment, water supply for buildings, shipbuilding, medical facilities, solar energy, mobile communication and electromagnetic microwave technology. Three kinds of tubes are manufactured in Mexico: smooth tubes, IGT, and pancake coils.[17]

5.1.2 GDG technology

GDG produces seamless refined copper (SRC) tubes. The technology used in the production of SRC pipes and tubes in the United States, China and Mexico has improved over the last two decades. GDG uses the most recent technology available, which consists of a continuous horizontal cast and roll process. It is an improvement over the extrusion method, since it is quicker and does not require the billet reheating and extrusion steps of the former. Hence, it has lower production costs, reduces defects in the final products and

---

16 In comparison to plain tubes, fins increase the surface area of the tube and improve the heat transfer efficiency.

17 http://www.gdcopper.com/en/ABOUT/Copindu/. Mexican producer IUSA and Luvata, a subsidiary of a multinational enterprise, also use this technology.

requires less energy and water for its manufacture. The process also has better control of wall thickness along the length of the mother tube compared to the extrusion process, making it possible to manufacture smaller diameter products that require less copper per meter.

The cast and roll process was developed by Outukumpu (now Luvata) in Finland, at the end of the 1980s, and its patent expired in 2008. It was introduced in China in 1991 through China National Technical Import and Export Corporation (GDG at present), which bought licenses from the Finnish company.[18] GDG has improved its technology considerably: originally, each line of production yielded 7,000 MT annually, but through re-engineering and machine improvement they are able to produce 25,000 MT at present.[19]

GDG has a strong R&D and innovation position for precise copper tube material research and has obtained around a hundred new patents. The company has an advanced quality control system with several certifications: OHSAS18001, ISO9001, ISO14001 and ISO/TS16949.[20]

GDG has incorporated several important environmental innovations in their products: it uses core technology of high-quality refrigeration copper tube; it produces an efficient heat-transfer threaded pipe that the company developed independently; and it has reduced the volume of air conditioners, increased the energy efficiency and reduced the use of the copper pipe since 2000.

5.2   Golden Dragon Affiliates S., de R.L. de C.V. (GDA), Coahuila, Mexico

5.2.1 Background and general performance

The subsidiary of GDG, GDA in Mexico made an initial investment of around USD 100 million and started operating in 2009. The company fabricates three kinds of tubes using the same technology as GDG in China, and has become a very important enterprise in this sector, with a capacity of 50,000 MT, although it has reached 40,000 MT in its three production lines. At present (2014), it has 420 employees (400 are Mexican and 20 are Chinese).

GDG set up GDA in Mexico with the purpose of exporting copper tubes to the United States. However, in 2009 the United States imposed a 60.6 percent

---

18 Interviews at GDA.
19 Interviews at GDA.
20 http://www.made-in-china.com/showroom/gdlvguan/companyinfo/
    Golden-Dragon-Precise-Copper-Tube-Group-Inc-.html

anti-dumping duty on the seamless refined copper pipe and tubes imported from Mexico and China.[21] In 2013, USTR overruled the antidumping duty it had imposed on GDA[22] but according to GDA executives in Monclova, exporting to the United States is still difficult.

As a result of this situation, GDA diversified its markets to Colombia, Japan and occasionally Europe, but it also made a special effort to expand its market in Mexico,[23] thereby strengthening its forward linkages, managing to cover 58 percent of the Mexican local market in 2012 (up from 27% in 2010).[24] During this period, the enterprise was able to gain some market share from its competitors in Mexico (particularly IUSA and NACOBRE, but not Luvata, which is very competitive). As to the GDA backward linkages, they frequently buy copper domestically. Local inputs also include nitrogen (GDA has its own plant), energy (it has a plant but is not self-sufficient) and plastic and other packaging materials (although some are also imported from China).

The complications faced in entering the US market, together with security problems in Mexico (GDA suffered repeated theft of its products – 12 full containers in 2012), among others, have caused certain financial problems for the company, which is striving to overcome them.

5.2.2 Environmental policy of the firm

Technology used by GDA is advanced and brought from GDG, China, since it has no R&D department in Mexico, while its modern nitrogen plant has French technology. The GDA plant has one person in charge of health, security and the environment. The firm was certificated by ISO 9000, in 2010, but does not yet have ISO 14000 or other environmental certifications in Mexico.

The production process of GDA is energy- and-water intensive (a scarce resource in northern Mexico). It has no direct atmospheric emissions, since it uses electricity for its smelting and its annealing processes (instead of using

21 US International Trade Commission, "Seamless Refined Copper Pipe and Tube from China and Mexico," *Investigation Nos. 731-TA-1174–1175*; Publication 4193, November, Washington, DC.
22 "Golden Dragon Won the 'Anti-dumping War' in the U.S."; State Intellectual Property Office of the PRC (SIPO), http://english.sipo.gov.cn/news/iprspecial/201309/t20130909_817185.html
23 Some of their national and international customers are: MABE, MESA, Panasonic, IMBERA, Whirlpool, Carrier, Hitachi, Samsung, Bohn, Lennox, and Rheem, among others.
24 31,100 MT, up from 27,300 MT (according to GDA).

natural gas, which would generate CO_2 emissions from the plant). However, the CO_2 generated from the electricity use must be considerable.

The production process uses abundant water (of various types) to cool down the tubes at different stages. First, when the mother seamless tube is formed; second, at different stretching phases; and, finally, after the annealing processes.

Water is treated before entering the facility because it is too rich in minerals to be used, especially in the first stage of production. All of the water used in the production process and in the sanitary facilities is recycled in the water treatment plants and reused. Water remnants are tested in laboratories certified by the official Mexican Certification Entity (EMA) before they are returned to the collection system of the city.

The most important component that needs to be recovered from the used water is oil, which is abundantly used to clean the copper tubes. GDA has a system to separate water from oil and once the latter is recovered, it is disposed of as hazardous waste.

Hazardous waste produced by GDA includes: oil, lubricants, coolants and waste that has been contaminated by chemicals. All of these are recovered and kept in special areas for hazardous waste, approved by SEMARNAT, until they are taken care of by private enterprises (authorized by SEMARNAT) that handle them. Other non-hazardous waste, such as plastics, discarded wood board and other leftovers from packaging materials are sold to Mexican firms for recycling. In short, all waste is either recycled or destroyed.

GDA, Monclova, has to meet several environmental standards and has to report its performance periodically on several fields. It has to file an annual report for SEMARNAT (Cédula de Operación Anual, COA) on its emissions to the atmosphere, its discharges into the water system and its hazardous waste and its disposal. The enterprise complies with this requirement, and it has been making an effort to improve its reports as a way to keep a better record of its own environmental performance. GDA does quite well in this, considering that the environmental authority in Coahuila has a very limited capacity to keep track of the 3,000 companies it needs to monitor. Very few companies prepare a COA – they pledge their accuracy under oath and only very seldom are they inspected.[25]

Each year the enterprise checks sound emissions, lights, vibration, oil mist and water quality, to make sure it is complying with the standards set for each one of these indicators.

---

25 Vanguardia, *Incumplen empresas con norma ambiental; la SEMA no verifica a todas.* 03/02/2013
    http://www.vanguardia.com.mx/incumplen_empresas_con_norma_ambiental%3B_
    la_sema_no_verifica_a_todas-1494962.html

As for environmental improvement programs, the firm has one to reduce hazardous waste and to lower energy consumption by using LED light bulbs; and to reduce oil mist, which may threaten workers' health.

The GDA case study has several characteristics in common with a group of 298 automobile and electronics assembly plants in three northern cities in Mexico interviewed for a survey on technical and environmental behavior carried out in 2002 (Carrillo and Schatan, 2005). GDA, like two-thirds of those plants, has an environmental policy and has personnel dedicated to this matter. It also resembles 30 percent of the surveyed enterprises in that it has obtained an ISO 9001 certification, but GDA still lacks ISO 14001, which 18 percent of the firms in the survey did have. The motives driving most of the enterprises to undertake an environmental policy in the survey (i.e., to comply with Mexican environmental standards) is similar to the GDA incentives to do so. However, many years have passed since such a survey, and the measures taken by GDA must certainly be much more advanced in emissions measurement, disposal of hazardous waste and recycling.

5.2.3 Labor conditions in GDA

Labor conditions in GDA comply with Mexican requirements overall,[26] but they have some specific problems. All Mexican workers are part of the Confederación de Trabajadores de México (CTM) trade union and earn a wage that is quite standard for such activities. Most workers are skilled, since the production process uses sophisticated technology and their job consists mostly of controlling machines and processes, rather than transforming inputs directly.

However, there seems to be a variety of difficulties that have to do mostly with differences between Mexican and Chinese working culture and an inadequate handling of overtime payments by the firm.

First, the incentives provided by Chinese and Mexican enterprises differ considerably. Chinese incentives are linked with productivity and the number of hours worked. So, while minimum wages are low in China, workers are capable of having relatively high salaries, by working very hard for long hours. Mexican workers are often not willing to sacrifice holidays and weekends, and they are protected by the law in this sense. However, at GDA laborers have often been required to do their jobs on non-working days and, although these should be paid accordingly, complaints have been raised because the firm has not honored this obligation. Also, there are some workers who claim to have been fired because they have refused to work on officially non-working days,

---

26 Various interviews with GDA staff.

and they maintain that they have not been compensated according to the law.[27] Since the CTM trade union in of Coahuila also has internal disputes, it seems not be able to act effectively in these cases.[28]

Second, there is a communication problem between Chinese and Mexican personnel. There are strong linguistic barriers: none of the Mexican employees speak or understand Chinese, and none of the Chinese workers speak Spanish. English is not an alternative, because only few staff members understand that language. This is why the knowledge transmission process is relatively difficult and imperfect and mostly done through interpreters, who are not technicians. Although several Mexican staff and workers have spent some time in China learning the technical aspects of the production process, this seems to have been insufficient. If we add a considerable labor turnover to this situation, then the capacity of human capital to respond to the enterprise's needs falls short.

Third, there is a very different social situation for Mexican and Chinese employees. The first live in their country, have social and family relations, and mingle in society without any problem. However, most of the Chinese staff come to Mexico without their families and are isolated from society because of the language barrier. This also deepens the differences already mentioned.

In short, GDA's characteristics are quite similar to other Chinese manufacturing enterprises abroad, which are technologically at the forefront in their sector. However, they face challenges to reach the targets set by their own group, due to market access and security problems and productivity shortcomings. Broadly speaking, GDA's environmental policies are in line with Mexican legislation, but there is room for improvement. Regarding labor policies, there is room for GDA to make a greater effort to surmount cultural and linguistic obstacles and comply appropriately with Mexican domestic labor laws.

6. Conclusions

This chapter has looked into the question of whether trade between Mexico and China has had an adverse incidence on environmental indicators (through exports to China) and labor issues (through imports from China) in Mexico, and whether Chinese OFDI has had a recognizable pattern of behavior regarding these issues. The analysis mostly concentrated in the manufacturing sector.

---

27 Periodico El Tiempo, *Actúa Golden Dragon en Represalia*, 02/12/2012; Zocalo Saltillo, *Cumplen las empresas con pago de utilidades*, 05/05/2012.

28 Periodico El Tiempo, *Truena Osvaldo Mata contra Tereso Medina*, 05/04/2012.

Mexico has only had a significant trade relationship with China through imports coming from that country and those that compete with Mexico in the US market. Exports from Mexico to China have been much more limited, but they have had an upward trend. The amount of OFDI coming from China is quite modest, still, especially compared with other LACs.

The issue of employment has been studied extensively, and most experts agree that displacement by Chinese imports contributed to important job losses in the first half of the 2000s, especially in the textile–apparel industry. However, there is no consensus on the strength of that phenomenon, or the extent to which the overall Mexican economy has been harmed by Chinese imports. This is because of the pervasiveness of illegal imports from China (which are hard to trace) and simultaneous technological innovations that have made the sector less labor-intensive (which make causation harder to attribute). Nonetheless, for this sector to strengthen, Mexico requires much more legal enforcement of rules on origin and illegal smuggling of products, especially apparel. The negotiations for China to be recognized as a market economy by Mexico before 2016 is also a critical issue because this new status could reduce the margins within which Mexico could claim unfair trade practices by China.

Regarding the environmental characteristics of Mexican exports, specifically GHG emissions arising from their production, a worrying sign is that the composition of these exports is changing towards more polluting sectors, particularly mining. This tendency is much more pronounced for Mexican exports to China than for those going to the rest of the world. Focusing specifically within the manufacturing sector, export to China favors less-polluting sectors, more so than it does for manufacturing exports from Mexico to the world. However, in all cases, it has been the rapid expansion of exports (scale effect) that has been, by far, the factor responsible for greater GHG emissions from exported goods. Improvements in technique have had an offsetting influence, but much less so for exports to China than for exports overall.

Chinese OFDI in Mexico has been very limited, most of it favoring the primary goods sector in recent years. The present study focused on OFDI in the manufacturing sector in Mexico and identified a group of 36 Chinese manufacturing companies. Our results indicate that the firms are quite heterogeneous in their structure as well as their environmental and social behavior.

Above all, it is quite clear that no unique environmental policy is being followed by these firms in Mexico, since their origins are varied. Few are wholly Chinese-owned; instead, many are either joint ventures or have other forms of relationships with firms from developed countries. They also vary considerably in size and sector, although the most important belong to sectors where China has traditionally had technological dominance. Of the group of enterprises identified, some are known to have adequate environmental standards, but for others it is not clear what their standards are, since access to information is very difficult. The case study – Golden Dragon Affiliates – shows, in general, a compliance with Mexican environmental standards in water treatment and hazardous waste handling as well as GHG emissions, although there is room for improvement.

Chinese OFDI projects receive guidelines from China on fulfilling local requirements, especially EIA, but following these guidelines is still mostly voluntary for subsidiaries abroad. Chinese banks that back enterprises abroad can apply greater pressure to comply with local standards, because they have inferred that a negative image of such firms abroad may end in a failure of the investment they are backing. The Mexican environmental legal and regulatory framework has greatly improved and now includes keeping records from the most polluting firms, but enforcement is still rather weak and needs to be improved. As is the case with FDI, in general, unless there is an explicit company policy regarding environmental and labor standards, or rules set by the country of origin of the investor, it is usually the local legal framework and its implementation that sets the limits of what these firms may or may not do. Chinese OFDI in Mexico is no exception.

The labor record of Chinese OFDI in the Mexican manufacturing sector, as in the case of the environment, is not homogeneous. Unfortunately, the apparel sector was the area hit the hardest by Chinese competition after China joined the WTO (2001) and MIA ended (2005). This sector is also one of the most vulnerable in terms of its labor conditions in Mexico, with informal work arrangements, low wages, fewer benefits and weak trade unions. Feeble regulations in this area and the still-important flow of illegal imports continue to affect this sector's employment and working conditions.

The common preconception that Chinese firms bring significant numbers of workers from China – doing so primarily in order to pay them lower wages, make them work longer and avoid social security expenses – seems more of an exception than a common practice. When firms are fully owned by Chinese capital we saw examples where the proportion of Chinese workers can be relatively high, but the reasons for this seems to lie more in the challenge of technical knowledge transfer and shortcomings in communication between Chinese and Mexican employees, rather than firms trying to profit from low compensation. As to the conditions of Mexican workers in purely Chinese-owned firms, there does not seem to be an overall trend toward labor law violations, but there are specific problems related to differences in Chinese and Mexican labor law regimes. The GDA case study shows these characteristics.

Wages in China itself have been rising very rapidly (with average real wages of the country's 700 million workers multiplying fivefold over the last two decades), and working conditions have improved. Meanwhile, the legal framework has transformed accordingly, with greater legal entitlements given to Chinese workers (Brown, 2013). This may create greater incentives for Chinese firms to invest in Mexico, but the latter should aim at competing with China by producing increasingly more sophisticated goods and attracting higher technology OFDI with greater value-added and better wages. Mexico needs to leapfrog in production of these kinds of goods, as it has been doing in the automobile and aerospace industries, with a greater integration of value chains at home to face the challenges posed by China.

One aspect that must draw attention and that needs to be studied in greater depth is that Chinese OFDI, although favoring the primary sector, is also diversifying. In fact, investments going to areas other than manufacturing (such as construction, agriculture and mining), while volatile, accounted for an average of about 40 percent of total Chinese OFDI between 2000 and 2012. Within this category there are very diverse activities, ranging from the construction of a large wholesale facility being built in the state of Quintana Roo (Dragon Mart), which is very controversial in terms of environmental impact, to high-technology enterprises such as Huawei, which provides telecommunication services and a training facility that are greatly needed in Mexico. New investments also include those of the Chinese Development Bank, which should help expanding China's involvement in several activities in Mexico.

Technical Appendix: Scale, Composition and Technique Analysis

This analysis is based on methodology used by Schatan (2000). We used the 3-digit SITC database for exports and the GTAP database for GHG emissions for 2004 and 2007 (Andrew and Peters, 2013; COMTRADE). From a list of 262 sectors, we focused on 164 sectors with over USD ten thousand in exports.

We analyzed trends from 2000 to 2012 by comparing an average of 2000 to 2002 and an average of 2010 to 2012. By taking averages, we compensated for volatility in emissions data. We also compared production for Mexican exports to China to production for Mexican exports to the world. We broke down the increase in GHG emissions into the three different components mentioned above:

$$\Delta P = \{ [xi_1 * (X_2/X_1)] * ti_1 - (xi_1 * ti_1) \} + \{ [(xi_2 * ti_1) - (xi_1 * ti_1)] - [(xi_1 * (X_2/X_1)) * ti_1 - (xi_1 * ti_1)] \} - [(xi_2 * ti_1) - (xi_2 * ti_2)]$$

$$\text{Scale effect} = \{ [xi_1 * (X_2/X_1)] * ti_1 - (xi_1 * ti_1) \}$$

$$\text{Composition effect} = \{ [(xi_2 * ti_1) - (xi_1 * ti_1)] - [(xi_1 * (X_2/X_1)) * ti_1 - (xi_1 * ti_1)] \}$$

$$\text{Technique effect} = [(xi_2 * ti_1) - (xi_2 * ti_2)]$$

where:
ΔP: is the pollution change between period 1 and period 2.
ti_1: pollution index for sector i in period 1.
ti_2: pollution index for sector i in period 2.
xi_1: exports of sector i in period 1.
xi_2: exports of sector i in period 2.
$X_1 = xi_1$
$X_2 = xi_2$
$i = 1, 2,..., 164.$

References

Andrew, Robbie M. and Glen P. Peters (2013). A Multi-Region Input–Output Table Based on the Global Trade Analysis Project Database (Gtap-Mrio), Economic Systems Research, 25:1, 99–121, DOI: 10.1080/09535314.2012.761953, Routledge http://dx.doi.org/10.1080/09535314.2012.761953

Ayala, Edgardo A. and Mario Villarreal (2009). "The Dragon Menace: Is China Displacing Mexico's Trade with the United States?" *Análisis Económico* 24, 55: 327–46. UAM, Mexico.

Berger, Axel (2013). "Investment Rules in Chinese Preferential Trade and Investment Agreements; Is China Following the Global Trend Towards Comprehensive Agreements?" Discussion Paper, German Development Institute, Bonn, July. http://www.die-gdi.de/CMS-Homepage/openwebcms3.nsf/(ynDK_contentByKey)/ANES-96KDZQ/$FILE/DP%207.2013.pdf

Brown, William (2013). "How China Works," *Cambridge Alumni Magazine*, https://www.alumni.cam.ac.uk/magazine/cam-70

Carrillo, Jorge and Claudia Schatan (eds) (2005). *El Medio Ambiente y la Maquila en México: un problema ineludible*, ECLAC Books no. 83.

China Council for the Promotion of International Trade: CCPIT (2013). *2013 China Outbound Foreign Direct Investment Survey.*

———. (2012). *Report on Chinese Enterprises' Outbound Investment and Operation.*

Duhamel, François and Diana Bank (2013), "¿México como plataforma para las inversiones directas chinas?," in Enrique Dussel Peters (coordinator), *América Latina y El Caribe – China; Economía, Comercio e Inversiones Economía, Comercio e Inversiones*, ALC-China and Cechimex, Udual, UNAM, Mexico.

Durán Lima, José and Andrea Pellandra (2013). "El efecto de la emergencia de China sobre la producción y el comercio en América Latina y el Caribe" in Enrique Dussel Peters (coordinator), *América Latina y El Caribe – China; Economía, Comercio e Inversiones Economía, Comercio e Inversiones*, ALC-China and Cechimex, Udual, UNAM, Mexico.

Dussel Peters, Enrique (2014). "Inversión Extranjera Directa de China en México, los casos de Huawei y Giant Motors de Latinoamérica," in Enrique Dussel Peters (coordinator), *China en América Latina: 10 casos de estudio*, Red ALC-China; Udual; UNAM and Cechimex, Mexico.

——— (2013). "Características de la inversión extranjera directa china en América Latina (2000–2011)," in E. Dussel Peters (coordinator), *América Latina y El Caribe – China; Economía, Comercio e Inversiones Economía, Comercio e Inversiones*, ALC-China and Cechimex, Udual, UNAM, Mexico.

——— (2012a). "Chinese FDI in Latin America: Does Ownership Matter?" Discussion Paper No. 33, Working Group on Development and Environment in the Americas, November.

——— (2012b). The Auto Parts-Automotive Chain in Mexico and China: Co-operation Potential? *The China Quarterly* 209, March.

——— (2009). "El Caso de México," in Rhys Jenkins and E. Dussel Peters (eds), *China and Latin America; Economic Relations in the Twenty-First Century*. Bonn and Mexico City: German Development Institute Studies (D.I.E) and Cechimex. http://www.economia.unam.mx/deschimex/cechimex/chmxExtras/repositorio/archivos/DIE.pdf

Dussel Peters, Enrique and Kevin Gallagher (2013). "NAFTA's Uninvited Guest: China and the Disintegration of North American Trade," *CEPAL Review*, No. 110, LC/G.2572-P/, Santiago, Chile, August.

ECLAC (2013). "Chinese Foreign Direct Investment in Latin America and the Caribbean: China-Latin America Cross-Council Taskforce," *Working Document*, LC/L.3729, ECLAC, Santiago, Chile.

——— (2010). *Foreign Direct Investment in Latin America and the Caribbean, 2010* http://www.cepal.org/publicaciones/xml/0/43290/Chapter_III._Direct_investment_by_China_in_Latin_America_and_the_Caribbean.pdf

El Tiempo, "Actúa Golden Dragon en Represalia," 02/12/2012 http://www.periodicoeltiempo.mx/index.php?option=com_content&view=article&id=42279:actua-golden-dragon-en-represalia-&catid=120:empresariales&Itemid=728

El Tiempo, Truena Osvaldo Mata contra Tereso Medina, 05/04/2012. http://periodicoeltiempo.mx/index.php?option=com_content&view=article&id=1874:truena-osvaldo-mata-contra-tereso-medina&catid=119:gobierno-y-politica&Itemid=728

Gallagher, Kevin and Roberto Porzecanski (2010). *The Dragon in the Room; China and the Future of Latin American Industrialization*. Stanford: Stanford University Press.

Gallagher, Kevin, Amos Irwin and Katherine Koleski (2012). "*The New Banks in Town: Chinese Finance in Latin America*," *The Interamercan Dialogue*, February, 83–108.

Guadarrama Olivera, Rocío, Alfredo Hualde Alfaro and Silvia López Estrada (2012). "Precariedad Laboral y heterogeneidad ocupacional: una propuesta teórico-metodológica," *Revista Mexicana de Sociología*, vol. 74 No. 2, Mexico April/June.

INEGI (2013). *La Industia Textil y del Vestido en México*, http://www.inegi.org.mx/prod_serv/contenidos/espanol/bvinegi/productos/integracion/sociodemografico/Textil/2013/702825056056.pdf

———. (2009). *La Industia Textil y del Vestido en México*, http://centro.paot.org.mx/documentos/inegi/textil_ves_09.pdf

——— (2000). *La Industia Textil y del Vestido en México*, http://www.inegi.gob.mx/prod_serv/contenidos/espanol/bvinegi/productos/integracion/sociodemografico/textil/2000/itvm%202000.pdf

Jenkins, Rhys and E. Dussel Peters (2009). *China and Latin America; Economic Relations in the Twenty-First Century*. Bonn and Mexico City: German Development Institute Studies (D.I.E) and Cechimex. http://www.economia.unam.mx/deschimex/cechimex/chmx-Extras/repositorio/archivos/DIE.pdf

Leung, Denise and Yingzhen Zhao, in collaboration with Tao Hu and Athena Ballesteros (2013). *Environmental and Social Policies in Overseas Investments: Progress and Challenges for China*. World Resource Institute (WRI), April. http://pdf.wri.org/environmental_and_social_policies_in_overseas_investments_china.pdf

Lin, Jianhua, (2007). "El Caso de Sinatex SA de CV en México, Oportunidades en la relación económica y comercial entre China y México," in E Dussel Peters (coordinator), *Oportunidades en la relación económica y comercial entre China y México*, 239–44.

Lin, Yue (2013). "Inversión extranjera directa de China en América Latina," in E. Dussel Peters (coordinator), *América Latina y El Caribe – China; Economía, Comercio e Inversiones Economía, Comercio e Inversiones*, ALC-China and Cechimex, Udual, UNAM, Mexico.

Lumsden, Andrew (2013). *Chinese Outbound Investment: The Growing Sophistication of China's "Go Global" Policy*. Corrs Chambers Westgarth, University of New South Wales, Sydney.   http://www.clmr.unsw.edu.au/article/risk/chinese-outbound-investment-growing-sophistication-chinas-go-global-policy

Ministry of Commerce People's Republic of China: MOFCOM (2013). *Guidelines for Environmental Protection in Foreign Investment and Cooperation*, http://english.mofcom.gov.cn/article/policyrelease/bbb/201303/20130300043226.shtml

OECD (2007). *Environmental Performance Reviews; China;* OECD, France.

Osvaldo Rosales and Mikio Kuwayama (2012). *China and Latin America and the Caribbean: Building a Strategic Economic and Trade Relationship*. Santiago, Chile: Libros de la CEPAL, ECLAC.

Schatan, Claudia (2000). "Mexico's Manufacturing Exports and the Environment under NAFTA," in *The Environmental Effects of Free Trade*, CEC, http://www.ecolex.org/server2neu.php/libcat/restricted/li/MON-068387.pdf

Schatan, Claudia and Liliana Castilleja (2005). "La Industria Maquiladora Electrónica en México," in J. Carrillo and C. Schatan (eds), *El Medio Ambiente y la Maquila en México: un problema ineludible*, ECLAC Books No. 83.

Sirkin, Harold L., Justin Rose and Michael Zinser (2012). *The US Manufacturing Renaissance; How Shifting Global Economics Are Creating an American Comeback*. Philadelphia: Knowledge@ Wharton.

UNCTAD (2013). *World Investment Report 2013; Global Value Chains: Investment and Trade for Development*. Geneva: United Nations http://unctad.org/en/PublicationsLibrary/wir2013_en.pdf

Watkins, Ralph (2013). "Meeting the China Challenge to Manufacturing in Mexico," in E. Dussel Peters, A. H. Hearn and H. Shaiken (eds) *China and the New Triangular Relationships in the Americas; China and the Future of U.S.-Mexico Relationship*, Center for Latin American Studies, University of Miami, Center for Latin American Studies and Cechimex. http://www.dusselpeters.com/62.pdf

Watkins, Ralph (2007). El Reto de China a las Manufacturas de México, in E. Dussel Peters, (2007), *Oportunidades en la relación económica y comercial entre China y México*, ECLAC, United Nations. http://www.economia.unam.mx/deschimex/cechimex/chmxExtras/repositorio/archivos/OportunidadesChina-Mexico2007.pdf

Zhang, Haiyan, Zhi Yang and Daniël Van Den Bulcke (2013). *Euro-China Investment Report 2011–2012*, Antwerp Management School, University of Antwerp http://www.antwerpmanagementschool.be/media/294010/report_exec_summ_english.pdf

CONTRIBUTORS

Nicola Borregaard is head of the Division of Sustainable Development at the Ministry of Energy of Chile. Between 2011 and 2014 she was head of energy and climate change at Fundación Chile. She was the former executive director of Centro de Investigación y Planificación del Medio Ambiente, and co-founder and director of RIDES NGO. Between 2005 and 2008 she was director of the National Energy Efficiency Program of the Chilean government. Her experience includes working as advisor to different ministers of economy and energy, and working for the Chilean National Commission on Environment. Borregaard was a member of the Presidential Commission on Energy (2012), the Presidential Commission on Urban Development (2013) and the Advisory Council to the Ministry of Environment (2010–2014). She holds a PhD in land economy from Cambridge University, England.

Mauricio Cabrera Leal is a policy coordinator in mining issues at WWF Colombia. He was comptroller of environment of Colombia, deputy director of Environmental Studies Institute of Hydrology, Meteorology and Environmental Studies – IDEAM, advisor to the Ministry of Environment of Colombia on environmental issues associated with mining and energy resources, specialist in energy and mining impacts, and coordinator and co-author of the Second National Communication of Colombia to the United Nations Framework Convention on Climate Change. He has been a consultant for international organizations such as IADB, IUCN and WBG. He has been a geologist at the Federal University of Amazonas-Brazil, remote sensing specialist at the CIAF-Bogotá and MA candidate in interdisciplinary studies in development in the Interdisciplinary Center for the Study of Development at Los Andes University.

Adam Chimienti is a PhD candidate at the Institute of China Asia Pacific Studies, National Sun Yat-sen University in Taiwan. He received his MA in international relations from St. John's University and BA in history and sociology from Queens College (CUNY). His research interests include

Chinese-Ecuadorian relations, the environmental and social issues stemming from major extractive projects throughout the Andean region, and the role of indigenous leaders across the Amazon. He is the author of several articles on Chinese foreign investment and contemporary issues in Latin America.

Victoria Chonn Ching is a doctoral student in political science and international relations at the University of Southern California. She has been a researcher at CIUP and assistant to the director of the Peru-China Center at UP. She has also interned at the National Committee on U.S.-China Relations in New York, and has provided research assistance to different public sector agencies. She has an MA in Chinese studies and a BA in political science and Asian languages and civilizations from the University of Michigan.

Julian Donaubauer is researcher at the chair for growth theory and business cycles at the Helmut-Schmidt-University in Hamburg, Germany. His research interests cover the fields of international economics and development economics. He was a visiting researcher at the Institute for the World Economy in Kiel as well as the Centro de Investigaciones para la Transformaciónin Buenos Aires. Prior to his academic career he worked for the Chamber of Industry and Commerce in Berlin. Julian holds a PhD in economics from the Helmut-Schmidt-University.

Annie Dufey is an economist from the Universidad de Chile with an MA in environment and development policies from the University of Sussex. She was lider and executive secretary of Energía 2050 – the participatory process for the long-term energy policy at the Ministry of Energy of Chile – and till April 2015 also head of the Division of Energy Policy and Prospective in the same ministry. Between 2009 and 2014 Dufey was director of policies, strategies and society at the Energy and Climate Change Area of Fundación Chile where she co-founded and was member of the Board of the Platform Energy Scenarios – Chile 2030. Between 2004 and 2008 she was in London working as senior researcher at the Environmental Economics Programme of the International Institute for Environment and Development, prior to which she held positions at the Centre of Environmental Research and Planning and Gemines Consultores in Santiago, Chile.

Philip M. Fearnside is research professor in the Department of Environmental Dynamics at the National Institute for Research in the Amazon, Manaus, Brazil. He completed his PhD in 1978 from the Department of Ecology and Evolutionary Biology, Division of Biological Sciences, University of Michigan. Fearnside's research from 1974 has been directed at the estimation of human carrying capacity of tropical agro-ecosystems. His work since 1992 has been organized around the objective of converting the environmental services of Amazonian forests into a basis for sustainable development for the rural population of the region, replacing the current pattern of forest destruction.

Adriano M. R. Figueiredo is professor of regional development and econometrics at the Federal University of South Mato Grosso. He is a researcher in applied economics, regional development and international trade, mainly using quantitative methods like computable general equilibrium models, spatial econometrics and time series econometrics.

Kevin Gallagher is professor of global development studies at Boston University's Frederick S. Pardee School of Global Studies, where he co-directs the Global Economic Governance Initiative. He is the author of *The China Triangle: Latin America's China Boom and the Future of the Washington Consensus and The Dragon in the Room: China and the Future of Latin American Industrialization* (with Roberto Porzecanski). With Daniel Chudnovsky he co-edited *Rethinking Foreign Investment: Lessons from Latin America*.

Andrés López is head of the Economics Department and full professor of development economics at the University of Buenos Aires. He is also director at the Centro de Investigaciones para la Transformación, Buenos Aires; executive director of the Red Sudamericana de Economía Aplicada; researcher at the National Council of Scientific and Technical Research; and invited professor at the universities of San Andrés and Torcuato Di Tella. He has edited and written several books and articles published in international academic journals, and consulted for international organizations such as ECLAC, IADB, UNCTAD, UNIDO, UNDP and WIPO.

Diana Piloyan teaches environmental economics at the Universidad Iberoamericana, Mexico City. She has a master's degree in global economic policy from the American University in Washington, DC, and a degree in economics from the Universidad Iberoamericana.

Adam Rua Quiroga is a Bolivian economist, with a master's degree in economics from ILADES – Chile (Georgetown University). He specializes in macroeconomics and environmental economics issues. He has done research in these areas along with Bolivian public research institutions like the Universidad Mayor de San Simon and also with NGOs like FAUNAGUA. The most relevant research is related to environmental impact assessment, environmental economic valuation and environmental regulation in developing countries.

Daniela Ramos has a master's degree in economics from the Instituto Torcuato Di Tella and a degree in economics from the Universidad de Buenos Aires. She is principal researcher at the Centro de Investigaciones para la Transformación and professor at the University of Buenos Aires. She has been consultant for different international organizations such as PNUD, ECLAC, IADB and IDRC. She is the author of several studies on foreign investment, entrepreneurship and trade in goods and services.

Rebecca Ray is research fellow at the Boston University Global Economic Governance Initiative, and a PhD student in economics at the University of Massachusetts-Amherst. She has also been a research associate at the Center for Economic and Policy Research, Washington, DC. She holds an MA in international development from George Washington University, and has conducted fieldwork in Ecuador, Nicaragua and Canada.

Guillermo Rudas Lleras is lecturer in environmental economics at Javeriana and Externado universities of Colombia. He is a researcher in monitoring and evaluation of environmental and social policy, particularly application of economic and financial instruments to environmental policy. He was titular professor in the Department of Economics at the Universidad Javeriana, where he taught and carried out research for more than twenty-five years. He is a member of the academic staff of the Foro Nacional Ambiental, Colombia.

Maria Teresa Ruiz-Tagle is a Chilean economist. Since 2012 she has been a consultant for the Economic Commission for Latin America and the Caribbean, and for UN-Habitat since 2015. Since 2004 she has been a research associate and visiting lecturer of the Faculty of Economics and Political Science, University of Chile, and also an affiliated lecturer in the Department of Land Economy, University of Cambridge, UK. Ruiz-Tagle received her PhD and MPhil in land economy from the University of Cambridge, UK; an MSc from the London School of Economics and Political Science, UK; and a BA in economics from the University of Chile. She is working on the Regional Report of Latin America and the Caribbean for Habitat III, Third Conference of the United Nations about Sustainable Development and Housing. Her research has focused on environmental and urban policy, sustainable development and institutional economics, with particular emphasis on cities in Latin America and the Caribbean.

Cynthia Sanborn is vice-rector for research at the Universidad del Pacífico, Lima, Peru. She is also president of the Board of the Peruvian Consorcio de Investigación Economica y Social and a founding member of Grupo Sofia:

Mujeres Profesionales en las Ciencias Sociales. She has held the William Henry Bloomberg Visiting Chair at Harvard University, and is a member of the advisory board of the South American office of the David Rockefeller Center for Latin American Studies at Harvard. Sanborn has written and edited articles and books on Peruvian and international politics, extractive industries and development, and Chinese investment in Peru. From 2007 to 2014 she was a member of the national Working Group of the Extractive Industries Transparency Initiative in Peru. Sanborn received her PhD and MA in government from Harvard University and a BA in political science from the University of Chicago.

Alejandra Saravia López is researcher and professor at the Universidad Mayor de San Simon, Cochabamba, Bolivia, where she is a part of the Instituto de Estudios Sociales y Económicos. Her research focuses on the environment-poverty relationship, and international trade and environmental deterioration issues. She has published work on the natural resource curse and its impact on poverty and the environment in Bolivia, and on the relationship between inequality and environmental degradation across Latin America. She holds an MA in economics from Tilburg University (The Netherlands) and is a PhD candidate at the same university.

Santiago Sinclair is an environmental engineer from Andrés Bello National University, Santiago, Chile. He is co-founder of and project manager in Regenerativa Consulting. Previously, he worked as a project engineer in Fundación Chile, developing local and regional energy strategies. Sinclair has also worked as a consultant in carbon management and sustainability strategies for companies in the wine and the retail industries. He has participated in the preparation of studies and publications on innovation and impact on issues of eco-labeling, sustainable public procurement, nonconventional renewable energies and climate change.

Claudia Schatan is a Mexican economist working as an international consultant for Foro Consultivo Científico y Tecnológico, Mexico. From 1990 to 2011 she worked with the Economics Commission for Latin America and the Caribbean in Mexico, where she was the head of the International Trade and Industry Unit. During 1980–1989 she was a researcher and professor in the Economics Department of the Centro de Investigación y Docencia Económica, Mexico City. Her research has focused on competition policy, trade, industry and environment. Among other publications, she co-authored a groundbreaking book, *Maquiladoras and the Environment in Mexico*.

INDEX

Lightning Source UK Ltd.
Milton Keynes UK
UKOW02n0117281216

290671UK00004B/51/P